D1293663

"Good Stuff is a winner!"

"This impressive paperback provides thousands of suggestions for games, toys, magazines, catalogs, videos, books, tapes, educational equipment and more. Parents will discover items that can feed a child's passion for a topic or spark an interest in a brand-new field. *Good Stuff* is a winner!"

Bay Area Parent

"This book is jam-packed with over ten chapters of information about where to find the best educational material in all subjects from writing to math to geography to life skills."

Priority Parenting Magazine

"*Good Stuff: Learning Tools for All Ages* by Rebecca Rupp is an excellent guide to the thousands of educational resources currently available for parents, kids, and teachers: Books, magazines, catalogs, videos, audiocassettes, games, computer programs, art and music resources, educational toys, and more. It is a comprehensive reference tool that every homeschooling family will enjoy."

Colorado Home Educator's Association

"Resource guide covering most subject areas and many new resources, includes recommended grade-level appropriate children's literature."

Home School: Taking the First Step

Good Stuff

Learning Tools for All Ages

by Rebecca Rupp

Home Education Press

Good Stuff
Learning Tools for All Ages

by Rebecca Rupp

published by
Home Education Press
Post Office Box 1083
Tonasket, WA 98855
509-486-1351

First printing 1993.
Second printing 1994.
Printed in the United States of America by
McNaughton & Gunn, Lithographers, Ann Arbor, Michigan.

ISBN 0-945097-20-4

Library of Congress Cataloging-in-Publication Data

Rupp, Rebecca.
  Good stuff : learning tools for all ages / by Rebecca Rupp.
    p. cm.
  Includes bibliographical references and index.
  ISBN 0-945097-20-4
  1. Home education--Textbooks.   2. Children--Books and reading.
  I. Title.
  LC40.R87   1993
  649'.68--dc20   93-39388

Original cover artwork and design by Chuck Trapkus, Rock Island, Illinois.
Layout and design by Mark Hegener, Wauconda, Washington.

For Randy
and because of
Joshua, Ethan, and Caleb

Table Of Contents

Preface

by Rebecca Rupp

Randy - my husband - and I made the decision to homeschool our three children some ten years ago, when Josh, our oldest, was just two, Ethan an infant, and Caleb still in the planning stage. We've never regretted that decision, and homeschooling, for us, has been everything we hoped it would be. It has also been more than we really bargained for: we didn't realize, in those early days of blocks and alphabet books, how much time, effort, and dedication it takes to provide a quality education. Our homeschool program has evolved somewhat bumpily over the years into a curriculum that now suits us all. We try to maintain an even flow of basic academics, while concentrating on child-led topics and projects - that is, zeroing in on the kids' present interests and incorporating them into our daily school sessions. We throw a few adult-led topics out there every so often too, just in case someone is eager to grab new bait: chemistry, candlemaking, Greek mythology, plane geometry, whales.

All this variety, as any parent/teacher quickly discovers, soon leads to an overwhelming feeling of too many spinning plates in the air. In our house, Josh wants to study philosophy, Ethan to learn Italic handwriting, Caleb to start an ant farm. Everyone wants to make pottery; Josh needs to know the scientific names of all his houseplants; Ethan, building a model of *The Spirit of St. Louis*, demands information about Charles Lindbergh. To support such interests is, as we see it, the job of educators everywhere. It's up to us, the adults, to provide a rich environment, both physical and mental, for learning. It's up to us to help and inspire, to suggest good books, to provide endless amounts of paper, paint, and glue, to plan trips to the science museum, to play games, to discuss, and to argue -often all at once, loudly, around the dinner table. Given that foundation, the kids will take it from there. Learning, after all, is what kids do best.

The resources listed in this book are intended to help parents and teachers provide a fertile learning environment for their children. The information supplied is as up-to-date as possible, though readers should be aware that, in this uncertain world, prices, addresses, and availabilities change, and businesses disappear.

For all the many people who have provided information for this book, many thanks - and a special thank you to Terry Deloney, whose talents as an educator and parent are an everlasting comfort and inspiration.

Becky Rupp
Shaftsbury, Vermont 1993

Introduction

by Mark and Helen Hegener

This book is an introduction to the wonderful world of learning resources. Use it as a place to turn for inspiration and ideas, a reference tool when you need the address or phone number of a favorite catalog or company, a book to browse for suggested titles just before your next trip to the library or bookstore, a jumping off place for your family's explorations in learning.

There are several indexes for this book: Catalogs, Audio/Video, Books, Authors, and Miscellaneous (magazines, games, companies, learning packets, etc.). If you're looking for a particular catalog, the Catalogs index will be the easiest place to find that particular listing. If you're looking for what else might also be offered by that catalog company, check the additional listings in the Miscellaneous index.

There is a set of reference books, updated annually, called *Books in Print*, carried by most bookstores and libraries. With these books you can find any book in print and learn the publisher, price, and current availability.

Librarians and bookstore personnel are generally very knowledgeable about books, and can be helpful in tracking down a particular book or resource. Extensive interlibrary loan programs allow access to hundreds of thousands of books, audiocassettes, records and videos through your local branch library.

We are very pleased to offer this compilation of educational resources. We are planning to update and revise this book biannually, and we welcome letters from readers who have information about the resources listed in this edition. Please send your ideas, suggestions for additional listings, and updates for the next edition to the publisher: Good Stuff, Home Education Press, PO Box 1083, Tonasket, WA 98855.

Mark and Helen Hegener
Publishers, Home Education Press

Chapter One

Reading and Literature

Beginners to Bookworms

Alphabet Books

Aardvarks, Disembark!   Ann Jonas   (Greenwillow; 1990) The animals leave the ark in alphabetical order; by the end of the book, there's a line of 132 species, including duikers, meerkats, numbats, and wallabies, all trailing down Mount Ararat.

Alphabears: An ABC Book   Kathlleen Hague   (Henry Holt; 1985) A short rhyming verse and a delightful illustration of busy teddy bears accompanies each letter of the alphabet.

Applebet   Clyde Watson   (Farrar, Strauss, & Giroux; 1982) A rhyming alphabet about a farmer and daughter taking apples to the county fair.

The Bird Alphabet Book   Jerry Pallota   (Charlesbridge Publishing; 1987) Full-color drawings of birds from A to Z, with a very brief explanatory text. By the same author and in the same format: *The Dinosaur Alphabet Book, The Flower Alphabet Book, The Frog Alphabet Book, The Furry Alphabet Book, The Icky Bug Alphabet Book, The Ocean Alphabet Book, The Underwater Alphabet Book, The Victory Garden Alphabet Book,* and *The Yucky Reptile Alphabet Book.*

A Caribou Alphabet   Mary Beth Owens   (Dog Ear Press; 1988) In this alphabet book, inspired by the Maine Caribou Transplant Project, each letter gives a piece of information about the caribou and their far northern habitat.

Curious George Learns the Alphabet   H. A. Rey   (Houghton Mifflin; 1963) George the little monkey learns all the letters of the alphabet, both upper- and lower-case. Each is presented is the shape of an appropriate letter word: the Ps, for example, are penguins; the Ks, kangaroos.

Dr. Seuss's ABC   Dr. Seuss   (Random; 1963) Typical Seuss, from Aunt Annie's alligator through the Zizzer-Zazzer-Zuzz. By the same author: *On Beyond Zebra,* a zany account of imaginary letters that come after Z in the alphabet.

Eating the Alphabet: Fruits and Vegetables from A to Z   Lois Ehlert   (Harcourt, Brace, Jovanovich; 1989) An alphabet based on colorful arrangements of fruits or vegetables, from apple to zucchini.

Eight Hands Round: A Patchwork Alphabet   Ann W. Paul   (HarperCollins; 1991) 26 alphabetically named quilt patterns, starting with Anvil, Buggy Wheel, and Churn.

A Farmer's Alphabet   Mary Azarian   (Four Winds; 1981) An alphabet
of rural life, illustrated with wonderful chunky woodcuts.

The Handmade Alphabet   Laura Rankin   (Dial; 1991) An American
Sign Language alphabet with realistic pictures of positioned
hands, plus visual cues for each letter: the G hand, for example,
wears a glove; the I hand is touching the tip of an icicle.

I Can Be the Alphabet   Marinella Bonini   (Viking; 1986) Colorful illustrations of cheerful kids in leotards forming the letters of the alphabet with their bodies.

On Market Street   Arnold Lobel   (Greenwillow; 1981) A boy works
his way down Market Street, buying presents that begin with each
letter of the alphabet. The shopkeepers themselves are made from
their wares: the apple vendor is made of apples; the quiltmaker of
quilts. Unusual and fascinating.

Nutshell Library   Maurice Sendak   (Harper & Row/HarperCollins;
1962) A series of four delightful little books: *Alligators All Around:
An Alphabet Book, Chicken Soup With Rice: A Book of Months, One
Was Johnny: A Counting Book,* and *Pierre: A Cautionary Tale in Five
Chapters and a Prologue.* For the dramatically inclined, all four
books, catchily set to music, are featured in Sendak's play, *Really
Rosie* (Harper & Row, 1975).

A Peaceable Kingdom: The Shaker Abecedarius   Alice and Martin
Provensen   (Viking; 1978) An enchantingly illustrated rhyming animal alphabet book, based on the art and lifestyles of the 19th-
century Shaker communities.

Pigs From A to Z   Arthur Giesart   (Houghton Mifflin; 1986) An imaginative alphabet book in which seven creative piglets build a treehouse.

Alphabet Books, Hands-On

The *Cuisenaire Alphabet Book* (Maria Rizzo Marolda) is a 64-page
workbook to be used with Cuisenaire rods. Each letter of the alphabet is represented in a double-page spread: on one page, kids
cover the letter with rods in a number of different ways; on the opposite page, they similarly cover pictures of objects whose names
begin with the relevant letter. (A, for example, is for Airplane, Apple Tree, and Alligator.) This hands-on approach to the alphabet

also teaches spatial relationships, counting, and early arithmetic concepts.

In *Alphagrams* (Teri Perl), kids cover letters and matching objects with colorful tangram-like pattern blocks (included in the book, in heavy-duty cardboard). Puzzle solutions are shown in the back. Both books are available from the Cuisenaire Co. of America, P.O. Box 5026, White Plains, NY 10602-5026; (800) 237-3142.

Susan Johnston's *Tangrams ABC Kit* includes two sets of tangram pieces (to cut out), plus 122 tangram puzzles based on the letters of the alphabet, starting with Acrobat and Bird. The kit costs $3.50 from Dover Publications, Inc., 31 East 2nd Street, Mineola, NY 11501. Also from Dover: ABC stickers and stencils.

For those who prefer to make their own alphabet books, KidsArt sells several alphabet rubber stamp kits, including basic sets of upper- and lower-case letters; *Alphabears*, a tumbling teddy bear alphabet, in which each fat little bear has an upper-case letter (A to Z) on the front of his T-shirt; *Alphazoo*, an animal-stamp upper-case alphabet, including 26 animals and upper-case letters, starting with A is for Alligator; and *Dinobet*, for dinosaur fans: a different prehistoric animal for each alphabet letter. Ink pads included. Available from KidsArt, P.O. Box 274, Mt. Shasta, CA 96067; (800) 959-5076.

Good Apple is another great source for hands-on alphabet activity books. Among these: *Alpha-Pets*, with which kids make 26 different puppets, one for each letter of the alphabet, and use these in a range of multidisciplinary projects; and *A is Amazing*, which includes suggestions for a large number of alphabetical activities, from sprouting Avocados and baking Banana Bread to tie-dyeing Flags and planting Zinnias. For a catalog, contact Good Apple, 1204 Buchanan St., P.O. Box 299, Carthage, IL 62321-0299; (800) 435-7234.

For a more challenging interaction with the alphabet, try *The ABC's of Origami* by Claude Sarasas (Charles Tuttle; 1964): instructions are included for 26 different origami objects and animals, beginning with the letters A-Z.

Alphabet Games

The United Art and Education Supply Co. carries an excellent assortment of reading readiness games for brand-new beginners. Included are *Alphabet Bingo* (playing cards include both upper- and lower-case letters), *Alphabet Lotto* (playing cards include upper- and lower-case letters and a bright-colored picture representing a word beginning with the printed letter), *Alphabet Match-Me Flash Cards* (players pair letter cards with picture cards, as in A with a big red Apple, H with a Hammer), and *Match the Letters Wipe-Off Cards* (kids match upper-case letters with their proper lower-case partners).

The Bull's-Eye Activity Cards are designed to teach beginning phonics: each card carries a colored picture and three possible lower-case letter choices; kids poke their fingers through the hole under the correct answer. Cards are self-checking; users just flip the card over to see if they chose the right answer. Bull's-Eye Cards are available in three sets: Beginning Consonants, Short Vowels, and Long Vowels. Each set contains 28 cards. Also available: *Consonant, Vowel, Rhyming, Sight Word, Parts of Speech*, and *Punctuation Bingos, Basic Picture Words Flash Cards, Basic Sight Words Flash Cards*, and *Make-Your-Own Flash Cards* (100 blank cards). Flash cards are also available in Spanish. For a catalog, contact United Art and Education Supply Co., Inc., Box 9219, Fort Wayne, IN 46899; (800) 322-3247.

Constructive Playthings is another excellent source of alphabet and reading readiness materials: the (immense) catalog includes crepe foam rubber and wooden alphabet puzzles, alphabet "stepping stones" for walk-on letter learning, *Build-A-Word* blocks, magnetic letters, letter stencils, and a wide assortment of card and board games for pre- and early readers. For a catalog, contact Constructive Playthings, 1227 East 119th St., Grandview, MO 64030-1117; (800) 255-6124.

Authors
Authors, an old-fashioned classic, is a rummy-type card game in which players collect matched sets of famous American and British writers. The game includes some 13 different famous writers: William Shakespeare, Charles Dickens, Nathaniel Hawthorne, Louisa May Alcott, Mark Twain, William Makepeace Thackeray, Robert Louis Stevenson, James Fenimore Cooper, Washington Irving, Henry Wadsworth Longfellow, Sir Walter Scott, Alfred Lord Tennyson, and Edgar Allan Poe. Cards list four different works written by each. Newer versions include *American Authors* (James

Baldwin, Theodore Dreiser, F. Scott Fitzgerald, Robert Frost, Ernest Hemingway, Eugene O'Neill, Herman Melville, Willa Cather, William Faulkner, Walt Whitman, John Steinbeck, Henry James, and Thomas Wolfe) and *Childrens' Authors* (A.A. Milne, Dr. Seuss, Isaac Bashevis Singer, Joel Chandler Harris, Hans Christian Andersen, Beatrix Potter, Meindert DeJong, Rudyard Kipling, Charles Perrault, J.M. Barrie, Brothers Grimm, Laura Ingalls Wilder, and Lewis Carroll). The games cost $6.00 apiece and are available from Aristoplay, P.O. Box 7529, Ann Arbor, MI 48107; (800) 634-7738.

Avon Books

Avon Books publishes a 72-page annotated catalog of fiction and non-fiction books for kids in the elementary grades through senior high school. All are available in paperback and are therefore relatively inexpensive. Among the selections: Lynne Reid Banks's *Indian in the Cupboard* books, in which Omri's toy Indian comes alive when placed inside a magical cupboard; Peggy Parish's *Amelia Bedelia* series for young readers, in which Amelia (who bakes a wicked pie) flounders through figures of speech; James Howe's *Bunnicula* series, in which Harold the dog and Chester the cat cope with a vampire bunny; and all the works of Beverly Cleary. For a catalog, contact Avon Books, 1350 Avenue of the Americas, New York, NY 10019; (800) 238-0658 (customer service); (901) 364-5742 (customer service in TN).

Betterway Books

A small, but nifty, selection of children's books, among them Judith St. George's *By George, Bloomers!*, the story of Mrs. Amelia Bloomer and the town's reaction to her first public appearance in pants; Kathy Henderson's *Market Guide for Young Artists and Photographers* and *Market Guide for Young Writers*, for publication-minded kids aged 8 and up; and, also by Henderson, *What Would We Do Without You?: A Guide to Volunteer Activities for Kids*. For a free brochure, write Betterway Books, 1507 Dana Avenue, Cincinnati, OH 45207.

Blue Mountain Book Peddler

The Blue Mountain Book Peddler publishes a charming 50-page newsprint catalog dotted with old-fashioned storybook illustrations. The carefully selected assortment of fiction and non-fiction books is divided into categories: Art, English, Geography, History,

Math, Science, Homeschool, and - under Additional - the apparently unclassifiable leftovers. A nice source for the classics; it's a rare catalog these days that carries *The Five Little Peppers and How They Grew*, *Rebecca of Sunnybrook Farm*, *Pollyanna*, *Little Lord Fauntleroy*, and *A Girl of the Limberlost*. For a free catalog, contact Blue Mountain Book Peddler, 15301 Grey Fox Road, Upper Marlboro, MD 20772; (301) 627-2131.

Bob Books

The Bob books - written by teacher Bobby Lynn Maslen - are reading booklets for beginning beginners. The booklets have bright-colored covers, but the innards are black-and-white, illustrated with simple - but hysterical - line drawings. The main characters here are a pair of buddies named Sam and Mat: Sam has a triangular head; Mat looks somewhat like a doughboy in checkerboard pants. The activities of Sam and Mat, summed up in very few words, aren't much from an adult point of view, but quickly give just-beginning readers the thrill of reading a whole book. Or set of books. The Bob Books are organized into sets, grouped by increasing level of difficulty: Set I contains 12 booklets, Sets II and III each contain eight. By Set III, the adventures of Mat and Sam have become wordier, and contain an occasional non-phonetic word. Bob Books cost $13.00 per set, and are available from Michael Olaf's Essential Montessori, P.O. Box 1162, Arcata, CA 95521; (707) 826-1557. Or from The Sycamore Tree catalog.

The Book Lady

The Book Lady is a bookworm, and her tightly packed catalog - the company stocks some 8000 titles - is out to create other bookworms. Catalog book categories include Favorite Stories, Multicultural Stories, Fairy Tales, Holidays, Stories for Older Children, Science (for the very young), Special Needs, and Parenting. For each title is listed a short plot summary and a recommended age range.

Also available: a series of theme packets, each containing four related books on a specific subject, an expanded bibliography, and 25 bookmarks. Packets are targeted at the early primary grades; topics include Bears, Dinosaurs, Trees, Millions, and Farm. For a catalog, contact The Book Lady, Inc., 8144 Brentwood Industrial Dr., St. Louis, MO 63144; (800) 766-READ.

Book Links

Book Links: Connecting Books, Libraries, and Classrooms is a bi-monthly publication of the American Library Association. It's described as "full of thematic articles that bring together books across the genres, subject areas, and age levels, and accompanied by suggestions for discussing and extending projects" - which means that each of the magazine's featured topics centers around a long list of related fiction and non-fiction books. Each listed book is accompanied by an age-range recommendation and a brief review. Flipping through a few past issues, grabbed at random, I came across an article on math books, with a superb 75-entry bibliography of counting books, math project and game books, non-fiction books about specific mathematical principles, and fiction books based on mathematical problems, such as David Birch's *The King's Chessboard* and E. Nesbit's *Melisande*, the story of a princess who wishes her hair "would grow an inch a day, and grow twice as fast every time it was cut." Other featured topics have included Mozart, trees, Japan, Russia, modern art, immigrants, and maps. And much more. A superb resource, especially for those who prefer a multidisciplinary approach to learning. Each issue also includes a reading calendar, "Year-Round Reading," which suggests books and book-related projects for specific holidays and anniversaries throughout each month. A one-year subscription to *Book Links* (6 issues) costs $14.95; order from Book Links: Connecting Books, Libraries, and Classrooms, American Library Association, 50 E. Huron St., Chicago, IL 60611; (800) 545-2433.

Book Wise

Book Wise publishes literature guides for use with individual children's books, intended to enhance and expand upon the initial reading experience. The guides run about 50 pages long, and include suggestions for discussion questions and writing assignments, project activities, reproducible workbook pages, and an associated bibliography. Guides are provided for some 24 different books, variously appropriate to grades 1-8, among them *The Story of Ferdinand* (Munro Leaf), *Amos and Boris* (William Steig), *Charlotte's Web* (E.B. White), *The Phantom Tollbooth* (Norton Juster), *Hatchet* (Gary Paulsen), and *The Witch of Blackbird Pond* (Elizabeth Speare). Literature guides cost $19.95 each. Those interested should contact Book Wise, Inc., 26 Arlington St., Cambridge, MA 02140; (617) 876-4014.

Cahill & Company

Though not specifically a catalog for children, the Cahill & Company catalog includes an excellent small selection of children's books, including such not-always-easy-to-find volumes as Frank Stockton's *The Griffin and the Minor Canon* and Gian Carlo Menotti's *Amahl and the Night Visitors*. The editors point out in horror that 60% of American households bought no books whatsoever in 1991; they hope to see that such a statistic never occurs again. For a free catalog, contact Cahill & Company, P.O. Box 39, Federalsburg, MD 21632-0039; (800) 462-3955.

Cambridge University Press

The Cambridge University Press ESL Catalog offers materials - textbooks and cassette tapes - for those learning English as a second language, at levels appropriate for beginning, intermediate, and advanced students. The bulk of the catalog is devoted to professional texts for language teachers, generally quite specialized and heavy in tone, as in *Research Methods in Language Learning* and *Communicative Methodology in Language Teaching*. Amid all this, there are some books that might be of interest to bilingual families, and a few selections that might appeal to less exalted educators: for example, *Five Minute Activities* (Penny Ur and Andrew Wright) purports to offer 100 quick ideas to spice up foreign language classrooms; *Literature in the Language Classroom* (Joanne Collie and Stephen Slater) presents an assortment of student-centered activities for use with literary works; and *Grammar Games* (Mario Rinvolucri) is a teacher's resource book containing materials for over 50 grammar games, targeted at kids for whom English is a first language. No actual description of the grammar games is provided by the catalog, but a blurb claims that they create an "atmosphere of trust." Those interested should contact Cambridge University Press, 40 West 20th Street, New York, NY 10011-4211; (800) 872-7423.

Can You Find It?   Randall McCutcheon   (Free Spirit; 1991)

This book is subtitled "25 Library Scavenger Hunts to Sharpen Your Research Skills;" the projects are designed to lure kids into the library reference section, tracking down the answers to real and intriguing research problems. Researchers use the card catalog, microfilm, dictionaries, indexes, directories, encyclopedias, and more, while finding out how to make restaurant reservations in Beijing, the name of the first R-rated movie, or the location of the world's largest shopping mall. For kids aged 14 and up. Cleverly written and illustrated. Available through bookstores, from Free Spirit Publishing, Inc., 400 First Avenue North, Suite 616, Minneapolis, MN 55401-1730; (800) 735-7323 or (612) 338-2068; or from Geode Educational Options, P.O. Box 106, West Chester, PA 19381.

Children's Book-of-the-Month Club

The kids' Book-of-the-Month Club works just like the grown-up version: you get three books cheap as an introductory offer; then, each month, thereafter, you get a Selections catalog, from which you choose books at not-quite-full prices. (*Always* lower than the publisher's prices, says the brochure.) There's also a Club-selected Book of the Month, which is sent to you automatically unless you mail off your Club postcard instructing otherwise. The Club attempts to offer books to children from six months to 12 years of age, which means that there's not a really huge selection for any one age group. What they've got, though, looks pretty good: initial selections (83 in all) include Robert McCloskey's *Make Way for Ducklings*, H.A. Rey's *Curious George*, Kenneth Grahame's *The Wind in the Willows*, Norton Juster's *The Phantom Tollbooth*, and Scott O'Dell's *Island of the Blue Dolphins*. For information, contact Children's Book-of-the-Month Club, Camp Hill, PA 17012.

Children's Book and Music Center

The Children's Book and Music Center publishes a 75-page catalog absolutely packed with books, cassette tapes, and videos for kids of all ages. The catalog lists *lots* of books, both time-honored classics and "new and wonderful" finds, plus a large assortment of less common resources, among them beginning science books in Spanish, American folk songs on tape, with accompanying songbooks, and many multicultural materials. There's also a selection of materials for special-needs kids, including the "Hal's Pals" dolls (variously available with leg braces, hearing aids, glasses and seeing-eye puppy, and wheelchair). For a free catalog, contact the Children's Book & Music Center, 2500 Santa Monica Blvd., Santa Monica, CA 90404; (800) 443-1856 or (213) 829-0215.

The Children's Small Press Collection

This 70-page catalog offers "hard to find, well-chosen books & music for tots to teens." Books are listed under such categories as "Self-Sufficiency," "Raising Up Readers and Writers," "Science and the Environment," "Self-Esteem Books," "Fun, Fantasy, and Fiction," "Non-fiction and Teen Issues," "Multicultural and Bilingual Materials," "History, Heroes, and Heroines," "Family Structures and Changes," "Parenting and Nurturing," and "Health, Sexuality, and Substance Abuse." Under "Raising Up Readers and Writers," for example, there's *Caught Ya! Grammar With a Giggle* (Jane Bell Kiester), in which kids learn English grammar by detecting errors in daily sentences, gleaned from an on-going "humorous soap opera;"*The Writing Book* (Inky Penguin), a collection of creative writing ideas for kids aged 8-11; and *1-2-3 Reading and Writing*, a collection of activities for preschoolers, designed to develop eye-hand coordination, auditory and visual discrimination, and rhyming, alphabet, and vocabulary abilities in preparation for actual reading and writing. Under "History" are included biographies of Chief Joseph, Cochise, W.E.B. DuBois, Thurgood Marshall, and Georgia O'Keefe; plus *History Comes Alive! 101 Activities for the Classroom* (Shari Steelsmith), a collection of multidisciplinary activities and projects related to young children's biographies and targeted toward 5-9-year-olds; and *American Adventures: True Stories from America's Past 1770-1870* (Morrie Greenberg), which relates, in chronological order, 15 "high interest" stories from American history, with accompanying activities, writing exercises, and debate topics.   And there's lots more. For a free catalog, contact the Children's Small Press Collection, 719 North Fourth Ave., Ann Arbor, MI 48104; (313) 668-8056.

Chinaberry Books

This is one of our all-time favorite children's book (and music) catalogs: 100 pages of books and tapes, each reviewed in reader-friendly detail. I *read* the Chinaberry catalog, cover to cover. The books are loosely grouped according to the age of the reader: Level I includes very simple - sometimes wordless - books for the absolute beginner; Level II, picture books; Level III, books for kids who can sit through longer stories; and Level IV, longer books for advanced readers or interested listeners. The books are selected with tender loving care: Chinaberry, writes the owner, "offers items to support families in raising their families with love, honesty, and joy, to be reverent, loving caretakers of each other and the earth." The stories are terrific too. Our latest Chinaberry acquisition: Patricia Wrede's *Dealing With Dragons* (Level IV), in which the contrary Princess Cimorene, who prefers fencing and Latin to embroidery and dancing lessons, ends up as Chief Cook and Librarian to the King of the Dragons. For a catalog, send $2.00 to Chinaberry Book Service, 2780 Via Orange Way, Suite B, Spring Valley, CA 91978; (800) 776-2242 (orders and customer service), or (619) 670-5200 (all other calls).

A Common Reader

Not a book catalog specifically for kids, but an invaluable resource for the imaginative and on-the-way-to-being-educated reader. The Common Reader catalog carries the *Library of America* series, which includes the writings of Willa Cather, Ralph Waldo Emerson, Benjamin Franklin, Washington Irving, Thomas Jefferson, and Mark Twain; the *Everyman's Library* series, which includes a vast list of classic volumes, by authors from Austen to Zola; and the *Loeb Classical Library*, which, in Greek and Latin, with facing English translations, includes the works of authors from Aeschylus to Xenophon.

There's also an eclectic collection of not-quite-so-classical fiction and non-fiction. Among these: *Idiom's Delight* (Suzanne Brock), which puts idioms in an international context (while, for example, it may rain cats and dogs in your backyard, it rains jugs in Spain, water basins in Italy, and ropes in France); the *Facts on File Visual Dictionary*, which, via 3000 labelled pictures, teaches readers the correct names for the parts of a castle, a motorcycle, and a pair of sneakers (and many others); and *British English from A to Zed*, which defines, for the ignorant American, such phrases as "peckish," "sticky wicket," and "bubble and squeak." Advanced and imaginative readers can obtain a free catalog from A Common Reader, 141 Tompkins Ave., Pleasantville, NY 10570; (800) 832-7323.

Creative Uses of Children's Literature   Mary Ann Paulin   (Library Professional Publications; 1982)

This 700+-page volume is an invaluable resource, creative in tone, encyclopedic is scope, and wonderful when its suggested techniques are put into practice. The (enormous) Bibliographical Index is difficult to read, but that's a quibble. This book is a gem.

Creative Uses of Children's Literature suggests multitudinous ways of introducing books to young children and of enhancing the book experiences of older readers. In chapter one, "Introducing Books in All Kinds of Ways," the author does just that: books are introduced through formal booktalks, through birthdays, through television, and through read-aloud sessions. Books are introduced by theme: dolls, pigs, mice, monsters, foxes, owls, time travel, science fiction, historical fiction, or mysteries, for example, with many suggested examples of each. There's a long list of related novels for Wilder lovers, titled "If You Like the *Little House Books*" and a series of lesson plans for enriching sixth-grade geography with storytelling programs. Other book chapters include "Experiencing Art Through Picture Books" (81 different subheadings), "Enhancing Books Through Music" (9 subheadings), "Enjoying Poetry" (93 subheadings), "Playing Stories" (live action and puppets; 48 subheadings), and "Using Riddles, Magic, Jokes, and Folk Themes" (82 subheadings). Book topics covered in this last chapter include multicultural riddles, Egyptian hieroglyphics, Japanese and Chinese calligraphy, cattle brands, codes and cyphers, Morse Code, Braille, American sign language, flag signals, music and mathematics, and "magic numbers" in children's literature, with lists of books revolving around the numbers 1-13.

A second book, *More Creative Uses of Children's Literature*, published in 1992, similarly suggests "all kinds of ways" to introduce all kinds of children's books to young readers. Available through libraries and bookstores, or from Shoe String Press/Library Professional Publications, P.O. Box 4327, 925 Sherman Ave., Hamden, CT 06514; (203) 248-6307; fax: (203) 230-9275.

Cricket and *Ladybug*

Cricket and *Ladybug* are monthly literary magazines for children. *Cricket* is targeted at kids aged 7-14; *Ladybug* ("The Magazine for Young Children") at kids aged 2-7. Both are superb. *Cricket* runs a bit over 60 pages long and is a nice mix of fiction, folklore, poetry, and non-fiction, plus projects, puzzles, and cheerful little bugs at the bottom of the pages who define anything difficult in the way of vocabulary words. *Ladybug* - 35 pages long - offers a similar mix of fiction, non-fiction, puzzles, songs, and projects, in bigger print, with bigger and brighter colored illustrations. Annual subscriptions cost $29.97 and are available from *Cricket*, Box 387, Mt. Morris, IL 61054, (800) 284-7257; or *Ladybug*, P. O. Box 592, Mt. Morris, IL 61054-0592, (800) 827-0227.

T.S. Denison and Co.

Denison's preschool and elementary catalog carries teacher-written resource books and teaching units: background information about well-known children's authors and their works, literature-associated activities books, and creative writing units. Included: *Distinguished Children's Literature*, a 260-page reference work listing, in chronological order, the Newbery and Caldecott Award-winning books, with information about the books, their authors and illustrators; *Launch Into Literature*, a whole-language approach to 36 classic children's books, including discussion questions, extended reading lists, and hands-on activities; and *Beasties*, which links poetry and natural science for kids in preschool through grade 3. There's also a series of teacher's guidebooks for teaching library skills to kids in kindergarten through grade 7. The introductory volume, targeted at kids through grade 3, covers visits to the library, library citizenship, and arrangement of books in the library; Book 1 (grade 4) teaches kids how to use the card catalog, with suggested check-up exercises; Book 2 (grade 5) introduces students to the Dewey Decimal system; Book 3 (grade 6) covers use of assorted library resources, including dictionaries, encyclopedias, almanacs, atlases, biographical dictionaries, and *The Reader's Guide to Periodical Literature*; and Book 4 (grade 7) is an overview of the research skills acquired in the previous books, in greater detail. For a free catalog, contact T.S. Denison & Co., Inc., 9601 Newton Avenue South, Minneapolis, MN 55431; (800) 328-3831 or (612) 888-8606.

Dover Publications
Dover publishes several catalogs, including a Children's Book Catalog, which lists over 650 books for kids, most of them in the $1.00-$4.00 price range. Dover carries a selection of children's classics in paperback, including selections by Beatrix Potter, Thornton Burgess, and L. Frank Baum; and all twelve of Andrew Lang's famous *Fairy Books*. Each of these contains a collection of 30 to 40 fairy tales from around the world, and each is bound in a different color: hence *The Blue Fairy Book*, *The Green Fairy Book*, and so on, through *Pink*, *Olive*, *Crimson*, and *Lilac*. Dover also carries a series of coloring and activity books for young readers, among them the *ABC Coloring Book*, the *Animal Alphabet Coloring Book*, the *Plant and Animal Coloring Book*, the *Fun With Letters Coloring Book*, the *Fun With Opposites Coloring Book*, and the *Fun With Spelling Coloring Book*. For older readers, there are a series of coloring books based on children's classics: *The Tale of Peter Rabbit: A Coloring Book*, *The Wind in the Willows Coloring Book*, *The Alice in Wonderland Coloring Book*, *A Child's Garden of Verses Coloring Book* (which includes 25 of Stevenson's poems), the *Rackham's Fairy Tale Coloring Book*, and the *Aesop's Fables Coloring Book* (with text). Dover also offers a Com-

plete Catalog, 72 pages of small print, listing some 4,500 paperback selections. Catalogs are free, from Dover Publications, Inc.,
31 East 2nd Street, Mineola, NY 11501.

Educational Record Center
If you've got a musical learner (or several), the Educational
Record Center carries assorted alphabet and phonics song collections on LP or audio cassette. Examples include *The Alphabet Oper-
etta*, a full-scale musical production featuring a song for each letter
of the alphabet; *Animal Alphabet Songs* (26 alphabetical animal
tunes), and *ABC's in Bubbaville* (musical descriptions of 26 alphabetical professions, including Kelly the Kindergarten Teacher and
Lori the Librarian). For a catalog, contact the Educational Record
Center, Inc., 3233 Burnt Mill Dr., Suite 100, Wilmington, NC
28403-2655; (800) 438-1637, fax: (910) 343-0311.

Fairytale Cards
These are decks of illustrated cards, each carrying illustrations
and lines of text from famous fairytales. There are four different
sets of cards: "Little Red Riding Hood," "Puss in Boots," "Sleeping
Beauty," and "Cinderella." Each set contains 15 pairs of illustrated
cards, which can be used for rummy-type card games or for reading activities, as children put the cards in proper order and participate in the telling of the story. Fairytale card decks cost $4.00
apiece, from Aristoplay, P.O. Box 7529, Ann Arbor, MI 48107;
(800) 634-7738.

Firefly Books
This is a big glossy colorful catalog of both adult and children's
books (mostly children's); the selection is excellent and there's always something that's bound to catch the booklover's eye. New
catalogs, complete with new selections, come out twice a year. To
get on the mailing list, contact Firefly Books, Ltd., 250 Sparks
Ave., Willowdale, Ontario M2H 2S4, Canada; (416) 499-8412. Firefly books can be ordered directly from the company or through
bookstores. The company offers a 10% discount to schools, if you
happen to be one.

The Folger Shakespeare Library
The Folger Shakespeare Library in Washington, D.C., sponsors
an "Education and Festivals Project," described as "an interdisciplinary, performance-based approach to teaching Shakespeare for
students of all ability levels, grades 4-12." In the course of the "fes-

tival," kids prepare and perform a scene or group of scenes from a selected Shakespearean play - which may be revised or edited to suit the age range of the performers. The Library offers day-long training workshops for teachers and others interested in throwing their own Shakespeare festivals; these run to $300 per session. For information, contact the Folger Shakespeare Library, Education Programs, 201 East Capitol Street, S.E., Washington, D.C. 20003-1094; (202) 544-7077 or (202) 675-0365.

Folktales: Teaching Reading through Visualization and Drawing   Laura Rose   (Zephyr Press; 1992)

This is a collection of ten (reproducible) traditional multicultural stories: in these, each page of text is accompanied by a drawing page, on which kids can draw illustrations to accompany the story as it is read aloud. At the end the reading, each kid will have a completed illustrated book of his/her own. *Folktales* costs $15.95, from Zephyr Press, 3316 N. Chapel Ave., P.O. Box 13448-E, Tucson, AZ 85732-3448; (602) 322-5090.

The Great Books Foundation

The Great Books Foundation is the Chicago organization best known for selling volumes of Plato, Aristotle, Shakespeare, and the like to improvement-minded adults. Along with its adult program, however, the Foundation also sponsors reading programs for children: the Junior Great Books Read-Aloud Program, targeted at kids in kindergarten and first grade; the Junior Great Books Program, for kids in grades 2-9; and Introduction to the Great Books, for high-school students. The programs are all designed to encourage kids to read interpretively, and to think critically and creatively about what they have read. This process is encouraged and developed in the course of post-book discussions. In each of the programs, according to the official program pamphlet, "students practice critical thinking skills in the context of discussion. They examine the grounds for their opinions, and determine the degree to which their ideas are valid and correct based on evidence in the text."

This all sounds a trifle stuffy, but it isn't: the story selections really are great, and the discussion questions listed in the accompanying Leader Aid manual really do generate enthusiastic debate. Generally about 12 selections - each chosen for literary merit - are covered each semester in the lower grades; fewer (but longer) selections in the upper grades. Grade 2 selections, for example, include "Cinderella," "Stone Soup," and "The Velveteen Rabbit;" Grade 4 selections include "The Emperor's New Clothes," "The Imp in the Basket," and "The Elephant's Child;" and Grade 5, Oscar Wilde's "The Happy Prince," Heywood Broun's "The Fifty-first Dragon," and Ray Bradbury's "All Summer in a Day." High-school kids (grades 10-12) get selections by Sigmund Freud, Anton Chekhov, John Locke, Isak Dinesen, Aristotle, and Virginia Woolf.

The program was originally designed for larger groups, but adapts beautifully to even very small groups, at home. Books and Leader Aids may be purchased as single copies by individuals; only schools, libraries, and trained discussion leaders - those who have completed a formal Great Books-sponsored Basic Leader Training Course - may purchase materials in bulk. Student books for grades 2-9, each containing a semester's-worth of selections, cost $9.25; Leader Aids, $3.75. For information and a free brochure, contact The Great Books Foundation, 35 East Wacker Dr, Suite 2300, Chicago, IL 60601; (800) 222-5870 or (312) 332-5870.

Greathall Productions

"It is the belief of Jim Weiss and Greathall Productions," reads the brochure, "that the joyful success of reading and writing begins on the lap of the storyteller" - and as storytellers go, Jim Weiss is our all-time favorite. To date, he has produced something over ten storytelling tapes, and we've - repeatedly - heard them all. The stories are wonderful, beautifully told. This, you think as you listen, is storytelling in its best incarnation, the sort of storytelling that should take place around the kitchen fire while snow falls in the woods outside.

Our first storytape acquisition was Weiss's *Greek Myths* - the stories of King Midas, Hercules, Perseus and Medusa, and Arachne. Our kids (and their parents) were promptly hooked. *Greek Myths* was thus rapidly followed by *King Arthur and his Knights, The Three Musketeers/Robin Hood, Arabian Nights,* and *Tales from the Old Testament.* Later selections have included *Sherlock Holmes for Children* (four Holmes stories, including "The Adventure of the Speckled Band"), *Tales from Cultures Near and Far* (stories from America, Japan, Spain, West Africa, China, and the Middle East), and *Rip Van Winkle/Gulliver's Travels.* All are superb. Tapes run about an hour and cost $9.95 each, with a 10% discount on orders of two or more. For a descriptive brochure, write Greathall Productions, P.O. Box 813, Benicia, CA 94510.

Harper Audio

For dedicated listeners, Harper Audio (a division of HarperCollins Publishers) publishes a 130+-page catalog of books, both abridged and unabridged, on tape. Tapes are listed by category: Biography and Autobiography, Business, Documentary, Gender Studies, History and Political Science, Humor, Languages, Literature, Fiction, Mystery and Suspense, Philosophy, Poetry, Psychology and Self-Help, Religion, Sports, and Theater. Sample selections include Anne Frank's *Diary of a Young Girl*, Ernest J. Gaines's *The Biography of Miss Jane Pittman*, Aesop's *Fables*, James Thurber's *Many Moons*, J.R.R. Tolkien's *The Hobbit* and *The Lord of the Rings*, Jules Verne's *Journey to the Center of the Earth*, and T.S. Eliot's *Old Possum's Book of Practical Cats*. And there's much more. To obtain a catalog, contact Harper Audio, HarperCollins Publishers, 1000 Keystone Industrial Park, Scranton, PA 18512-4621; (800) 242-7737.

The Horn Book

Horn Book Magazine - "everything you need to know about books for children and young adults" - is a fat bimonthly collection of book reviews, essays, and articles by or about children's authors and illustrators. Also available is the biannual *Horn Book Guide*, which contains "reviews of virtually every hardcover trade children's and young adult book published in the U.S. in the previous season." A one-year subscription to *The Horn Book Magazine* costs $34.00; a subscription to *The Horn Book Guide*, $45.00; and a dual subscription to both *Magazine* and *Guide*, $65.00. To order, contact, The Horn Book, Inc., 14 Beacon St., Boston, MA 02108-9765; (800) 325-1170 or (617) 227-1555.

How A Book is Made   Aliki   (Thomas Y. Crowell; 1986)

This little volume gives kids aged 7 and up the real nitty-gritty on how a book is made, from author through artist, editor, publisher, designer, production director, color separator, printer, and salesperson. Clever diagrams explain such unfamiliar concepts as color separation, printing plates, and color proofs; and there's a great double-page spread showing the inner workings of a four-color offset printing press. There's also a labeled picture showing all the parts of a finished bound book: dust jacket, front and back flaps, endpapers, spine, and signatures. Delightful drawings; all the characters are cats. Available from libraries and bookstores.

International Learning Systems, Inc.

International Learning Systems is known for the "Sing, Spell, Read & Write" (SSR&W) program, a compact kit of songs, games, storybooks, workbooks, charts, and little plastic prizes that leads children into "independent reading ability" in 36 sequential steps. SSR&W is action-oriented: kids cut, paste, and color in their phonics workbooks, sing catchy little songs designed to teach short and long vowel sounds and letter clusters, play phonetic versions of rummy, bingo and "Go Fish!," and read through a series of 17 phonetic storybooks. Along the way they track their progress by moving a magnetic car along the 36 steps of the "Raceway Chart" and - for extra motivation - are allowed to pick a prize from the treasure sack as they complete each step. The illustrations throughout are pretty awful, but the concept is appealing; our two youngest kids enjoyed this one. The SSR&W programs are available both as Classroom Kits and as individual Home Tutoring Kits. The latter comes packaged in a convenient heavy cardboard "Treasure Chest." Users will need separate sets of workbooks for each participating child. For more information, contact International Learning Systems, Inc., P.O. Box 16032, Chesapeake, VA 23328; (800) 321-TEACH or (804) 366-0227.

International Reading Association

The International Reading Association is a professional organization of persons and institutions concerned with the improvement of reading at all levels nationwide. It publishes four professional journals, including *The Reading Teacher*, targeted at preschool and elementary-level educators. The Association's (free) catalog includes a wide selection of books and pamphlets on all aspects of reading. The Association also offers a number of free resources for parents and teachers, among them a series of parent brochures focusing on "practical reading concerns" - examples include "You Can Help Your Child Connect Reading to Writing" and "Your Home is Your Child's First School" - and a series of annual booklists, including "Children's Choices," in which kids pick their favorites of the new children's books, and the analogous "Young Adults' Choices," and "Teachers' Choices." A basic membership in the International Reading Association costs $19.00, and includes a subscription to the bimonthly newspaper, *Reading Today*. For information or a copy of the catalog, contact the International Reading Association, 800 Barksdale Rd, PO Box 8139, Newark, DE 19714-8139; (302) 731-1600.

Ladybird Books
   The Ladybird Readers are a series of small (4 1/2 x 6 1/2") hard-bound books, all colorfully illustrated. Most are re-tellings of classic fairy tales, in vocabulary keyed to the just-barely-beginning reader. Available volumes - 20 in all - include *The Elves and the Shoemaker*, *The Enormous Turnip*, *Peter and the Wolf*, *The Three Little Pigs*, *The Ugly Duckling*, and *Jack and the Beanstalk*.
   A second set, for slightly older readers, collectively called the Ladybird Classics, are similarly small and heavily illustrated re-tellings of heftier classics, among them *Alice in Wonderland*, *Tom Sawyer*, *Treasure Island*, *Gulliver's Travels*, *Black Beauty*, *Oliver Twist*, and *Robin Hood*. Again, the simple language allows early readers access to these classic stories and prepares them for future reading of the original texts. Ladybird Readers and Classics cost $3.50 per volume and are available (individually) from Michael Olaf's Essential Montessori, P.O. Box 1162, Arcata, CA 95521; (707) 826-1557; Ladybird Readers (in sets only) are also available from John Holt's Book and Music Store, 2269 Massachusetts Ave., Cambridge, MA 02140; (617) 864-3100.

Learning Links
   Learning Links sells study guides, thematic units, and a vast selection of children's books, all designed to connect literature and hands-on activities across the curriculum. Guides are available for a wide range of literature-based topics. The "Reading Quilts Study Guide," for example, presents "an integrated unit that focuses on the handicraft of quilting" through 8 elementary-level picture books, among them *The Josefina Quilt Story*, *The Keeping Quilt*, *The Patchwork Farmer*, and *Sam Johnson and the Blue Ribbon Quilt*. The "Journeying Through the Middle Ages Study Guide," aimed at grades 5-9, coordinates 21 fiction and non-fiction books about the medieval period, including Marguerite de Angeli's *The Door in the Wall*, Rosemary Sutcliff's *Dragon Slayer: The Story of Beowulf*, and David Macauley's *Castle* and *Cathedral*. Other study guide themes include "Folktales," "Greek and Roman Myths," "Poetry," "Giants," "Native Americans," "Colonial America and the Revolution," "Westward Expansion and the Frontier," and "The Civil War." Study guides are sold separately, or in packages with all the accompanying book selections. For a catalog, contact Learning Links, Inc., 2300 Marcus Ave., New Hyde Park, NY 11042; (800) 724-2616 or (516) 437-9071.

Long Ago & Far Away

Though much commercial television programming, the discerning public agrees, consists of total glup, public television has produced a number of notable series for young readers, among them "Reading Rainbow," "Wonderworks," and "Long Ago & Far Away." "Long Ago & Far Away" is targeted at children aged 5-9, and presents re-enactments of classic stories from around the world, using a variety of dramatic techniques, including live action, animation, and puppetry.

To accompany the programs, WGBH publishes a series of "Discussion and Activity Guides" for parents and teachers. For each "Long Ago & Far Away" selection, the Guide provides a list of suggested discussion questions, an assortment of hands-on activities, and a bibliography of related books. After viewing "Beauty and the Beast," for example, children are encouraged to build a beautiful room for the Beast's castle, using a shoe box and collage materials, to pretend to be Beauty and keep a diary about her life with the Beast, and to write a story about someone or something ugly on the outside but beautiful within. The bibliography lists assorted retellings of the tale of Beauty and the Beast, and (many) other stories of magical transformations, including Lloyd Alexander's *The Cat Who Wished to Be a Man*, Sumiko Yagawa's *The Crane Wife*, and John Steptoe's *Mufaro's Beautiful Daughter*.

The Guides also list sources for videotapes of the "Long Ago & Far Away" programs. (It's okay, however, to tape them right off your own TV, provided you do so for educational purposes.) Copies of the "Long Ago & Far Away" Discussion and Activity Guides cost $3.00 each, from WGBH, Print Projects, 125 Western Ave., Boston, MA 02134. Also see *Reading Rainbow: A Guide for Teachers*; the book (softcover) costs $10.95 from GPN, P.O. Box 80669, Lincoln, NE 68501; (800) 228-4630.

Magazines for Children   David R. Stoll, Ed.   (International Reading Association)

This guidebook/bibliography lists upwards of 120 "worthwhile" children's periodicals, variously suitable for kids over a large range of ages, from toddlers through teenagers. Single copies cost $5.25; there are quantity discounts for those ordering 10 copies or more. Available from the International Reading Association, 800 Barksdale Road, P.O. Box 8139, Newark, DE 19714-8139; (302) 731-1600.

McGuffey Readers

McGuffey's Eclectic Readers still look pretty much the same as they did in 1836, when our several-times-great-grandparents were learning how to read. There are six of these little red-bound books: the *Primer*, the *Pictorial Primer*, and the *First* through *Fourth Readers*. The *Primers* are appropriate for kids in kindergarten through grade 2; the *Readers* progressively for kids in grades 2-3, 3-5, 6-8, and 9-12. The earliest books begin with the alphabet, then move through simple one-syllable words to short sentences. Stories, when you get to them, are highly moral in tone. Available through bookstores or from Sycamore Tree, 2179 Meyer Pl, Costa Mesa, CA 92627; (714) 642-6750 (orders) or (714) 650-4466 (information).

The Mind's Eye

The Mind's Eye catalog specializes in books on tape. Their audiocassette selection is superb, ranging from tales for the very young (*The Complete Winnie-the-Pooh, The Velveteen Rabbit, Cinderella*) to stories for the slightly older (*The Chronicles of Narnia, The Wind in the Willows, The Hobbit*, Anne of Green Gables, *Charlotte's Web*) to classics for all ages (*A Tale of Two Cities*, the complete works of Sir Arthur Conan Doyle, the tragedies of Shakespeare, *The Adventures of Huckleberry Finn, The Odyssey*, the short stories of Edgar Allan Poe). A not-to-be-missed source for families of listeners. For a free catalog, contact The Mind's Eye, Box 1060, Petaluma, CA 94953; (800) 227-2020.

NAPPS

The National Association for the Preservation and Perpetuation of Storytelling (NAPPS) offers an assortment of books on storytelling for those eager to try it on their own, such as *Tell Me A Story: Creating Bedtime Stories Your Children Will Dream On* (Chase Collins), *Creative Storytelling: Choosing, Inventing and Sharing Tales for Children* (Jack Maguire), and *Awakening the Hidden Storyteller: How to Build a Storytelling Tradition in Your Family* (Robin Moore). The organization also sells audiocassettes of stories told by the very best present-day storytellers, many of them recorded live at the National Storytelling Festival - "unforgettable stories," reads one description, "gathered from cultures around the world and America's most colorful corners." For a free packet of information, contact NAPPS, P.O. Box 309, Jonesborough, TN 37659; (615) 753-2171. (Also for storytellers, see Creative Thinking: Life Stories/ Future Stories.)

Novel Units

Novel Units, Novel Unit Themes, and *Novel Activities* are innovative workbooks, designed to enhance reading ability, foster creative thinking, and inspire literature-related projects and activities. *Novel Units* are teacher's guides, each containing vocabulary lists, comprehension questions, and activity suggestions for one novel. Over 200 of these are available, for books appropriate for kids in grades 1-12. The *Novel Unit Themes* deal with lists of related books, each with the same central theme: examples include "Dinosaurs," "Inventions," "Native Americans," "Pigs," and "Tropical Rain Forests." The Theme guides contain reading lists, suggestions for math, art, and writing activities, vocabulary exercises, discussion questions, and a resource bibliography. The *Novel Activities* series, organized similarly, concentrates on literature-related hands-on projects. The catalog also offers all the books featured in the guides, in paperback, plus a large assortment of video recordings. For a copy of the catalog, contact *Novel Units*, P.O. Box 1461, Palatine, IL 60078; (708) 253-8200.

Oxford University Press

Oxford is, of course, famous for its reference works, of which the *Oxford English Dictionary* ("a scholarly Everest") is the supreme example. The *Dictionary*, which provides meanings, detailed histories, and pronunciations for over half a million words, runs to 20 volumes full-size; it's also available in compact form, in extremely small print, decipherable with the (accompanying) magnifying glass. Even compacted, the OED costs $295, but it is, indeed, a "treasure-house of the language" - language-lovers denied one of their very own should try their local library. Also, and more affordably, from Oxford: *The Oxford Dictionary of Modern Quotations, The Oxford Companion to the English Language, The Oxford Book of English Verse, The Oxford Book of Short Poems, The Oxford Book of Essays, The Oxford Companion to Children's Literature*, and *The Oxford Book of Nursery Rhymes*. And much more. A free catalog, for serious scholars, is available from Oxford University Press, 200 Madison Ave., New York, NY 10016; (800) 451-7566.

Perfection Learning Corporation

Resources for readers and writers in grades K-9, including a sizeable list of books, literature-based activity guides, "Storysong" cassettes, poetry workbooks, book-and-cassette sets, and blank books for journal- or story-writing in several different shapes and sizes. For a free catalog, contact Perfection Learning Corporation, 1000 North Second Avenue, Logan, IA 51546-1099; (800) 831-4190.

Playing Shakespeare

Playing Shakespeare is a board game of Shakespearean charades. Players, organized into teams, attempt through creative acting to fill in missing words in famous Shakespearean quotations. Examples include "To be, or not to be; that is the *QUESTION*" and "Why then the world's *MINE OYSTER*, which I with sword will open." Quotations are included from all 37 of Shakespeare's plays, divided into Comedies, Tragedies, and Histories - which you draw depends on where you land on the gameboard, which is illustrated with photographs of modern Shakespearean performances. The game is recommended for 4 to 24 players, aged 12 or over - this is definitely not a game for the very small - but for those interested older kids, no special knowledge of Shakespeare's plays is necessary. Just a talent for charades. An accompanying booklet includes short summaries of all 37 of the plays. "Playing Shakespeare" costs $40.00 and is available from Aristoplay, P.O. Box 7529, Ann Arbor, MI 48107; (800) 634-7738.

Poets' Audio Center

"If it's poetry and it's available on tape," reads the brochure, "we have it - or we'll get it!" Readings of poets old and new, among them Carl Sandburg, W.H. Auden, Ezra Pound, Sylvia Plath, William Carlos Williams, Dylan Thomas, Alfred Lord Tennyson, Pablo Neruda, and Langston Hughes. For a brochure or additional information, contact the Poets' Audio Center, P.O. Box 50145, Washington, D.C., 20091-0145; (202) 722-9106.

Puffin Books

The catalog is subtitled "The Best in Paperbacks for Children." Many selections for all ages: picture books, poetry, multicultural tales, mysteries, historical fiction, and natural science. For a catalog, contact Puffin Books, 375 Hudson St., New York, NY 10014; (800) 526-0275.

Quickword

In this, "The Ultimate Word Game," players draw colored challenge cards as they hop their tokens around the game board. The cards challenge players to come up with appropriate words: a list of hardware store items beginning with the letter B, for example, or nursery rhyme characters whose names begin with the letter C.

Each player has 90 seconds in which to answer, which is where the "quick" comes in; a timer is included. The game costs $29.95, and is available from toy and game stores or from Zephyr Press, 3316 N. Chapel Ave., P.O. Box 13448, Tucson, AZ 85732-3448; (602) 322-5090.

Readers' Guides

The following, all useful resources for book-choosing parents and teachers, include collections of reviews of recommended children's books:

Best Books for Children in Preschool through Grade 6   John T. Gillespie and Corinne J. Naden   (R.R. Bowker; 1992)

The Best in Children's Books: The University of Chicago Guide to Children's Literature 1985-1990   Zena Sutherland   (University of Chicago; 1991)

Best of the Best for Children   Denise Perry Donavin, ed.   (American Library Association; 1992)

Eyeopeners! How to Choose and Use Children's Books About Real People, Places, and Things   Beverly Kobrin   (Viking Penguin; 1988)

For Reading Out Loud! A Guide to Sharing Books With Children   Margaret Mary Kimmel and Elizabeth Segel   (Dell; 1983)

Magazines for Children   Selma Richardson   (ALA Publishing; 1991)

The New Read-Aloud Handbook   Jim Trelease   (Penguin; 1982)

The New York Times Parent's Guide to the Best Books for Children Eden Ross Lipson   (Times Books/Random House; 1991)

Reading For the Love of It   Michelle Landsberg   (Prentice Hall; 1987)

Also see entries under *Book Links*, *The Horn Book*, and International Reading Association.

Recorded Books

A catalog of books on tape. "Unabridged on audio cassette," states the catalog front cover, and *The New York Times* , which recommends it, adds, "The human voice adds dimensions of color and feeling lost to the printed page." The 30-page catalog of selections includes recorded books both for young restless listeners and for older booklovers with Olympic attention spans. Young children's selections include Lewis Carroll's *Alice's Adventures in Wonderland* (2 cassettes, 2.5 hours), E.B. White's *Stuart Little* (2 cassettes, 2 hours), and Kipling's *Just So Stories* (3 cassettes, 4.5 hours); selections for older listeners include Harper Lee's *To Kill a Mockingbird* (9 cassettes, 13.5 hours), Stephen Crane's *The Red Badge of Courage* (3 cassettes, 4.5 hours), Charles Dickens's *A Tale of Two Cities* (10 cassettes, 13.5 hours), Frances Hodgson Burnett's *The Secret Garden* (5 cassettes, 7.25 hours), and Anna Sewall's *Black Beauty* (4 cassettes, 6 hours). And many more.

All titles may be either purchased outright or rented for 30-day periods (you pay rental charges and two-way shipping costs). For a free catalog, contact Recorded Books, Inc., 270 Skipjack Rd. Prince Frederick, MD 20678; (800) 638-1304.

The RIF Guide to Encouraging Young Readers   Ruth Graves (Doubleday;1987)

The "RIF" in the title stands for "Reading is Fundamental," and, given that, the book sets out to provide an immense collection of appealing activities, designed to encourage kids from infancy to age 11 to learn and love to read. Among the suggestions: wear special hats to read special stories (a witch's hat for *Strega Nona*, a pot for *The Story of Johnny Appleseed*); reward kids' reading with stickers kept in a special sticker book, which can be redeemed for treats or prizes; read your way around the world, marking the settings of your books on a world map with colored pins; make a family card catalog; make foods to go with special books (a bowl of popcorn to accompany *The Popcorn Book*, a jam sandwich while reading *Bread and Jam for Frances*); play rhyming and letter games in the car; hold a newspaper scavenger hunt (the list of things to find might include a picture of a world leader, the high temperature reading from a major U.S. city, an advertisement for a puppy, the price of fruit, the word "book," and so on); make your own photo phone book; make a Halloween monster dictionary; make your own bookmarks; write sequels to some of your own favorite books. Includes an annotated list of books and reading resources. Available through bookstores.

Scattergories Junior

A game of words for 2-4 players. Participants roll a die to determine the key letter of play and are then given a list of categories for which they must come up with a list of words or phrases beginning with the key letter. Answers are written on the included score pads; players win points for unique words and phrases that do not match those of other players.

Sample challenges might involve identifying Wild Animals, Things You Feed Your Pet, Names for a Dog or Cat, Animals That Make Bad Pets, Animals That Fly or Swim, and Stuffed Animals, all beginning with the letter M. *Scattergories Junior* is appropriate for kids aged 8-11; the original version of the game, *Scattergories*, for older kids and adults. Available from toy and game stores.

Scholastic Books

Scholastic publishes a 118-page catalog packed with inexpensive paperback titles, both fiction and non-fiction, suitable for kids in grades K-9. A must for new library-builders. For a free copy, contact Scholastic, Inc., P.O. Box 7502, Jefferson City, MO 65102; (800) 325-6149.

School Zone

Our oldest son learned to read from School Zone's "Start to Read" books, and the tattered remains of particularly favored volumes are still kicking around in one of our bookcases. There are over 30 books available in the series now, all 16-page paperbacks, available either individually or grouped in sets by difficulty of vocabulary level. The series is generally recommended for children aged 4-7.

The "Start to Read" books stand out among beginner books in that, through clever illustrations and turns of phrase, they manage to be funny - which is no small accomplishment when working with a preschool reading vocabulary, at three to six words per page. In *Jog, Frog, Jog*, for example, an athletic-looking frog decoys an infuriated pursuing dog into a log, where he gets stuck; at the end a cheerful party of frog joggers mills about the wedged dog and the log is hung with a sign reading, "Feed the Dog in the Log." In *Beep, Beep*, a frustrated driver tries to maneuver his truckload of mattresses through an uncooperative herd of sheep; at the end, all curl up together and fall asleep. "Start to Read" books cost $2.25 apiece, or $12.95 per set of six. School Zone also sells workbooks, flash cards, and simple educational games. For a brochure, contact the School Zone Publishing Company, 1819 Industrial Dr., P.O. Box 777, Grand Haven, MI 49417; (800) 253-0564.

Spalding Education Foundation

The Spalding Foundation promotes an innovative method of

teaching reading, based on integrating hearing, saying, writing, and seeing, all presented such that "every avenue into the mind is used." The gist of the method is presented in Romalda Spalding's *The Writing Road to Reading*, which explains the teaching of the 70 common English phonograms (25 letters and 45 fixed combinations of 2, 3, or 4 letters). Kids initially write from dictation, as they repeat the sounds of the 150 most used English words; then write original sentences; and soon branch off into the reading of books. No gimmicks: kids just use pencils, papers, and their brains. The multi-faceted approach is especially recommended for children who are somewhat dyslexic. For more information and a brochure, contact the Spalding Education Foundation, 15410 N. 67th Ave., Suite 8, Glendale, AZ 85306; (602) 486-5881.

Sundance

This is a 125-page catalog of resources for "literature-based learning across the curriculum," appropriate for preschoolers through sixth-graders. The Sundance programs, which generally consist of an assortment of paperback books, a teacher's guide containing project suggestions and background information, and a collection of reproducible student activity sheets, are cross-curricular teaching units, designed to connect literature to other academic disciplines, notably science, social studies, American history, and creative writing. A "Connect/Science" unit, for example, targeted at kids in grade 3, correlates hands-on science activities with five different popular books: Aliki's *Corn is Maize*, Sharmat's *Gregory, the Terrible Eater*, Baylor's *Hawk, I'm Your Brother*, Callenback and Leefeldt's *Humphrey the Wayward Whale*, and Cole's *The Magic Schoolbus at the Waterworks*. The "Wild About" units provide cross-curricular activities centering around specific favorite themes: in "Wild About Dinosaurs," for example, kids do math, science, social studies, history, and art projects centered around ten different books about dinosaurs, among them *My Visit to the Dinosaurs* and *Dinosaurs Are Different* (Aliki), *Patrick's Dinosaurs* (Carrick), and *The Enormous Egg* (Butterworth).

The catalog offers a large selection of paperback books (all those required for their literature programs), available individually or as "Classroom Library" sets, along with audiocassettes, and videotapes. Among others, Sundance carries the "Newbery Cassette Collection," dramatizations of 55 different Newbery titles, including *Across Five Aprils, Blue Willow, Cricket in Times Square, Johnny Tremain, Mr. Popper's Penguins, Sounder, The Witch of Blackbird*

Pond, and *Zlateh the Goat*. For a free catalog, contact Sundance, P.O. Box 1326, Newtown Road, Littleton, MA 01460; (800) 343-8204 or (508) 486-9201.

Teach Your Child to Read in 100 Easy Lessons Siegfried Engelmann, Phyllis Haddox, and Elaine Bruner   (Simon and Schuster; 1983)

This 395-page book is an entire reading program between two covers, complete right down to what the helping parent/teacher should say along the way. (Adult lines are printed in red.) Lesson 1 begins with the "m" and "s" sounds; by Lesson 100, the participating child is reading at a second-grade level. I found the stories generally unappealing and unimaginative ("The Dog That Dug," "The Singing Bug," "The Pig Who Liked to Hide"), but this didn't seem to bother our children, who liked the things enough to request them as read-alouds. A solid, sequential, phonics-based approach to reading. *Teach Your Child to Read* is available through bookstores, or from The Timberdoodle, E. 1510 Spencer Lake Rd., Shelton, WA 98584; (206) 426-0672.

Tiger Lily Books

This is a delightful little newsprint catalog, spattered with drawings, poems, quotations, recipes, and chatty little notes from Kathy Epling, the owner, mother of Garth, Gabriel, and Laurel. The book selection is terrific. Included are many of our family's all-time favorites: Susan Cooper's *The Dark is Rising* series, Frances Hamerstrom's *Walk When the Moon is Full*, L.M. Boston's *Green Knowe* series, and the books of Edward Eager. Kathy Epling describes Eager's books as splendid, and we enthusiastically agree. There are several of these: in *Half Magic*, four children find a magic coin that, maddeningly, grants only half of every wish made upon it; in *The Time Garden*, four (different) children meet a cranky (but talkative) toad in a magical garden of thyme and embark on a series of time-traveling adventures; and in *Knight's Castle*, an ancient toy soldier transports a quartet of kids back to the days of Ivanhoe. This last inspired our oldest son to tackle Sir Walter Scott. For a catalog, contact Kathy Epling, Tiger Lily Books, P.O. Box 111, Piercy, CA 95587.

T'N'T

T'N'T ("Tips & Titles of Books: Grades K-8") is a pithy collection of book reviews published three times annually by Jan Lieberman, a children's librarian from Santa Clara, California. Lieberman reviews about 25 books per issue, both fiction and non-fiction, all carefully chosen as the current "best" in children's books. To receive *T'N'T*, send three legal-sized, stamped self-addressed envelopes, plus $1.00 in cash or stamps, to Jan Lieberman, 121 Buckingham Dr. #57, Santa Clara, CA 95051.

Tongue Twisters

A gem among phonics games, *Tongue Twisters* is a lotto game, with accompanying audiocassette. Players listen to the alliterative tongue twisters (say, "Two tired tigers take a taxi to town") and identify the "t" on their lotto board, marking it with a colored plastic counter. The game can be played at two levels: lotto boards are illustrated on one side (the "t" is accompanied by a pair of yawning tigers in a pale-green taxi) for those young enough to need hints; the reverse side carries only the unadorned letter. The game is suitable for 1-4 players, aged 4-8. The game costs $10.95, and is available from Constructive Playthings, 1227 East 119th St., Grandview, MO 64030; (800) 255-6124 or (816) 761-5900.

The WEB

WEB stands for Wonderfully Exciting Books; this hefty booklet, published three times yearly (Fall, Winter, Spring/Summer), contains detailed reviews of children's books, with associated suggestions for classroom use. Each issue has a central theme: a general subject, book title, or children's author. In the past these have included Folk and Fairy Tales, Beatrix Potter Books, Dragons and Monsters, the Middle Ages, Music, Celebrating Snow, Focus on the American Revolution, Dinosaurs and Digs, Exploring Mythology, the Wild West, and Columbus. Approximately 25 books are reviewed in each issue. An annual subscription to *The WEB* (three issues) costs $10.00; single back issues (available from Fall 1976), $3.00 apiece. To order, contact *The WEB*, Ohio State University, Room 200, Ramseyer Hall, 29 West Woodruff, Columbus, OH 43210.

Word Works: Why the Alphabet is a Kid's Best Friend   Catheryn Berger Kaye   (Little, Brown; 1985)

This book, one of the "Brown Paper School Book" series, is crammed full of information, fascinating facts, puzzles, and activities, all about the magic of words. "Words are tools," explains the (short and wordy) introduction. "You can build castles in the air with some highfalutin words or craft a tiny poem for your friend's valentine. You can invent new words and find lost ones or make a record of current events to bury inside a time capsule."

The book covers the written word, including pictographs, invisible writing, codes, and ciphers; grammar; story-telling; poetry; newspapers; plays; diaries ("Who Was Samuel Pepys?"); reference works; slang; and censorship - with tips on word histories, Leonardo da Vinci's backward handwriting, American Sign Language, and a quick guide to graphology. Available through bookstores.

World Almanac Education

World Almanac Education publishes a 40+-page catalog of "books for the whole language classroom." Books, fiction and non-fiction, are grouped together by theme. Sample themes include the Solar System, Native Americans, World Neighbors, African Americans, Insects, Early America, Weather, Celebrations, Prehistoric Life, Under the Water, Save Our Planet, Animals, Transportation, Our Earth, Families, Birds, Food, Pets, Language Skills, and Ancient Civilizations. The African-American section, for example, includes an assortment of biographies of famous black Americans (Matthew Henson, Jackie Robinson, Guion Bluford, George Washington Carver, Scott Joplin, Sojourner Truth, Jesse Jackson); short histories of the Underground Railroad, the Gettysburg Address, John Brown's raid on Harper's Ferry, and the Montgomery bus boycott; personal (fictional) stories of black kids coping with growing up; and a selection of African folktales. For a free catalog, contact World Almanac Education, 1278 West Ninth St., Cleveland, OH 44113-1067; (800) 321-1147.

Good Books For Kids

Age recommendations here are loose at best; our kids read some of these books earlier than suggested, and some later - and some they've enjoyed steadily over a period of years. Book-picking, inevitably, is a process of trial and error. If your kids are sitting on your lap, enthralled, while you read aloud, or poring over the pages on their own before they fall asleep at night, you'll know you're right on.

Books for Grade Levels K-1:

Alastair's Time Machine   Marilyn Sadler   (Simon and Schuster; 1986)   Alastair Grittle, boy of science, builds a time machine in his basement for Twickadilly's Second Annual Science Competition. Hilarious illustrations. In the same series: *Alastair in Outer Space* and *Alastair's Elephant*.

Alexander and the Terrible, Horrible, No Good, Very Bad Day Judith Viorst   (Atheneum; 1972)   Alexander has a dreadful day: gum sticks in his hair, his teacher doesn't appreciate his picture of the invisible castle, his mother forgets to put dessert in his lunch, the dentist finds a cavity in his teeth, and he has to wear his railroad train pajamas. (He hates his railroad train pajamas.) He wants to go to Australia. Some days, his mother tells him, are like that. By the same author: *Alexander Who Used to Be Rich Last Sunday* and *I'll Fix Anthony*.

Amelia Bedelia   Peggy Parish   (Harper & Row/HarperCollins; 1963)   Amelia Bedelia is a scatty (but lovable) housekeeper who gets into continual trouble through her literal interpretations of figures of speech. When asked to "draw the drapes," for example, Amelia sits down with sketch pad and pencil; when told to "put out the lights," she hangs all the lightbulbs on the clothesline. There are eleven more books in the series, including *Come Back, Amelia Bedelia* and *Good Work, Amelia Bedelia*.

Blueberries for Sal Robert McCloskey   (Viking; 1948)   Sal and her mother are out picking blueberries at the same time that a mother bear and her cub are in the blueberry patch, stocking up for the winter. Somehow, to the upset of everybody, kids and mothers get exchanged, but all sorts itself out happily at the end. By the same author: *One Morning in Maine*, in which Sal loses a tooth, and *Make Way for Ducklings*.

Bread and Jam for Frances   Russell Hoban   (Harper & Row; 1964)   Frances, an endearing song-singing little badger, decides to eat nothing for breakfast, lunch, and dinner but her favorite bread and jam. Other Frances books include *A Baby Sister for Frances*, *A Bargain for Frances*, *Bedtime for Frances*, and *A Birthday for Frances*.

Corduroy Don Freeman   (Viking; 1968)   Corduroy is a spunky little up-for-sale teddybear who - in search of his missing overall button - has after-hours adventures in the closed department store. Eventually he is bought by Lisa, a little girl who not only loves him, but knows how to sew on buttons. There's a sequel: *A Pocket for Corduroy*.

Frederick   Leo Lionni   (Random House; 1967)   Frederick the field mouse doesn't gather food for the winter; instead he gathers memories and poems. Enchanting collage illustrations.

Frog and Toad Together Arnold Lobel   (HarperCollins; 1972)   The adventures of Frog and Toad make for delightful and clever easy-readers. Toad is disaster-prone: he falls off sleds and loses buttons; his seeds don't grow fast enough, his kite won't fly, his ice-cream cones melt, and he looks silly in his bathing suit. He manages to overcome most of this, however, with the help of his level-headed friend, Frog. Frog and Toad also star in *Frog and Toad Are Friends*, *Days With Frog and Toad*, and *Frog and Toad All Year*.

George and Martha   James Marshall   (Houghton Mifflin; 1972)   Five very short stories about two large friends. George and Martha are a pair of hippos who, though best friends, still have a few lessons to learn about getting along with each other.

Gregory the Terrible Eater   Mitchell Sharmat   (Four Winds; 1980)   Gregory, a goat, spurns neckties and newspaper in favor of fruits, vegetables, and other healthy foods. His worried parents take him to a doctor.

Hill of Fire   Thomas P. Lewis   (Harper & Row; 1971)   Nothing ever happens in the little Mexican village - until one day a volcano erupts in the middle of a cornfield. Reading Rainbow selection.

Little Bear Else Holmelund Minarik   (HarperCollins; 1957)   Every little kid can relate to Little Bear's activities, from his demand for snowpants for playing in the snow to his imaginary trip to the moon. For more of Little Bear, there's also *Little Bear's Friend, A Kiss for Little Bear, Little Bear's Visit,* and *Father Bear Comes Home.*

Madeline Louis Bemelmans   (Viking; 1930)   In an old house in Paris all covered with vines, live twelve little girls in two straight lines - including the obstreperous red-headed Madeline. Several sequels detail the further (rhyming) escapades of Madeline, including *Madeline and the Bad Hat* and *Madeline and the Gypsies.*

Mike Mulligan and His Steam Shovel Virginia Lee Burton   (Houghton Mifflin; 1939)   Mike Mulligan and his steam shovel, Mary Ann, bravely set out to dig the cellar for the Popperville town hall in just one day. By the same author: *Katy and the Big Snow,* the tale of an intrepid snow shovel.

Millions of Cats Wanda Gag   (Coward; 1928)   A very old man sets out to find one pet kitten, but comes home with hundreds of cats, thousands of cats, millions and billions and trillions of cats.

Miss Rumphius Barbara Cooney   (Viking; 1982)   In this enchanting book, Miss Rumphius sets out to see the world, and then returns home, determined to do something to make the world more beautiful. She hits upon the perfect solution. By the same author: *Island Boy.*

Mouse Tales Arnold Lobel   (HarperCollins; 1972)   A mustached father mouse puts his offspring to sleep by telling seven (very short) clever stories: "one for each of you." Stories involve a testy wishing well that says "Ouch!" when pennies are dropped in it; a (very clean) mouse whose bathtub floods the town; and a scary cat-shaped cloud. In the equally delightful *Mouse Soup,* an imaginative mouse, nabbed by a hungry weasel, manages to talk his way out of the soup pot by telling (four) stories.

The Red Balloon Albert Lamorisse   (Doubleday; 1957)   Pascal, a small boy in Paris, makes friends with a magical red balloon that seem to have a life of its own. Illustrated with photographs.

Rotten Ralph Jack Gantos   (Houghton Mifflin; 1976)   Ralph is Sarah's bright-red and totally rotten cat, but in spite of all the mischief he gets into, Sarah loves him anyway. Sequels, full of further feline bad behavior, include *Worse Than Rotten, Ralph* and *Rotten Ralph's Rotten Christmas.*

The Story of Ferdinand Munro Leaf (Viking; 1936) The classic tale of the peaceful bull who would rather sit under the cork tree and smell the flowers than fight.

Tikki Tikki Tembo Arlene Mosel (Henry Holt; 1968) Once upon a time, first-born sons in China had very long names - until Tikki tikki tembo-no sa rembo-chari bari ruchi-pip peri pembo fell down the well.

William's Doll Charlotte Zolotow (Harper &Row/HarperCollins; 1972) William wants a doll. He gets, instead, a basketball and an electric train - until finally his sensible grandmother buys him a doll, "so he can practice being a father."

The Worst Person in the World James Stevenson (Puffin; 1980) The Worst Person in the World, who eats lemons and lives in a house covered by poison ivy, becomes a lot less crochety after meeting up with a cheerful (but ugly) creature named Ugly. By the same author: *What's Under My Bed?, Could Be Worse!, No Friends, That Dreadful Day, That Terrible Halloween Night, The Great Big Especially Beautiful Easter Egg, We Can't Sleep, Worse Than Willy!, We Hate Rain!,* and *Will You Please Feed Our Cat?* All feature Mary Ann and Louie's Grandpa, whose disastrous and improbable boyhood experiences make their own problems look like pretty small potatoes.

Books for Grade Level 2:

The Amazing Bone William Steig (Farrar, Straus, & Giroux; 1976) Pearl, a piglet, finds a talking bone (dropped by a witch) in the woods on the way home from school. Together, they manage to escape from an evil, but elegant, fox, who plans to have Pearl for dinner. By the same author: *Sylvester and the Magic Pebble, Solomon the Rusty Nail, Brave Irene, Doctor DeSoto,* and *Amos and Boris.*

A Bear Called Paddington Michael Bond (Houghton Mifflin; 1960) Paddington Bear, who arrives in London's Paddington Station from Darkest Peru with nothing but a scrapbook, an old hat, and an empty jar of marmalade, is adopted by the Brown family. Paddington is a well-meaning, but trouble-prone bear, and the stories of his adventures continue through ten more volumes: *Pad-*

dington Helps Out, More About Paddington, Paddington Abroad, Paddington At Large, Paddington At Work, Paddington Goes to Town, Paddington Marches On, Paddington On Top, Paddington Takes to the Air, and *Paddington Takes to TV.*

The Bed Book Sylvia Plath (Harper & Row; 1976) An imaginative and poetic account of anything-but-plain little beds, including Acrobat Beds, Submarine Beds, and Jet-Propelled Beds.

The Church Mouse Graham Oakley (Atheneum; 1972) Arthur, the church mouse, shares the vestry with Sampson, the ginger church cat, who, after years of listening to sermons about brotherhood, has taken a vow never to harm mice. In this, the first book of the series, Arthur brings home a large population of rambunctious friends and saves the church from a burglary. Very cleverly written, with a tongue-in-cheek British twist. Sequels include: *The Church Mice Spread their Wings, The Church Mice Adrift, The Church Mice At Bay, The Church Mice in Action, The Church Mice and the Moon, The Church Mice and the Ring, The Church Mice at Christmas,* and *The Church Cat Abroad.*

Cross-Country Cat Mary Calhoun (Mulberry; 1979) Henry, a Siamese cat, is left behind in a mountain cabin after a family ski vacation. He manages to get back to civilization on a pair of homemade cross-country skis. In a sequel, *Hot-Air Henry,* Henry takes an inadvertent trip in a hot-air balloon.

Curious George H.A. Rey (Houghton Mifflin; 1942) George, an adventurous little monkey, is captured in Africa and taken home to the city by the man in the yellow hat. There, his curiosity leads him into many difficulties. There are eighteen other books starring George, including *Curious George Rides a Bike* and *Curious George Flies a Kite.*

Donna O'Neeshuck Was Chased by Some Cows Bill Grossman (Harper Trophy; 1988) It started one day, when Donna at play, patted a cow on the head - and then, in riotous verse, is chased by cows, and mooses and gooses and sows - and eventually horses, goats, bears, a herd of buffalo, and a whole townful of people.

Do Not Open Brinton Turkle (E.P. Dutton; 1981) Miss Moody, who lives with her cat, Captain Kidd, in a cottage by the ocean, finds a mysterious purple bottle washed up on the beach. Scratched on the side is the warning phrase "Do not open." (She opens.)

Elbert's Bad Word Audrey Wood (Harcourt, Brace, Jovanovich; 1988) Elbert catches a bad word, which loudly escapes at a garden party when a croquet mallet falls on his big toe. The estate gardener, who happens to be a magician, finds a cure.

Ellen's Lion Crockett Johnson (David R. Godine; 1984) Ellen and her stuffed lion have twelve make-believe (and real-life) adventures together. Ellen provides the imagination; the lion provides the common sense.

Everyone Knows What a Dragon Looks Like Jay Williams (Four Winds; 1976) Everybody in the city of Wu knows what a dragon looks like - but nobody, except Han, the little gate-sweeper, believes that a dragon looks like a small, fat, bald, old man.

Georgie Robert Bright (Doubleday; 1944) Georgie, a shy little ghost, haunts Mr. and Mrs. Whittaker's old New England farmhouse where, every night, he squeaks the parlor door and creaks the stairs at bedtime. Then, one upsetting day, Mr. Whittaker oils the door and mends the stairs. Georgie's adventures occupy several sequels: *Georgie and the Robbers, Georgie to the Rescue, Georgie the Magician,* and *Georgie's Halloween.*

The Glorious Flight: Across the Channel With Louis Blériot Alice and Martin Provensen (Viking; 1983) The (true) story of Papa Louis Blériot (father of Alceste, Charmaine, Suzette, Jeannot, and Gabrielle) who finally, in his eleventh airplane, manages to fly across the English Channel.

The 500 Hats of Bartholomew Cubbins Dr. Seuss (Vanguard; 1965) Bartholomew Cubbins tries to take off his hat before the king, but more and more hats keep magically appearing on his head, each more wonderful than the last. For further adventures of Bartholomew, see *Bartholomew and the Oobleck,* in which the king demands something different to fall from his kingdom's sky. He gets awful green goo.

The House on East Eighty-Eighth Street Bernard Waber (Houghton Mifflin; 1968) When Joshua and his parents move into the new house on East 88th Street, they find the upstairs bathroom occupied by Lyle, a talented caviar-loving crocodile. Sequels include *Lyle, Lyle, Crocodile, Lovable Lyle, Lyle and the Birthday Party,* and *Lyle Finds His Mother.*

The Jolly Postman, or Other People's Letters Janet and Allan Ahlberg
(Little, Brown; 1986) A birthday invitation to Baby Bear from
Goldilocks, an advertising circular for the Wicked Witch, and a
postcard to the giant from Jack - all (and more) tucked into the en-
velope-like pages of the book.

Jumanji Chris Van Allsburg (Houghton Mifflin; 1981) Two kids find
an abandoned board game called Jumanji in the park; as they play
it, the game comes alive, complete with lions, snakes, and kitchen-
destroying monkeys. Wonderful illustrations. Also by Van Allsburg: *The Stranger, The Wreck of the Zephyr, The Witch's Broom,* and
The Polar Express. All haunting and beautiful.

The Legend of the Indian Paintbrush Tomie de Paola (Putnam;
1988) Little Gopher, a small artist who dreams of capturing the
colors of the sunset on his buckskin canvas, brings the flowering
sunset-colored Indian paintbrush to earth. By the same author: *The
Legend of the Bluebonnet.*

The Littles John Peterson (Scholastic; 1970) The Littles, a family of
tiny people (with tails), live in the walls of the Bigg family's house.
The story of their adventures is told in a series of short chapter
books, of which this is the first. Sequels include *The Littles and the
Big Storm, The Littles and the Trash Tinies, The Littles Have a Wed-
ding, The Littles Go to School, The Littles' Surprise Party,* and *The Littles to the Rescue.*

Keep the Lights Burning, Abbie Peter and Connie Roop (Carolrhoda;
1985) Abbie has to keep the lighthouse lights burning through a
storm at sea after her father rows to the mainland to get medicine
for her sick mother. Based on a true story.

Many Moons James Thurber (Harcourt, Brace, Jovanovich; 1943) The
Princess Lenore falls ill of a surfeit of raspberry tarts and will only
be well again if she can have the moon. The clever court jester gets
it for her.

Ming Lo Moves the Mountain Arnold Lobel (Scholastic; 1982) Ming
Lo and his wife live miserably in the dark shadow of a mountain.
With the help of the village wise man, they manage, after a little
trial and error, to make the mountain (more or less) move.

Mufaro's Beautiful Daughters John Steptoe (Lothrop, Lee & Shepard;
1987) A West African tale of Mufaro's two beautiful daughters,

one nasty and ambitious, one generous and kind, who both set out to marry the king.

Paul Bunyan Steven Kellogg (Morrow Junior Books; 1984) The story of the legendary lumberjack, his gargantuan pet, Babe the Blue Ox, and his larger-than-life adventures. More by Kellogg along the same lines: *Peco Bill*, the story of the tall-tale cowboy, *Mike Fink*, the tale of the world's greatest riverboat man, and *Johnny Appleseed*, the story of the famous apple-tree-planter.

The Quilt Story Tony Johnston (G.P. Putnam's Sons; 1985) A home-made quilt, patterned with falling stars, comforts two generations of little girls.

Stone Soup Marcia Brown (Scribner's; 1947) The classic tale of the clever soldiers who feed a whole village with soup made out of a stone.

The Story About Ping Marjorie Fleck and Kurt Wiese (Viking; 1933) Ping, a yellow duck, lives with all his family aboard a boat in the Yangtze River, until one day he ventures off on his own and gets lost.

The Tale of Peter Rabbit Beatrix Potter (Frederick Warne; 1902) The beloved classic about the disobedient little rabbit who wriggles into Mr. McGregor's garden and then has a hard time getting out again. For fans of Peter, there are many other exquisitely illustrated little animal tales by Potter, among them *The Tale of Benjamin Bunny*, *The Tale of Squirrel Nutkin*, *The Tale of Mrs. Tiggy-winkle*, and *The Tale of Jemima Puddle-duck*.

Thy Friend, Obadiah Brinton Turkle (Puffin; 1969) Obadiah is an adventure-prone small Quaker boy, who lives with his large and understanding family in 19th-century Philadelphia. Sequels include *Obadiah the Bold*, *Rachel and Obadiah*, and *The Adventures of Obadiah*.

The Velveteen Rabbit Margery Williams (Doubleday; 1926) The enchanting story of the dearly loved little stuffed rabbit who becomes real.

Winnie -the-Pooh A.A. Milne (Dutton, 1926) The classic tale of the plump and endearing Bear of Little Brain who, along with Piglet, Owl, Eeyore the doleful donkey, and Rabbit and all of his friends and relations, lives in Christopher Robin's Enchanted Forest. The adventures of Pooh and company continue in *The House at Pooh Corner*.

Books for Grade Level 3:

Arabel's Raven Joan Aiken (Doubleday; 1974) The adventures of Arabel and her pet raven, Mortimer, who sleeps in the bread box, looks for diamonds in the coal bin, and keeps croaking "Nevermore!" Sequel: *Arabel and Mortimer*.

The Best Christmas Pageant Ever Barbara Robinson (Harper & Row/ HarperCollins; 1972) The five hideous Herdman kids take over the annual Christmas pageant, with surprising and heart-warming results for everyone.

The BFG Roald Dahl (Farrar, Straus & Giroux; 1982) Sophie, an eight-year-old orphan, and the BFG, the Big Friendly Giant who blows dreams in the windows of sleeping children, manage to rid the world of a band of people-eating giants. The language, from "snozzcumber" to "scrumdiddlyumptious," is wonderful.

Bunnicula: A Rabbit Tale of Mystery Deborah and James Howe (Atheneum; 1979) Harold the lethargic dog and Chester the excitable cat cope with the arrival of Bunnicula, a (possibly vampire) bunny found by their owners in a movie theatre during a showing of "Dracula." Further, and equally funny, adventures of Harold and Chester follow in *Howliday Inn, The Celery Stalks at Midnight, Nighty-Nightmare*, and *Return to Howliday Inn*.
Catwings Ursula LeGuin (Orchard Books; 1988) All the kittens in Mrs. Jane Tabby's latest litter are born with wings; when they grow up, they fly away from the city to find a new safer home. There's a sequel: *Catwings Return*.

Charlie and the Chocolate Factory Roald Dah (Knopf; 1963) Charlie Bucket finds a winning golden ticket in his chocolate bar and embarks on a fantastic tour of Mr. Willie Wonka's magical chocolate factory, along with a company of greedy and horrible children, all of whom get their comeuppance. In the sequel, *Charlie and the Great Glass Elevator*, Charlie and Willie Wonka rocket into space, where they tangle with the Vermicious Knids.

Charlotte's Web E.B. White (Harper & Row/HarperCollins; 1952)
Charlotte, a wise, creative, and literate spider, saves the life of Wilbur the pig.

The Cricket in Times Square George Selden (Farrar, Straus & Giroux; 1960) Chester, a misplaced and musical country cricket, lives in a subway station in New York City's Times Square, along with friends Harry (the cat), Tucker (the mouse), and a boy named Mario, whose parents run a newstand.

Encyclopedia Brown: Boy Detective Donald Sobol (Lodestar/Morrow; 1963) Encyclopedia (really Leroy) Brown looks like an ordinary ten-year-old, but is really the world's greatest boy sleuth. This is the first collection of Encyclopedia Brown mysteries; there are many more.

The Enormous Egg Oliver Butterworth (Little, Brown; 1956) A mysterious and enormous egg from the Twitchell family's chicken coop hatches out an infant Triceratops.

Fantastic Mr. Fox Roald Dahl (Puffin; 1988) The truly fantastic Mr. Fox permanently tricks a nasty trio of fox-hunting farmers, Boggis, Bunce, and Bean.

Flat Stanley Jeff Brown (Harper & Row; 1974) A bulletin board falls on Stanley in the night, squashing him flat as paper. He has several adventures in his new shape until his younger brother finally restores him to normal, with a bicycle pump.

Freddy the Detective Walter R. Brooks (Knopf; 1932) Freddy the versatile pig becomes a detective and, with the help of his friends on the Bean farm, manages to bring Simon the rat and gang to justice. There are several more volumes of Freddy's entertaining adventures, among them *Freddy Goes Camping, Freddy and the Men From Mars, Freddy and the Perilous Adventure, Freddy the Cowboy,* and *Freddy the Pilot.*

Homer Price Robert McCloskey (Viking; 1943) Homer Price of Centerburg deals with skunks and burglars, a crazed automatic doughnut-making machine, the world's biggest ball of string, a musical mousetrap on wheels, and more. Warm, delightful, and funny. For more on Homer, try *Centerburg Tales: More Adventures of Homer Price.*

Jacob Two-Two and the Dinosaur   Mordicai Richler (Knopf; 1987)   Jacob Two-Two got his name because, being the youngest in the family, he always has to say things twice before anybody pays attention. People do pay attention, however, to his pet lizard - which turns out to be a (pizza-loving) Diplodocus dinosaur. For more adventures of Jacob, try *Jacob Two-Two Meets the Hooded Fang*, in which Jacob is convicted of insulting a grown-up (he asked for two pounds of tomatoes two times) and is sentenced to Slimers' Isle, a nightmarish prison guarded by wolverines and the child-hating Hooded Fang.

James and the Giant Peach Roald Dahl   (Knopf; 1961)   James, an orphan, lives with his evil aunts, Spiker and Sponge, until he encounters a gigantic magic peach and sets off on a strange journey with the equally overgrown Spider, Centipede, Glow-worm, Grasshopper, and Earthworm.

Just So Stories Rudyard Kipling   (Viking; 1902)   A collection of perennial favorites, including "How the Rhinoceros Got His Skin," "How the Leopard Got His Spots," "The Cat Who Walked By Himself," and "The Elephant's Child." Every childhood should include an imaginary trip to the great, grey-green greasy Limpopo River, all set about with fever trees, to see what the Crocodile has for dinner.

Lafcadio, The Lion Who Shot Back   Shel Silverstein (Harper; 1963)   Lafcadio, the sharp-shooting lion, leaves home to become the star of Finchfinger's Circus and to live on toasted marshmallows and buttermilk. He becomes famous, but not quite happy.

Mary Poppins Pamela Travers   (Revised Edition: Harcourt, Brace, Jovanovich; 1962)   The story of the acerbic and magical nanny with the parrot-headed umbrella who arrives on the East Wind at Cherry-Tree Lane to take care of Jane, Michael, and the twins. Sequels include *Mary Poppins Comes Back*, *Mary Poppins Opens the Door*, and *Mary Poppins in the Park*.

The Mouse and the Motorcycle Beverly Cleary   (Morrow Junior Books; 1965)   Ralph, the mouse, meets the (toy) motorcycle and Keith, its owner, who is staying with his parents at the Mountain View Inn. After a series of escapades and adventures, he gets to keep the motorcycle for his very own. Further adventures of Ralph in *Runaway Ralph* and *Ralph S. Mouse*. (The S stands for Smart.)

My Father's Dragon   Ruth Stiles Gannett   (Random House; 1948)   Elmer Elevator, with a knapsack full of tangerines and lollipops, travels to Wild Island to save a small captive dragon. Sequels include *Elmer and the Dragon* and *The Dragons of Blueland*.

Mr. Popper's Penguins   Richard and Florence Atwater   (Little, Brown; 1938)   Mr. Popper, a housepainter, is given a penguin (Captain Cook) by Captain Drake of the Antarctic Expedition. He next acquires a female penguin (from the Aquarium in Mammoth City); and soon the Poppers are the surprised owners of twelve penguins. To support his growing family, Mr. Popper decides to take the penguins on the stage.

Pippi Longstocking Astrid Lindgren   (Viking; 1950)   The adventures of Pippi, the strongest girl in the world, who lives insouciantly all by herself, and keeps a horse on the porch and a chest of gold coins under her bed. Sequels include *Pippi in the South Seas, Pippi Goes on Board*, and *Pippi on the Run*.

Rabbit Hill Robert Lawson   (Puffin; 1941)   All the animals on the hill, especially Little Georgie the rabbit, are in a turmoil: new folks are moving into the long-empty Big House.

The Reluctant Dragon Kenneth Grahame   (Holiday; 1938)   The dragon, a retiring type, wants only to sit in his cave and write poetry - but then St. George comes to town. An understanding solution satisfies everyone.

The Shrinking of Treehorn   Florence Parry Heide   (Holiday; 1971)   Treehorn is definitely shrinking, but his parents don't seem to notice. Great illustrations by Edward Gorey. By the same author: *Treehorn's Treasure* and *The Problem With Pulcifer*.

Tintin Series Hergé   (Little, Brown)   Not-just-another comic book series, these wordy animated adventures of Tintin, the globe-trotting boy detective, and his talking dog, Snowy, have probably lured more kids into reading than all the basal readers put together. There are 21 available titles in the series, all in oversized paperback: *Tintin and the Black Island, Tintin and the Blue Lotus, Tintin and the Broken Ear, Tintin and the Calculus Affair, Tintin and the Castafiore Emerald, Tintin and the Cigars of the Pharoah, Tintin and Flight 714, Tintin and King Ottokar's Sceptre, Tintin and the Land of Black Gold, Tintin and the Picaros, Tintin and the Red Sea Sharks, Tintin and the*

Seven Crystal Balls, Tintin and the Shooting Star, Tintin: The Crab with the Golden Claws, Tintin: Destination Moon, Tintin: Explorers on the Moon, Tintin: Prisoners of the Sun, Tintin: Red Rackham's Treasure, Tintin: The Secret of the Unicorn, Tintin in America, and *Tintin in Tibet.*

Books for Grade Level 4:

The Adventures of King Midas Lynne Reid Banks (Morrow Junior Books; 1976) A delightful retelling of the tale of the unhappy king with the golden touch, who finally gets back to normal with the help of a mumbo - which, as everyone knows, is the proper name for a baby dragon.

Alice's Adventures in Wonderland Lewis Carroll (Macmillan; 1865) The classic tale of Alice, who tumbles down a rabbit hole while chasing after the elegantly outfitted White Rabbit.

The Bat-Poet Randall Jarrell (Macmillan; 1964) "Once upon a time," begins the book, "there was a bat - a light brown bat, the color of coffee with cream in it." The bat is a poet and an explorer; he stays awake in the daytime, composing poems about the new and colorful world around him - but his masterpiece turns out to be a poem about the dark familiar world of bats.

Bedknobs and Broomsticks Mary Norton (Harcourt, Brace, Jovanovich; 1943) Carey, Charles, and Paul meet Miss Price, amateur witch, when she tumbles off her broomstick into their Aunt Beatrice's garden. She gives them an enchanted bedknob which, when twisted on the bedpost, carries them into magical adventures - and finally takes them back in time to meet necromancer Emelius Jones. There's a Disney movie of the same name, but the makers obviously never read the book.

The Black Stallion Walter Farley (Knopf; 1941) After a shipwreck, a young boy, stranded on an island, tames a magnificent black stallion. There are eighteen Black Stallion sequels for dedicated horse-lovers.

The Borrowers Mary Norton (Harcourt, Brace, Jovanovich; 1953) The enchanting story of Pod, Homily, and Arriety, the Borrowers, tiny people who live under the floor of Great-Aunt Sophy's Victorian mansion. Arriety, against all Borrower tradition, makes friends with a human boy. Sequels include *The Borrowers Afield*, *The Borrowers Afloat*, *The Borrowers Aloft*, and *The Borrowers Avenged*.

The Boxcar Children   Gertrude Chandler Warner   (Whitman; 1942)   Henry, Jessie, Violet, and Benny are orphans who - rather than risk being separated - make a home for themselves in an abandoned boxcar. There are 19 Boxcar Children books in all, in which the children solve an assortment of mild mysteries.

Caddie Woodlawn   Carol Ryrie Brink   (Macmillan; 1935)   The story of tomboyish Caddie Woodlawn and her 19th-century adventures on the Wisconsin frontier. In a subplot, the family decides whether or not to leave America for England, when the father turns out to be the heir to a great estate.

Chronicles of Narnia   C.S. Lewis   (Macmillan; 1950)   In the first book in this series, *The Lion, the Witch, and the Wardrobe*, four children pass through the back of a magical wardrobe into the land of Narnia. Narnia is ruled by the wicked White Witch, who keeps the land in eternal winter and turns her enemies into stone. The children, with the help Aslan, the great lion, overthrow the witch and free the kingdom. A seven-volume series; other titles are *Prince Caspian*, *The Voyage of the Dawn Treader*, *The Silver Chair*, *The Horse and His Boy*, *The Magician's Nephew*, and *The Last Battle*.

David and the Phoenix   Edward Ormondroyd   (Follett; 1957)   David, while mountain-climbing, stumbles upon the erudite Phoenix, and embarks upon a series of adventures with griffins, leprechauns, witches, and sea serpents - and a Phoenix-stalking Scientist.

The Devil's Storybook   Natalie Babbitt   (Farrar, Straus & Giroux; 1974)   A collection of thought-provoking stories starring the very sly and clever devil. Sequel: *The Devil's Other Storybook*.

The Dolls' House   Rumer Godden   (Puffin; 1948)   The dolls' house once belonged to Emily and Charlotte's great-grandmother, as did the dolls: Totty, the gallant little farthing doll, who never forgets that she was made of wood from a strong tree; and the elegant, conceited, and villainous Marchpane.

From the Mixed-Up Files of Mrs. Basil E. Frankweiler   E.L. Konigsberg   (Macmillan; 1967)   Two children run away from home and, using a number of creative subterfuges, hide out at the Metropolitan Museum of Art, where they solve a mystery about an angel, sculpted by Michelangelo.

Half Magic Edward Eager (Harcourt, Brace, Jovanovich; 1954) Four children find a magic token that - maddeningly - grants only half of every wish made upon it. The Eager books are thoroughly delightful: others include *Magic by the Lake, Knight's Castle, Seven-Day Magic, Magic or Not?*, and *The Time Garden*.

Harriet the Spy Louise Fitzhugh (Harper Trophy; 1964) Harriet Welsch, child spy, keeps a secret notebook filled with (totally honest) notes and observations on the people around her. All goes well until the notebook falls into the wrong hands.

Miss Hickory Carolyn Sherwin Bailey (Viking Press; 1946) Miss Hickory is a country woman made of an apple twig with a hickory-nut head; she lives in a cabin made of corncobs and sleeps under a patchwork quilt of sumac leaves. Her adventures with her assorted animal neighbors during the long New Hampshire winter - including a magical Christmas - are delightful. At the end, however, Miss Hickory's head is eaten by the hungry Squirrel and her body, miraculously, becomes a blossoming graft on an apple tree. Miss Hickory, the author tells us, is completely happy about this, but our kids weren't.

The Indian in the Cupboard Lynne Reid Banks (Doubleday; 1981) Omri's toy Indian comes to life when placed inside a magical cupboard, bringing excitement, adventure, and great difficulties. Sequels include *The Return of the Indian, The Secret of the Indian*, and *The Mystery of the Cupboard*.

Knights of the Kitchen Table Jon Scieszka (Viking; 1991) Joe gets *The Book* as a birthday present from his uncle, a magician. *The Book* has the power to transport Joe and his two best friends through time, where they stumble through a series of humorous adventures. Sequels include *The Not-So-Jolly Roger* and *The Good, the Bad, and the Goofy*.

Martin's Mice Dick King-Smith (Crown; 1988) Martin, a very unusual cat, keeps pet mice in a bathtub in the barn attic. By the same author: *Harry's Mad*, in which Harry inherits, from an American uncle, an extremely intelligent talking parrot named Madison.

Owls in the Family Farley Mowat (Little, Brown; 1961) The adventurous story of a nature-loving boy growing up on the Saskatchewan prairies, along with his pet owls, Wol and Weeps.

The Phantom Tollbooth Norton Juster (Random House; 1961) Milo passes through the Phantom Tollbooth into a strange and magical country where, in company with Tock, a Watchdog, and the Humbug, he sets out to find Rhyme and Reason and restore peace to the warring kingdoms of Dictionopolis and Digitopolis. A brilliant tour-de-force with words and numbers.

The Search for Delicious Natalie Babbitt (Farrar, Straus & Giroux; 1969) The trouble began over the Prime Minister's dictionary: the Prime Minister claims "Delicious is fried fish;" the General of the Armies opts for a mug of beer; the king for apples; and the queen for Christmas pudding. Young Gaylen is sent out to take a survey of "delicious" throughout the kingdom, and along the way has a series of strange adventures, (almost) participates in a war, and finds the true meaning of delicious.

The Secret Garden Frances Hodgson Burnett (Lippincott; 1912) Mary, a cross and skinny orphan from India, is brought to her uncle's lonely house on the English moors. There she meets Dickon, a wise country boy, and Colin, her spoiled and sickly cousin; and restores to life a long-locked and secret rose garden.

The Sign of the Beaver Elizabeth George Speare (Houghton Mifflin; 1983) Twelve-year-old Matt, waiting alone for his father to return to their cabin in the Maine wilderness, is befriended by the chief of the nearby Beaver clan and his grandson, Attean.

Soup Robert Newton Peck (Knopf; 1974) Soup is the author's trouble-prone boyhood pal; the stories of their activities in rural Vermont in the 1920's are funny and delightful. Several sequels.

Stone Fox John Gardiner (Crowell; 1980) Ten-year-old Willy and his dog, Searchlight, must win the dog-sled race to pay off the taxes on his grandfather's farm - but his chance seems slim, since he'll be racing against the powerful legendary Indian, Stone Fox.

The Whipping Boy Sid Fleischman (Greenwillow; 1986) Jemmy, the whipping boy, and Prince Brat, the heir to the throne, run away together and stumble into a series of adventures with the villanous Hold-Your-Nose Billy and Cutwater that change both boys' lives for the better.

The Wish Giver Bill Brittain   (Harper; 1983)   Wishes, purchased for fifty cents from the mysterious Wish-Giver at the church social, do come true - but don't turn out quite as planned.

The Wonderful Flight to the Mushroom Planet Eleanor Cameron (Little, Borwn; 1954)   David and Chuck come upon a notice, printed in green, in the newspaper: "Wanted: A small space ship about eight feet long, built by a boy, or by two boys, between the ages of eight and eleven." With that begins their association with the mysterious Mr. Tyco M. Bass and a marvelous trip through space to Basidium, the pale-green Mushroom Planet. There are five other titles in the series, including *Stowaway to the Mushroom Planet*.

Books for Grade Level 5:

Abel's Island William Steig   (Farrar, Straus & Giroux; 1976)   Abel, a very civilized city mouse, is swept off in a storm and stranded on an island, where he survives by a combination of luck, imagination, and hard work. Before he manages to return home, he learns an important lesson about life.
Be a Perfect Person in Just Three Days!   Stephen Manes   (Clarion; 1982)   Milo Crinkley checks *Be a Perfect Person in Just Three Days!* by Dr. K. Pinkerton Silverfish out of the library and follows the instructions to the letter - until he decides that perhaps he doesn't want to be perfect after all. By the same author: *Make Four Million Dollars by Next Thursday!*

The Cat Who Went to Heaven   Elizabeth Coatsworth   (Macmillan; 1930)   A poor Japanese artist paints a miraculous picture with the help of his little white cat, Good Fortune.

Cheaper By the Dozen Frank B. Gilbreth, Jr., and Ernestine Gilbreth Carey   (Bantam; 1948)   The riotous (and true) story of the innovative, red-headed Gilbreth clan, all twelve of them.

Children of Green Knowe   L.M. Boston   (Harcourt, Brace, Jovanovich; 1954)   Tolly goes to stay with his great-grandmother at ancient Green Knowe and finds the house haunted by three children who lived there in the 17th century: Toby and his horse, Feste, little Linnet, and Alexander, the flute-player. Strange and magical. Sequels include *Treasure of Green Knowe, The River at Green Knowe, A Stranger at Green Knowe,* and *An Enemy at Green Knowe.*

The 13 Clocks James Thurber (Donald I. Fine; 1957) The simultaneously poetic, clever, and comic tale of a prince who, with the help of the fabulous Golux, rescues the Princess Saralinda from the cold and evil Duke of Coffin Castle. Also by Thurber: *The Wonderful O, The Great Quillow, and The White Stag*.

D'Aulaire's Book of Greek Myths Ingri and Edgar Parin D'Aulaire (Doubleday; 1962) All of Greek mythology, enticingly presented and colorfully illustrated. By the same authors: *D'Aulaire's Norse Gods and Giants* (Doubleday; 1967).

Dealing With Dragons Patricia C. Wrede (Harcourt, Brace, Jovanovich; 1990) The contrary Princess Cimorene, who prefers fencing to embroidery, deals with wizards, witches, jinns, and an enchanted stone prince, and ends up as Chief Cook and Librarian to the King of the Dragons. The adventures of Cimorene are continued in *Searching for Dragons*.

The Fifty-First Dragon Heywood Broun (Cooper; 1921) Gawaine le Coeur-Hardy is the least promising pupil at knight school, until the Headmaster gives him a magic word ("Rumplesnitz") for protection from dragons. Thus armed, Gawaine triumphantly deals with fifty dragons - until the Headmaster tells him that there's no such thing as a magic word.

Mrs. Frisby and the Rats of NIMH Robert C. O'Brien (Atheneum; 1971) Mrs. Frisby, a widowed field mouse, goes to the super-intelligent Rats of NIMH, escapees from the labs of the National Institute of Mental Health, for help in moving her home, and is able to give them some help in turn. Sequels, by the author's daughter, Jane Conly, include *Racso and the Rats of NIMH* and *R-T, Margaret, and the Rats of NIMH*.

The Gammage Cup Carol Kendall (Harcourt, Brace, Jovanovich; 1959) The Minipins, who live along the river that runs through a hidden valley, are all very much alike, right down to the color of their front doors (green). Five rebels, ostracized from their village for contrary behavior - Muggles isn't tidy, Curley Green paints pictures, Gummy composes poems, Walter the Earl spends his time digging for ancient artifacts, and Mingy just doesn't like being told what to do - together save the country from invasion and change the Minipin way of thinking forever. Sequel: *The Whisper of Glocken*.

The Hobbit J.R.R. Tolkien   (Houghton Mifflin; 1937)   Bilbo the Hobbit runs out of his door one day without so much as a pocket handkerchief, and sets off with a band of the dwarves to battle the dragon Smaug in his cavern under the Lonely Mountain.

The House With a Clock in its Walls   John Bellairs (Dial; 1973)   Lewis, his Uncle Jonathan, a practicing wizard, and their next-door neighbor, Mrs. Zimmerman, a witch with a penchant for purple, struggle to stop the hidden clock designed by an evil sorceror to end the world. Scary and exciting. Similar books by the same author include *The Figure in the Shadows, The Letter, the Witch, and the Ring, The Curse of the Blue Figurine, The Eyes of the Killer Robot, The Lamp from the Warlock's Tomb, The Secret of the Underground Room, The Trolley to Yesterday*, and *The Mansion in the Mist*.

The Jungle Book   Rudyard Kipling   (Viking; 1896)   The story of Mowgli, the Man-Child, raised by wolves in the jungles of India, his friend Bagheera, the wise panther, and his enemy, the giant tiger Shere Khan.

Peter Pan and Wendy J.M. Barrie   (Charles Scribner's Sons; 1927)   The original book has a much eerier and more dramatic flavor than the Disney version, to say nothing of suspense, fascination, and a real vocabulary.

The Pushcart War Jean Merrill   (Addison-Wesley; 1964)   The war between the pushcart peddlers and the truckers in New York City begins with the Daffodil Massacre, in which the cart of flower peddler Morris the Florist is flattened by a Mammoth Moving Truck. Funny, clever, and thought-provoking.

Sadako and the Thousand Paper Cranes   Eleanor Coerr   (Putnam; 1977)   The story of young Sadako, who has leukemia, contracted as a result of the atomic bombing of Hiroshima. A friend visits her in the hospital and brings her a gold-paper crane: "Don't you remember the old story about the crane?" Chizuko said. "It's supposed to live for a thousand years. If a sick person folds one thousand paper cranes, the gods will grant her wish and make her healthy again." Sadako does not live long enough to fold her one thousand cranes, but her courage becomes an inspiration to people everywhere.

Sarah, Plain and Tall   Patricia MacLachlan (Harper & Row/ HarperCollins; 1985)   Anna and Caleb's mother has died, so their father writes away for a mail-order bride. When Sarah arrives from the coast of Maine, she changes all their lives.

Tuck Everlasting Natalie Babbitt (Farrar, Straus & Giroux; 1975)   Ten-year-old Winnie meets the Tuck family, who have drunk from a spring whose waters give eternal life. A beautiful and thoughtful book.

The Twenty-One Balloons William Pène Dubois (Viking; 1947)   The story of Professor Sherman's fabulous trip by hot-air balloon to the island of Krakatoa, a land of elaborate restaurants and diamond mines. He arrives shortly before the island is destroyed in a volcanic explosion.

The Wind in the Willows Kenneth Grahame (Scribner's; 1908)   The classic tale of the Water Rat, the Mole, the wise old Badger, and the flighty and effervescent Mr. Toad, and their adventures along the River and in the Wild Wood.

Books for Grade Level 6:

Anne of Green Gables   L.M. Montgomery (Grosset & Dunlap; 1908)   The story of the red-headed, talkative, and talented eleven-year-old orphan who comes to live with Marilla and Matthew Cuthbert on their farm on Prince Edward Island. There are several sequels, including *Anne of Avonlea, Anne of the Island,* and *Anne of Windy Poplars.*

The Black Cauldron Lloyd Alexander (Henry Holt; 1965)   The land of Prydain, where the action takes place, is a landscape akin to ancient Wales. There young Taran, Assistant Pig-Keeper, sets bravely out with his companions to destroy the Black Cauldron, used by the evil magician Arawn to conjure up a diabolical army. Though the book stands on its own, there are four other volumes in the "Chronicles of Prydain:" *The Book of Three, The Castle of Llyr, The High King,* and *Taran Wanderer.*

Ghosts I Have Been Richard Peck (Viking; 1977)   The story of the oddly gifted Blossom Culp and her adventures in the spirit world - which include meeting the ghost of young Julian Poindexter, drowned in the sinking of the *Titanic.* By the same author: *The Ghost Belonged to Me.*

The Great Brain John D. Fitzgerald   (Dial; 1967)   The story of young John D. and his brainy big brother, Tom, and their escapades growing up in turn-of-the-century Mormon Utah.

The Haunting   Margaret Mahy   (Atheneum; 1982)   Eight-year-old Barney, youngest son of a strangely magical family, is frightened by eerie messages proclaiming "Barney is dead."

The House of Dies Drear   Virginia Hamilton   (Macmillan; 1968)   A modern black family moves into an old Ohio farmhouse, once a stop on the Underground Railroad. There, 100 years ago, the owner, Dies Drear, and two escaping slaves had been murdered. An enthralling mystery.

The Little Prince   Antoine de Saint-Exupery   (Harcourt, Brace, Jovanovich; 1943)   The mystical tale of the Little Prince who comes to earth from his own tiny planet, leaving behind a sheep and a rose.

Little Women   Louisa May Alcott   (Little, Brown; 1868)   The classic story of Meg, Jo, Beth, and Amy, growing up in Massachusetts in the days of the Civil War. Sequels include *Little Men, Jo's Boys,* and *Rose in Bloom.*

My Side of the Mountain   Jean Craighead George   (E.P. Dutton; 1959)   Young Sam Gribley, tired of crowded New York City, takes off for the Catskill Mountains where, equipped with a penknife, a ball of cord, an ax, and some flint and steel, he survives - in fascinating fashion - on his own. Sequel: *The Other Side of the Mountain.*

Redwall   Brian Jacques   (Philomel; 1986)   An action-packed knights-in-shining-armor tale of the community of gallant mice who live in Redwall Abbey. The mice battle to keep their Abbey safe from enemies; in this, the first book of the series, the enemy is a thoroughly evil rat named Cluny with his accompanying band of vicious cutthroats. Other Redwall books: *Mossflower, Mattimeo, Mariel of Redwall, Salamandastron.,* and *Martin the Warrior.*

Shakespeare Stories   Leon Garfield   (Houghton Mifflin; 1991)   An excellent collection of prose re-tellings of twelve of Shakespeare's plays: "Twelfth Night," "King Lear," "The Tempest," "The Merchant of Venice," "The Taming of the Shrew," "King Richard the Second," "Henry IV, Part One," "Hamlet," "Romeo an Juliet," "Othello," "A Midsummer Night's Dream," and "Macbeth."

Treasure Island Robert Louis Stevenson (Scribner's; 1911) The rousing story of young Jim Hawkins and his voyage in search of pirate treasure in company with the villainous (but fascinating) Long John Silver.

The White Mountains John Christopher (Macmillan; 1967) Will lives in the future, in a world that has been enslaved by the Tripods, huge three-legged machines. No one even questions the Tripods' power: all humans, at the age of thirteen, are Capped, fitted with a brain-modifying device that ensures obedience. As the time for Will's Capping approaches, he meets a stranger who tells him that there is a way of escape, and sends him off on the long journey to the White Mountains. Sequels: *The City of Gold and Lead* and *The Pool of Fire*.

Books for Grade Level 7:

The Call of the Wild Jack London (Grosset & Dunlap; 1965) More than just a dog story, set in the days of the Klondike gold rush. By the same author: *White Fang*.

A Christmas Carol Charles Dickens (Holiday; 1983) The stingy and uncaring Ebenezer Scrooge is visited by three spirits one snowy Christmas Eve, and undergoes a miraculous change of heart.

Fahrenheit 451 Ray Bradbury (Simon and Schuster; 1950) In the world of the future, all books are banned: a Fireman is a book-burner, and the "Fahrenheit 451" of the title is the temperature at which paper incinerates. By the same author: *The Illustrated Man* and *The Martian Chronicles*.

Island of the Blue Dolphins Scott O'Dell (Houghton Mifflin; 1960) This is the story of Karana, a young Indian girl, who spent 18 years alone on an island off the California coast. The story of her survival - battling the pack of wild dogs that killed her younger brother, fashioning weapons, hunting for food, building a house with a fence of whalebone - makes fascinating reading.

Never Cry Wolf Farley Mowat (Little, Brown; 1963) Reports claim that wolves are slaughtering the Arctic caribou; naturalist Farley Mowat is sent to investigate, with the words of his chief still ringing in his ears: "The wolf, Lieutenant Mowat, is now *your* problem!" Mowat spends months on the tundra learning to know the wolves, and finding the official reports to be far from the truth. His story is fascinating, often hysterically funny, and, ultimately, sad.

The Neverending Story Michael Ende (Doubleday; 1983) Bastian Balthazar Bux discovers a magical book through which he steps into the kingdom of Fantastica, where, with Atreyu and Falkor the luck-dragon, he participates in a great quest.

Over Sea, Under Stone Susan Cooper (Harcourt, Brace, Jovanovich; 1965) This is the first volume of Cooper's superb "The Dark is Rising" series, a present-day tale of the great battle between good and evil, with roots in the legendary past of King Arthur and Merlin. The main characters are children whose daily lives suddenly become intertwined with the ancient conflict taking place about them. A spellbinder. Subsequent volumes in the series include *Greenwitch, The Dark is Rising, The Grey King,* and *Silver on the Tree.*

The War of the Worlds. H.G. Wells (Scholastic; 1974) Wells's classic tale of the Martian invasion. By the same author: *The Time Machine.*

The Westing Game Ellen Raskin (E.P. Dutton; 1978) The 16 heirs to the fortune of Samuel Westing must compete by solving a series of clues to win their inheritance, a game that turns out to be positively dangerous.

The Witch of Blackbird Pond Elizabeth George Speare (Houghton Mifflin; 1958) Kit Tyler, sent to relatives in Connecticut from her home in Barbados after her grandfather's death, is homesick and lonely in the strict Puritan colony - until she meets Hannah, a Quaker, known as the "witch of Blackbird Pond."

A Wrinkle in Time Madeleine L'Engle (Farrar, Straus & Giroux; 1962) It was a dark and stormy night when Meg Murry, her remarkable younger brother Charles Wallace, and her scientist mother meet Mrs. Whatsit - who remarks, as she pulls on her boots, "Speaking of ways, pet, by the way, there *is* such a thing as a tesseract." A tesseract is a wrinkle in time, and through it the adventures of Meg, her brother, and their friend Calvin begin. Sequels include *A Wind in the Door, A Swiftly Tilting Planet,* and *Many Waters.*

Chapter Two

Writing

From ABC to
the Great American Novel

Ball-Stick-Bird Publications

The Ball-Stick-Bird phonics program, developed by research psychologist Renée Fuller, takes its name from the three shapes need to make all the letters of the alphabet: a circle (ball), a straight line (stick), and a V-shaped angle (bird). Using these shapes, color-coded for easy recognition, kids learn to write upper- and lower-case letters, starting with the simplest and most frequently used letters rather than proceeding in strict alphabetical order. By letter number two, kids are beginning to write words; and by number four, the stories begin, a series of catchy sci fi tales starring Vad of Mars, who has rockets for feet, and his evil enemies, the Vooroos of Venus. Ball-Stick-Bird stories aren't pap either: topics covered include ecology, authoritarianism, overpopulation, and other thought-provoking issues - and happily for all, the good guys always win and the bad guys learn a lesson. A real plus here, for beginners, is that actual reading is not put on hold, pending mastery of a long, and sometimes discouraging, list of "readiness facts." In fact, since the stories are written as curiosity-provoking cliffhangers, kids are motivated to move ahead, if only to find out what happens next. The Ball-Stick-Bird program is appropriate for kids aged 3 and up, and has had marked success with kids with learning disabilities. Available as two sets of five books each, with accompanying teacher's manual. Each set costs $74.95, plus $6.50 shipping and handling. For more information or a brochure, contact Ball-Stick-Bird Publications, Inc., Box 592, Stony Brook, NY 11790; (516) 331-9164.

Calligraphy Supplies

Our kids - all of whom kicked like steers at the sight of conventional handwriting practice workbooks - adored calligraphy. There are many calligraphy kits on the market, in a range of prices, for those interested in the art of decorative handwriting. Ours comes from the Schaeffer Pen people: it contains a high-quality fountain pen, 3 different nibs (fine, medium, and broad), 20 ink cartridges in 7 different colors (including emerald-green and peacock-blue), a pad of calligraphy paper, and an instruction booklet. The instruction booklet even includes a page of tips for left-handers, which helped our middle calligrapher, who is. Calligraphy kits cost $12.95 from KidsArt, P.O. Box 274, Mt. Shasta, CA 96067; (800) 959-5076.

Creative Writing

The best way for kids to learn to write, of course, is simply to write: stories, poems, essays, letters, lists, notes, daily journals. In our house, we've helped this process along a bit by making an "Imagination Box for Writers": a collection of index cards in a kid-decorated box, each listing a suggestion for a writing project. Try making one of your own.

From the Imagination Box:

1. You have just built a time machine. Where would you go? Write a story about what happens to you there.
2. Write a poem about your favorite season.
3. Imagine that you are the cabin boy or girl on a pirate ship.
4. Is it better to be a kid or a grown-up? Why?
5. Imagine you are shipwrecked on a desert island. What do you do? Tell about your adventures.
6. Write about your favorite trip. Where did you go? What was it like?
7. What do you suppose it feels like to be an endangered species? Write a story from the point of view of an endangered animal.
8. Write a letter to a boy or girl who lives in colonial times. Explain what life is like for kids now.
9. What do you suppose happens at the zoo at night after all the people go home?
10. Write a story about the most wonderful birthday present possible.

Design-A-Study

For those who want to learn to spell the old-fashioned way, Design-A-Study publishes an "all-in-one" spelling program for grades 1-8, available as either a spiral-bound notebook or a packet of 3-hole-punched separate sheets. The program, titled "Natural Speller," includes grade-level-appropriate spelling lists, lists of spelling and punctuation rules, and as assortment of exercises designed to build skills in spelling, grammar, and vocabulary.

There's also an equivalent "all-in-one" writing program, "Comprehensive Composition," for kids from preschool age through high school. "Natural Speller" costs $22.00, spiral bound, or $20.00 as a 3-hole-punched packet; "Comprehensive Composition,"in the same format, $14.00 or $12.00. For order forms or additional information, contact Design-A-Study, 408 Victoria Ave., Wilmington, DE 19804-2124.

The Elements of Style   William Strunk, Jr. and E.B. White   (Macmillan; 1979)

A classic of language usage for would-be writers young and old, written by William Strunk, Jr., professor of English at Cornell University, and his eminently successful student, E.B. White, known to children as the author of *Stuart Little, Charlotte's Web,* and *The Trumpet of the Swan.* Our home boasts two copies (one upstairs, one down), which have for years provided sage advice on the use of "shall vs. will," "that vs. which," and that awful bugbear of English composition, "hopefully."

Also for grammarians: *The Well-Tempered Sentence: A Punctuation Handbook for the Innocent, the Eager, and the Doomed;* and *The Transitive Vampire: A Handbook of Grammar for the Innocent, the Eager, and the Doomed,* by Karen Elizabeth Gordon   (Times Books, 1984)   All the rules of English grammar, illustrated in Victorian black-and-white, with riotous examples: "I had moped for five days before I would touch my gruel;" "After they removed the leeches, she showed them to the door;" "Those who are leap-frogging on the front lawn are in for a big surprise;" and - my favorite - "Not only were we naked, crazed, and starving (and far from our warm little homes); we were without any good books as well." These are books for grown-ups and sophisticated older kids; portions of them are naughty (under "Gerund Phrases": "Ogling stevedores is his penchant") and the vocabulary is adult. Rules of grammar learned from them, however, will remain locked in your mind forever. Available from bookstores or A Common Reader, 141 Tompkins Ave., Pleasantville, NY 10570; (800) 832-7323.

Families Writing   Peter R. Stillman   (Writer's Digest Books, Cincinnati, OH; 1989)

The cover blurb promises "a lifetime of family writing activities," and that's exactly what the book delivers: ideas for journals, field notebooks, memory books, family stories (with and without photographs), family newsletters, family recipe books. Then, under "How to Start a Tradition," there's the following:

"Dear Grandma,

This is to wish you a Merry Christmas. Instead of giving you a typical present this year, I promise instead to write you a letter every week."

In this world of families disintegrating, it's a joy to think of families building together, on paper. Available through bookstores or from John Holt's Book and Music Store, 2269 Massachusetts Ave., Cambridge, MA 02140; (617) 864-3100.

GNYS AT WRK: A Child Learns to Write and Read   Glenda Bissex   (Harvard University Press, Cambridge, 1980)
A detailed account of how one five-year-old learned to write, first using his own invented spellings, and then gradually correcting his mistakes and developing literary fluency. The featured child is the author's son; her observations of his "genius at work" developed into a doctoral thesis. Available through bookstores and from John Holt's Book and Music Store, 2269 Massachusetts Ave., Cambridge, MA 02140; (617) 864-3100.

Grammar Songs
Grammar Songs is a music-based kit generally recommended for upper-level elementary students, designed to teach kids the parts of speech and the basic rules of grammar and punctuation. Definitions and rules are taught through songs - which, if not precisely musical masterpieces, are highly effective memory aids. The 16 songs cover definitions of verb, noun, pronoun, adjective, and adverb, basic sentence structure, use of apostrophes, prepositions, capital letters, plurals, commas, and quotation marks, and Greek and Latin suffixes and prefixes. The kit contains an audiocassette, a 68-page student workbook containing all song lyrics plus associated written exercises, and a teacher's guide, with suggestions for activities, instructions for grammar games, and answers to the workbook exercises.
The *Grammar Songs* kit costs $16.95, from Audio Memory Publishing, 2060 Raymond Ave., Signal Hill, CA 90806; (800) 365-SING (orders) or (310) 494-8822 (information).

Heller, Ruth
This series of books, written and illustrated by Ruth Heller, may be the most appealing introduction to the parts of speech around. Each is a gorgeous picture book, brilliantly illustrated, with grammatical information presented in short, catchy verse. Appropriate for grammarians as young as 3 or as old as 12.
All are published by Putnam; titles include *Merry-Go-Round: A Book About Nouns, Kites Sail High: A Book About Verbs, Many Luscious Lollipops: A Book About Adjectives, Up, Up, and Away: A Book About Adverbs*, and *A Cache of Jewels and Other Collective Nouns.* Available through bookstores or from Michael Olaf's Essential Montessori, P.O. Box 1162, Arcata, CA 95521; (707) 826-1557.

If You're Going to Teach Kids How to Write, You've Gotta Have This Book!   Marjorie Frank   (Incentive Publications; 1979)
 The first slice of this book is a pep talk for teachers and students who don't like - or think they don't like - to write, followed by suggestions for starting points, a nine-part plan for producing a finished written piece, a commentary on criticism and technical writing skills, many ideas for writing projects (make a collection of home remedies, write a mixed-up fairytale, list six reasons for tomatoes, write an epitaph, make a pinwheel and write a poem about the wind), and a book list.
 More for creative writers: *Any Child Can Write: How to Improve Your   Child's Writing Skills from Preschool Through High School*, by Harvey S. Weiner,(McGraw-Hill; 1978); *Growing Up Writing: Sharing With Your Children the Joys of Good Writing*, by Linda Leonard Lamme (Acropolis Books; 1984) *In Your Own Words*, by Sylvia Cassedy (Doubleday; 1979). Available through bookstores.

Journal Writing
 There's nothing like a daily journal for encouraging kids to write. Some resources for journal-keepers include:

The Creative Journal for Children: A Guide for Parents, Teachers, and Counselors   Lucia Cappachione   (Shambhala Publications; 1982) Activities to encourage very young diarists. Suggestions include drawing a self-portrait, making a design using your own name, making a personal history timeline, making a list of life goals, creating an imaginary friend, making a family tree, drawing and/or describing your own home, drawing a dream, making three wishes. Activities can be adapted for preschoolers through older children. Available through bookstores.

Make Beliefs   Bill Zimmerman   (Bantam Books; 1992)
 A do-it-yourself diary and an imaginative delight. Sample pages: "MAKE BELIEVE that every time you stepped outside you had to sing a song. What would your song say?" "MAKE BELIEVE you could sleep on a cloud. What would you cover yourself with?" "MAKE BELIEVE it rained butterflies." "MAKE BELIEVE you could live in the sea." There are pages for wishes, jokes, smiles, longings, dreams, surprises, and just for being curious. Anybody can use it, but older, more articulate children will get more out of it. The writing spaces are designed for kids who can write fairly small. The book is available through bookstores.

Rainbow Writing   Mary Euretig and Darlene Kreisberg
(Dream Tree Press; 1990)
This is not an instruction book, but an actual diary for beginners. The format is oversized paperback, divided into twelve sections, one for each month of the year. (Each month's pages are a
different Necco-wafer pastel color, hence "Rainbow.") For each
month, there's a calendar to complete and a number of fill-in-the-
blank-type pages for kids who feel they have nothing to say: "List
your three favorite books." "Sit outside for five minutes. Write
down all the sounds you hear." "If I could make three wishes, I
would wish for these three things." There's a place for filling in the
best surprise of the month, a favorite new book title, something
new that was learned. There are also blank lined pages with
framed spaces for pictures where kids can write or draw whatever
they please. Appropriate for journal-writers under eight. *Rainbow
Writing* costs $9.95 and is available through bookstores or from
Dream Tree Press, 3836 Thornwood Dr., Sacramento, CA 95821;
(916) 488-4194, fax: (916) 488-4194, orders: (800) 769-9029.

*Writing Down the Days: 365 Creative Journaling Ideas for
Young People*   Lorraine M. Dahlstrom   (Free Spirit; 1990)
Writing ideas and activities for every single day of the year,
starting with the making of New Year's resolutions on January 1.
Other examples: on March 14, Albert Einstein's birthday, kids are
asked to discuss Einstein's saying "Imagination is more important
than knowledge;" on May 1, International Labor Day, they're
asked to discuss their future jobs; on May 27th, Vincent Price's
birthday, they're asked to describe the scariest movie they ever
saw. On Jim Henson's birthday, they discuss their favorite Mup-
pet (or invent a new one); on Evel Knievel's birthday, they write
about definitions of danger. On Guy Fawkes Day, the anniversary
of Great Britain's famous Gunpowder Plot, they're asked to write
about a time when they behaved mischievously, which seems a little understated; on Madame Curie's birthday, they deal with
women in traditional "male careers." Recommended for seventh-
graders and older, but certainly usable for younger writers. Available at bookstores or from Free Spirit Publishing, 400 First Avenue
North, Suite 616, Minneapolis, MN 55401; (612) 338-2068.

Kid-Written Publications
The following magazines all publish the work of young writers
and artists. For information order a sample copy and/or submission guidelines for contributors:

Boodle is a quarterly literary magazine for kids aged 6-12. *Boodle* publishes ("imaginative") stories, poems, articles, and illustrations by young writers and artists. They accept over 50 contributions per issue; those who get published receive two free copies of the magazine. An annual subscription (4 issues) costs $10.00; single samples are available for $2.50. Order from *Boodle*, P.O. Box 1049, Portland, IN 47371.

Creative Kids is a magazine for writers aged 5 to 18: accepted material includes fiction and non-fiction articles, poetry, games and puzzles, cartoons, songs, plays, book reviews, artwork, and photographs. The magazine, states the staff, "includes young people's work that represents their ideas, questions, fears, concerns, and pleasures. It does not dwell on any one aspect. The material never contains sexist, racist, or violent expression." Subscriptions cost $24.00 per year (8 issues) and are available from *Creative Kids*, P.O. Box 637, Holmes, PA 19043-9937. Submissions must include name, birthdate, grade, home address, school name, and school address; a statement signed by a legal guardian or teacher attesting to the originality of the work; and a self-addressed stamped envelope. Art work must be done in black ink or felt pen. Send to *Creative Kids*, P.O. Box 6448, Mobile, AL 36660.

Merlyn's Pen, "The National Magazine of Student Writing," is available in two editions: a junior version, for writers in grades 7-10, and a senior version for kids in grades 9-12. The magazine is a thoroughly professional publication, about 40 pages long on glossy paper, and is entirely kid-written and illustrated, right up to the front cover. Aspiring authors and artists may submit short stories, science fiction stories, movie, book, and music reviews, essays, poems, parodies, photographs, drawings, or cartoons. For writers' and artists' guidelines, contact the address below. *Merlyn's Pen* is published four times per year; an annual subscription costs $18.95, from *Merlyn's Pen*, P.O. Box 1058, East Greenwich, RI 02818; (800) 247-2027.

Stone Soup may be *the* literary magazine for children, containing high-quality stories, poems, book reviews, and art by kids up to age 13. Also included is an insert page of suggested writing and art projects based on the selections in the current magazine issue. *Stone Soup* is published five times a year; the subscription ($23.00 annually) accompanies membership in the Children's Art

Foundation. Send submissions, along with a self-addressed, stamped envelope, or subscription fees to the Children's Art Foundation, P.O. Box 83, Santa Cruz, CA 95063-9990; (800) 447-4569.

Young Voices, "The Magazine of Young People's Creative Work," publishes poems, stories, essays, non-fiction articles, interviews, and drawings by kids of all ages, elementary-level through high school. The magazine functions like a real-world adult magazine: interested writers are directed to submit a query letter, describing their proposed topic, and including some basic information about themselves, plus a self-addressed, stamped envelope. If a proposal is accepted, writers are paid for their work. Artists are not required to send a query letter, but submissions of work must be accompanied by a self-addressed, stamped envelope. A subscription to *Young Voices* costs $15.00 annually (six issues); for information, contact *Young Voices Magazine*, P.O. Box 2321, Olympia, WA 98507; (206) 357-4683.

Market Guide for Young Writers Kathy Henderson (Shoe Tree Press; 1990)

This 191-page book provides a comprehensive and descriptive list of (many) markets for work by young writers and literary contests open to young writers, sponsored by everything from the Young Playwrights' Festival to the Young Entomologists' Society. Also included: interviews with successful young writers and not-quite-so-young editors of young writers, and information on preparing and submitting a finished manuscript. Available at bookstores or from Betterway Books, 1507 Dana Avenue, Cincinnati, OH 45207.

National Writing Institute

The National Writing Institute was founded by Dave Marks, a public-school writing teacher and homeschooler, whose writing program - *Writing Strands* - is a real find. This, for me, is saying something, since, by and large, I am unfond of prepackaged writing programs. *Writing Strands*, however, strikes a nice balance between technical accuracy and creativity, all delivered in a day-by-day lesson format that gives kids just enough work to keep them busy and interested, but not so much that repetition makes them resentful and bored. Step-by-step instructions are clear and reader-friendly. (Caleb, now 8: "I like it. It sounds like the book is talking to you.") Progression through the *Writing Strands* books is so gradual and graceful that kids are writing fluently almost before they know it.

Writing Strands books are available in seven levels: Level 1 contains oral work for kids aged 3-8; Level 2 is appropriate for kids in grade 2; Level 3 for kids in grades 3-7; Level 4, 5, 6, and 7, respectively, for kids in grades 8, 9, 10, and 11-12. There are 15 assignments, for example, in Level 2, each taking several days to complete; topics include Adjectives, Listing, Reporting, Paragraphing, Ordering Actions, Grouping and Variety, Story Writing, Convincing, Writing Dialogue, Letter Writing, Personal Narration, Comparing, Greeting Cards, Projection, and Imagination. Level 3, for middle-grade kids, covers Following Directions, Sentence and Paragraph Control, Rewriting Sentences, Description (people), Description (people's thoughts), Organization (activities), Organization (objects), Description (perspective), Story Creation, Description (organization), Description (action), Organization (narrative events), and Creative (narrative). To order or for more information, contact the National Writing Institute, 7946 Wright Road, Niles, MI 49120; (616) 684-5375.

On-Words

On-Words is a game of word structure, from Wff 'n Proof, the instructional gaming people who came up with *Equations* (see Mathematics). In *On-Words*, players use letters to reach established goals (example: a 5-letter word) under play-determined rules, which may require, ban, or allow use of certain letters. Take it a step up in difficulty and a whole new range of grammatical restrictions may apply: the established goal may be a specific part of speech (noun, verb, adjective), with a required suffix or prefix, and so on. Depending on the selected rules of play, the inventors explain, the game can teach spelling, counting, grammar, phonetics, word roots, infectional endings, prefixes, and suffixes. It's also great preparation for the *New York Times* crossword puzzle. *On-Words* costs $22.50, from Wff 'n Proof Learning Games, 1490-JR South Boulevard, Ann Arbor, MI 48104-4699; (313) 665-2269.

Penmanship

Some kids like penmanship workbooks; some don't. Some parents support them; some don't. We tend collectively toward the "don'ts:" our kids all write reasonably legibly, having used assorted homemade penmanship exercises ("Write in cursive: The cat put on the green snorkle and leaped into the fish bowl") administered by their mother, and, given that, we've decided to leave well enough alone.

For those with higher standards, however, there are large numbers of penmanship workbook series on the educational market. Prominent among them are the *Palmer Method Handwriting* books, published by Macmillan, still demonstrating the standard slanty script I was taught in third grade (and promptly dropped in eighth); the Portland State University *Italic Handwriting Series*, which looks much more elegant; and Scott, Foresman and Company's *D'Nealian Handwriting* series, which eases the manuscript-to-cursive transition by starting kids off writing their letters at a slant, with little hooks at the bottom, suitable for future cursive connections. There's also the *Spencerian Penmanship Classic Curriculum* from Mott Media, a series of old-fashioned copybooks that promote a graceful copperplate script, taught in part by having the teacher count aloud while Spencerian students write rhythmically in concert.

Original sources for the above include Macmillan Publishing Company, Front and Brown Streets, Riverside, NJ 08075-1197; (800) 323-9563 (*Palmer Method Handwriting*); Tena Spears at Portland State University Continuing Education Press, Box 1394, Portland, OR 97207; (800) 547-8887, ext. 4891, or, in Oregon, (800) 452-4909, ext. 4891 (*Italic Handwriting Series*); Scott, Foresman, and Company, 1900 E. Lake Ave., Glenview, IL 60025; (312) 729-3000 (*D'Nealian Handwriting*); and Mott Media, 1000 E. Huron St., Milford, MI 48402; (800) 348-6688 or (313) 685-8773 (*Spencerian Penmanship Classic Curriculum*). All series are also available from Home School Supply House, P.O. Box 7, Fountain Green, UT 84632; (800) 772-3129; or the Sycamore Tree, Inc., 2179 Meyer Place, Costa Mesa, CA 92627; (714) 642-6750 (orders and fax).

Poetry Writing

Resources for young poets include:

Beyond Words: Writing Poems with Children   Elizabeth McKim and Judith W. Steinbergh (Wampeter Press; 1983)   A collection of poetry projects, with samples of student work, and ideas to stimulate the imagination. Kids write about special places, animals, fruits and vegetables, old people, occupations, feelings. They listen to a recording of "Songs of the Humpback Whales" and write whale poems; they collect objects from the outdoors - weeds, sticks, shells - and write poems about what they've found; they draw words written on slips of paper from a "word bowl" and compose poems using their selections. Available through bookstores.

Calliope Greta Barclay Lipson and Jane A. Romatowski (Good Apple; 1981) *Calliope* is subtitled "A Handbook of 47 Poetic Forms and Figures of Speech." Using it, young poets will turn out alphabet and acrostic poems, cinquains and quatrains, sonnets, ballads, and limericks, and learn a lot of basic poetic terminology: for example, the meaning and use of metaphor, simile, onomatopoeia, personification, hyperbole, and alliteration. Appropriate for grades 4-8, according to the authors, but many of the exercises are fun for younger children. Available from Good Apple, Inc., Box 299, Carthage, IL 62321; (800) 435-7234 or (217) 357-3981.

Rose, Where Did You Get That Red?: Teaching Great Poetry to Children Kenneth Koch (Random House; 1973); *Wishes, Lies, and Dreams: Teaching Children to Write Poetry* (Random House; 1970) A superb pair of books for young poets. *Wishes, Lies, and Dreams* is appropriate for children in kindergarten through grade 6; *Rose, Where Did You Get That Red?* for grades 3 and up. Both are filled with ideas for encouraging students to write poetry: projects, teaching suggestions, and samples of student work. *Wishes, Lies, and Dreams* includes ideas for poems based on wishes, noises, weather, colors, and animals; *Rose, Where Did You Get That Red?* uses the work of great poets - William Blake, William Shakespeare, Walt Whitman, Federico Garcia Lorca, Percy Bysshe Shelley, Frank O'Hara - as inspirational jumping-off points for kids' own poems. This technique expands readily and rapidly to poems not included in the book, and is a delight for creative poetry lovers. Available at bookstores, in paperback.

Poetry Books for Kids

As: A Surfeit of Similes Norton Juster (Morrow & Company; 1989) A great rhyming introduction to the art of simile - your kids will never ask what one is again - by the author of *The Phantom Tollbooth*.

Custard and Company Ogden Nash (Little, Brown; 1980) Vintage Nash, including the story of Custard, the realio, trulio, little pet dragon.

I'm Nobody! Who Are You?: Poems of Emily Dickinson for Young People Emily Dickinson (Stemmer House; 1978) 45 favorite poems.

Imaginary Gardens: American Poetry and   Art for Young People Charles Sullivan, ed. (Abrams; 1989) The poems, by Marianne Moore, Henry Wadsworth Longfellow, Phillis Wheatley, Edgar Allan Poe, Delmore Schwartz, and others, are illustrated by the works of noted American artists, such as Roy Lichtenstein, Grandma Moses, John James Audubon, and Winslow Homer.

A Light in the Attic Shel Silverstein (Harper & Row; 1981) By the same author: *Where the Sidewalk Ends*. Funny and extremely funny poems for kids.

A New Treasury of Poetry Philip Neil (Stewart, Tabori & Chang; 1990) 288 poems, arranged by theme, by such poets as Langston Hughes, Walt Whitman, e.e. cummings, William Carlos Williams, and Dylan Thomas.

Old Possum's Book of Practical Cats T.S. Eliot (Harcourt, Brace, Jovanovich; 1939) Fifteen masterly poems about marvelous cats, from Growltiger and Old Deuteronomy through Mr. Mistoffelees and Macavity the Mystery Cat.

The Random House Book of Poetry for Children (Random House; 1983) 528 poems in 14 categories, including "Alphabet Stew," "Children, Children Everywhere," and "Where Goblins Dwell."

Ride a Purple Pelican Jack Prelutsky (Greenwillow; 1986) Big-print rhymes especially appealing to younger kids, with colorful full-page illustrations.

Reflections on a Gift of Watermelon Pickle...and Other Modern Verse (Lothrop,Lee & Shepard; 1967) 114 poems by modern poets, including Phyllis McGinley, Ezra Pound, Carl Sandburg, and Lawrence Ferlinghetti, on subjects ranging from giraffes and toasters to arithmetic and the atom bomb.

Sing A Song of Popcorn: Every Child's Book of Poems (Scholastic; 1988) A wonderful collection of 128 poems from such poets as Edward Lear, Robert Louis Stevenson, Emily Dickinson, Edna St. Vincent Millay, and Nikki Giovanni.

Talking to the Sun: An Illustrated Anthology of Poems for Young People Kenneth Koch and Kate Farrell, eds. (Metropolitan Museum of Art; Henry Holt; 1985) A simply beautiful book, illustrated with full-color photographs of art works from the collection of the Metropolitan Museum of Art. There are native American, African, and ancient Chinese poems, poems by William Shakespeare, Robert Herrick, and Percy Bysshe Shelley, and poems by modern poets.

Tomie de Paola's Book of Poems   (G.P. Putnam; 1988)   Poems by Lewis Carroll, William Blake, Langston Hughes, Robert Frost, and more; lovely illustrations by Tomie de Paola.

A Visit to William Blake's Inn   Nancy Willard   (Harcourt, Brace, Jovanovich; 1981)   A poetic trip to William Blake's magical inn, where dragons bake the bread, and visitors include the King of Cats and the Man in the Marmalade Hat.

Starwords

A cooperative spelling game, in which players collaborate to make words to cover as many "Star Spaces" on the playing board as possible. Each word must apply to what you see in a displayed picture and must use the available letter tokens. It gets tricky quickly: pictures change; letters are irrevocably discarded.

There's an Advanced version of the game in which a roll of the dice determines the kind of word to be formed: antonym, synonym, adverb, adjective, noun, verb, rhyme, and the like. The game includes a colorful playing board, 100 letter tokens, and a collection of unusual pictures. Available from Bluestocking Press, P.O. Box 1014, Dept. GS, Placerville, CA 95667-1014; (916) 621-1123.

Treetop Publishers

For those writers who want something special to write *in*, Treetop Publishing produces a series of inexpensive hardbound blank books ("Bare Books") for children. The books are available in two sizes: small (6 3/8 x 8 1/8 inches) and large (8 3/8 x 11). There's also a horizontal version, wider than it is high, that opens sideways. The books are 28 pages long and are unlined; line guides are available for those whose handwriting tends to wander.

Bare Books come in a variety of cover styles, all black and white, to be colored by the owner: bears, balloons, butterflies, clowns, dinosaurs, dragons, or - if you want it all your own way - absolutely blank. Small books cost about $1.00 apiece; large books about $1.50. Minimum order: 10 books. For information and order forms, contact Treetop Publishing, P.O. Box 085567, Racine, WI 53408-5567; (414) 633-9228.

Typing

These days, with typing an essential skill for use of the ubiquitous computer keyboard, the earlier kids learn, the better off they are. One good resource for young typists is Christine Mountford's *Kids Can Type Too!* (Barron's; 1985). This is a stand-up typing manual, wire-bound along the top edge like a stenographer's notebook, with a fold-out base, for easy reference as kids sit at the keyboard or typewriter. The book comes with an assortment of stick-on textured dots that, attached to the keyboard keys, help keep beginners' hands in the right place. Each simple lesson is illustrated with a color-coded keyboard, plus a pair of kid's hands with matching color-coded fingers. For each lesson, there's a short typing exercise, to be repeated until the typist has it down cold. There are 22 lessons in all, covering all the letters of the alphabet, numbers, and punctuation marks, and the use of the shift key. Available through bookstores or from the Home School Supply House, P.O. Box 7, Fountain Green, UT 84632; (800) 772-3129.

A software program appealing to young typists is "Stickybear Typing:" a three-fold program in which kids begin with basic drills (reinforced by juggling bears), then proceed to speed and accuracy practice, and finally to the real nitty-gritty of typing, reproducing whole paragraphs of an entertaining story text. Available in IBM, Apple, or Commodore format from Optimum Resource, Inc., 5 Hiltech Lane, Hilton Head Island, SC 29926.

Write From the Start: Tapping Your Child's Natural Writing Ability Donald Graves and Virginia Stuart   (E.P. Dutton; 1985)

This book describes "a revolutionary method of letting young children discover their innate writing ability." Graves and Stuart object to the traditional "component model" of learning to write, in which kids first copy letters, then words, then construct simple sentences, learn proper use of punctuation marks, identify parts of speech, memorize lists of spelling and vocabulary words, and finally - after endless amounts of drill - are allowed to tackle real writing. Instead, they propose that young children be liberated from the restrictive rules of grammar and composition, permitting them to write as they please, using invented spelling. Children, allowed to "write from the start," produce articulate and involved work; knowledge of conventional spelling and grammar develop naturally, from a process of discussion, re-writing, and editing. Many specific examples. Available through bookstores.

Zaner-Bloser

These are basically workbook people, but their workbooks are better than most: their interdisciplinary spelling series ("Spelling Connections") features color illustrations and photographs, creative writing activities, excerpts from well-known children's books, exercises in the use of the dictionary and the thesaurus, vocabulary riddles, and - nobody's perfect - assorted drill assignments, along the lines of "Write the spelling words that have the long e sound spelled ee." Also available: color-illustrated handwriting workbooks for grades K-8; lined blank books is assorted sizes and styles; and lots of that red-and-blue lined paper (by the ream, $4.29) recommended for just-beginning printers. For a free catalog, contact Zaner-Bloser, 2200 West Fifth Avenue, P.O. Box 16764, Columbus, OH 43216-6764; (800) 421-3018.

Chapter Three

Mathematics

Counting to Calculus

The Academy for Economic Education

The Academy of Economic Education is a nonprofit organization, "dedicated to improving understanding among K-12 students of our economic system." Their prime publication along these lines is *Ump's Fwat: An Annual Report for Young People*, delightfully illustrated by Marilyn Sadler. Ump is a entrepreneurial caveperson; a fwat is a Stone-Age-type baseball bat; and the *Annual Report* is a pint-sized economics book, providing elementary-level explanations of the laws of supply and demand, and the associated concepts of profit, investment, stocks, and dividends.

Ump's Fwat, for all that talk about profit and loss, is absolutely free upon request; along with it, the Academy provides a couple of informational fliers, a copy of their newsletter, and an order form for additional economic educational materials, including an *Ump's Fwat* Instructor Guide and "The Economic Baseball Game" ($7.00), in which baseball-buying and -selling players experience firsthand how supply and demand affect the market price of a product. For additional information and a free copy of *Ump's Fwat*, contact the Academy for Economic Education, 125 Nationsbank Center, Richmond, VA 23277; (804) 643-0071.

Activity Resources

Activity Resources is a math manipulatives company, and each of their manipulative sets, they explain, "can be used at each of the four levels of thinking by making them available, first for play and then for investigations appropriate to the skill level of the children." Boiled down, that means that little kids can happily fool around with the things, and older kids can use them to solve increasingly complex arithmetical problems.

The Activity Resources catalog carries many mathematical manipulatives, including fraction tiles in seven colors, base ten blocks in red, blue, and purple, geoblocks, Cuisenaire rods, hundreds boards, tangrams, and Unifix and Multilink cubes, plus a large assortment of mathematical games and activity books. These last include *Cartesian Cartoons*, an "amusing collection" of graphing puzzles; *Pholdit*, an instruction book for making paper geometric solids, suitable for kids in grade 2 and up; *Bucky for Beginners*, presenting the geometry of Buckminster Fuller for kids in grades 4-12; *Hands-On Logic*, which allows kids to combine math skills with social studies, science, art, or language arts; and a statistics series for primary students titled *Used Numbers: Real Data in the Classroom* (see review below). For a catalog, contact Activity Resources Co., Inc., P.O. Box 4875, Hayward, CA, 94540; (510) 782-1300.

The Allowance Game

This is a simple money-based board game for the small: kids hop their pieces around a colorful homey gameboard, earning or spending small, manageable (and realistic) amounts of cash as they go. Players earn money by delivering newspapers, walking the neighbor's dog, selling lemonade, or losing a tooth; they spend on library fines, ice cream cones, and teddybears. Play money (coins, and one- and five-dollar bills) is included. The *Allowance Game* costs $14.95, from Toys to Grow On, Box 17, Long Beach, CA 90801; (800) 542-8338 or (310) 603-8890. In a similar board game, *Presto-Change-O*, kids also variously earn, spend, and save: the winner is the first player to accumulate $10.00. Available from Educational Insights, 19560 S. Rancho Way, Dominguez Hills, CA 90220; (800) 933-3277 or (213) 637-2131. There's also the old money-making classic, *Monopoly*, available at toy and game stores everywhere.

Anno, Mitsumasa

Award-winning illustrator and author Anno is justly famed for his thought-provoking picture books. Our children were introduced to Anno as toddlers, with *Anno's Counting Book* (HarperCollins; 1977), an enchanting little volume covering the numbers 1 to 12, with the growth of a small village through the seasons of the year. The book begins (0) with an empty snow scene; by (1) there's one house, one snowy pine tree, one bridge over the river, one snowman, and one skier; by (7), there are seven buildings, seven pine trees, seven spotted cows, a clothesline hung with seven sheets, and a rainbow with seven stripes of color; and so on. It's a beauty.

Anno's Math Games, *Anno's Math Games II*, and *Anno's Math Games III* (Philomel Books; 1987,1989,1991) cover a variety of mathematical concepts, through the creative activities of a pair of curious little characters in peaky hats named Kriss and Kross. The first, and simplest, of the books covers comparing and classifying, combinations and mixtures, number sequence, measurement, graphs, and ratio. *Games II* covers classification, comparison, points, number symbolism, and liquid measures; *Games III* tackles topology, triangles, mazes (there's an Anno-rendered version of mathematician Leonhard Euler's classic Konigsberg bridge problem), and the concepts of left and right. Problems are absorbing; illustrations are wonderful. Recommended for kids in kindergarten through grade 3. *Anno's Hat Tricks* (with Akihiro Nozki; Philomel;

1985) introduces logic problems, by way of kids wearing red or white hats (plus one mysterious "Shadow Child," whose hat color must be determined by the reader); *Anno's Mysterious Multiplying Jar* (with Masaichiro Anno; Philomel; 1983) introduces the concept of factorials; *Socrates and the Three Little Pigs* (with Tsuyoshi Mori; Philomel; 1983) - recommended for kids in grades 4-6 - introduces readers to probability theory, as Socrates, a hungry wolf, tries to determine which of three houses is most likely to harbor the three little pigs. All are terrific. Available through bookstores.

Burns, Marilyn

Marilyn Burns, if her books are anything to go by, is the sort of math teacher we all should have had in elementary school. *The I Hate Mathematics! Book* (Little, Brown; 1975), according to the back cover, "was written especially for kids who have been convinced (by the attitudes of adults) that mathematics is (1) impossible, (2) for those smart kids who can't play stickball, and (3) no fun anyhow." *The I Hate Mathematics! Book* is one of the superb Brown Paper School Book series, originally devised by a group of California teachers, writers, and artists who believe that learning occurs only when kids want it to; and that the process should be not only a challenge, but a joy. The books work. Burns's contribution to the series is largely mathematical: along with *The I Hate Mathematics! Book*, there's *Math for Smarty Pants, This Book is About Time,* and *The Book of Think (Or How To Solve a Problem Twice Your Size)*. The first two are entrancing introductions to real mathematics: concepts covered include topology, prime numbers, binary numbers, infinity, "The Preposterous Googol," and the parabola. All are presented through hands-on activities, puzzles, and mind-benders - no arithmetical drill here - kids make boxes (without topses), solve popcorn puzzles ("How much popcorn would fit in your sock drawer?"), do shoelace surveys, perform magic tricks with quarters and paperclips, play "Poison" ("A Friendly Game") and "Pig" (ditto).

This Book is About Time is another charmer; it covers the history of watches and calendars, explains time zones, timelines, and biorhythms, and delves into the science of the split second. Among the suggested activities: making sundials, sand timers, and water clocks, testing your reaction time, recording the phases of the moon, and building a pendulum (and using it to play a game of bowling).

Burns has also written a trio of books for the teaching adult: *A Collection of Math Lessons From Grades 1 Through 3, From Grades 3*

Through 6, and *From Grades 6 Through 8* (The Math Solution Publications). In these, she shows teachers how to implement her ideas in group or classroom situations: little kids solve riddles with bags of color tiles, estimate numbers with jars of beans, learn number place with popcorn and lentils, and experiment with boxes, toothpicks, and spinners; older kids estimate with raisins, multiply with rectangles, and are introduced to statistics by compiling a usage chart for the letters of the alphabet. ("Why, in a game of Scrabble, is Q worth more than E?")

Also by Burns: *Math and Literature*, which interfaces mathematical problems and children's storybooks, suitable for kids in grades K-3. Marilyn Burns's books and the rest of the Brown Paper School Books series are available through bookstores; *A Collection of Math Lessons* (all levels) and *Math and Literature* can be ordered from the Cuisenaire Company of America, 12 Church St., New Rochelle, NY 10805; (800) 237-3142.

Chess

Chess, with all its mathematical connotations, is a great game for kids of (almost) all ages. For beginners, Workman Publishing offers an introductory chess kit, consisting of a set of black and white plastic pieces, a large board, and an instruction manual, *The Kids' Book of Chess*, which explains both the mechanics of play and gives some information about the history of the game. Available through bookstores or from Workman Publishing, 708 Broadway, New York, NY 10003; (212) 254-5900. For a complete line of chess sets, books, and products, contact the U.S. Chess Federation, 186 Route 9W, New Windsor, NY 12553; (800) 388-5464. The federation also publishes a bimonthly children's chess magazine, targeted at kids aged 8 and up, *School Mates: The U.S. Chess Magazine for Beginning Chessplayers*. Annual subscription (6 issues) costs $7.50.

Chip Trading Activities

The Chip Trading Activities Program is a basic skills program for kids in grades K-8, designed to teach addition, subtraction, multiplication, division, and place value through the use of manipulatives, games, and hands-on activities. Number place is represented by plastic chips of different colors (ones are yellow, tens blue, hundreds green, and thousands red). The "Chip Trading Starter Set" includes an introductory (Book I) activities book, suitable for grades K-8, a teacher's guide, 150 chips, numeral cards (in coded colors), operation cards, dice, and ten chip tills (color-coded boards for trading activities). Additional manipulatives are available separately, and there is a supplementary series of student activity books: *Book II-Addition and Subtraction* (grades 2-8), *Book III-Multiplication* (grades 3-8), *Book IV-Division* (grades 4-8), *Book V-Place Value and Numeration* (grades 5-8), and *Book VI-Bases Other Than Ten* (grades 6-8). Available from Cuisenaire Co. of America, Inc., P.O. Box 5026, White Plains, NY 10602-5026; (800) 237-3142.

Counting Books

Anno's Counting Book: An Adventure in Imagination   Mitsumasa Anno   (Harper; 1977)   See above.

The April Rabbits   David Cleveland   (Scholastic; 1988)   More and more rabbits mysteriously appear for each day of the month, through 30 rabbits on April 30th. (Then, on May 1st, 1 hippo.)

Count on Your Fingers African Style   Claudia Zaslavsky   (Harper; 1980)   A survey of how different African tribes use their fingers for counting.

Counting Wildflowers   Bruce Macmillan   (Lothrop, Lee & Shepard; 1986)   Kids learn numbers by counting American wildflowers, in beautiful full-color photographs.

Demi's Count the Animals 123   Demi   (Grosset & Dunlap; 1986)   Big bright animal pictures with which kids can collectively count up to 100, starting with 1 pink-and-purple rhinoceros.

1 Hunter   Pat Hutchins   (Greenwillow; 1984)   A cross bespectacled hunter stalks right past 1 elephant, 2   giraffes, and so on, up through 10 parrots.

Moja Means One: Swahili Counting Book   Muriel Feeling   (Dial; 1971)   Kids count their way through East African culture.

One Woolly Wombat   Rod Trinca and Kerry Argent   (Kane-Miller; 1985)   Kids count Australian animals, one to fourteen.

Rooster's Off to See the World   Eric Carle   (Picture Book Studio; 1987)   Rooster (sequentially) collects a group of animals together and sets off to see the world. The book also introduces the concepts of addition and subtraction.

Ten in a Bed   Mary Rees   (Little, Brown; 1988)   Ten crowded kids are sequentially bumped out of bed.

When Sheep Cannot Sleep: The Counting Book   Satoshi Kitamura
(Farrar, Straus & Giroux; 1986)   Woolly the sheep can't sleep, so he sets
off on a walk, chasing 1 butterfly, watching 2 ladybugs, and so on.

Creative Teaching Associates

Creative Teaching Associates carries (many) manipulatives,
games, and puzzles for teaching mathematical concepts and skills
to kids of all ages. Games include the *Chase* series, played like par-
cheesi, designed to teach place value and decimals; *One*, an inexpensive card game that teaches fractions; and a large array of
"Consumer Math" games, intended to familiarize players with the
math skills necessary for daily living. Titles include *Budget*, *Travel
Math*, *Department Store Math*, *Bank Account*, *Shopping Bag*, *Purchase*,
Grocery Cart, and *Stock Exchange*. In *Bank Account*, for example,
players progress around the board paying bills (by check), making
deposits, balancing their checkbooks, and dealing with interest
and taxes. For a free catalog, contact Creative Teaching Associates,
P.O. Box 7766, Fresno, CA 93747; (209) 291-6626, (800) 767-4CTA.

Cuisenaire Company of America

The company publishes a gorgeous, glossy, full-color catalog,
125+ pages long, filled with math and science resources for kids in
grades K-9. Their namesake manipulative is the famous Cuisenaire rod kit, an assortment of brightly colored rods in graduated
lengths which - with accompanying activity cards and instruction
books - is intended for use in elementary- and middle-school-level
mathematics programs. (A starter set, 155 wooden rods, costs
$35.50.) They also carry all kinds of counting and sorting manipu-
latives, from beads to teeny dinosaurs; pattern blocks; color tiles;
dominoes; geometric blocks; fraction bars; decimal squares; mathematical balances; and all kinds of mathematical game materials,
including 7 different kinds of spinners and dice. And much else.
Books include a wide selection of both innovative mathematical
projects books and fiction books, recommended as springboards
for the teaching of mathematical concepts. For a free catalog, contact Cuisenaire Company of America, P.O. Box 5026, White Plains,
NY 10602-5026; (800) 237-3142. (Also see Science.)

Delta Education

Delta Education, Inc., publishes a pair of comprehensive full-
color catalogs, the *Hands-On Math Catalog* and the *Hands-On Science Catalog* (see Science). The company is dedicated to providing
"materials for educators who believe that children learn by doing,"

and accordingly, the catalog offers a wealth of educational good-ies suitable for hands-on investigation. Included, among the base ten blocks, Cuisenaire rods, and Unifix cubes, is the "Fraction Bur-ger," a wooden puzzle in which the buns are wholes, and the meat patty is divided into halves, the onion into thirds, cheese into fourths, tomato into sixths, and lettuce into eighths; *Quizmo*, a bin-go-like game designed to teach addition/subtraction or multipli-cation/division facts; *Fractions are Easy as Pie*, a puzzle game in which players assemble whole pies from different-sized slices; ge-ometry and clock dominoes; inexpensive student thermometers; sets of plastic beakers for liquid measurement activities; and a large assortment of mathematical activity and resource books.

For those just embarking on a mathematics program, Delta has organized some of their most popular materials into age-appropriate kits: their "Basic Math Manipulatives Kit," for exam-ple, includes a set of base ten blocks (100 units, 10 rods, 10 flats, and 1 1000-cube), a set of play money (coins and bills), a set of Learning Links, six plastic geoboards with rubberbands, and 6 sets of tangrams in different colors, plus a couple of instructional booklets. The whole shebang costs $79.00. For a free catalog, con-tact Delta Education, Inc., P.O. Box 950, Hudson, NH 03051; (800) 442-5444 (orders).

Design-A-Clock

Creativity for Kids (see Arts and Crafts) produces a terrific se-ries of boxed activity kits for children. Of particular interest to young mathematicians is "Tick Tock Design-a-Clock," with which kids aged 4 and up can make their own decorated (working) time-piece. The kit includes a folding heavy-cardboard clock form, hands and clock mechanism (some simple assembly required), an assortment of interchangeable paper clockfaces (one marked with Roman numerals), and collage materials and colored markers for decorating. The finished product is about nine inches square, can be stood on a bedside table or hung on the wall, and, once you in-stall your own AA battery, runs like a charm. Available from toys-tores or from Creativity for Kids, 1802 Central Avenue, Cleveland, OH 44115; (216) 589-4800.

Donald in Mathmagic Land

Producing an appealing math video for kids is no mean trick, but Disney has done it: *Donald in Mathmagic Land* is not only math-ematical, but clever, creative, and delightful. It starts with the an-cient Greeks, and ends up demonstrating mathematical aspects of cathedrals, baseball diamonds, starfish, and the *Mona Lisa*. Running time: 27 minutes. Available through Movies Unlimited, 6736 Castor Ave., Philadelphia, PA 19149; (800) 523-0823.

Easy to Make 3D Shapes in Full Color   E.G. Smith   (Dover; 1989)
There are many make-your-own-geometric-shapes activity books on the market, but this may be the pick of the litter. The shapes - cube, tetrahedron, pentagonal prism, octahedron, cuboctahedron, and icosahedron - really are easy to make; young mathematicians simply cut, fold, and tape or glue. Shapes are made of thin, glossy-coated cardboard, in appealingly bright colors; final products are not only good-looking, but solid enough for mathematical experimentation. *Easy to Make 3D Shapes* costs $2.95, from Dover Publications, Inc., 31 East 2nd Street, Mineola, NY 11501.

Extra Editions
Touted as "Good News for Students Who Needs Something Extra," *Extra Editions* is a series of math units in newspaper format, conceived and written by Earl Ockenga and Walt Rucker, a pair of mathematics educators from Urbana, Illinois. Each math "newspaper" is 15 pages long, with a headline reading EXTRA EDITION in red; they are available in sets of eight, grouped by grade level from kindergarten through grade six. Within sets, each *Edition* concentrates on a different mathematical skill. Titles in the Grade 3 set, for example, include *Place Value to 1000, Telling Time, Money, Addition, Subtraction, Multiplication Facts, Division Facts*, and *Fractions*.

Within each *Edition*, a cartoon - usually featuring a trio of homely little mice - appears at the top of each lesson page, introducing and demonstrating the featured mathematical topic. Each lesson also includes an illustrated "higher order thinking skill": logic problems, pattern identifications, mental math tricks, or word problems. The word-problems are often based on eye-catching real-world situations, such as comparing heights of the world's most spectacular waterfalls.

Extra Editions is not intended as a math program in and of itself, but as an enriching extra. Its authors state that it "augments and enhances all elementary math programs for grades K through 6 in a manner that nurtures and challenges students." It's not especially pretty, but it is efficient and inexpensive: individual *Editions* cost $1.25 apiece; sets of eight, $10.00. For a descriptive brochure and order form, contact *Extra Editions*, P.O. Box 38, Urbana, IL 61801-0038; (800) 423-9872.

Eyewitness Series: *Money*

For general information on the superb and ever-growing Eyewitness series (Alfred A. Knopf, NY), see Multipurpose Resources.

The volume of particular interest to mathematicians is the *Money* book, a worldwide overview of money from its origin to its use in the present day, illustrated with spectacular photographs. The book begins with photographs of unusual money used by past societies: stone disks from the island of Yap, Ethiopian salt bars, Sudanese hoe blades, native American wampum, Pacific island "feather money," and Chinese cowrie shells. It then moves on to discuss the first coins, the first paper money, the processes by which coins are minted and banknotes printed, money in trade, war, myth, and magic, and international money, then and now. There's also a brief dissertation on the piggy bank, some hints for coin collectors, and an index listing the notes and coins presently issued by various countries of the world. Available through bookstores.

Family Math Jean Kerr Stenmark, Virginia Thompson, and Ruth Cossey   (Lawrence Hall of Science; 1986)

Family Math is a 320-page book of projects and activities designed to encourage parents and kids to learn mathematics together. Each project, game, or activity is coded for level of difficulty (primary, elementary, junior high); the book is targeted at kids in grades K-8. For each, there is a list of necessary (simple) materials, an explanation of the mathematical skill the activity reinforces, and instructions for directing the activity. Mathematical activities are grouped into eleven basic categories: "Beginning," "Word Problems and Logical Reasoning," "Measurement," "Numbers and Operations," "Probability and Statistics," "Time and Money," "Geometry and Spatial Thinking," "Patterns and Number Charts," "Estimation, Calculators, and Microcomputers," and "Careers." Participants variously make odd and even cards using beans as counters, make their own tangrams, build a square meter, determine the ratio between diameter and circumference by using strips of ribbon and assorted jar lids, perform probability experiments with (homemade) spinners and dice, experiment with mathematical palindromes, and identify patterns on a hundred chart. And, of course, much more.

The book is also source of reproducible master sheets for all forms of mathematical activities: there are tangram patterns, game boards, blank calendars, graph paper in several grid sizes (including one- and four-quadrant graph paper), coin boards, number place boards, and hundred charts. Available from the Lawrence Hall of Science, University of California, Berkeley, CA 94720; (415) 642-1016.

Fictional Books About Math
Many fictional books deal with mathematical concepts, and these often make wonderful introductions to new mathematical ideas or enriching supplements to on-going mathematical programs.

Alexander Who Used to Be Rich Last Sunday Judith Viorst (Macmillan; 1987) Alexander gets a dollar as a present and makes some very unwise monetary trades.

All the Money in the World Bill Brittain (Harper & Row; 1979) Quentin catches a leprechaun and wishes for all the money in the world. He gets it - and then has to cope with the consequences, world-wide and local.

Arithmetic Carl Sandburg (Harcourt Brace; 1993) A picture book version of Sandburg's poem, which begins "Arithmetic is where numbers fly like pigeons in and out of your head." Both text and pictures are fun for young mathematicians: the illustrations are all anamorphic images, which means they are distorted until viewed with the (included) piece of reflective Mylar.

The Doorbell Rang Pat Hutchins (Greenwillow; 1986) Sam and Victoria have just divided up a dozen freshly-baked cookies, when the doorbell rings - again and again - bringing visiting friends. The cookies, accordingly, must be divided several times.

The Dot and the Line Norton Juster (Random House; 1963) The line falls in love with a purple dot, and in order to impress her, learns to form squares and triangle, hexagons, parallelograms and polyhedrons, and spectacular complex curves.

A Gebra Named Al Wendy Isdell (Free Spirit; 1993) Julie embarks on a magical tour of the Land of Mathematics, in company with a zebra-like Gebra (Al) and his friends, scientific "horses" representing the elements of the periodic table. The trip takes her through the Concentric Caves, the lands of Multiplication and Division, Addition Mountain, and the Valley of Subtraction.

The Go-Around Dollar Barbara Johnston Adams (Four Winds;

1992)   A clever explanation of how money is created, distributed, exchanged, and replaced. The book combines a fictional story of a single dollar bill, first found abandoned in the park and finally, after many travels, framed, as the first dollar earned at a new store, with catchy non-fictional information about paper money. The fascinating non-fictional tidbits appear on each page, printed on an oversized dollar bill.

Grandfather Tang's Story   Ann Tompert   (Crown; 1990)   A Chinese grandfather tells his granddaughter a story, illustrating the tale with tangram puzzle pieces arranged in the shapes of the animal characters.

Half Magic   Edward Eager   (Harcourt, Brace, Jovanovich; 1954)   Four children find a magic token that - maddeningly - grants only half of every wish made upon it. This leads to a lot of creative calculation.

The King's Chessboard   David Birch   (Dial; 1988)   When the king demands that his wise counselor accept a reward, the counselor asks for a single grain of rice, the quantity to be doubled each day for as many days as there are squares on the king's chessboard. Before many days have passed, the king learns his mistake and a valuable lesson. Set in India. For a Chinese version of the same tale, try Helen Pittman's *A Grain of Rice* (Hastings House; 1986).

Make Four Million Dollars By Next Thursday!   Stephen Manes   (Bantam Books; 1991)   Jason Nozzle checks Dr. K. Pinkerton Silverfish's book, *Make Four Million Dollars by Next Thursday!*, out of the library, and follows its hilarious instructions for becoming a multi-millionaire.

Melisande   E. Nesbit   (Harcourt, Brace, Jovanovich; 1989)   The tale of a bald princess who unwisely wishes that her hair "would grown an inch a day, and grow twice as fast every time it was cut." Her problems are eventually solved by a mathematically clever prince.

One Hundred Hungry Ants   Elinor J. Pinczes   (Houghton Mifflin; 1993)   An exercise in division. A group of hungry ants, zeroing in on a picnic, is halted by one mathematically-minded small ant who claims they will get the food more quickly if they split up into ranks. The group then splits itself into halves, quarters, fifths, and so on. Once they've finally got themselves in order, however, the picnic food is all gone.

The Phantom Tollbooth Norton Juster (Alfred A. Knopf; 1961) A fascinating and infinitely creative fantasy in which Milo passes through the Phantom Tollbooth and visits the warring countries of Dictionopolis (where he meets the Spelling Bee and has to eat his own words at a royal banquet) and Digitopolis (where he encounters the Dodecahedron and visits the Mathemagician's numbers mine).

Ts'ao Chung Weighs An Elephant Ludwig Lundell (Creative Arts; 1983) An adaptation of an old Chinese folktale, in which clever young Ts'ao Chung figures out how to weigh his father's elephant.

Go

Go is an ancient Chinese strategy game, played with black and white stones on a cross-hatched playing board. It's the kind of game, the president of the American Go Association writes, "that one can learn in a day - and spend a lifetime perfecting." Players basically attempt to stake out territories on the grid by building "walls" of stones, while simultaneously capturing and eliminating the stones of their opponents - but, as players gain more experience, the game quickly becomes more challenging and complex. There's more to Go than initially meets the eye. Generally available from toy and game stores.

Hands-On Equations

Hands-On Equations is an introduction to algebra, using manipulatives; and by the time kids work their way through the first few lessons, they'll know how to solve a simple algebraic equation. The system itself is simple. Student kits include a packet of manipulatives (blue and white chess pawns represent the unknown "x;" nice chunky red and green number cubes the positive and negative integers), a plastic sheet with a picture of an arm balance on it, and a stack of printed lesson sheets. To solve a given equation - say "$4x = 2x + 6$" - kids line up the requisite pawns and number cubes on each arm of the balance; then remove pieces in a balanced manner (a pawn off one arm, a pawn off the other arm) until the value of x can be determined.

The program has a couple of particularly nice aspects: for one thing, the kids get a charge out of solving complex-looking, grown-up-type equations; and, for another, the system does clearly demonstrate some basic algebraic principles. Kids quickly grasp the concept of the balanced equation (as in "If you're going to take a 3 off one side of the balance, you have to take a 3 off the other side, too") and learn that equation-solving is largely a matter of logical and sequential simplification. Our kids, having used the program, can now solve equations. The system definitely works.

The drawback of *Hands-On Equations* is its lack of connection. Our kids were willing to master this cute new mathematical trick, but they wanted a reason. "What do people do with this? What's algebra *for*?" Be prepared to deal with this one on your own.

The *Hands-On Equations Learning System* (manipulatives, plastic balance sheet, lesson pages, and instruction booklets) costs $34.95 plus $4.50 shipping and handling, from Borenson and Associates, P.O. Box 3328, Allentown, PA 18108; (215) 820-5575.

Hap Palmer

For musical mathematicians, singer Hap Palmer has produced a number of math-oriented records and cassettes. His "Learning Basic Skills Through Music" series includes numbers for the very small: In Volume I, kids aged 2-5 learn colors, numbers, and the alphabet through a series of catchy interactive songs; Volume II takes things a bit further, and includes counting to 20, colors, beginning subtraction, time-telling, and reading readiness. Both are available on either LP or cassette, in English or Spanish. "Math Readiness - Vocabulary and Concepts" teaches preschoolers the "language of math:" big, little, long, short, same, alike, before, and after. "Math Readiness - Addition and Subtraction," for elementary-aged kids, sets the basic addition and subtraction facts to music; "Swinging Multiplication Tables" does the same for the 2- through the 12-times tables. This last is particularly insidious; listeners, without conscious effort, seem to absorb the facts by osmosis. All are available on either LP or cassette, with accompanying guide, from the Educational Record Center, Inc., 3233 Burnt Mill Dr., Suite 100, Wilmington, NC 28403-2655; (800) 438-1637.

How Much is a Million David Schwartz (Lothrop, Lee & Shepard; 1985)

A delightful introduction to enormous numbers - a million, a billion, and a trillion - all stage-managed by Marvelosissimo the Mathematical Magician. Examples: "If a goldfish bowl were big enough for a million goldfish, it would be large enough to hold a whale." "If a billion kids made a human tower, they would stand up past the moon." And much more, all cleverly illustrated. By the same author: *If You Made a Million* (Lothrop, Lee & Shepard; 1989), in which Marvelosissimo explains money and interest. ("A MILLION DOLLARS! That's a stack of pennies ninety-five miles high, or enough nickels to fill a schoolbus, or a whale's weight in quarters." Illustrations include pictures of real cash. Available through libraries and bookstores.

In One Day   Tom Parker   (Houghton Mifflin; 1984)

In One Day, reads the introduction, "illustrates the human size of the United States. If all 236 million Americans were squeezed together into one standing-room-only crowd, they would take up 12.7 square miles of floor space... If all 236 million people stood single-file in a line, they would stretch 67,000 miles, or more than 26 times the width of the United States." The book contains 365 different entries, each detailing what all those collective Americans do in a day. Readers learn that in one day, Americans use 18,000 bushels of tea leaves, which is enough to make six million gallons of tea. They also eat 90,000 bushels of carrots, finish building 3000 new houses, weave 640 acres of carpet, and write 20,000 letters to the President of the United States. Many of the entries are accompanied by terrific graphics: a person stands next to a pile of 52 million tablets, for example, to show how much aspirin Americans consume in a day; a page of 10,000 dots shows how many babies are born daily; a mammoth cauliflower perches next to the heads on Mount Rushmore to show the size of the 750-ton head that Americans (collectively) eat each day. A fascinating education in real numbers. Available through libraries and bookstores. (Also see below: *On an Average Day* and *In an Average Lifetime*, by Tom Heynman)

Innumeracy: Mathematical Illiteracy and its Consequences   John Allen Paulos   (Hill and Wang; 1988)

This is an essential and thoroughly enthralling book for all families bent on combating mathematical illiteracy. "I am always amazed and depressed," writes the author, "when I encounter students who have no idea what the oopulation of the United States is, or the approximate distance from coast to coast, or roughly what percentage of the world is Chinese." A failure to grasp basic number concepts or to develop a feel for probabilities, Paulos explains, leaves us all prey to deception, confusion, or outright exploitation. The book, by way of countless fascinating examples, clearly demonstrates that a lack of mathematics in our daily lives can be the equivalent of P.T. Barnum's "This Way to the Egress!" The uninformed find themselves abruptly out in the street. The book leaves its readers with a solid appreciation of matters numerical. In our family, it also led to a spirited two-day discussion of how long it would take a continuous stream of dump trucks to cart away Mt. Fuji. Also by the author: *Beyond Numeracy: Ruminations of a Numbers Man.* Available through bookstores.

Institute for Math Mania

The Institute for Math Mania was founded in 1984 by educator Rachel McAnallen ("Ms. Math"), whose public-school "Mathematician in Residence" programs are aimed at teaching kids that math can both make sense and be fun. The Institute's catalog carries a large assortment of puzzles and games, mathematical models and manipulatives, origami materials ("a delightful way to explore geometry informally"), tangrams, pentominoes, and math books intended to promote problem-solving and thinking skills. The Institute has also organized a "truly cross-disciplinary" math immersion program known as the "Mozart, Escher, and Math" program, which has been notably successful in sparking math interest in school systems while demonstrating the relationship of mathematics of all aspects of real life. For more information and a free catalog, contact Institute for Math Mania, P.O. Box 910, Montpelier, VT 05601; (802) 223-5871.

Invicta Math Balance

This is a sturdy plastic arm-balance: arms are marked off at intervals with the numbers 1-10 and fitted with pegs, upon which can be hung 1-gram rectangular plastic weights. An alternative design has hanging plastic buckets on each arm, which can be filled with plastic counters. In either incarnation, this is an excellent tool for the hands-on demonstration of simple mathematical principles, such as greater than, lesser than, addition, subtraction, multiplication, and division. Equivalent quantities balance; non-equivalent quantities tilt the scale. A supplementary activity book, *The Balance Book* by Lee Jenkins, describes over 90 different balance-based activities, suitable for kids in grades K-8. Available from Activity Resources Co., Inc., P.O. Box 4875, Hayward, CA 94540; (510) 782-1300; or from Cuisenaire Co. of America, Inc., P.O. Box 5026, White Plains, NY 10602-5026; (800) 237-3142.

J C Cassettes

Number facts on cassette tapes. Three different "kits" are available, each containing a cassette, a teacher's guide, and a master "Answer & Award" sheet. Kit A (grade 1+) covers addition and subtraction facts; Kit B (grade 3+), multiplication and division; and Kit C ("For Experts" in grade 5+), a conglomeration of all of the above. Side one of each cassette introduces listening kids to the facts in question; side two is a quiz, in which kids try to come up with the correct answer before hearing it from the "Answer Lady." Each kit costs $19.95, plus $1.00 shipping. For a brochure: J C Cassettes, Box 73, Route 2, Calumet, OK 73014; (405) 893-2239.

Key Curriculum Press

Key Curriculum Press ("Innovators in Mathematics Education") produces creative math materials for kids in grades 1-12. Their primary program, the Miquon Math Materials, was by far our pick among early math series. Miquon Math, designed for use with Cuisenaire rods, includes a set of six color-coded workbooks - the Orange, the Red, the Blue, the Green, the Yellow, and the Purple - for kids in grades 1-3. The books are fat and attractive, and - unlike most workbooks series - really do stress problem-solving skills and creative thinking. Conventional workbooks, which rely on repetitive drill and rote memorization of rules, tend to give users mathematical tunnel vision. Miquon students, on the other hand, develop a broad understanding of number patterns and relationships. The Key Curriculum Press also publishes the "Key to" series: *Key to Fractions* (4 booklets), *Key to Decimals* (4 booklets), *Key to Percents* (3 booklets), *Key to Algebra* (10 booklets), and *Key to Geometry* (8 booklets), appropriate for kids in grades 4-12; and an array of geometry materials for secondary students. For a free catalog, contact Key Curriculum Press, P.O. Box 2304, Berkeley, CA 94702; (415) 548-2304 or (800) 338-7638.

Lakeshore Learning Materials

Lakeshore sells a collection of whole-language math packets for primary students. Each includes a mathematically-based picture book, a multidisciplinary activity guide, storytelling props, and equipment for hands-on activities. Eric Carle's *The Grouchy Ladybug*, for example, is accompanied by a bright red-and-black ladybug fingerpuppet, a pair of practice clockfaces on plastic stands, a clock stamp, and a sandtimer; Pamela Allen's *Who Sank the Boat?* comes with a mouse fingerpuppet, a small plastic scale, a 1-ounce weight, and a collection of colorful little sailboats for float-or-sink experiments; Pat Hutchins' *The Doorbell Rang*, a clever introduction to the concept of fractions as kids share cookies, comes with 12 vinyl cookies and a small cookie sheet, and a ringable bell; and Judith Viorst's *Alexander Who Used to Be Rich Last Sunday*, comes with a pack of play money (paper bills and plastic coins) and a set of five coin rubber stamps. Each packet costs $19.95; for a complete list, contact Lakeshore Learning Materials, 2695 E. Dominguez St., P.O. Box 6261, Carson, CA 90749; (800) 421-5354.

Math Products Plus

This plump little black-and-white catalog carries, according to the blurb on the back, "products that educate, entertain, and challenge" and "products that help demystify and popularize mathematics." They succeed on both counts. The product line includes items from the lighter side of math: there are math T-shirts, including, for small fry, a great triangular cat, captioned "How Many Triangles Can You Find?" and, for older fry, a kindly Einstein, saying "Do not worry about your difficulties in mathematics. I can assure you that mine are still greater." There are also math mugs, magnets, stamps, posters, and puzzles.

Then there are logic games, including "Crossing the River," in which players try to get a wolf, a goat, and a cabbage safely across the water; mathematical card games, including "Operations," designed to improve the mental math skills of persons aged 8 and up; and page after page of math books. "Math book" here doesn't mean those stultifying workbooks crammed with colums of double-digit addition problems: Math Products Plus offers fiendish collections of mathematical mindbenders, wonderful maze books, solve-it-yourself mystery books, and mathematical puzzle collections by such super-puzzlers as Lewis Carroll and Martin Gardner. Some of the "Instruction Math Books" sound interesting: there's a *Notable Numbers Book* for kids in grades 5-9, designed to introduce students to "the world of unique numbers and the patterns numbers make;" *Math Sponges* for grades 3-6 (quickie brain boosters for blank moments); and *From Recreation to Computation Around the World*, a collection of multicultural mathematical games, with reproducible gameboards included. There is also a *Mathematical Curiosities* series: paper models to make, all with "curious properties;" and several books of brightly colored geometric shapes to assemble, from the simple (cubes) to the complex (Escher kaleidocycles). For a free catalog, contact Math Products Plus, P.O. Box 64, San Carlos, CA 94070; (415) 593-2839.

Math Songs

These mathematical song "kits" include an audiocassette and a 25 x 36 inch sing-along poster of printed mathematical facts. Kits include *Multiplication Songs* (the multiplication tables, 2-12), *Addi-*

tion Songs (basic facts from 1+1 to 9+9), and *Subtraction Songs* (basic facts from 1-1 to 20-12). The songs are musically monotonous, but do - like commercial jingles - tend to worm themselves into the memory. Songs are sung echo style, and then repeated without the answers, allowing listeners to test themselves. Each kit costs $8.00, from Audio Memory Publishing, 2060 Raymond Ave., Signal Hill, CA 90806; (800) 365-SING (orders) or (310) 494-8822.

Math Trivial Pursuit

This board game comes in workbook form, with a pull-out paper board, 230 question cards (you cut them out yourself), and a fold-and-assemble card box; you provide playing pieces and dice. Once you've got that all together, players can tackle the game, answering questions in four different categories (concepts, computations, geometry, and math for daily living). Questions are all pretty straightforward: this is math drill, but it comes in an attractive package. *Math Trivial Pursuit* is available at three levels: Primary (grades 1-3), Intermediate (grades 4-6), and Junior High (grades 7-9). Each game costs $12.95, from Good Apple, 1204 Buchanan St., Box 299, Carthage, IL 62321-0299; (800) 435-7234 or (217) 357-3981.

Math...Who Needs It?

This 60-minute videotape, from the PBS television special, demonstrates exactly who needs it, with examples from a wide range of fascinating professions from robot builder to roller coaster engineer. The tape also features a visit to the classroom of master math teacher Jaime Escalante, famed for his success in teaching mathematics to inner-city students. Expanding upon the program, PBS has also produced a three-part series, *Futures,* hosted by Escalante, demonstrating specific uses of mathematics in a variety of professions. Volume I covers agriculture, aircraft and automotive design, and architecture; Volume 2, optics, cartography, fashion design, and hydro-engineering; Volume 3, NASA, pro sports, and audio engineering. Each tape runs 60 minutes. The tapes cost $29.95 each; all are available from The Video Catalog, P.O. Box 64428, Saint Paul, MN 55164-0428; (800) 733-2232.

A Mathematical Mystery Tour   Mark Wahl   (Zephyr Press; 1988)

A Mathematical Mystery Tour is subtitled "Higher-Thinking Math Tasks," and is, accordingly, targeted at kids in sixth grade or older, since mathematical tourists will need conventional math skills to fully appreciate the higher-thinking tasks. A good deal of it, however, can be easily adapted for younger children, and we, at one point, had our seven-year-old happily looking for Fibonacci numbers in pine cones and pineapples. If Fibonacci numbers and the like are not your usual cup of tea, do not be mathematically intimidated; all is clearly explained in the reader-friendly text.

The first unit in the book is titled "Living Things Count": kids identify number patterns in pine cones, sunflowers, pineapples, and daisies; calculate the maddening reproductive rate of rabbits; play a game based on the hexagonal cells of the honeycomb; learn a lot of tricks with Fibonacci numbers; and end up with prime numbers. In "Finding the Gold," they learn about the Greeks and their "golden ratio;" identify the golden ratio in themselves, their families, and assorted statuary; and move on to (golden) pentagrams and spirals. In "Mathematical Artforms," they make a spectacular assortment of polyhedra; in "Geometry, the Pyramid, and the Moon," they derive pi, build a model pyramid and measure it, and make accurate scale drawings of the earth and moon. The book includes both student and teacher's guide pages, and is accompanied by a student newletter stuffed with information, games, and puzzles. Also included: an interview with Plato, a quick history of Cheops and his pyramid, and an account of how Eratosthenes, in 231 B.C., managed to measure the circumference of the earth. (Recommended: one newsletter per kid.) *A Mathematical Mystery Tour* is available from Zephyr Press, P.O. Box 13448, Tucson, AZ 85732-3448; (602) 322-5090; or from John Holt's Book and Music Store, 2269 Massachusetts Ave., Cambridge, MA 02140; (617) 864-3100.

Mathematics: A Human Endeavor   Harold R. Jacobs   (W.H. Freeman; 1982)

This is a case in which the book, most emphatically, cannot be told by its cover; it's 600+ pages long and looks, at a casual glance, like a run-of-the-mill mathematics textbook. It isn't. The book opens with a quote from *Huckleberry Finn*: "Well, three or four months run along, and it was well into winter, now. I had been to school most all the time, and could spell, and read, and write just a little, and could say the multiplication table up to six times seven is thirty-five, and I don't reckon I could ever get any farther than that if I was to live forever. I don't take no stock in mathematics, anyway."

If mathematical education were left up to Harold Jacobs, however, no student would ever feel this way again. *Mathematics: A Human Endeavor* is a real treasure trove of information mathematical; readers, irresistably fascinated, are pulled into mathematics through an imaginative deluge of puzzles, paradoxes, jokes, cartoons, games, photographs, and magic tricks. Our children, enthralled, spent days plotting the paths of billiard balls, trying to invent a five-color map, playing games with cards, pennies, and paper clips, experimenting with ciphers, and studying the cross-sectional curves generated by slicing up candles. Illustrations demonstrating mathematical principles are both superb and unexpected: there are pictures of postage stamps, penguins, star clouds, and spiralling leaves; of snowflakes, honeycombs, and Escher mosaics; of ostrich eggs, ice cream cones, and the Golden Gate bridge. Spend a few weeks or months with Harold Jacobs, and those who don't take no stock in mathematics, will. The book costs $31.95; and is available through bookstores, from Math Products Plus, P.O. Box 64, San Carlos, CA 94070; (415) 593-2839; or from John Holt's Book and Music Store, 2269 Massachusetts Ave., Cambridge, MA 02140; (617) 864-3100.

Mathematics Their Way   Mary Baratta-Lorton   (Addison-Wesley; 1976)

Mathematics Their Way is an "activity-centered mathematics program" for kids in grades K-2. The premise here is that kids should be allowed to learn math concepts "their way," through hands-on manipulations of familiar materials. The program is described in a 416-page spiral-bound book, containing instructions for over 200 different suggested activities, plus reproducible student worksheets. Topics covered include counting, pattern-making, sorting and classification, measurement and comparison (of quantity, length, weight, volume, and time), addition and subtraction, and simple word problems. Kids master these concepts by playing around with tiles and counters, buttons, bottle caps, mirrors, cups and jars, blocks, and linking cubes. An attractive and popular introduction to the basics. From bookstores, Cuisenaire Co. of America, P.O. Box 5026, White Plains, NY 10602-5026; (800) 237-3142; or Creative Teaching Associates, P.O. Box 7766, Fresno, CA 93747; (800) 767-4CTA or (209) 291-6626.

Math-It

Math-It, brainchild of Elmer W. Brooks, is a collection of memorize-and-practice-type games for those "who want to be better at simple math and are willing to follow the directions page by page." Kids learn addition and multiplication facts using a number of simple memory tricks ("To add 9 to a number, you count back one and say *teen*"), and then practice, matching little color-coded problem cards to an answer board, until they've got the solutions down cold. An instruction manual is included for parents or teachers, but kids can handle this one pretty much on their own. *Math-It* is appropriate for kids aged 6 or older. There's an equivalent *Pre-Math-It* program, using double-nine dominoes, for kids aged 5-7; and an expert version, *Advanced Math-It*, for older kids, through eighth grade. All are beautifully packaged, in heavy plastic cases, and include cassette tapes with game instructions, all necessary cards, game boards, and playing pieces, and an instructor's manual. *Pre-Math-It* ($29.95), *Math-It* ($34.95), and *Advanced Math-It* ($28.95) are available from The Sycamore Tree, Inc., 2179 Meyer Place, Costa Mesa, CA 92627; (714) 650-4466 (information) or (714) 642-6750 (orders).

Mathematicians Are People, Too   Luetta Reimer and Wilbert Reimer   (Dale Seymour;1990)

This is a (nearly) 150-page collection of "Stories From the Lives of Great Mathematicians" - all of which are short, friendly, clever, and clearly mathematical, in an intriguing fashion, which is no small feat. The first story in the book is that of Thales of Miletus, who, using proportions of heights and shadows, managed to figure out the height of the Great Pyramid of Giza. This one even roped in our oldest son, ordinarily math-resistant to the point of immoveability; and all of our children promptly set off, armed with tape measures and curiosity, to measure the heights of the apple tree, the garage, and the neighbor's flagpole. The book covers fifteen mathematicians, among them Pythagoras, Archimedes, Pascal, Newton, Gauss, Euler, and Ramanujan. For each, mathematical achievements are meshed with attention-getting biographical information: along with the Pythagorean theorem, for example, readers learn that the sacred symbol of the followers of Pythagoras was the pentagram, or five-pointed star; along with an explanation of Pascal's Triangle, there's mention of Pascal's lesser-known invention: the one-wheeled wheelbarrow. And much more. Available through bookstores or from the Cuisenaire Company of America, P.O. Box 5026, White Plains, NY; (800) 237-3142.

Mortensen Math

Mortensen Math is a manipulative-based math program, with workbook series at several levels, appropriate for all ages. The ma-

nipulatives are nowhere near as aesthetically appealing as Cuisenaire rods, but are more versatile: they're plastic bars, which come
in eleven color-coded sizes, from units through 100-squares. The
bars, unlike Cuisenaire rods, are scored on one side and blank on
the others. The scoring is a plus; you can look at a Mortensen six-
bar and know right off that the thing is a six-bar. Comparisons
and manipulations are therefore more straightforward.

Mortensen students use these manipulatives along with a series
of workbooks, available at three different levels. Workbooks at
each level are divided into five different mathematical categories:
Arithmetic, Measurement, Problem-Solving, Algebra, and Calculus. There are 10 workbooks per category. The workbooks, unfortunately, lack spark: they're flimsy little newsprint productions,
poorly printed, and grindingly repetitive. (To be fair, they're also
cheap.) The Mortensen program has enjoyed considerable popu-
larity and success nationwide; it is especially recommended for
older students who are floundering, due to an inadequate early
background in arithmetical basics. For further information, contact Mortensen Math Academic Excellence Institute, 2450 Fort Union Blvd., Salt Lake City, UT 84121; (801) 944-2500.

National Council of Teachers of Mathematics

The NCTM is a professional organization "for all persons interested in the teaching and learning of mathematics." Annual membership fees ($40) include a subscription to either *Arithmetic Teach-
er*, a monthly (September through May) magazine for elementary-
school educators, or *Mathematics Teacher*, an equivalent publication for secondary-school educators. The NCTM also sponsors a
number of national conferences on mathematics in education, and
several national math competitions for students in grades 7-12.
They also publish a "Catalog of Educational Materials" which offers a large assortment of instructional and activity books for
teachers, among them *Curriculum and Evaluation Standards for
School Mathematics*, a 258-page document describing projected
standards for mathematics curricula and achievements for students in grades K-12. For additional information, contact the National Council of Teachers of Mathematics, 1906 Association
Drive, Reston, VA 22091-1593; (703) 620-9840.

O! Euclid

O! Euclid is touted as "an amusing and scholarly card game for
ages 9-99." It comes with an informational sheet including some

biographical facts about Euclid, a brief explanation of the essentials of Euclidean geometry, and a poem, "Euclid," by Vachel Lindsay. The game consists of a series of puzzle cards with which players can form 14 different geometrical shapes (equilateral, isosceles, and right triangles, square, rectangle, parallelogram, trapezoid, pentagon, hexagon, octagon, circle, ellipse, parabola, and hyperbola), a series of true-false question cards about each shape, and a series of name cards, to be matched to each completed puzzle. Rules for four different games, at various levels of difficulty, are listed on the instruction sheet. Younger kids simply enjoy assembling the geometrical puzzles and matching the shapes with their proper names. Available from Ampersand Press, 8040 N.E. Day Rd West #5-A, Bainbridge Island, WA 98110; (206) 780-9015.

On An Average Day and *In An Average Lifetime*   Tom Heynman   (Fawcett Columbine; 1991)

These books, at the rate of one large-print fact per page, detail what happens to the average American in the short-term, during the average day, or in the long-term, during the average lifetime. In an average lifetime, for example the average American eats 450 pounds of peanut butter, makes 184,702 telephone calls, walks 92,375 miles, and produces 95,685 pounds of garbage. (There are a few sex statistics at the back that parents might want to censor for the under-aged.) A fascinating slant on statistics. By the same author: *On An Average Day in the Soviet Union* and *On An Average Day in Japan*. Available through bookstores. (Also see above book: *In One Day*.)

Pappas, Theoni

Theoni Pappas has published a number of delightful and innovative mathematics books, notable among them *The Joy of Mathematics: Discovering Mathematics All Around You*, an entrancing volume in which readers are introduced to the mathematics of the real world, including the mathematical aspects of soap bubbles, ocean waves, and the *Mona Lisa*. There's a sequel on the same lines, *More Joy of Mathematics: Exploring Mathematical Insights and Concepts*. Our current favorite is *Fractals, Googols, and Other Mathematical Tales* (Wide World Publishing/Tetra; 1993), in which kids learn a good deal about the greater world of mathematics with Penrose the cat, Leonhard, the topological turtle, and Fibonacci the rabbit. Curious readers find themselves making Mobius strips, translating mysterious numbers from the Planet Dodeka into base

10, learning the histories of zero and pi, and solving Chinese magic squares. By the same author: *Math Talk*, a collection of math *poems*, designed to be read by two voices. There are 25 poems in the collection, including "Circles," "Fractals," "Zero," "The Even Numbers," and "Googols."

Pappas also designs a yearly *Children's Mathematics Calendar*. Each month has one major mathematical feature (among them, origami, tessellation, fractals, logic puzzles, and polyominoes), plus a single mathematical problem for each day. The daily problems are straightforward and suitable for a range of ages: included are quick exercises in addition, subtraction, multiplication, division, measurement, time-telling, geometry, fractions, percent, decimals, square numbers, prime numbers, ancient number systems, and money. Available through bookstores or from the catalog offered by Math Products Plus, P.O. Box 64, San Carlos, CA 94070; (415) 593-2839.

Powers of Ten: About the Relative Size of Things in the Universe Philip Morrison and Phylis Morrison (Scientific American; 1982)

The text itself is in tiny, adult-level print, but the core of the book, the authors point out, is the series of 42 spectacular photographs that detail the size of things in the universe in ten-fold steps. The series begins at 10^{25} meters (a billion light-years), in almost-empty space, and gradually narrows down through the galaxy, the solar system, and the planet, to an aerial view of Chicago, a close-up of picnickers in a city park, a microscopic view of the skin on one picnicker's hand, a view of intracellular DNA, and, at 10^{-14} meters, the nucleus of a single carbon atom. The video is even better. Both are available from Creative Learning Systems, Inc., 16510 Via Esprillo, San Diego, CA 92127; (800) 458-2880 or (619) 675-7700; the *Powers of Ten* video is also available from The Video Catalog, P.O. Box 64428, Saint Paul, MN 55164-0428; (800) 733-2232.

Saxon Math

John Saxon threw his math philosophy into the ring in 1981, in the introduction to his algebra textbook: "Repetition is necessary to permit all students to master all of the concepts, and then the application must be practiced for a long time to ensure retention. This practice has an element of drudgery in it, but it has been demonstrated that people who are not willing to practice fundamentals often find success elusive. Ask your favorite athletic coach for his opinion on the necessity of practicing fundamental skills." There, in a nutshell, you have the Saxon textbooks: a thorough, no-nonsense approach to math, with lots of practice exercises in basic skills. There are Saxon books for kids from kindergarten through grade 12 (counting through calculus); K-3 materials are provided in workbook form, with accompanying teacher's manuals; older kids (fourth grade, plus) get hardcover texts, at prices ranging from approximately $30-$40. *Math 54*, for example, is appropriate for fourth-graders who have completed Saxon's *Math 3* workbook materials or for "average fifth-grade students who previously studied from a conventional textbook;" *Math 65* is appropriate for advanced fifth-graders and average sixth-graders, and so on. For most of the Saxon publications, "Homeschool Packets" are available for home educators, containing single copies of student texts, answer keys or teacher's manual, and tests.

The Saxon texts, despite all that ominous talk about "drudgery," do work: the program has been shown to increase scores on standardized achievement tests, which most educators see as success. For catalogs and order forms, contact Saxon Publishers, Inc., 1320 West Lindsey St., Norman, OK 73069; (405) 329-7071. Books can be ordered directly, by mail only, from the Thompson Book Depository, P.O. Box 60160, Oklahoma City, OK, 73146.

Set

In this clever card game, players develop mathematical thinking skills by identifying patterns. The game consists of a deck of 81 cards, each printed with shapes (diamonds, lozenges, or bean-shaped blobs) in different colors, shadings, and numbers. Players lay out 12 cards at a time, face up, and attempt to identify sets: three cards in which each feature is either the same or different. Sounds simple, but isn't. Appropriate for all ages. *Set* costs $12.00, and is available from toy and game stores, or from Zephyr Press, 3316 N. Chapel Ave., P.O. Box 13448, Tucson, AZ 85732-3448; (602) 322-5090.

Texas Instruments

Texas Instruments publishes a free newsletter for educators, *It's About T.I.M.E.*, in which "T.I.M.E." stands for Technology in Math Education. The theme of the newsletter is, overwhelming, student use of calculators, and calculators are, of course, the company's reason for being. TI produces calculators of all capacities, from the red-and-yellow "Math Mate," targeted at early elementary students, through the "Math Explorer" ("the only calculator designed for teaching fractions"), to the "TI-81 Graphics Calculator," a scientific superstar for the advanced calculus student. TI also produces a children's speaking calculator, dubbed "Super Speak and Math," programmed for 8 different activities and over 250,000 "exciting problems," all based on standards set by the National Council of Teachers of Mathematics.

For catalogs, information, and a list of regional Texas Instruments distributors, contact Texas Instruments, P.O. Box 53, Lubbock, TX 79408-9955; (800) TI-CARES.

Twenty-Four

This innovative game was designed to "develop the mental habits of creative mathematicians." It consists of a collection of big, colorful, heavy-duty cards, each printed with four numbers. Players must combine these numbers, using addition, subtraction, multiplication, and division, to reach the answer: 24. All numbers must be used, and each number can be used only once. A solution for a card bearing the numbers 7,5,7, and 2, for example, might be $5 \times 2 = 10$; $7 + 7 = 14$; $10 + 14 = 24$. Cards are coded by level of difficulty, with one, two, or three dots. Three-dot cards are dillies. Both fun and challenging. The game costs $17.00, and is available through toy and game stores or from Zephyr Press, 3316 N. Chapel Ave, P.O. Box 13448, Tucson, AZ 85732-3448; (602) 322-5090.

United Art and Education Supply Co.

The United Art and Education Supply Company sells a number of materials and games for just-barely-beginning mathematicians. Among these: a number line (0-120, in segments), wipe-off graphing grids in 2 sizes (both large), "Count and Match" puzzles, and flash cards listing number, time-telling, and money facts. Games include *Numbers Lotto*, in which young players match numbers (1-10) with the proper number of pictures of objects; and *Addition, Subtraction, Multiplication*, and *Money Bingo*. For a free catalog, contact United Art and Education Supply Co., Inc., Box 9219, Fort Wayne, IN 46899; (800) 322-3247.

Used Numbers

This series, devloped by Susan Jo Russell, Rebecca Corwin, and Susan Friel, introduces elementary-level students to statistics through the use of "real data in the classroom." Lesson units involve collecting, organizing, graphing, and interpreting real-world numerical information. There are six books in the series (available separately): *Counting: Ourselves and Our Families* (grades K-1), *Sorting: Groups and Graphs* (2-3), *Measuring: From Paces to Feet* (3-4), *Statistics: The Shape of Data* (4-6), *Statistics: Prediction and Sampling* (4-6), and *Statistics: Middles, Means, and In-Betweens* (5-6). The books are attractive and well-written; the projects look like fun. Many of the activities assume a classroom or large-group situation for the collecting of raw data (Examples: "How much taller is a fourth-grader than a first-grader?" "How many people are in a family?" "How many cavities do kids have?"); homeschoolers will need to poll friends, acquaintances, and relatives. The *Used Numbers* books are available from the Cuisenaire Co. of America, Inc., P.O. Box 5026, White Plains, NY 10602-5026; (800) 237-3142 or Activity Resources Co., Inc., P.O. Box 4875, Hayward, CA 94540; (510) 782-1300.

Wff'n Proof Learning Games
The Wff'n Proof Instructional Gaming Program, designed to increase math achievement and develop problem-solving skills, was developed by a team of math educators from the University of Michigan. The games, after extensive classroom testing, were proved to make learning both more enjoyable and more effective; effectiveness claims are supported by studies showing that game use increases standard achievement test scores and decreases absenteeism. The games, which definitely do make one think, are appropriate for players over a wide range of ages: *Equations: The Game of Creative Mathematics*, a 5-game kit, is appropriate for ages 7-adult; *Wff'n Proof: The Game of Modern Logic*, a 21-game kit, for ages 6-adult. Other games include *On-Sets*, a 30-game kit based on set theory; *The Real Numbers Game* (prepares beginners for *Equations*); *Configurations*, a collection of geometrical and numerical puzzles for the single player (aged 12 and up); and *Quik-Sane*, a perfectly maddening topological puzzle. For those who prefer to wet their mental toes before plunging in all the way, the first two games from *Wff'n Proof* are available as a separate smaller package: it's called *Wff* and costs $5.50. For an informational brochure and order forms, contact Wff'n Proof Learning Games, 1490-JR South Blvd., Ann Arbor, MI 48104; (313) 665-2269.

Whatever Happened to Penny Candy?   Richard J. Maybury
(Bluestocking Press; 1991)
Penny Candy is a short, snappy introduction to economics, writ-

ten as a series of letters to a curious ninth-grader - Chris - from his economically with-it Uncle Eric. Uncle Eric deals with everything from why quarters have little grooves around the edges to the phenomenon of runaway inflation, and sneaks in a lot of fascinating information along the way: the origin of the word "dollar," the reason Kublai Khan invented paper money, and the sad story of tulipomania and its awful effect on the finances of the Dutch. Generally recommended for teenagers and adults, but our youngest child enjoyed it at seven. Available from Bluestocking Press, P.O. Box 1014-GS, Placerville, CA 95667-1014.

The Wonder Number Game

A colorful board game with which a large number of different mathematical games can be played at varying skill levels. Mathematical concepts reinforced through various games include odd and even number patterns, place value, addition, subtraction, multiplication, division, prime numbers, lowest common denominators, greatest common factors, measurement, and geometry. "In a way," one teacher writes, "it's almost like a deck of playing cards. You can use the same deck to play a simple child's game like 'Go Fish' and a highly sophisticated and complex game such as Contract Bridge." The game comes with a colorful playing board, laid out like a giant hundred chart, a numerical spinner, and an assortment of playing chips. Instructions are included for 25 games and game variations. For those who wish to expand upon the basic *Wonder Numbers* game, three lesson plan books are available, variously appropriate for kids in grades K-3, 3-6, and 6-8. Game and books are available from Activity Resources Co., Inc., P.O. Box 4875, Hayward, CA 94540; (510) 782-1300.

Wonderful Ideas

This is a math newsletter, published monthly during the school year, targeted at teachers and students in the elementary and middle grades. The newsletter contains creative activities, puzzles, games, and reproducible worksheets for student use. An annual subscription (8 issues) costs $24.00, from *Wonderful Ideas*, P.O. Box 64691, Burlington, VT 05406, (617) 239-1496.

World Records

Our kids, who all balked at arithmetic workbooks, have been consistently fascinated with numerical records. Accordingly, a good deal of math around here has been absorbed via the world's smallest butterfly, fastest airplane, closest star, tallest tree, and largest dinosaur. References for record-lovers include:

The Big Book of Animal Records   Annette Tison and Talus Taylor
(Grosset & Dunlap; 1984)

Guinness Book of World Records (Bantam Books)   Updated yearly, this is the ultimate in record books, listing hundreds of world records from the seriously scientific to the simply silly.

The Kids' World Almanac of Amazing Facts About Numbers, Math and Money   Margery Facklam and Margaret Thomas   (World Almanac; 1992)

Young Math Books

This many-volume series, published by Thomas Y. Crowell, is intended to introduce (a range of) young readers to the basics of mathematics. The books are short picture books, heavily illustrated, and include assorted hands-on activities or suggestions for demonstrations to reinforce the principles presented in the books.

Titles include *Angles Are Easy As Pie* (Robert Froman), *Bigger and Smaller* (Robert Froman), *Circles* (Mindel and Harry Sitomer), *3D, 2D, 1D* (David A. Adler), *The Ellipse* (Mannis Charosh), *Estimation* (Charles F. Linn), *Exploring Triangles: Paper-Folding Geometry* (Jo Phillips), *Fractions Are Parts of Things* (J. Richard Dennis), *The Greatest Guessing Game: A Book About Dividing* (Robert Froman), *666 Jellybeans! All That?: An Introduction to Algebra* (Malcolm E. Weiss), *Odds and Evens* (Thomas C. O'Brien), *Roman Numerals* (David A. Adler), *Statistics* (Jane Jonas Srivastava), *Straight Lines, Parallel Lines, Perpendicular Lines* (Mannis Charosh), *Venn Diagrams* (Robert Froman),*Weighing and Balancing* (Jane Jonas Srivastava), *What is Symmetry?* (Mindel and Harry Sitomer), and *Zero is Not Nothing* (Mindel and Harry Sitomer). Available through libraries.

Chapter Four

History and Geography

When, Where, Who, What, and Why

American Heritage

American Heritage is so beautifully done that it seems more akin to a book than a magazine. It was, in fact, originally published as a bimonthly book, bound in hardcover. We often stumble over old hardbound issues in used-book stores - and immediately snap them up, since *American Heritage* is a superb resource for the home-style historian. The modern magazine, richly illustrated with color photographs, covers all aspects of American history, from pre-Columbian native civilizations to the present day. Topics are interesting; writing is reader-friendly; historical information is accurate. Each issue generally contains four or five major long articles, and a number of regular short features, among them "The Life and Times," a biographical profile of a famous American, "American Made," an account of a well-known American invention or product (such as the Waterman pen or the Boston rocker), "History Happened Here," the story of a famous (or not-so-famous) American place, and "The Time Machine," a collection of short pieces on historical happenings 200, 100, 75, 50, and 25 years ago. An annual subscription (8 issues) costs $29.00, from *American Heritage* Subscription Department, P.O. Box 5022, Harlan, IA 51593-2522; (800) 777-1222.

American Heritage Illustrated History of the United States

Our *American Heritage Illustrated History of the United States* came from a book barn in Maine. The set consists of 16 heavily illustrated volumes which collectively cover 500 years of American history from the pre-Columbian civilizations to John F. Kennedy. It cost us $20.00, which we then thought sinfully cheap, and still do. The modern up-dated version is an 18-volume series, and costs $89.95. Even at that, it's a steal.

The books are superb. Each is just under 100 pages long; the text presents a straightforward chronological account of American history, covering political, economic, military, and cultural happenings. In conjuction with this, the present series also contains over 2500 full-color illustrations: maps, sketches, photographs, political cartoons, diagrams, portraits. Titles include *The New World, Colonial America, The Revolution, A New Nation, Young America, The Frontier, War With Mexico, The Civil War, Winning the West, Age of Steel, The Gilded Age, A World Power, World War I and the Twenties, The Roosevelt Era, World War II, Decades of the Cold War, The Vietnam Era,* and *America Today*. To order, contact *American Heritage*, P.O. Box 10934, Des Moines, IA 50340; (800) 876-6556.

American History Illustrated

American History Illustrated is a bimonthly magazine aimed at exploring "The Adventure of the American Past." Articles include individual biographies of famous Americans, features on military, political, and cultural events or periods, and stories of personal encounters with history. All are lavishly illustrated with pictures and photographs, both in color and black-and-white. The magazine also lists on-going historical exhibits, programs, and museum presentations all over the country and reviews new history books, audio cassettes, and videos. An annual subscription (6 issues) costs $20.00; order from *American History Illustrated*, P.O. Box 8200, Harrisburg, PA 17112; (800) 435-9610 or (717) 657-9955.

Americard USA

Americard USA, subtitled "A Fun Game for the Curious," is a geographical card game devised by educator Robert Allen of the National Academic Games Project. The game, packaged in a nice solid plastic box, consists of a pack of state cards, each with an unlabeled state map on the front and a pair of multiple-choice historical challenge questions on the back, a fold-out map of the United States, and an instruction booklet including directions for five different games at varying levels of complexity. Games are appropriate to a wide range of age groups, from small beginners just learning to identify states by shape ("Spotter") to advanced geographers capable of answering questions about the Gadsden Purchase, the Missouri Compromise, and the New Deal ("Answer It").

There's also a version in which kids draw a state card and then write their own multiple-choice questions. *Eurocard*, of similar format, is designed to teach kids the geography and history of the countries of Europe. Available from Wff 'n Proof Learning Games, 1490-JR South Boulevard, Ann Arbor, Michigan 48104-4699; (313) 665-2269.

Ancient Civilization Games

This beautifully done game series consists of high-quality reproductions of ancient board games. Of these, our family's favorite is *Senet*, "the most popular board game of ancient Egypt." *Senet*, deceptively simple, is played on a hieroglyphic-patterned wooden board, and comes with either dice (which our children scorn) or two-sided throwsticks. Also in the series: *Ur*, a 5000-year-old game from ancient Sumeria; *Go*, from China; and *Mankala*, from Africa. The games cost $22.00 to $28.00 each, and are available from toy and game stores, or from Michael Olaf's Essential Montessori, P.O. Box 1162, Arcata, CA 95521; (707) 826-1557.

Archaeology Kits

These hands-on kits are a delight for young ancient-history buffs: each contains a replica of an ancient ceramic vase or vessel, in shards, embedded in a block of clay. Budding archaeologists unearth the pieces, re-assemble their find, and paint it with historically accurate designs. Pottery pieces are pretty good-sized: it's a challenging project, but not inordinately difficult. Several different kits are available, including Etruscan, Greek, and Roman vases, and a Roman bowl, based on a sample discovered during the excavation of Pompeii. Each comes with an informational instruction booklet. Available from Carolina Biological Supply Company, 2700 York Road, Burlington, NC 27215; (800) 334-5551; or Learning Things, Inc., 68A Broadway, P.O. Box 436, Arlington, MA 02174; (617) 646-0093.

Audio Forum

Audio Forum claims to be the publisher of "the greatest number of audio cassettes in the world." Of particular interest to historians is their American History Cassette-of-the-Month program, in which participants, via monthly cassette, can listen to the story of America from the first settlers through modern times, presented in "interesting and dramatic vignettes." For the less committed, there's a 2-cassette program of dramatized biographies titled "American Patriots," which includes, among others, the stories of Thomas Jefferson and Patrick Henry; the 3-cassette "Facts, Foibles, and Fancies about Our Early Presidents;" "Yesterday's Headlines - Today's History," which includes accounts of world news events as they were originally broadcast, among them Lindbergh's transatlantic flight, the destruction of the Hindenburg, the invasion of Pearl Harbor, and the assassination of John F. Kennedy; and "The Good Old Days - They Were Terrible!," a one-cassette account of life as it really was in turn-of-the-century America. For a catalog, contact Audio Forum, 96 Broad Street, Guilford, CT 06437-2635; (800) 243-1234 or (203) 453-9794.

Avalon Hill Game Company

Avalon Hill specializes in games of military strategy: many of the gameboards are accurate maps and playing rules mesh with the course of landmark historical battles ranging in time from the Peloponnesian to the Gulf War. Examples include *Napoleon's Bat-*

tles, Gettysburg, Stonewall Jackson's Way, Bull Run, The Battle of the Bulge, Guadalcanal, and *Russian Campaign.* Other games are less specific: examples include *Republic of Rome, Circus Maximus, Blackbeard* (with deck of 64 action/pirate cards), and *Civilization.* The catalog - which lists all available games with absolutely no accompanying description - also includes a "Leisure Time/Family Games" section, under which are listed *Dinosaurs of the Lost World* (with gameboard, set of 60 dinosaur cards, and pad of adventure sheets), *Legends of Robin Hood* (card deck and map board), and *Shakespeare* (gameboard, pawns, and 112 quotation cards). Games are generally appropriate for older children and adults. Avalon Hill also sponsors an annual boardgaming championship contest ("Avaloncon") and publishes a bimonthly magazine for war-game enthusiasts, *The General Magazine.* An annual subscription (6 issues) costs $15.00. For further information or a product list, contact The Avalon Hill Game Company, 4517 Harford Road, Baltimore, MD 21214; (410) 254-9200.

Bellerophon Books

Bellerophon Books publishes a vast list of coloring and activity books with predominately historical themes. Books are detailed, accurate, and inexpensive, and our kids have enjoyed them since they first learned to scribble purple wings on Wilbur and Orville Wright's fledgling airplane. Examples of coloring book titles include *Myths and Legends of the Vikings, The Middle Ages, Ancient Rome, Ancient Greece, Ancient China, Tutankhamun, The Story of Africa, Great Explorers, Aces and Airplanes of World War I, Indian Chiefs, Heroes of the American Revolution, Incas, Aztecs, and Mayas,* and *Shakespeare.* Also available are historically accurate paperdoll collections and cut-and-assemble books, including three-dimensional paper castles, Viking ships, and trains. For a catalog, contact Bellerophon Books, 36 Anacapa Street, Santa Barbara, CA 93101; (800) 253-9943.

Big Bird in China/Japan/Israel

These videos provide multicultural education to fans of *Sesame Street.* In each, the Sesame Street characters are introduced to the culture, language, and historical and geographical landmarks of another country (China, Japan, or Israel). In *Big Bird in China,* Big Bird and his rambunctious canine pal Barkley set off for China in search of the legendary phoenix: along the way, they visit a Chinese school, watch a tai ji demonstration, walk along the Great Wall, travel by sampan, and learn how to say "I love you" in Chinese. In *Big Bird in Japan*, Big Bird and Barkley, separated from their sight-seeing tour, visit a Japanese restaurant and experiment with chopsticks, stay overnight with a Japanese family and learn Japanese manners, see Mount Fuji, learn to say "Good morning" in Japanese, ride the bullet train, and hear the story of the magical Bamboo Princess. Each video runs about 60 minutes. In the *Shalom Sesame* series, the Sesame Street crew visits Israel, touring Jerusalem, Tel Aviv, and the Ein Gedi kibbutz, and participating in the celebration of Chanukah. There are eight videos in the series, each about 30 minutes long. Available from Movies Unlimited, 6736 Castor Avenue, Philadelphia, PA 19149; (800) 523-0823 (orders) or (215) 722-8398 (customer service).

Bluestocking Press

Jane Williams' catalog of "products and ideas" contains a wonderful assortment of unusual resources for young historians. For starters, the catalog is *the* source for fans of Laura Ingalls Wilder's *Little House* series: Bluestocking Press carries all of the *Little House* books (separately or as a boxed set), detailing Laura's late-nineteenth-century childhood on a midwestern homestead, as well as associated biographies, posters, and photo essays. There's also a Little House cookbook ("over 100 authentic recipes bring to today's tables the foods that Laura Ingalls and her family ate as they traveled from the woods of Wisconsin to the Dakota territory"), an Ingalls family Time Line Reference, and a Little House song tape. Historical resources, however, don't stop with Laura: there are also cassette tapes of colonial and Civil War era music, and excellent collections of books fictional and non-fictional, listed by period in American history. For the dedicated hands-on historian, there's Peggy Parish's *Let's Be Early Settlers With Daniel Boone*, which includes instructions for making colonial costumes, frontier dioramas, and model log cabins, flatboats, and covered wagons, and Plimoth Plantation's*The Thanksgiving Primer*, which gives complete instructions for re-creating the first Thanksgiving, from the Governor's Proclamation through the menu, the table manners, and the after-dinner games. A catalog costs $2.00; order from Bluestocking Press, P.O. Box 1014-GS, Placerville, CA 95667.

The Book of Where (Or How to Be Naturally Geographic)   Neill Bell   (Little, Brown; 1982)

The Book of Where, one of the Brown Paper School Book series (see Multipurpose Resources), is described as "a trip around the world in 119 pages." The trip begins with mapping close to home, with the reader's house, street, and town ("Most towns and cities have street patterns that make them look like GIANT WAFFLES"), and then proceeds to the use of the compass, formal map-reading, U.S. geography, globes and world maps, plate tectonics, and the undersea mapping of the ocean bottom. The text, interesting and informative, is spattered with clever diagrams, cartoons, puzzles, quizzes, riddles, and projects for the curious young geographer. Appropriate for kids aged 9-12; available through bookstores.

Boomerang!

Boomerang! is a monthly children's audio magazine, presented on 70-minute cassette tapes, "designed to delight, inform, and challenge 7-12-year-olds." "Take the best of National Public Radio's 'All Things Considered,'" writes one admirer, "convert it to something of interest and importance for kids, and you've got *Boomerang!*" Standard *Boomerang!* format includes "Turning Points," in which a time-traveling young reporter interviews historical figures such as Abraham Lincoln, Mohandas Gandhi, Sacajawea, and Louis Braille; "American Journey," in which a roving reporter gives an overview of points of interest all over the United States; and "The Big Idea," the monthly cover story, which offers "an explanation of a selected current events topic from a child's perspective." Big Ideas to date have included gun control, rain forest conservation, prejudice, animal rights, world hunger, and the discovery of America by Christopher Columbus ("Who Discovered Whom?") A balanced picture is presented of each, through interviews with persons with differing points of view. There's also a "Money" segment (economics as demonstrated by Freddie Baxter's Rhubarb and Banana Sandwich business) and "Natural Wonder," which covers the world of nature from cicadas and dolphins to raindrops and volcanoes. *Boomerang!* can be purchased as individual cassettes or by yearly subscription. For information, contact *Boomerang!*, 13366 Pescadero Road, La Honda, CA 94020; (800) 333-7858.

Buck Hill Associates

Buck Hill's catalog offers some 600 reproduction posters, handbills, broadsides, prints, maps, and advertisements from America's past, most of which cost under a dollar. Among the selections: Paul Revere's print of the Boston Massacre, a bill of sale for a slave, Francis Scott Key's handwritten draft of "The Star-Spangled Banner," a gold mine map drawn by William Tecumseh Sherman,

Civil War recruiting posters, a poster commemorating the opening of the Union Pacific Railroad, advertisements for Buffalo Bill's Wild West Show and P.T. Barnum's Greatest Show on Earth, and a 1902 cartoon showing Teddy Roosevelt refusing to shoot a bear cub, thus giving a name to the ever-popular Teddy bear. For a free catalog, write Buck Hill Associates, Box 501, North Creek, NY 12853-0501.

The Buck Stops Here   Alice Provensen   (HarperTrophy; 1990)

This delightful book covers all the U.S. presidents from George Washington to George Bush. There's not much text - a short, memory-sticking couplet for each president ("Teddy Roosevelt, Twenty-six/Whisper softly, wave big sticks") - but the colorful folk-art pictures are simply packed with information for the discerning reader. The double-page spread on Franklin Roosevelt, for example, shows the president in his wheelchair, surrounded by poster-sized postage stamps picturing Eleanor Roosevelt, Fala, Frances Perkins, the repeal of prohibition, the recognition of the U.S.S.R., Jesse Owens and his four Olympic gold medals, Albert Einstein, the attack on Pearl Harbor, the "Four Freedoms," the Yalta Conference, and the formation of the United Nations. Looks like a picture book, but is appropriate for kids of all ages. Available through libraries and bookstores.

Center for Learning

The Center for Learning is a nonprofit corporation "dedicated to publishing student-centered, value-based materials that will improve the quality of home education." The materials are essentially collections of interdisciplinary lesson plans, variously appropriate for kids in grades 1-9, each containing instructions, background information, bibliographies, reproducible student worksheets, and suggestions for supplemental activities. Among these is the "U.S. Biography Series," targeted at students in grades 4-8. The series consists of seven books, each covering 14 influential persons from a different period in American history. Book 1 ("Beginning to 1800"), for example, includes biographies of Benjamin Banneker, King Philip, Pocahontas, Pontiac, Paul Revere, and Phillis Wheatley; Book 2 ("1800-1830"), Dolley Madison, John Marshall, Zebulon Pike, Sacajawea, Samuel Slater, Sequoyah, and Emma Willard; Book 3 ("1830-1850"), Elizabeth Blackwell, Dorothea Dix, Washington Irving, Samuel Morse, and Sojourner Truth. Each includes both teacher resources and student booklets, for a total cost of $19.95; additional student booklets can be ordered separately, for $4.95 each.

An equivalent "International Biographies Series" includes seven books, each concentrating on a different world region, which makes for an interestingly mixed bag of famous characters: Book 1 ("Africa and the Middle East") covers, among others, Kahlil Gibran, Miriam Makeba, Nelson Mandela, Mansa Musa, and Queen Nefertiti; Book 2 ("Asia, Australia, and Oceania"), Corazon Aquino, Matsuo Basho, Indira Gandhi, Hammurabi, Hirohito, Kublai Khan, and Queen Liliuokalani.

Also available: lesson units on famous scientists and inventors, a "Basic Skills" series covering the essentials of U.S. and World history, and a "Social Studies Activities Series," in which lesson plans center around hands-on projects and activities. The Activities Series covers both "World History and Geography" and "U.S. History and Geography." There are two books for available for each topic, each containing approximately 20 lesson plans and 50 student hand-outs. Under World History and Geography Book 1 ("The East"), for example, lessons plans include re-telling African folktales, making a "picture safari" through Kenya, studying the art of the Byzantine Empire, keeping a South Pole journal, making Chinese papercuts, celebrating a Japanese festival, and creating an Australian aboriginal myth. To obtain a catalog, contact The Center for Learning, P.O. Box 910, Villa Maria, PA 16155; (800) 767-9090.

Center for Research and Development in Law-Related Education (CRADLE)

CRADLE, in association with Wake Forest University's Schools of Law and Education, publishes a 70-page catalog of lesson plans and classroom resources on the law and the Constitution. Lesson plans are coded by appropriate grade level (primary, middle, high school). The selection is large; and plan prices generally range from one to four dollars. Included are "Was It the Pied Piper's Fault?," in which kids in grades 1-4 consider the question of responsibility and hold a mock trial in Hamelin Town; "Humpty Dumpty's Assault," a re-enactment of the entire judicial process from crime to sentence, for kids in grades 5-7; and "Buyer Beware," a consumer fraud unit for grades 7-9 based on "The Emperor's New Clothes." Other units cover everything from Roman justice to DNA fingerprinting. The organization also publishes a quarterly newsletter, *SPLICE*, listing legal news and reporting on new law-related educational resources. For a free catalog or information, write CRADLE, Wake Forest University School of Law, 2714 Henning Drive, Reynolda Station, Winston, Salem, NC 27109; (919) 721-3355; fax: (919) 721-3353.

Chatham Hill Games

We discovered Chatham Hill's line of historical adventure games at the tail end of a museum trip, in an unplanned (but lucky) stop-off at the museum gift shop. We're now in the process of collecting the entire set, with considerable intrafamily bickering over which one is the best of the bunch. The games are attractive, inexpensive, clever, and solidly historical; all are printed on heavy paper in earthy old-fashioned colors, and packaged in manila envelopes. Each includes do-it-yourself cut-out playing pieces and spinners. Games vary in complexity: the two simplest - *The Redcoats Are Coming!* and *The Battle of Bunker Hill* - are probably appropriate for kids as young as 5 or 6, though the little paper playing pieces may be finicky for small fingers. In *The Redcoats are Coming!*, Paul Revere and William Dawes race the British regulars to Concord; in *The Battle of Bunker Hill*, Americans battle the British on a grid-like board in an effort to defend their redoubt.

Thar She Blows!, a game of 19th-century whaling, is a step up in difficulty; whaling ships *Essex* and *Emelia* encounter fogs and icebergs in their search for whales, which, once spotted, must be pursued and captured. Players chase whales, harpoon whales, lose their boats to whales, and take off on Nantucket sleigh rides. In*The Monitor and the Merrimack*, players re-enact the most famous Civil War sea battle; in *Frigates!*, *Old Ironsides* tackles the *Guerriere*; and in *Don't Give Up the Ship!*, Commodore Perry struggles for control of Lake Erie in the War of 1812. In *The Voyage of the Mayflower*, players attempt to get their ships across the Atlantic before supplies run out, battling stormy weather and contrary winds.

In the works, says designer Ron Toelke, are games based on the Underground Railroad, the Gold Rush, and the Alamo. A descriptive brochure is available from Chatham Hill Games, Ray Toelke Associates, P.O. Box 253, Chatham, NY 12037.

Childhood of Famous Americans series

These biographies are not new. They were originally published in the early 1940's, and you can occasionally come across them in used-book stores, in hardcover. The original series was extensive, and many of the books, unfortunately, are now out of print. A number of the volumes, however, are still with us, available nowadays in blue-and-orange paperback editions, and the series has been updated in recent years to include, among others, Martin Luther King, Jr., and John F. Kennedy. Other Famous Americans available include Daniel Boone, Davy Crockett, Henry Ford, Benjamin Franklin, Molly Pitcher, Paul Revere, George Washington, Robert E. Lee, Clara Barton, Susan B. Anthony, and Wilbur and Orville Wright. These are about right for 8- or 9-year-olds to read on their own; as read-aloud books, they're chatty and appealing enough to hold the attention of younger children. Books in the Childhood of Famous Americans series are available from libraries and bookstores, or can be ordered from Sycamore Tree, Inc., 2179 Meyer Place, Costa Mesa, CA 92627; (714) 642-6750 (orders) or (714) 650-4466 (information).

The Civil War

Ken Burns' renowned nine-part documentary on the Civil War is superb, wholly fascinating, and an education in itself, on videotape. Each episode is 70 to100 minutes long and features period photographs, quotes from Civil War diarists, and narration by modern historians. The final episode, which covers the surrender at Appomatox and the assassination of Abraham Lincoln, includes a heart-rending account of the fiftieth anniversary of the Battle of Gettysburg in 1915. The survivors, re-enacting Pickett's Charge, suddenly burst from their ranks and ran across the fields to embrace each other. It's history made human and unforgettable. Age appropriateness is difficult to gauge here. Our family watched *The Civil War* together: it only held the attention of our 7-year-old in bits and pieces, but our 9- and 10-year-olds were enthralled. *The Civil War*, in a 9-tape boxed set, is available from Time-Life Video, 777 Duke Street, Alexandria, VA 22314; (800) 621-7026; or from Movies Unlimited, 6736 Castor Avenue, Philadelphia, PA 19149; (800) 523-0823 (orders) or (215) 722-8398 (customer service).

Cobblestone Publishing

Cobblestone publishes a trio of excellent children's history and social studies magazines: *Cobblestone* ("The History Magazine for Young People"), *Calliope* ("World History for Young People"), and *Faces* ("The Magazine About People"). *Cobblestone* concentrates on American history; *Calliope* on world history from ancient times through the Renaissance period; and *Faces* on multicultural themes. All are published monthly, and each issue is organized around a single central topic.

In my experience, *Faces* has the most appeal for younger children; we first subscribed when our sons were aged 5, 6, and 8, and that seemed about right. Past *Faces* topics have included "Around the Arctic," "Desert Life," "Hats," "Horses," "Islands," "Masks," "Maps," "Money," "Witches and Wizards," and "Writing." Each topic is dealt with from several different angles: there are non-fiction articles, related folktales from around the world, recipes, puzzles, and craft projects.

Cobblestone and *Calliope* are targeted at older readers; to me, they look appropriate for kids aged nine or ten and older. *Cobblestone* issues cover all aspects of American history: topics have included "The Alamo," "American Architecture," "The Beaver Trade," "Helen Keller," "Newspapers in America," "Old-Time Schools," "The Oregon Trail," and "Whaling." *Calliope* concentrates on ancient history: sample topics have included "Ancient Inventions," "Epic Heroes," and "Lost Cities." Both run a little longer than *Faces*, but similarly contain a range of fiction and non-fiction articles, puzzles, projects, and short plays. Back issues of all three magazines are continuously available. For a complete list and subscription information, write Cobblestone Publishing, Inc., 7 School Street, Peterborough, NH 03458; (603) 924-7209; fax: (603) 924-7380.

Count Your Way Books

There are twelve of these small books, written by Jim Haskins, in which kids can count their way through Africa, Canada, China, Germany, India, Israel, Italy, Japan, Korea, Mexico, Russia, and the Arab world. Each page presents a number (1-10) with its foreign-language name, a pronounciation guide, and a picture and description of the number of relevant cultural items to be counted. In *Count Your Way Through China*, for example, 1 (yee) shows a map of China, 2 (uhr) a pair of giant pandas, and 3 (sahn) the Great Wall, up through 10 (shur), a list of the ten major ruling dynasties in Chinese history. Kids can also learn to write the numbers 1-10 in Chinese. The books cost $4.95 apiece, and are available through bookstores or from Carolrhoda Books, 241 First Ave North, Minneapolis, MN 55401; (800) 328-4929 or (612) 332-3344.

Creative Minds Biographies

This series of short (56-64 pages) biographies, published by Carolrhoda, are targeted at kids in grades 3-6. Titles include: *America, I Hear You: A Story about George Gershwin; Between Two Worlds: A Story about Pearl Buck; Click!: A Story about George Eastman; The*

Country Artist: A Story about Beatrix Potter; Fine Print: A Story about Johann Gutenberg; Frontier Surgeons: A Story about the Mayo Brothers; Go Free or Die: A Story about Harriet Tubman; "Good Morning, Mr. President:" A Story about Carl Sandburg; Healing Warrior: A Story about Sister Elizabeth Kenny; Mr. Blue Jeans: A Story about Levi Strauss; Pioneer Plowmaker: A Story about John Deere; A Pocketful of Goobers: A Story about George Washington Carver; Raggin': A Story about Scott Joplin; Rooftop Astronomer: A Story about Maria Mitchell; Shoes for Everyone: A Story about Jan Matzeliger; Stateswoman to The World: A Story about Eleanor Roosevelt; Tales for Hard Times: A Story about Charles Dickens; To the Point: A Story about E.B. White; Walking the Road to Freedom: A Story about Sojourner Truth ; We'll Race You, Henry: A Story about Henry Ford; What Are You Figuring Now?: A Story about Benjamin Banneker; What Do You Mean?: A Story about Noah Webster; The Wizard of Sound: A Story about Thomas Edison. Available through bookstores or from Carolrhoda Books, Inc., 241 First Avenue North, Minneapolis, MN 55401; (800) 328-4929 or (612) 332-3344.

Don't Know Much About Geography   Kenneth C. Davis   (William Morrow; 1992)

The subtitle, "Everything You Need to Know About the World but Never Learned," is more like it: this book is a goldmine of geographical information, with fascinating ties to history, science, literature, and mathematics. Chapter titles include "The World is a Pear," "What's So Bad About the Badlands?," "If People Were Dolphins, the Planet Would be Called Ocean," "Elephants in the Alps," "Paradise Lost?: Geography, Weather, and the Environment," and "Lost in Space," plus three appendices: "What the Hell is a Hoosier?: Names and Nicknames of the 50 American States," "Table of Comparative Measures," in which readers can look up the mathematical definitions of such unfamiliar terms as hectare, league, and furlong, and "The Nations of the World," which lists all of them, in alphabetical order. The (addictive) text is written largely in question-and-answer format. Sample questions: "Who invented the compass? Are there Amazons on the Amazon River? What do tides have to do with tidal waves? Why did Hannibal take elephants across the Alps, and did Napoleon know how far it was to Moscow? Which is colder, Antarctica or the Arctic Circle?" Also included is "Geographical Voices," a collection of quotes from the journals of famous explorers and geographers, and "Geographical Milestones," a timeline of geographical events and discoveries stretching from 5000 B.C. to the present. By the same author: *Don't Know Much About History: Everything You Need to Know About American History but Never Learned* (Crown; 1990). Available through bookstores.

Dover Publications

Dover's complete catalog contains some 4500 paperback selections from all fields, described in 72 pages of small print; if you don't feel up to all that, there's a separate Children's Book Catalog, listing 650 different selections, with color illustrations. The children's catalog is an excellent source of historical project books. There is, for example, a large assortment of detailed historical coloring books, among them *The Story of the Civil War*, *The History of the American Automobile*, *Life in a Medieval Castle*, *Indian Tribes of North America*, *History of Flight*, *Historic Sailing Ships*, *The Lewis and Clark Expedition*, *Life in Ancient Egypt*, *The Story of the American Revolution*, and *Cowboys of the Old West*. There are cut-and-assemble paper models in varying degrees of difficulty, including a western frontier town, a southern plantation, a medieval castle, and a Columbus diorama; and collections of historical paperdolls with appropriate costumes, among them a Pilgrim family, a colonial family, and a Civil War era family, George Washington, Abraham Lincoln, and Theodore Roosevelt, with their respective families, and famous American women paperdolls: 16 paper women, including Emily Dickinson, Mary Cassatt, Jane Addams, Margaret Mead, and Georgia O'Keefe. Free catalogs can be obtained from Dover Publications, Inc., 31 East 2nd Street, Mineola, NY 11501.

Eliza Records

Eliza Records produces "Abe Lincoln in Song and Story," a 40-minute cassette tape that combines narration and music to detail the life and times of Honest Abe, from his boyhood through the years of the Civil War. The songs - "toe-tapping tunes and authentic ballads from American history" - are accompanied by banjo, guitar, and harmonica. There is also an "Educational Guide" booklet. "Abe Lincoln in Song and Story" costs $14.98 from Eliza Records, 1304 Rittenhouse St., N.W., Washington, D.C. 20015.

Empire Builder

A board game for players aged 12 and up, in which participants build the transcontinental railroad across frontier America. The game costs $24.95 from Rand McNally Catalog, P.O. Box 182257, Chattanooga, TN 37422-7257.

Everything is Somewhere: The Geography Quiz Book   Jack McClintock and David Helgren   (William Morrow; 1986)

This book is a collection of over 30 different geography quizzes, each consisting of questions ranging from the solidly serious to the off-the-wall. Examples include: "Where would you find the world's largest spider? Where is the Sphinx's beard? Where are the best Panama hats made? How many words do the Eskimos have for snow? Which country has the most lawyers? What country has a cockroach named after it? Which is the biggest lake in the world?" There is also a series of map identification quizzes. Answers, luckily, are included. Available through bookstores and from Zephyr Press, 3316 N. Chapel Ave., P.O. Box 13448-E, Tucson, AZ 85732-3448; (602) 322-5090.

Explorers

This is an inexpensive rummy-type game in which players collect sets of cards carrying pictures and information about famous explorers, among them, Leif Ericson, Marco Polo, Alexander the Great, Columbus, Magellan, Vasco da Gama, James Cook, Meriwether Lewis and William Clark, and Robert Peary. Cards can also be used for other educational purposes: as research challenges or for ordering on a timeline. Available from Michael Olaf's Essential Montessori, P.O. Box 1162, Arcata, CA; (707) 826-1557; or Aristoplay, P.O. Box 7529, Ann Arbor, MI 48107; (800) 634-7738.

Explorers

This is a cooperative board game, appropriate for kids aged 8 and up, in which players embark on past journeys of discovery, tracing the routes of such great explorers as Marco Polo, Christopher Columbus, and Roald Amundsen. Players must collect supplies, assemble crews, and set off along the explorer's original route, facing (authentic) problems such as mutiny, bandits, sickness, hurricanes, and blizzards. The game board is a world map; playing accessories include land and sea logs, paper currency, and navigational charts. The game costs $22.00 from Michael Olaf's Essential Montessori, Box 1162, Arcata, CA 95521; (707) 826-1557.

Facts-A-Nation

A board game of U.S. geography (plus) for players aged 8 and older. The board features a large (unlabeled) map of the United States; players proceed by answering questions on American geography, history, science, arts, and sports. Included are 300 question-and-answer cards. *Facts-A-Nation* costs $26.00 from the Smithsonian Institution, Department 0006, Washington, D.C. 20073-0006; (800) 322-0344.

Fireworks Educational

Fireworks Educational - their motto is "Learning is a blast!" - publishes a series of integrated study units based on the travels of Maude Marmot, Rodent Scholar. Maude variously visits Japan, Brazil, and Russia, getting her educational money's worth out of each journey. Each unit aims at interdisciplinary integration: Maude's visits incorporate reading, writing, math, science, geography, and social studies, plus assorted hands-on projects. Each of the current Maude modules - "Maude Visits Japan," "Maude Visits Brazil," and "Maude Visits Russia" - includes a 90-page teacher's sourcebook, including reproducible storybooks, science experiment instructions, maps, an introduction to the relevant foreign language, and a book list, a color photo filmstrip, and an audio cassette. In the near future, Maude will also be visiting Egypt and Mexico. Maude is a bit pricey: each module costs about $60.00. The publisher points out, however, that it's easy to share. For more information on Maude, contact Fireworks Educational, Inc., P.O. Box 2325, Joliet, IL 60434; (815) 725-9057.

Foster, Genevieve

Genevieve Foster's superb history books, published in the 1940's by Charles Scribner's Sons, are all out of print now, but they're generally available through libraries, who know better than to discard such gems, and we've tracked down occasional volumes through used-book stores. So far we've acquired *The World of Captain John Smith*, *George Washington's World*, and *Abraham Lincoln's World*, and we have high hopes - someday - of finding a copy of *The World of Augustus Caesar*. These are all good-sized books - around 400 pages long - but are divided into manageable chunks, like a collection of short stories. They read well at bedtime.

The delight of the Foster books is the way in which they demonstrate the interconnectedness of world history. World events are related to periods in the life of the title character. *George Washington's World*, for example, is divided into six parts: when George was a boy, a soldier, a farmer, a commander-in-chief, a citizen, and the first president. During Washington's boyhood, Daniel Boone was growing up in Pennsylvania, John Adams was studying Latin in Massachusetts, and John Hancock was living with his rich Uncle Thomas in Boston. Benjamin West was just teaching himself to paint, making brushes with bits of fur pulled from his cat's tail; and Benjamin Franklin was experimenting with electricity. Fray Junipero Serra was setting out for California; Johann Sebastian Bach was writing flute music for King Frederick of Prussia; and Catherine (not yet the Great) had just arrived in Russia, at the age of fourteen, ready to marry the Grand Duke Peter. Louis XV was king of France; Voltaire was in jail; James Cook, aged thirteen, had just run away to sea; James Watt was doing experiments in Glasgow. By the time Washington was a farmer, Captain Cook was exploring the Antarctic, Joseph Priestley had just discovered oxygen; and James Watt had patented his steam engine. Marie Antoinette was a little girl; Napoleon Bonaparte was a baby. Mozart was composing; Goya was painting; Catherine (now the Great) was fighting the Sultan of Turkey; and Japan was ruled by feudal lords called shoguns. The books are packed with information and they're fun to read. Keep an eye out for them. See Out-of-Print Books.

Fritz, Jean

The books of author Jean Fritz comprise some of the most reader-friendly American history available for kids aged 7-10. Her history series is published by Coward-McCann and is available in paperback. The books include *Where Do You Think You're Going, Christopher Columbus?*, *Can't You Make Them Behave, King George?*, *Why Don't You Get a Horse, Sam Adams?*, *Where Was Patrick Henry on the 29th of May?*, *And Then What Happened, Paul Revere?*, *Will You Sign Here, John Hancock?*, and *Shh! We're Writing the Constitution!* All are about 50 pages long, and are informative, accurate, and delightful.

For readers on the younger end of the scale, there's also *George Washington's Breakfast*, in which young George Allen learns a great deal about Washington while finding out what the great man ate for breakfast (hoecakes and tea); for older readers, there are longer and more detailed biographies of Pocahontas (*The Double Life of Pocahontas*), Benedict Arnold (*Traitor*) and James Madison (*The Great Little Madison*). The Fritz books are available from libraries and bookstores, and many are offered by Bluestocking Press, P.O. Box 1014-GS, Placerville, CA 95667; (916) 621-1123.

Fun With Hieroglyphics

Fun With Hieroglyphics, by Catharine Roehrig, is published by the Metropolitan Museum of Art. This is essentially a rubber-stamp kit, beautifully packaged, containing 24 hieroglyphic stamps, an inkpad, and an informational guidebook on the meaning and use of hieroglyphics. (It also includes a hieroglyphic crossword puzzle and instructions for making your own cartouche.) A wonderful hands-on resource for young Egyptologists. The kit is available from bookstores or from the Metropolitan Museum of Art, 255 Gracie Station, New York, NY 10028-9998; (800) 468-7386.

Genealogy for Kids

A good start for beginning historians is often their very own families. Along these lines, one good resource for young genealogists is Rosemary Chorzempa's *My Family Tree Workbook*. This is a do-it-yourself family history scrapbook; kids record information about themselves, their parents, their brothers and sisters, their grandparents, and their great-grandparents, and then fill in a preprinted family tree. They then go on to record information about immigrant ancestors, collect family autographs, record and illustrate family stories and legends, describe their ancestors' homelands (geography, language, ethnic foods, arts and crafts, folksongs and dances, and traditional holidays), and design a family coat-of-arms. There are lots of spaces throughout for pasting in photographs. There are also lists of helpful research sources and suggestions for additional projects. If the coat-of-arms project catches your students' fancy, Chorzempa has also written a workbook introducing kids to heraldry, titled *Design Your Own Coat of Arms*. Both workbooks are available from Dover Publications, Inc., 31 East 2nd St., Mineola, NY 11501. Good informational books for kids on genealogy include: *Do People Grow on Family Trees? Genealogy for Kids and Other Beginners,* by Ira Wolfman (Workman; 1991), *The Great Ancestor Hunt: The Fun of Finding Out Who You Are*, Lila Perl (Clarion; 1989), *Roots for Kids: Genealogy Anyone Can Understand*, Susan Beller (Betterway; 1989), *Where Did You Get Those Eyes?* Kay Cooper (Walker and Company; 1988).

Geografacts

Geografacts, "The Game of the World," is a board game for young geographers. It consists of a world map playing board, two colorful map sheets covering the continents of Asia, Africa, North America, South America, and Europe, with numbered (not labeled) countries, and over 350 question-and-answer cards. Cards are color-coded by continent, and numbered to correspond to the numbered countries on the map sheets. Players advance around the board depending on their ability to answer geographical questions, which range from the simple ("What's the continent?") to the challenging ("Name the most populous city in Canada."). The game is right up to geographical date, and includes the new Commonwealth of Independent States (once the U.S.S.R.). *Geografacts* costs $24.95 from Edutainment Group, 1445 N. Rock Rd. #200, Wichita, KS 67206; (800) 752-5262 or (316) 634-0441.

The Geography Coloring Book   Wynn Kapit   (HarperCollins; 1991)
"Coloring," explains one reviewer, "enables you to reach an unusual level of concentration and awareness" - and this is a book for the absolutely serious colorer, a 50-page collection of highly detailed maps with encyclopedic amounts of information in small print. An excellent resource for older geographers, but definitely not for the scribble-with-crayons set. Available through bookstores.

Geography Songs
For musically-minded geographers, Audio Memory publishes the *Sing Around the World* geography kit. The kit contains a pair of cassette tapes which, through 18 songs, teaches the names of the countries on each continent, the planets in the solar system, and the states in the United States. The words are no great shakes but, set to music, they do stick firmly in the head: after a few days we found ourselves pattering about the house, humming - to a tune vaguely resembling "This Land Is Your Land" - "In Southeast Asia, there is Malaysia/Laos and Burma/And Campuchea..." The accompanying workbook includes all the song lyrics, outline maps to label and color, and 24 geographical crossword puzzles. Also included: a 25 x 36 inch map of the world poster, on which kids can label and color countries while listening to the music.

The *States and Capitals* kit teaches names of states and their capitals through the "United States Song" and the "Capitals Song." Capitals are sung echo-style, and repeated for self-testing. A 25 x 36 inch U.S. map poster is included, for labeling and coloring. Available separately: *50 State Crosswords*, a reproducible collection of crossword puzzles, one for each state, covering state history, geography, industry, agriculture, and famous landmarks and citizens. The *Sing Around the World* kit costs $24.95; *States and Capitals*, $9.95, from Audio Memory Publishing, 2060 Raymond Ave., Signal Hill, CA 90806; (800) 365-SING (orders) or (310) 494-8822 (information).

Geography: The United States of America Frances Stewart
(Harper & Row; 1990)

This is a sticker book, containing - according to the cover blurb -
122 moveable stickers. Each sticker pictures a memorable state feature (the Statue of Liberty, the Alamo, Mt. Rushmore, Crater Lake,
the Boston Tea Party) and are meant to be stuck upon a a large
fold-out map of the United States. Also included are maps of Canada and Mexico, and an alphabetical chart listing all the states,
their two-letter abbreviation, the date they were admitted to the
Union, their rank in size, and - in case you didn't figure it out on
your own - which sticker they were supposed to get.

The book is made of nice sturdy coated paper, which means
that it lasts well; and we bought only one of them, which was a
mistake. Available through bookstores or from Chinaberry Book
Service, 2780 Via Orange Way, Suite B, Spring Valley, CA 91978;
(800) 776-2242 (orders, customer service) or (619) 670-5200 (info).

Geosafari

Geosafari, from its recent prominence in the catalogs, seems to
have made quite a splash in the world of educational products. It's
an electronic geography quiz game; the basic unit comes with 20
different maps, political and physical, of all the continents of the
world, a detailed United States map, and a map of the solar system. Kids identify (numbered) countries, cities, and planets by
keying in numbers on the answer panel. At first glance, Geosafari
is a glitzy little set-up: questions and answers are accompanied by
beeps and flashing lights; but our children adore it, and since its
introduction into our household, have become little storehouses of
information geographical. Geosafari is expensive: the introductory
set-up (plus maps) runs around $100, batteries not included. Once
you've got it, however, there is a large assortment of additional
lesson card sets available, including Advanced U.S. Geography,
Advanced World Geography, World Animals, Puzzles, Science,
American History, and even a blank set of lesson cards, upon
which you can create your own electronic question-and-answer
quizzes. There's also a GeoSafari, Jr., version, targeted at 4-7-year-
olds, with lesson card sets covering time-telling, money, math and
phonics facts, animal habitats, and basic map skills. GeoSafari is
available from Educational Insights, 19560 South Rancho Way,
Dominguez Hills, CA 90220; (800) 933-3277.

Geo-Whiz! Susan M. Tejada   (National Geographic Society; 1988)

Geo-Whiz! is a spectacular photographic tour of the world, designed for kids by the National Geographic Society. Nobody does pictures better. The photographs include an Alaskan ice cave, glittering with blue ice, an erupting Hawaiian volcano, a little girl floating on an immense Amazon lily pad, an Antarctic nursery crammed with penguins, towering Chinese sand dunes, a Saudi Arabian camel race, and - from Australia - the world's biggest rock. Chapter titles are "Looking at the Land," "'Waterful' Worlds," "Land Alive," and "Meeting People." The text is peppered with colorful maps and "Geo-Quizzes," short catchy questions about the world's biggest wave, loudest noise, biggest iceberg, highest geyser, and driest desert. *Geo-Whiz!* costs $8.95 from the National Geographic Society, Washington, D.C. 20036; (800) 447-0647.

Global Pursuit

This is a geographical board game for families, in which players assemble a world map from a collection of pentagonal map puzzle pieces ("a new view of the world every time you play") and then, from the included pack of trivia cards, answer "intriguing" questions about geographical facts. *Global Pursuit* costs $21.95 from the National Geographic Society, Washington, D.C. 20036; (800) 447-0647.

Globe Pequot Press

The Globe Pequot Press sells 100-piece state puzzle maps, in colorful heavy-duty cardboard. Each map features state counties, major cities, geographical features, and agricultural and industrial products, plus the state seal, flag, flower, bird, and tree. States currently available include Arkansas, California, Colorado, Connecticut, Illinois, Iowa, Kansas, Louisiana, Massachusetts, Minnesota, Missouri, Nebraska, New Jersey, New Mexico, New York, Oklahoma, Pennsylvania, Texas, Washington, and Wisconsin, with more in the works. Puzzles cost about $10.00 each. For a catalog or additional information, contact the Globe Pequot Press, P.O. Box 833, Old Saybrook, CT 06475; (800) 243-0495 or (203) 395-0440.

Gonick, Larry

Larry Gonick, says the blurb on one back cover, "is the author or co-author of many books of graphic non-fiction on scientific and historical subjects. A graduate of Harvard in math, he dropped out of graduate school to pursue something really difficult: rendering information in little pictures." His books - a favorite in our family - contain almost overwhelming amounts of (accurate) information, rendered in zillions of clever (and hilarious) little pictures. Young historians should look for *The Cartoon History of the Universe*, which starts with the Big Bang and ends - some 358 illustrated pages later - with Alexander the Great; and *The Cartoon History of the United States*, which starts with the crossing of the Asia-to-Alaska land bridge some 15,000 years ago (picture of Indian throwing off parka, saying "This sure beats Siberia!") and ends with the Gulf War. Gonick's cartoon histories are available from bookstores or from A Common Reader, 141 Tompkins Ave., Pleasantville, NY 10570-3154; (914) 747-3388.

Great Women Biographical Card Games

There are three sets of the *Great Women* card games, each played like rummy, and suitable for children in grade 3 and up. Games consist of a deck of 52 cards, each carrying a photograph and selected biographical information about ten different famous American woman. Set I, "Foremothers," includes Susan B. Anthony, Mary Shadd Cary, the Grimke sisters, Lucretia Mott, Ernestine Rose, Elizabeth Cady Stanton, Lucy Stone, Susette La Flesche Tibbles, Sojourner Truth, and Harriet Tubman. Set II, "Founders and Firsts," includes Clara Barton, Mary McLeod Bethune, Elizabeth Blackwell, Nellie Bly, Antoinette Brown, Amelia Earhart, Emma Goldman, Belva Lockwood, Mary Lyon, and Margaret Sanger. Set III, "Poets and Writers," includes Louisa May Alcott, Emily Dickinson, Margaret Fuller, Charlotte Perkins Gilman, Frances E.W. Harper, Julia Ward Howe, Sarah Orne Jewett, Emma Lazarus, Harriet Beecher Stowe, and Phillis Wheatley. Games cost $7.95 each, from the National Women's History Project, 7738 Bell Road, Windsor, CA 95492; (707) 838-6000, or from Aristoplay, P.O. Box 7529, Ann Arbor, MI 48107; (800) 634-7738 or (313) 995-4353.

Hail to the Chief

Hail to the Chief is subtitled "The Presidential Election Game." The gameboard is a map of the United States (crisscrossed with campaign trails). Players become presidential candidates by answering historical and constitutional questions about the presidency; then succeed on the campaign trail by answering questions about the history and geography of the fifty states. 91 President cards (652 questions) and 91 State cards (364 questions) are included. Suitable for 2 to 4 politically-minded players aged 10 and up. The game costs $25.00 from Aristoplay, P.O. Box 7529, Ann Arbor, MI 48107; (800) 634-7738 or (313) 995-4353.

Hands Around the World: 356 Creative Ways to Build Cultural Awareness & Global Respect Susan Milord (Williamson; 1992)

This is a big information-and-activity book, targeted at kids aged 4-10, and designed to encourage appreciation for other cultures around the world and for the planet itself. Using it, kids will make Javanese shadow puppets, weave Guatemalan friendship bracelets, cook an Israeli dinner, create their own wildlife sanctuaries, and celebrate a long list of new holidays, including World Environment Day. And much more. The book is stuffed with interesting facts, information on worldwide celebrations, new recipes, games, and arts and crafts. A wonderful and worthwhile resource. Available through bookstores or from Williamson Publishing Company, Church Hill Road, P.O. Box 185, Charlotte, VT 05445; (800) 234-8791.

Hands-On History

The Hands-On History units are the brainchildren of a pair of homeschoolers who espouse the philosophy of "immersion learning," in which kids learn by immersing themselves - via books, games, and manipulatives - in a given historical period. To further such immersion learning, they have assembled an assortment of packaged units, each centering around a certain period or event in history. Our sample - the "Christopher Columbus Unit" - was a delight. It arrived in a sturdy cardboard sea-chest, an absolute treasure trove of historical goodies: there was a stuffed parrot (now hanging goonily from our kitchen ceiling), a full-color "Columbus Discovers America" diorama to cut out and assemble, and a set of heavy-duty Christopher Columbus paperdolls, including all the main players in the Columbus saga, plus historically accurate clothes. There was a compass, a nautical knot-tying kit, and an antique-parchment-like "Days of Columbus" document, with a reproduction of the pre-voyage agreement between Columbus and the King and Queen of Spain, and a map showing the routes of his (four) journeys across the "Ocean Sea." There was a paperback book - *I Sailed With Columbus* by Miriam Schlein - and an assortment of (fake) gold doubloons, a Columbus-type hat, and a Queen Isabella-type crown, for formal skits or informal make-believe. Accompanying the unit is an "Idea Guide" for parents or teachers, and a list of additional available Columbus materials, including an excellent assortment of books, a Columbus map puzzle, and wooden model kits for making small replicas of the *Nina*, the *Pinta*, and the *Santa Maria*.

On History units include "Revolutionary War
ationary War Girl" - each containing a "hook"
and toys, replica Revolutionary War-era money,
ell, and ink, and Revolutionary War documents
the works: units of the Pilgrims, pioneers, Ore-
gon Trail, Gold Rush, Civil War, and the turn of the century. Units
retail for $59.95 each, but you get a *lot* for your money. For a cata-
log and order forms, write Hands On History, 201 Constance Dr.,
New Lenox, IL 60451.

Hear & Learn Publications

The Hear & Learn people offer a small hand-picked selection of
history and geography books and workbooks, but the cream of
their catalog is definitely the *History Alive! Through Music* series.
So far there are three of these are book-and-cassette-tape sets:
"America 1750-1890: The Heart of a New Land," "Westward Ho!,"
and "Musical Memories of Laura Ingalls Wilder." "Heart of a New
Land" traces early American history in song from the Revolution
through the building of the transcontinental railroad: featured
songs include "Old Dan Tucker," "Erie Canal," "When Johnny
Comes Marching Home," and, of course, "Yankee Doodle." "West-
ward Ho!" - our kids' favorite - includes "Home on the Range,"
"Little Old Sod Shanty," "Boll Weevil," "The San Juan Pig," and
"Gooey Duck." "Musical Memories" features favorite songs from
the Laura Ingalls Wilder *Little House* books, among them "Wait for
the Wagon," "Buffalo Gals," "Pop! Goes the Weasel," and "The Girl
I Left Behind Me."

The accompanying illustrated books explain the historical background and associations of each song; also included are music and
lyrics. *History Alive! Through Music* book-and-tape sets cost $17.95,
plus $3.00 shipping and handling. For a catalog, contact Hear &
Learn Publications, 603 S.E. Morrison Road, Vancouver, WA
98664-1545.

Historical Literacy: The Case for History in American Educa-tion Paul Gagnon (Macmillan; 1989)

This book, a compelling defense of historical literacy, is based
on studies by the Bradley Commission on History in Schools. The
authors list the important topics and themes to be covered in the
general study of history, and suggest effective methods for presenting this material to children. In lieu of the conventional "expanding horizons" history curriculum used in the elementary
grades, in which kids study families and neighborhoods, then

towns and cities, and gradually branch out to the study of the nation and the world, the Commission recommends a more wide-
ranging perspective, based on "good narrative storytelling." Such
a program would include: Grade K: children's adventures long
ago and far away; Grade 1: stories of the people who made America; Grade 2: traditions, monuments, and celebrations; Grade 3: inventors, innovators, and immigrants; Grade 4: heroes, folktales,
and legends of the world; Grade 5: biographies and documents in
American history; Grade 6: biographies and documents in world
history. Studies in the upper grades become more detailed: Grade
7: regional history and geography; Grade 8: U.S. history and geography; Grade 9: Western civilizations; Grade 10: world history and
geography; Grade 11: U.S. history and geography; Grade 12:
American government.

The authors further propose more in-depth connection to the
study of history: the use of real historical documents, such as diaries, journals, letters, and newpaper articles; the connection of history to current events, as in "What is the historical background of
this event?;" the combination of history with creative writing; the
use of historical artifacts as hands-on aids; and the importance of
using timelines. Using such approaches and techniques, the Commission hopes, children will begin to view history as a complex,
fascinating, and on-going process. Check libraries and bookstores.

Historical Photographs

We discovered these historical photograph packets in the Michael Olaf Essential Montessori catalog and have found them to be
a banner addition to our history program. These are not teeny
snapshots, but 8 1/2 x 11" reproductions (on paper) of photographs or painted portraits. Available sets are "Famous Women in
U.S. and World History," "Famous Men in U.S. History (born in
1779 or earlier)," "Famous Men in U.S. and World History (born
1783-1817)," "Famous Men in U.S. and World History (born 1819
or later)," "U.S. Presidents," and "Famous Composers." All are fascinating: this is history brought up close and personal. Pictures include the Wright brothers, in lock step, wearing identical bowlers;
Carrie Nation wielding her hatchet; Robert Peary, squinting in a
fur parka; Henry David Thoreau, looking uncomfortable in high
collar and tie; Sojourner Truth knitting; Mohandas Gandhi in
spectacles; Alexander Graham Bell talking on the telephone; John
Paul Jones on deck, with sword and a beltful of pistols; and Helen
Keller with Annie Sullivan.

We combined all ours in a pair of looseleaf binders and they've been a continuing source of interest, conversation, and historically-based storytelling. Historical Photograph sets cost $4.50 each, or $26.50 for the entire series; they are available from Michael Olaf's Essential Montessori, P.O. Box 1162, Arcata, CA 95521; (707) 826-1557.

Historical Products

The products here are T-shirts and sweatshirts, each printed with the portrait of a famous person. Nearly a hundred different famous portraits are available, among them Jane Austen, Ludwig von Beethoven, Leonardo Da Vinci, Emily Dickinson, Amelia Earhart, Sherlock Holmes, Malcolm X, Michelangelo, Isaac Newton, William Shakespeare, Henry David Thoreau, Vincent Van Gogh, and Frank Lloyd Wright. Our oldest son owns an Edgar Allan Poe, which he seldom takes off. Descriptive fliers are published quarterly, and include terrific 3-month calendars of historical and literary events. For information, contact Historical Products, P.O. Box 403, E. Longmeadow, MA 01028; (413) 525-2250.

Homestyle Geography

Despite the enormous selection of excellent commercial resources for young geographers, our kids' favorite continues to be homemade. Our game consists simply of a big bright-colored world or United States map, tacked to the dining room wall at kid-level, and a large tatty pack of index cards, each inscribed with a geography trivia question or challenge. Kids, in more or less cooperative turns, answer the questions and find the correct geographical feature on the map.

Sample Questions for Homestyle (World) Geographers
1. Where were fireworks invented? (*China*)
2. Which African country has the most people? (*Nigeria*)
3. Where did Howard Carter find King Tut's tomb? (*Egypt*)
4. Which country's flag has a red maple leaf on it? (*Canada*)
5. Show how Marco Polo traveled to Cathay.
6. Which continent has the most countries? (*Africa*)
7. Where is the world's highest waterfall? (*Venezuela*)
8. Where did William Shakespeare live? (*England*)
9. Find the longest river in the world. (*Nile*)
10. Where is the deepest part of the ocean? (*Marianas Trench*)
11. In what country was Jesus born? (*Israel*)
12. Find the Rock of Gibralter.

13. Where did the ancient Romans live? (*Italy*)
14. Find the Panama Canal.
15. Where is the Sahara Desert? (*northern Africa*)
16. Find the Cape of Good Hope.
17. Find Pakistan.
18. Where are the world's highest mountains? (*Himalayas*)
19. Where did the dodo come from? (*Mauritius*)
20. What country has the only manmade structure that can be seen from the moon? (*China, the Great Wall*)

Sample Questions for Homestyle (U.S.) Geographers
1. Which state has a meteor crater one mile wide? (*AZ*)
2. Which state has the highest mountain in the U.S.? (*AK*)
3. Where is Pearl Harbor? (*HI*)
4. Which state is named for Queen Elizabeth? (*VA*)
5. Which is the smallest state? (*RI*)
6. Where is the oldest town in the U.S.? (*FL*)
7. Where would you go to see Mt. St. Helens? (*WA*)
8. Where did the Wright Brothers fly their airplane? (*NC*)
9. Where did George Washington live? (*VA*)
10. Where did the Pilgrims land? (*MA*)
12. Where would you go to see the Statue of Liberty? (*NY*)
13. Which is the biggest state in the continental U.S.? (*TX*)
14. Which state is named for the country's biggest river? (*MS*)
15. Where is the Alamo? (*TX*)
16. Where is Yellowstone National Park? (*WY*)
17. Where was the Battle of Gettysburg? (*PA*)
18. Where was the first shot of the Civil War fired? (*SC*)
19. Where is the Great Salt Lake? (*UT*)
20. Which state is a peninsula? (*FL*)

If You...Series
Scholastic, Inc., publishes a great little series of history books, written in entertaining question-and-answer format. This format works: our kids plunged right in, answering questions and discussing answers. Books in the series include *If You Grew Up With Abraham Lincoln, If You Lived in Colonial Times, If You Lived With the Sioux Indians,* and *If You Sailed on the Mayflower* by Ann McGovern; *If You Grew Up With George Washington* by Ruth Belov Gross; *If You Lived at the Time of Martin Luther King, Jr., If You Lived At the Time of the Great San Francisco Earthquake,* and *If You Traveled West in a Covered Wagon* by Ellen Levine; and *If You Were There When*

They Signed the Constitution by Elizabeth Levy. The books run 80 (small) pages and cost a mere $2.95 apiece. Order from Scholastic, Inc., P.O. Box 7502, Jefferson City, MO 65102; (800) 325-6149.

It Happened in America: True Stories from the Fifty States   Lila Perle   (Henry Holt; 1992)

The meat of this delightful book is the collection of short true stories from each of the fifty states, plus one (on Dolley Madison) from the District of Columbia. The stories, which are irresistable, come from all periods of American history, from pre-colonial days to modern times. The book is organized in alphabetical order by state: each story is preceded by a short general introduction describing the state's original inhabitants, explaining the state nickname, and mentioning any notable historical or geographical state features. Among the stories: "The Day Rosa Parks Said No to 'Jim Crow'" (Alabama), "Hadji Ali and the Camel Experiment" (Arizona), "Mr. Studebaker's Horseless Carriage" (Indiana), "Jean Lafitte, Pirate or Patriot?" (Louisiana), "Breakfast from Battle Creek" (Michigan), "Atlantic City, Monopoly's Hometown" (New Jersey), "Yours till Niagara Falls" (New York), "Casey Jones and the Cannonball Express" (Tennessee), "All Those Dinosaur Bones" (Utah), and "The Ringling Brothers Start a Circus" (Wisconsin).

Available through bookstores.

Jolie Coins

Jolie Coins sells coins and stamps from all over the world, and as such is an excellent source both for active or potential collectors, and for educators on the look-out for hands-on materials to supplement geography and history lessons. Coins and stamps are offered individually, for discerning collectors, and in inexpensive packets, for curious beginners. Jolie Coins also offers "Flags of the World" and "Coats of Arms of the World" stickers, and a pen-pal club for kids aged 7 to 16. (See Penpals, International.) For a catalog, contact Jolie Coins, P.O. Box 68, Roslyn Heights, NY 11577-0068.

Kids' America   Steven Caney   (Workman; 1978)

Kids' America, according to the introduction, is "a book about America's spirit, its history, ingenuity, and life-styles." It's also a terrific project book, jam-packed with clever information, illustrations, photographs, and activities for the creative kid-sized historian. Projects include making butter, soap, candles, and weathervanes, telling the temperature by listening to the crickets, building a teepee, a treehouse, and a scarecrow, holding a frog-jumping contest, making your own time capsule, dowsing for water, making dried apple rings, cheese, and peanut butter, mixing up your own ink and cutting a quill pen, making a gravestone rubbing and a snow globe, learning to use hobo sign language, playing charades, and making a piggy bank. And much more. Our copy has been so much loved and used that the cover has gone ragged. Available through libraries and bookstores, or from Workman Publishing, 708 Broadway, New York, NY 10003; (212) 254-5900.

Kids Learn America!   Patricia Gordon and Reed C. Snow   (Williamson; 1992)

Kids Learn America! is subtitled "Bringing Geography to Life With People, Places, and History" - which it does, delightfully, in 175 heavily illustrated pages. The book covers the United States, state by state, listing for each an assortment of geographical and historical information, project suggestions, quick quizzes, quotes from famous state citizens, games, stories, and clear, uncluttered outline maps. Under Connecticut, for example, you find "Yankee Doodle" (the State Song), Nathan Hale, Noah Webster, Mark Twain (who lived in Connecticut for 30 years), Connecticut inventors, whaling ships, and the story of the Charter Oak, with instructions for making your own ancient-looking Charter. Under Kansas: sunflowers, buffalo, Dwight David Eisenhower, Wyatt Earp, Amelia Earhart, tornadoes, and *The Wizard of Oz*, with suggestions for making your own Oz map. *Kids Learn America!* is available at bookstores or can be ordered from Williamson Publishing Company, Church Hill Road, P.O. Box 185, Charlotte, VT 05445; (800) 234-8791. The book costs $12.95, plus $2.00 postage and handling.

Kidsprint Times

The *Kidsprint Times* is a national monthly newspaper for kids aged 7-12. It's written in true newspaper format: there's national and world news, a kid-level business report, science and technology news briefs, a "How Things Work" feature (examples: elevators, soap), an "Earth News" section dealing with current environmental issues, book reviews, sports, games, and puzzles. For subscription rates and information, write or call *Kidsprint Times*, P.O. Box 7391, San Jose, CA 95150; (800) 697-4537.

Knights and Castles

An "adventure-in-chivalry" board game for young medievalists. The playing pieces are bright-colored knights, equipped with shields and banners. Players advance in rank from page to squire to full-fledged knight by answering questions about medieval life and knighthood, as they move around the "questing trail" toward the castle. The game includes 48 question-and-answer Chivalry cards. Suitable for 2-4 players aged 6 and up. *Knights and Castles* costs $25.00 from Aristoplay, P.O. Box 7028, Ann Arbor, MI 48107; (800) 634-7738 or (313) 995-4353.

Land Ho!/Tierra! Tierra!

This bilingual "Discovery of America" board game looks at first glance like an antique map. Players on board the *Nina, Pinta,* or *Santa Maria* advance through the perils of the 15th century ocean ("Sea of Seaweed! Go back 2 spaces.") to the new continent of America. An accompanying informational ship's log gives the historical details of the voyage. *Land Ho!/Tierra! Tierra!* costs $22.00 from Aristoplay, P.O. Box 7028, Ann Arbor, MI 48107; (800) 634-7738 or (313) 995-4353.

Lawson, Robert

Robert Lawson's historical fiction is a must for young history lovers. The books are witty, clever, and endearing - and confirm what most of us have always suspected: that the bumbling greats of history must have had some help somewhere along the way. Lawson's best-known book along these lines is *Ben and Me,* the story of Benjamin Franklin as told by his mouse, Amos - who, it turns out, invented the Franklin stove, took a ride on the famous kite, and did a lot of Revolutionary plotting on his own, from his perch in Ben's fur hat. *Capt. Kidd's Cat* details the life of the famous pirate from the point of view of his ship's cat, McDermot, who, in true pirate fashion, wore a ruby earring in one ear; *I Discover Columbus* describes Columbus's landmark voyage through the eyes of Aurelio, a cross and displaced Central American parrot; and *Mr. Revere and I* reveals the truth about Paul Revere through the words of his horse, Scheherazade, one-time pride of His Majesty's 14th Regiment of Foot. Available still - and, with luck, forever - through libraries and bookstores.

Legends of the World Series

This collection of short, brightly illustrated paperbacks is published by Troll; each presents a single world legend, followed by a short non-fiction account of the associated native culture with a small map showing its country of origin. Titles to date include *The Llama's Secret* (Argentina Palacios), a Peruvian legend, *The Hummingbird King* (Argentina Palacios), a Guatemalan legend, and *The Sea Serpent's Daughter* (Margaret H. Lippert), a Brazilian legend. Available from Troll Learn and Play, 100 Corporate Drive, Mahwah, NJ 07430; (800) 247-6106.

Macauley, David

David Macauley has written and illustrated a superb series of books for young historians: *Castle* (Houghton Mifflin; 1977) details the construction of a thirteenth-century Welsh castle; *Cathedral* (Houghton Mifflin; 1973), the building of a thirteenth-century French cathedral; *City* (Houghton Mifflin; 1974), the planning and construction of a Roman city; *Pyramid* (Houghton Mifflin; 1975), the erection of an Egyptian pyramid; and *Mill* (Houghton Mifflin; 1983), the building and operation of an early 19th-century New England textile mill. Available through bookstores. Video versions of *Castle*, *Cathedral*, and *Pyramid* are also available. All combine narration, real-life photography, and animation, and are excellent. Available from PBS Video, 1320 Braddock Place, Alexandria, VA 22314-1698; (800) 424-7963.

Made for Trade

A board game of early American life, in which players, represented by playing pieces printed with pictures of colonists, travel throughout the town, attempting to accumulate the goods on their Inventory Lists from the potter, the tinsmith, the cabinetmaker, the blacksmith, and others. As they proceed, they deal with taxes, tithes, custom duties, and tavernkeepers, and respond to Event cards, detailing the historical happenings of the time. ("The Treaty of 1763 ended the seven-year French and Indian War. Go directly to the Printer's Shop and pay 1 shilling to get a broadside telling about it." "Theaters are rare in America, but a playhouse just opened in your town. Pay 1 shilling for a ticket to the first production, a Shakespeare comedy.") The game includes 8 Character cards, 48 Object cards, with accurate drawings of early American artifacts, 60 Events cards, and 60 plastic replicas of 1652 shillings. Suitable for 2-4 players aged 8 and up. *Made for Trade* costs $22.00 from Aristoplay, P.O. Box 7529, Ann Arbor, MI 48107; (800) 634-7738 or (313) 995-4353.

The Map Corner Arnold B. Cheyney and Donald L. Capone
(Scott, Foresman; 1983)

This is a collection of clever map activities and exercises for upper-elementary to junior-high-level students. The book, in softcover workbook format, is divided into four sections. "Things to do with Maps" lists 35 simple map-using assignments; kids are asked, for example, to locate and label the birthplaces of the U.S. presidents, to locate the places discussed in a national network news program, to trace the flow of the Gulf Stream, and to draw and label the world's 12 longest rivers. "Map Corner Lesson Plans" include background information and suggested activities for six different geographical lessons, variously involving geographical term definitions, road map use, weather maps, in the tracking of thunderstorms and hurricanes, and the mapping of bird and monarch butterfly migrations. "Map Activity Quizzes," of which there are 13, are work-on-your-own-type projects involving the reading and labeling of maps, covering such topics as map scale, latitude and longitude, time zones, and various countries and continents. "The Explorer Series" includes background information and suggested map projects related to a series of famous explorers: Marco Polo, Christopher Columbus, Vasco da Gama, Ferdinand Magellan, Sir Walter Raleigh, Henry Hudson, Captain James Cook, Meriwether Lewis and William Clark, Amelia Earhart, and Wiley Post. Under Amelia Earhart, for example, kids are challenged to find and label all the stops the famous flyer made on her ill-fated attempt to fly around the world: 29 in all, with a final "unknown."

To accompany these exercises, the book also includes 50 reproducible outline maps. *The Map Corner* is available through bookstores or from Good Year Books, 1900 East Lake Avenue, Glenview, IL 60025; (800) 628-4480, ext. 3038.

Maps

A free index to the topographic mapping of each state, plus a pamphlet explaining topographic map symbols, is available from the National Cartographic Information Center, 507 National Center, Reston, VA 22092. The index allows you to identify, by name and number, which maps cover which specific areas. Using this information, individual topographical maps can be ordered directly, by check or money order, from the United States Geological Survey, Map Distribution, Federal Center Building 41, P.O. Box 25286, Denver, CO 80225. A must for map-lovers or serious young orienteers. (See Orienteering Services, below.)

Maus and *Maus II*   Art Spiegelman (Pantheon Books; 1986, 1991)

Maus and *Maus II* tell the story of the author's father, a Jewish survivor of the Holocaust, from the time of his incarceration in a concentration camp in Hitler's Germany through the post-war years in America. The story is told in cartoon form - Art Spiegelman is a noted cartoonist - in which the Nazis are portrayed as cats, and the Jews as mice; but these are not cartoons as most of us have come to think of them. Reviewers have described the books as "a brutally moving work of art," and the cartoon approach as "a new kind of literature."

Our 11-year-old son read these and found them both horrifying and fascinating; like all of us, he's now coming to grips with the human tragedy of history. These are not - repeat, *not* - books for the very young. For the rest of us, they're impressive. Available through bookstores or from John Holt's Book and Music Store, 2269 Massachusetts Ave., Cambridge, MA 02140; (617) 864-3100.

My Backyard History Book   David Weitzsman   (Little, Brown; 1975)

"This book is about you," the book begins, "and your grandfather and his grandmother and the songs they used to sing and picnics and the wagon they used to drive and the house where your mother was born and the uncle on your mother's side that everyone used to whisper about. This book is about attics and your father's grandfather's famous horse. It's about long ago and not so long ago - big things, little things, and all the things that make the history of your place and your people and you special."

This is one of the Brown Paper School Book series, over 100 pages of information, projects, puzzles, and challenges for young hands-on historians. Suggested projects include making a birthday time capsule, drawing a family map and several different kinds of family trees, putting together a family photograph album or historical scrapbook, recording oral history, playing "Thingamajig," in which players identify old-fashioned artifacts (watch fobs, stereoscopes, bottle cappers), checking out antique shops (hold a Thingamajig-type treasure hunt) and cemeteries, making rubbings, starting an old building collection (with camera), and auctioning off the contents of the 1897 *Sears, Roebuck Catalog*. Available through bookstores.

Name That State

The board is a colorful map of the United States surrounded by a playing path; players proceed around it by answering questions about geographical locations, capital cities, and important features of all fifty states. Suitable for 2-4 players in grades 3-8. *Name That State* costs $19.95 and can be ordered from Educational Insights, 19560 S. Rancho Way, Dominguez Hills, CA 90220; (800) 933-3277 or (213) 637-2131.

National Geographic Society

An unparalleled source for resources geographical, prominent among them the famous lushly illustrated yellow-covered *National Geographic Magazine*. (Subscriptions, for 12 fat issues with enclosed maps, cost $22.50, unless you're an educational institution, in which case you pay $21.00.) For young geographers, there's a kid-level magazine, *National Geographic World*: an annual subscription (12 issues) costs $12.95. The Society catalog is a rich source of books, games, and videotapes - and, of course, atlases, globes, and maps, in every conceivable form, detailing everything from Shakespeare's Britain to the ocean floor to Mars. For catalogs or subscription information, contact the National Geographic Society, Washington, D.C. 20036; (800) 447-0647.

National Women's History Project

The National Women's History Project publishes a catalog of books, posters, curriculum guides, and miscellaneous resources, all related to women's history. Included are a selection of women's history coloring books (*Civil War Heroines, Cowgirls, Women in U.S. History*), famous women paperdolls, great women biographical card games, and an assortment of biographies of famous women for young readers. Subjects of these biographies include Harriet Tubman, Juliette Gordon Low, Elizabeth Blackwell, Rosa Parks, Susan B. Anthony, Amelia Earhart, and Eleanor Roosevelt. Also available: a Harriet Tubman game and study set, suitable for children in grades 2-6; materials and lesson plans for a quilt-making art unit ("introducing history and geometric principles") appropriate for grades 1-6; and "Woman of the Month" display kits, each of which consists of twenty-four 8 x 10" black-and-white captioned photographs of remarkable women. Catalogs are available from the National Women's History Project, 7738 Bell Road, Windsor, CA 95492-8518; (707) 838-6000.

Native American Legends series   Terri Cohlene   (Watermill Press)

There are many excellent collections of native American legends for kids, but this series strikes an unusual balance between traditional fiction and historical truth. Each 48-page book begins with a beautifully illustrated traditional legend from a specific Indian tribe, among them *Quillworker: A Cheyenne Legend, Dancing Drum: A Cherokee Legend, Turquoise Boy: A Navajo Legend, Ka-ha-si and the Loon: An Eskimo Legend, Little Firefly: An Algonquin Legend*, and *Clamshell Boy: A Makah Legend*. The story is followed by a non-fiction historical and cultural account of the Indian tribe which originated the legend, illustrated with terrific photographs, plus a map showing the tribe's geographical range, a timeline of important dates concerning the tribe, and a glossary of native terms. The books, published by Watermill Press, are available through libraries and bookstores.

Old News

Old News, published in Marietta, Pennsylvania, is a great find for young history buffs: it's a monthly (except in August) history magazine, printed in newspaper format on heavy white paper. Each issue is 12 over-sized pages long, and the articles - with accompanying maps, photographs, and picture reproductions - report very old news. Headlines in our sample issue announce "Gold Found in Klondike Hills!" and "English Monarch Is a Fugitive in His Own Kingdom!" - which last is an account of the 17th-century adventures of King Charles II, with a nice picture showing the king hiding in an oak tree to avoid capture by Cromwell's soldiers. The stories are well-researched, interesting, and chatty, and a list of supplementary historical resources is included for each. Subscriptions cost $14.00 per year. For information write or call *Old News*, 400 Stackstown Rd., Marietta, PA 17547-9300; (717) 426-2212.

On Assignment With National Geographic

In this creative board game, players become photojournalists. Each player is given a general "portfolio list" of photographs to be collected from various parts of the globe; players then attempt to collect pictures in each of the assigned categories while answering geographical questions. The game board is a world map.

The game includes 144 Photo cards, each a terrific photographic reproduction: there are pictures of the Great Wall of China, the Taj Mahal, St. Basil's Cathedral, a Colombian coffee plantation, a Panamanian mola, Tuareg goatherds, the Eiffel Tower, the Parthenon, Big Ben, the Colosseum, the Great Barrier Reef, and the Pyramids of Giza. And much more. There are also six sets of question cards, color-coded by continent: Africa, Asia, Europe, North America, South America, and Oceania/Antarctica. The game costs $29.95 from the National Geographic Society, Washington, D.C. 20036; (800) 447-0647.

Oregon Trail

This award-winning computer software program is a simulation of a trip westward by wagon train along the Oregon Trail in 1848. Players select the members of their party, stock their wagons, choose their starting date, and set off, dealing along the way with snakebite, illness, nasty weather, and food shortages. They obtain useful information, specific and general, from persons they meet along the trail; try their hands at hunting deer and buffalo; follow their progress on a moving United States map; and finally embark on an exciting journey by raft down the Columbia River. Successful travelers make it safely to the Willamette Valley of Oregon. Available for Apple, IBM/Tandy, and Macintosh computers from MECC, 6160 Summit Drive North, Minneapolis, MN 55430-4003; (800) 685-MECC, ext. 549.

Orienteering Services

This is a resource for people who like their geography out of doors. For those interested in traveling by map and compass, Silva Orienteering Services provides a free information packet containing a catalog of orienteering teaching aids, a list of U.S. Orienteering Clubs, an introductory informational booklet and an "Orienteering Planning Guide," and a sample orienteering map. The catalog sells compasses, orienteering books, workbooks, and teaching outlines, and map and compass games. Potential orienteers should contact Silva Orienteering Services, U.S.A., Box 1604, Binghamton, NY, 13902; (607) 724-0411.

Out-of-Print Books

Many used-book stores have search services for tracking down out-of-print books; check the Yellow Pages of your telephone directory for possibilities near you. The following companies also provide free book search services: Peninsula Booksearch, P.O. Box 1305, Burlingame, CA 94011-1305; Avonlea Books, Box 74, Main Station, White Plains, NY 10602, (914) 946-5923; and M.F. Adler Books, Box 627, Stockbridge, MA 01262, (413) 298-3559.

Oxford University Press

Oxford University Press publishes a superb line of history books for children. Among the selections is a three-volume series for middle-grade readers on truly extraordinary explorers, authored by geography buff Rebecca Stefoff. *Women of the World: Women Travelers and Explorers* covers such feisty females as Florence Baker, a former Hungarian slave who searched for the source of the Nile, Alexandra David-Neel, the first Western woman to reach Lhasa, Tibet, and Louise Arner Boyd, who made it to the Arctic. *Accidental Explorers: Surprises and Side Trips in the History of Discovery* covers, among others, Christopher Columbus and his annoying encounter with the Americas while en route to India, and Coronado's unexpected discovery of the Grand Canyon; while *Scientific Explorers: Travels in Search of Knowledge,* covers three centuries of scientific expeditions, including Charles Darwin's travels on board the *Beagle,* Lewis and Clark's cross-country journey, Robert Ballard's undersea explorations in search of the sunken *Titanic,* and *Voyager'*s high-tech trip through the solar system. Each volume is lavishly illustrated with photographs and maps, and includes quotations from the explorer's diaries, letters, and published accounts of their landmark journeys. Oxford has also published an excellent 10-volume series, *A History of US,* by writer and former elementary teacher Joy Hakim. The books are both well-researched and entertaining, aimed at returning the "concept of story" to history. Titles in the series (all available in paperback) include *The First Americans, Making Thirteen Colonies, From Colonies to Country, The New Nation, Liberty for All?, War, Terrible War, Reconstruction and Reform, An Age of Extremes, War, Peace, and All That Jazz,* and *All the People.* The books are available through libraries or bookstores, or from Oxford University Press, Order Dept, 2001 Evans Road, Cary, NC 27513; (800) 451-7556.

Passtimes

Passtimes is subtitled "The Game of History." Players (alone or in teams) advance pairs of tokens around the game board from Yesterday to Today by answering historical questions. There are four questions on each of the 320 question cards, ordered by increasing difficulty. Examples of easy questions: "Which New World colony was founded first, Plymouth colony or the Jamestown settlement?" "Who was president of the United States during the Civil War?" "Who was prime minister of Great Britain during most of World War II?" " What modern U.S. city used to be called New

Amsterdam?" Examples of hard questions: "How old was Edgar Allan Poe when he died of unknown causes in 1849?" "In 1981, what man became the first person of Mexican descent to be elected mayor of a major U.S. city?" "Name the book that Adam Smith wrote which includes many ideas that are accepted as the basis for private enterprise." "In what year did General Hideki Tojo become premier of Japan?" For those who find this isn't enough, there's an *Advanced Passtimes* card set available. *Passtimes* can be ordered from Edutainment Group, 1445 N. Rock Road #200, Wichita, KS 67206; (316) 634-0441.

Paul Harvey's The Rest of the Story and *More of Paul Harvey's The Rest of the Story*   Paul Aurandt   (Doubleday; 1977)
The Rest of the Story and its sequel are both collections of very short (1-2 pages) and absolutely enthralling historical mysteries, so cleverly told that even the most suspicious and knowledgeable readers seldom guess the answer until the final punchline. Stories deal with the famous and the not-so-famous: John Paul Jones, John Wilkes Booth, Zachary Taylor, Joe DiMaggio, Charles Lindbergh, Anne Boleyn, the inventors of Coca-Cola and potato chips, and "Dear Abby." An addictive addition to any history program. Available through bookstores.

Penpals, International
Kids looking for correspondents in other countries can try contacting these penpal organizations: Jolie Coins: Perfect Penpals, P.O. Box 68, Roslyn Heights, NY 11577-0068; Kids Meeting Kids, Box 8H, 380 Riverside Drive, New York, New York 10025 (matches kids aged 7-18 with penpals); Student Letter Exchange, 630 3rd Avenue, New York, NY 10017; (212) 557-3312 (for potential penpals aged 10-21; send SASE for application forms); World Pen Pals, 1694 Como Ave., St. Paul, MN 55108; (612) 647-0191.

Perkins, Lucy Fitch
Lucy Fitch Perkins wrote most of her Twin series back in the 1920's: these are definite oldies, and in some cases are abysmally incorrect politically-speaking, but they continue to appeal to kids aged 7-9 or so. The entire series consists of something over twenty books, each featuring a set of fraternal twins from a different culture or historical period. Examples include *The Eskimo Twins, The Cave Twins, The Indian Twins, The Spartan Twins, The Japanese Twins, The French Twins, The Colonial Twins of Virginia,* and *The Pioneer Twins.* Our kids at one point went through stacks of these;

they enjoyed the stories, and the stereotypes circa 1920 only impressed on them how much the world has changed. Libraries still carry these. They're worth a look.

Pocahontas Press

Pocahontas Press specializes in books about "real people who aren't well known but who have done something interesting or remarkable." Their selection, though small, includes *From Lions to Lincoln - The Life of Dan French* (Fran Hartman), the story of the American sculptor who made Concord's famous Minuteman and the seated Lincoln for the Lincoln Memorial in Washington, D.C. For a brochure, contact Pocahontas Press, P.O. Drawer F, Blacksburg, VA 24063; (703) 951-0467, (800) 446-0467.

Project Earth

Project Earth is a make-your-own-globe kit: kids assemble a styrofoam sphere (it comes in four pieces), cover it with papier-maché, trace on the outlines of the continents using the enclosed templates, paint in oceans and countries, and plant national flags (on toothpicks). The finished product is 14 inches in diameter and sits on a cardboard base. Educational Insights, which sells it, calls it the "best geography experience ever" - and in our hands, it came close. Project Earth costs $29.95 from Educational Insights, 19560 S. Rancho Way, Dominguez Hills, CA 90220; (800) 933-3277 or (213) 637-2131.

Pyramids and Mummies

This game features an exquisitely illustrated game board that folds up to form a three-dimensional pyramid. Players assemble the pyramid as they solve quasi-Egyptian rebus puzzles, and then proceed to the inner mummy chamber, dealing en route with such perils as snake pits and ancient curses. *Pyramids and Mummies* costs $32.00 from Aristoplay, P.O. Box 7529, Ann Arbor, MI 48107; (800) 634-7738 or (313) 995-4353.

Quackenbush, Robert

Robert Quackenbush is one of the very few authors around who writes catchy and informational biographies for younger children. The books are appropriate for kids aged 7-10 or so. Each is about 35 factual pages long, and in each, kids, cats, pigs, or Rooseveltian Teddy bears help the text along, with irreverent comments in cartoon balloons at the bottom of each page. The biographies, published by Prentice-Hall, include *Ahoy! Ahoy! Are You There?: A Sto-*

ry of Alexander Graham Bell; The Beagle and Mr. Flycatcher: A Story of Charles Darwin; Clear the Cow Pasture, I'm Coming in for a Landing!: A Story of Amelia Earhart; Don't You Dare Shoot That Bear!: A Story of Theodore Roosevelt; Here A Plant, There A Plant, Everywhere A Plant, Plant!: A Story of Luther Burbank; I Did It With My Hatchet: A Story of George Washington; Mark Twain? What Kind of Name is That?: A Story of Samuel Langhorne Clemens; Oh, What an Awful Mess: A Story of Charles Goodyear; Old Silverleg Takes Over!: A Story of Peter Stuyvesant; Once Upon a Time!: A Story of the Brothers Grimm; Pass the Quill, I'll Write a Draft: A Story of Thomas Jefferson; Quick, Annie, Give Me a Catchy Line!: A Story of Samuel F.B. Morse; Quit Pulling My Leg!: A Story of Davy Crockett; Take Me Out to the Airfield: How the Wright Brothers Invented the Airplane; Watt Got You Started, Mr. Fulton?: A Story of James Watt and Robert Fulton; What Has Wild Tom Done Now!!!?: A Story of Thomas Alva Edison; Who Let Muddy Boots Into the White House?: A Story of Andrew Jackson; Who's That Girl With the Gun?: A Story of Annie Oakley; Who Said There's No Man on the Moon?: A Story of Jules Verne. Available through libraries and bookstores.

Rand McNally

Maps, globes, adult atlases, kids' atlases (several kinds), geography games, travel videos, and even geography placemats (world and U.S.), so that lunch can be a learning experience. For a free catalog, contact Rand McNally Catalog, P.O. Box 182257, Chattanooga, TN 37422-7257.

Roots

This six-part video series, based on Alex Haley's best-selling book of the same name, is an extraordinary experience for all viewers. It begins in Africa, with the birth of young Kunta Kinte who, in young adulthood, is captured by slavers and shipped to the American South. Kunta is enslaved, but never defeated: his legacy of defiance and determination is passed on to his descendants, to his daughter, Kizzy, and his grandson, Chicken George. By the final episode, the Civil War is over and the slaves have been freed; Chicken George, who fought with the Union Army, returns home and takes his family away to start a new life in Tennessee. There, generations later, author Alex Haley was born, another descendant of the indomitable Kunta Kinte.

This series is not easy viewing: it's cruel and heart-rending; but it's also fascinating and unforgettable. Available from PBS Video,

1320 Braddock Place, Alexandria, VA 22314-1698; (800) 424-7963; Movies Unlimited, 6736 Castor Avenue, Philadelphia, PA 19149; (800) 523-0823 (orders) or (215) 722-8398 (customer service).

Skipping Stones

Skipping Stones is a multicultural children's quarterly magazine, designed to "encourage cooperation, creativity and celebration of cultural richness." It's almost entirely kid-written, filled with stories, poems, pictures, and non-fiction articles by children from all over the world. Foreign language submissions appear in both the original and in English translation. There are a number of regular features, including "Bookshelf" - a list of short book reviews; "Taking Action" - accounts of persons working to solve world problems; "Pen Pals;" and the "Multicultural Calendar," which lists holidays and happenings around the world. The magazine is ecologically, as well as multiculturally, oriented, and is printed on recycled paper using soybean-based ink. *Skipping Stones* welcomes submissions of writings and artwork from children and young adults: send an S.A.S.E. along with your submission if you'd like your work returned. If published, you'll get a free copy of the magazine issue in which your work appears. Magazine subscriptions cost $15.00 per year; single or back issues are available for $5.00 each. Order from *Skipping Stones*, P.O. Box 3939, Eugene, OR 97403-0939; (503) 342-4956.

Sloane, Eric

Our children - all boys - never quite fell for Laura Ingalls Wilder's *Little House* books, but they did love Eric Sloane's *Diary of an Early American Boy* (Wilfred Funk; 1962), based on a (real) diary kept by 15-year-old Noah Blake in 1805. Like all of Sloane's books, *Diary* is beautifully illustrated with detailed line drawings of early American buildings and tools, which particularly fascinated our mechanically-minded second son. Also written and illustrated by Sloane: *An Age of Barns*, *A Reverence for Wood*, *Our Vanishing Landscape*, and *Museum of Early American Tools*.

An excellent bet for younger kids is Sloane's *ABC Book of Early Americana* (Henry Holt; 1963), a treasure-trove of pictures and information, from A (as in Axe, Almanack, Arm-rest, and Apple Cider Press) through Z (as in Z-bridge, Zig-Zag fence, Zax, and Zany). And a zax, for those of you who don't own this invaluable book, is a slate axe, used for cutting slate roof shingles. All are still available through bookstores.

Smithsonian Games

This assortment of beautifully illustrated history games has been licensed (and authenticated) by the Smithsonian Institution. Among them is *Presidential Lotto*, which comes with five (illustrated) lotto boards and 45 cards, bearing full-color portraits of all the U.S. presidents (plus pictures of an occasional historical artifact to make the boards come out even). Board are labeled with the president's name; cards aren't. For card players, there are *Presidential* and *American History* rummy games: in each, players collect sets of related cards, each with a brief historical description and a color picture or portrait. *American History Quiz* and *Presidential Quiz* are question-and-answer card games: each contains 40 large color-illustrated cards, each bearing 10 general history or presidential questions. Sample *American History Quiz* cards carry photographs of the Alamo, the Transcontinental Railroad's golden spike, a Charles Lindbergh poster, a World War II gas ration coupon, and a brand-new Model T. All games are available from Scientific Wizardry, 9925 Fairview Ave., Boise, ID 83704; (208) 377-8575.

Sourcetapes

Sourcetapes is a catalog of spoken-word recordings, featuring "eyewitness accounts, actualities, and oral history interviews on audio cassettes." Among these is "The Decade Series," available in 3-cassette sets, covering the 1930's, 1940's, 1950's, and 1960's. Within each set, one cassette is devoted to politics, one to society, and one to technology. Cassette selections are arranged in chronological order, with a narrator providing background information, and run 40-60 minutes. The 1940's set, for example, features over 50 on-the-spot recordings, including Franklin Roosevelt's request for a declaration of war, a campaign speech by Harry Truman, a radio broadcast explaining World War II rationing, news reports on the bombing of Hiroshima, and William Shockley's description of the first transistor patent. Other cassette sets include eyewitness accounts of the San Francisco Earthquake and Fire, Custer's Last Stand, the Iwo Jima Landing, Homesteading, the Sinking of the Titanic, and the Scopes Monkey Trial. For a catalog or additional information, contact Sourcetapes, Visual Education Corporation, 14 Washington Road, Box 2321, Princeton, NJ 08543; (609) 799-9200.

Spizzirri Publishing Company

The Spizzirri catalog carries lots of educational coloring books on assorted topics, available with (or without) accompanying story cassettes. Of interest to young historians: *Colonies, Pioneers, Cowboys, Eskimos, Cave Man, Indians* (six different books), *Texas, Kachina Dolls,* and *California Missions.* Coloring books alone cost $2.25; book/cassette sets $5.95. For a free catalog, contact Spizzirri Publishing, P.O. Box 9397, Rapid City, SD 57709; (605) 341-4451.

Strait of Magellan

This is a 51-minute cassette tape, breathtakingly narrated by master storyteller Jay O'Callahan, in the guise of Antonio, who accompanied the great explorer Magellan on his epic voyage around the world. History made real. The tape costs $10.00, and is available from Chinaberry Book Service, 2780 Via Orange Way, Suite B, Spring Valley, CA 91978; (800) 776-2242 (orders, customer service) or (619) 670-5200 (information).

Swamp Gas Visits Europe/Swamp Gas Visits the United States of America

This pair of prize-winning geography software programs feature a perky little alien in a space ship who tours either Europe or the United States; players direct the tour on a colorful full-screen map, landing at designated locations. The United States game teaches states, capitals, major cities, and notable landmarks; the European version, countries, capitals, major cities, and landmarks. Stumped players can get geographical hints; winners get to play short arcade-style games. Clever and effective. Programs in the works will send Swamp Gas to visit Asia, Africa, North America, South America, and the world. Available for the Macintosh computer, from Inline Software, 308 Main Street, Lakeville, CT 06039-1204; (203) 435-4995, (800) 453-7671.

Time-Life

Our own library includes two of the Time-Life book series: *The Old West* (bound in brown) and *The Time-Life History of the United States* (maroon). The children have been unceasingly fascinated with both, primarily for the illustrations - period photographs, maps, paintings, and pictures of artifacts - which are wonderful. Books can be purchased individually, or the truly interested can subscribe to an entire series, in which a new volume arrives (with bill) each month. Current series of potential interest to historians include *The American Indians, The Civil War, The Third Reich,* and *Lost Civilizations.* For information, contact Time-Life, 1450 East Parham Road, Richmond, VA 23280.

Timelines

There's nothing like a timeline for giving kids a concrete sense of their - and everybody else's - place in history. Creative Teaching Press sells six different timelines, suitable for intermediate science and history students. Each consists of eight lushly illustrated full-color panels, with a total measurement of 8 3/4 inches by 18 1/2 feet. Titles include *Transportation* (48 landmark developments in land, sea, and air transportation), *Inventions* (from the wheel to the video camera), *Building a Nation* (American history from the first European settlements through the signing of the Constitution), *Civil Rights in America* (20 famous Civil Rights leaders and acts of legislation), *Explorers* (from the ancient Egyptians to the space shuttle), and *Famous Scientists* (from the ancient Greeks to the present day). Also available: equivalent blackline reproducible timelines for individual student use and correlating activity books. Each timeline costs $6.95, from Creative Teaching Press, Inc., P.O. Box 6017, Cypress, CA 90630-0017; (800) 444-4CTP.

Knowledge Unlimited sells the *American History Timeline*, which covers 500 years of American history (1490 to the present) in ten full-color illustrated posters. The posters are ordered in columns, by decade, with color-coded strands that help students connect initial historical cause with subsequent effect. *The American History Timeline*, with accompanying teacher's guide, costs $22.95, from Knowledge Unlimited, Box 52, Madison, WI 53701-0052; (800) 356-2303 or (608) 836-6660.

Creative Home Teaching sells an interactive *North American Time Line*: the seven-chart set, illustrated with reproductions of famous paintings, sculptures, and notable documents, covers North American history from 1565 to the present. The chart includes a series of blank "event" spaces for students to fill in themselves. All in a row, the seven charts measure about 18 feet long, total. The set costs $11.50 from Creative Home Teaching, P.O. Box 152581, San Diego, CA 92195; (619) 263-8633.

Michael Olaf's Essential Montessori carries a notably ambitious timeline, titled *A Graphic History of Mankind*, which covers human history from the dawn of civilization to the present. Each developing (or declining) civilization or nation is shown by a different-colored band on the chart. Students can thus follow the history of a particular group by following a single band vertically from top to bottom or, horizontally, can compare developments and events in all parts of the world at a particular point in time. The publisher manages to squash all of human history into a mere 50 x 19 inches. *A Graphic History of Mankind* costs $8.00, from Michael Olaf's Essential Montessori, P.O. Box 1162, Arcata, CA 95521; (707) 826-1557.

The Timetables of History Bernard Grun (Simon and Schuster; 1975); *The Timetables of American History* Lawrence Urdang, ed. (Simon and Schuster; 1981)

The Timetables of History is subtitled "A Horizontal Linkage of People and Events," which is what it provides, from 5000 B.C. through the present. This is an annotated time line, in book form. For each year (or, early on, group of years) are listed happenings worldwide in seven different categories: "History, Politics," "Literature, Theatre," "Religion, Philosophy, Learning," "Visual Arts," "Music," "Science, Technology, Growth," and "Daily Life."

The Timetables of American History covers the years from 1000 A.D. to the present; for each year, happenings in America and "Elsewhere" are listed under four different categories: "History and Politics," "The Arts," "Science and Technology," and "Miscellaneous," which last includes, for example, the dates of the publication of the first Indian newspaper, New York City's first cricket match, and the opening of the first women's medical school. Both fascinating for browsers and excellent historical references. Available through bookstores.

Tommy Tricker and the Stamp Traveller

A geographical adventure video in which a young boy shrinks to the size of a postage stamp and travels, via envelope, all over the world. Mystery, excitement, and an introduction to several foreign countries and cultures, all packed into 101 minutes. Available from Live Home Video, 15400 Sherman Way, P.O. Box 10124, Van Nuys, CA 91410; (800) 423-7455; or from Movies Unlimited, 6736 Castor Avenue, Philadelphia, PA 19149; (800) 523-0823 (orders) or (215) 722-8398 (information).

Traveling the U.S. Through Children's Literature Virginia Williams

Virginia Williams' 33-page bibliographical booklet is a great idea: its aim is to enrich and personalize U.S. geography by linking it to novels and storybooks. The books, all 235 of them, are listed by geographical region: Northeast, Southeast, Northwest,

Southwest, Far West, and, as an extra, Canada. Under the Northeast, for example, are included Elizabeth Speare's *Sign of the Beaver* (Maine), Sydney Taylor's *All-of-a-Kind Family* (New York), and Marguerite Henry's *Misty of Chincoteague* (Maryland); plus, for younger readers, Barbara Cooney's *Miss Rumphius*, Donald Hall's *Ox-Cart Man*, and Robert McCloskey's *One Morning in Maine*. Under the Southwest: *Old Yeller*, *Brighty of the Grand Canyon*, *The Legend of the Bluebonnet*, and *Pecos Bill*. And many more. Each title is followed by a brief plot summary. Inevitably you'll find some omissions on the regional lists - but if you want to read your way across the country, this should give you a good start. *Traveling the U.S. Through Children's Literature* costs $7.99; order from Virginia Williams, 13 Woodside Circle, Sturbridge, MA 01566.

Troll Learn & Play

Troll publishes a series of inexpensive paperback biographies, most about 48 pages long, targeted at kids aged 7-12. Illustrations are blah, but the text is usefully informational. Titles include *Abe Lincoln: The Young Years*, *Amelia Earhart: Adventure in the Sky*, *Babe Ruth: Home Run Hero*, *Black Hawk: Frontier Warrior*, *Chief Joseph: Leader of Destiny*, *Clara Barton: Angel of the Battlefield*, *The Courage of Helen Keller*, *Daniel Boone: Frontier Adventures*, *Davy Crockett: Young Pioneer*, *Elizabeth Blackwell: The First Woman Doctor*, *George Washington: Young Leader*, *Harriet Tubman: The Road to Freedom*, *James Monroe: Young Patriot*, *Jesse Owens: Olympic Hero*, *Jim Thorpe: Young Athlete*, *John Adams: Brave Patriot*, *John Paul Jones: Hero of the Seas*, *Lafayette: Hero of Two Nations*, *Lou Gehrig: Pride of the Yankees*, *Louis Pasteur: Young Scientist*, *Louisa May Alcott: Young Writer*, *Marie Curie: Brave Scientist*, *Narcissa Whitman: Brave Pioneer*, *Osceola: Seminole Warrior*, *Patrick Henry: Voice of the American Revolution*, *Paul Revere: Son of Liberty*, *Pocahontas: Girl of Jamestown*, *Pontiac: Chief of the Ottawas*, *Robert E. Lee: Brave Leader*, *Sacajawea: Wilderness Guide*, *Sequoyah: Cherokee Hero*, *Sitting Bull: Warrior of the Sioux*, *Squanto: The Pilgrim Adventure*, *Tecumseh: Shawnee War Chief*, *Teddy Roosevelt: Rough Rider*, *Thomas Alva Edison: Young Inventor*, *Wilbur and Orville Wright: The Flight to Adventure*, *Willie Mays: Young Superstar*, *Young Albert Einstein*, *Young Ben Franklin*, *Young Eleanor Roosevelt*, *Young Frederick Douglass*, *Young Mark Twain*, *Young Queen Elizabeth*, and *Young Thomas Jefferson*. Troll generally sells the books in sets (10 biographies for $19.95). For a catalog, contact Troll Learn & Play, 100 Corporate Drive, Mahwah, NJ 07430; (800) 247-6106 (orders) or (800) 942-0781 (information). Individual books are available for $2.50 apiece, from Brook Farm Books, P.O. Box 246, Bridgewater, ME 04735.

UniSet Maps

Kids assemble these maps themselves, using an assortment of brightly colored reusable stickers. Maps sets include the United States, Europe, and the World. Each consists of a folding play-board picturing an unlabeled outline map, a sheet of press-and-peel vinyl stickers in the shapes of states or countries, and an information sheet. Stickers are labeled with state or country names, names of capital and major cities, and symbols showing notable industries or natural resources.

Available from Sycamore Tree, Inc., 2179 Meyer Place, Costa Mesa, CA 92627; (714) 642-6750 (orders) or (714) 650-4466 (information).

We Were There

The *We Were There* books were published by Grosset & Dunlap (NY) during the 1950's and 60's, and have since vanished from print, which means that the only available sources nowadays are libraries and used-book stores. In its heyday, the series included over 30 books, appropriate for middle-grade readers, in which assorted pairs of children (male and female) participated in many of the major events of history. Accordingly, kids were there at the Battle of Gettysburg, the Boston Tea Party, the Alamo, Pearl Harbor, and the Normandy Invasion; they were with Admiral Byrd at the South Pole, with Charles Darwin on board the *Beagle*, with Richard the Lionhearted in the Crusades, with Jean Lafitte in New Orleans, with Cortez in Mexico, with Caesar's legions in ancient Britain, and with Lewis and Clark on their way cross-country.

The books are written by several different authors, each in conjunction with an historical consultant; for card catalog purposes, your best best is W, since all the books are similarly titled, as in *We Were There At the First Airplane Flight* and *We Were There With the Mayflower Pilgrims*. Worth a look. (See Out-of-Print Books.)

Whatever Happened to Justice?   Richard J. Maybury   (Bluestocking Press; 1993)

Fans of Uncle Eric, the letter-writing sage of *Whatever Happened to Penny Candy?* (see Mathematics), will be delighted at his return, this time to explain to his nephew, Chris, the ins and outs of the law. The information here, again, is presented in small bite-sized chunks, as a series of topic-centered letters. The letters are master-pieces: Maybury has a talent for explaining difficult material to children without either oversimplifying or condescending. The book covers the history of law, the difference between scientific and political law, the components of common law, the reasons for government - all with intriguing examples - and ends with a thought-and-loud-discussion-provoking series of letters about un-solved legal problems: capital punishment, drugs, war, and the environment. The book is peppered with quotations from famous political thinkers and includes - a special bonus - a story titled "I Pencil," the world's best explanation of how, under the principles of common law, people manage to get things done. We just fin-ished *Whatever Happened to Justice?* and the boys are already clam-oring to read it again. Highly recommended. Available from Blue-stocking Press, P.O. Box 1014-GS, Placerville, CA 95667; (916) 621-1123.

Where in America's Past is Carmen Sandiego?/Where in Time is Carmen Sandiego?

In this prize-winning computer software series, players must track arch-crook Carmen Sandiego and her gang of no-goods through time, responding to historical clues to determine their destinations. *Where in America's Past is Carmen Sandiego?* covers five different regions of the United States, and nine time periods in American history, from A.D. 986 to the present. *Where in Time?* is of broader scope, covering world history from the Middle Ages through the Modern Age through China, Japan, India, Mexico, Peru, and Europe. Graphics are superb: players are treated to views of famous monuments and landmarks, portraits of famous people, and representations of famous historical periods and events. Available in Apple, IBM/Tandy, Macintosh, Commodore, and Amiga format from Broderbund Software, Dept. 15, P.O. Box 6125, Novato, CA 94948-6125; (800) 521-6263.

Where in Europe is Carmen Sandiego?/Where in the U.S. is Car-men Sandiego?/Where in the World is Carmen Sandiego?

In this series of prize-winning geography software programs, kids pursue arch-thief Carmen Sandiego and her gang of baddies across the maps of Europe, the United States, or the world, follow-ing geographical clues, and assimilating geographical, historical, and cultural information along the way. Each program includes an enormous array of creative graphics. Outstanding. Available in

Apple, IBM/Tandy, Macintosh, Commodore, and Amiga format, from Broderbund Software, Dept. 15, P.O. Box 6125, Novato, CA 94948-6125; (800) 521-6263.

Where in the World?

Where in the World? is a geographical board game, much touted in the educational literature. It consists of six colorful map boards, instructions for six different games of varying difficulty, and a pack of country cards, detailing capital city, population, literacy rate, major languages, and major religions for some 174 countries. Despite its obvious educational worth, our kids, who showed no interest in learning the capital of Zaire or the literacy rate of Argentina, condemned it as dull.   Generally available, including from Michael Olaf's Essential Montessori, P.O. Box 1162, Arcata, CA 95521; (707) 826-1557; and Learning Alternatives, 2370 West 89A, Suite 5, Sedona, AZ 86336; (800) HANDS ON.

Who Put the Cannon in the Courthouse Square?   Kay Cooper
(Walker and Company; 1985)

A how-to book for local historians, with suggestions for close-to-home historical research projects: How did your town get its name? How about your street? How about local bridges, hills, old buildings? What can you find out about your area's first settlers, oldest houses and cemeteries, first industries, famous people? Do you know the stories behind any local lore? Cooper then provides young reseachers with lists of potential sources and instructions for using them, suggestions for conducting oral history interviews, and ideas for organizing and presenting findings. Available through libraries or bookstores.

Windows to the World and More Windows to the World   Nancy Everix   (Good Apple; 1984, 1985)

Using this pair of activity books, kids - as tourists, armed with homemade passports - hop about the globe, sopping up information and tackling creative multidisciplinary projects along the way. *Windows to the World* covers China, Mexico, Australia, Brazil, British Columbia, Canada, West Germany, and Egypt; *More Windows to the World*, Norway, Japan, Kenya, Quebec, Canada, Italy, Peru, and India. Under China, for example, kids label a map, with special attention to the Great Wall, try Chinese calligraphy, read about giant pandas, design a junk, bake fortune cookies, make and play tangrams, construct a paper pagoda lantern, and dress Chinese paperdolls. Under India, they label a map, make a model of the Taj Mahal, graph monsoon rainfall, write and illustrate a travelogue on Indian wildlife, read and illustrate the story of the elephant-headed god, Ganesh, taste Indian spices, decorate a royal elephant, learn about the caste system, read about Mahatma Gandhi and try fingerweaving, and design a sari for an Indian paperdoll. The books cost $11.95 each, and can be ordered from Good Apple, 1204 Buchanan St., P.O. Box 299. Carthage, IL 62321-0299; (800) 435-7234 or (217) 357-3981.

Worldwide Penpals

Worldwide Penpals is a geography game for younger kids: players earn points by locating countries on the world map, which then allows them to hop along the game board. Occasionally they land on a "Postcard Square" and draw a postcard from a Mystery Penpal whose home country they have to guess from the accompanying clues. Example: "Dear Penpal, Buenos dias! My country is named after the equator. Name my country! Adios, Hernando." The gameboard includes a spinner, a world map, and a playing path decorated with foreign stamps. The game costs $19.95 from Educational Insights, 19560 S. Rancho Way, Dominguez Hills, CA 90220; (800) 933-3277 or (213) 637-2131.

Yo, Millard Fillmore!   Will Cleveland and Mark Alvarez   (Fundamentals; 1992)

"Once you've read this book once (maybe twice)," states the "For Kids Only" introduction, "you'll know all the presidents backwards and forwards. You will know them without trying and you will know them forever." Each double-page spread carries a black-and-white portrait of a president, selected biographical information, and dates of his life and presidential terms - but the real nitty-gritty is, on the facing page, the memory-grabbing cartoon, one for each president. Readers start out by imagining a giant washing machine on the lawn of the White House, big enough to *wash a ton* - get it? - of dirty clothes. Wash a ton = Washington. On the next page, you imagine yourself lifting up the lid of the washing machine and there, swirling around through the soap bubbles, are several giant *atoms*. Atoms = Adams. And so on, up through the present day. Our kids, who thought it screamingly hilarious, each read it twice and promptly memorized all the presidents forever. At the end, there's a 112-question "Jeopardy"-style quiz about the presidents. Available through bookstores.

Zephyr Press

Zephyr Press offers "cutting-edge materials for innovative education" - including a large assortment of creative workbooks, games, and multidisciplinary units for young historians and geographers. Of particular interest are Zephyr's self-directed learning packets, packaged in comb-bound reproducible 50- to 80-page booklets, appropriate for kids in grades K-8. These are collections of interdisciplinary projects and activities related to a specific topic, plus a resource bibliography. The *Ancient Greece and Rome* packet, for example, suggests that kids make a chart comparing Greek and Roman gods, write a Grecian-style myth, draw a map of the empire of Alexander the Great or the Roman Empire, research the Olympic games, build a "marble" statue, make a mural of life in ancient Greece or Rome, build a model temple, and trace the etymology of various Greek- and Latin-derived modern words.

Learning packets of interest to historians: *American History, The Blue and the Gray: America's Civil War, The Industrial Revolution of the 19th Century, The Renaissance, Early Japan, Ancient Civilizations, The Middle Ages, The Jade Garden: Ancient to Modern China, Ancient Greece and Rome, Old Russia, The Americas, Ancient Egypt, Columbus Encounter, Archaeology,* and *Early People.* Learning packets cost $19.95 each. For information and a free catalog, contact Zephyr Press, 3316 N. Chapel Ave., P.O. Box 13448, Tucson, AZ 85732-3448; (602) 322-5090.

An American History Book List: Almost True Books

History, for us, has often been first discovered through stories. For those who use historical fiction to introduce or enhance their history programs - or for just plain reading enjoyment - a list of possibilities follows.

Aaron and the Green Mountain Boys   Patricia Lee Gauch   (Shoe Tree Press; 1988)   Historical fiction for small fry. In the early days of the Revolution, young Aaron hopes to accompany Ethan Allen and the Green Mountain boys in their attack on Fort Ticonderoga. Instead, he ends up helping his grandfather bake bread to feed the hungry soldiers.

Across Five Aprils   Irene Hunt   (Tempo; 1965) During the first April, in 1861, Jethro Creighton is nine years old, planting potatoes with his mother on their farm in southern Illinois. His story, through the next four Aprils, is that of the Civil War and its powerful impact on the family. Older readers.

Araminta's Paintbox   Karen Ackerman   (Atheneum; 1991) Araminta, traveling west by covered wagon in 1847, loses her paintbox. The box passes through the hands of a Mennonite family, a doctor's wife en route to a fort in Colorado, a family of Mormons on the way to Utah, and a gold prospector, before returning once again to Araminta in California. Young to middle-grade readers.

The Baker's Dozen: A Colonial American Tale   Heather Forest   (Harcourt, Brace, and Jovanovich; 1988)   In colonial Albany, NY, a baker cheats his customers while baking the St. Nicholas Day cookies. Bad luck follows, until the baker learns a lesson about generosity and begins giving out 13 cookies to the dozen. For young readers.

Before You Came This Way   Byrd Baylor   (E.P. Dutton; 1969)   The story of the southwest before the Europeans arrived, with illustrations derived from prehistoric rock drawings. Young readers.

A Book of Americans   Rosemary Benét and Stephen Vincent Benét   (Henry Holt, 1933; reissued 1986) Fifty-six delightful biographical poems about historic Americans. Appropriate for all ages.

The Boston Coffee Party   Doreen Rappaport   (HarperCollins; 1988)   In the days before the Revolutionary War, a greedy merchant takes advantage of the colonists' refusal to drink taxed tea by overcharging customers for coffee and sugar. He gets his comeuppance. Simple text for young readers.

Buttons for General Washington   Peter and Connie Roop   (Carolrhoda; 1986)   Young John smuggles coded messages concealed in his coat buttons out of British-occupied Philadelphia to George Washington's camp. Based on a true story. Young to middle readers.

By the Great Horn Spoon!   Sid Fleischman   (Little, Brown; 1963)   In the days of the Gold Rush, Jack Flagg, a twelve-year-old orphan, and Praiseworthy, an imperturbable English butler, are en route to California to win a fortune for Jack's Aunt Arabella. Middle-grade to older readers.

The Courage of Sarah Noble   Alice Dalgliesh   (Macmillan; 1986)   Based on the true story of a little girl who came with her father in 1707 when he built the first house in New Milford, Connecticut. Young Sarah then stays behind with the Indians while her father returns to Massachusetts to fetch her mother and younger brothers and sisters. Suitable for kids in grades K-3.

Dakota Dugout   Ann Turner   (Macmillan; 1985)   A short simple story of life in a sod house on the prairie in the late 19th century. For young readers.

Death of the Iron Horse   Paul Goble   (Bradbury; 1987)   Based on a true story, the tale of the young Cheyenne warriors who bravely destroyed the Iron Horse, the Union Pacific freight train. Young to middle-grade readers.

The Drinking Gourd   F. N. Monjo   (Harper & Row; 1970)   Young Tommy Fuller helps escaping slaves on the Underground Railroad. Simple text for young readers.

The Erie Canal   Peter Spier   (Doubleday; 1970)   The history of the canal is recounted in brief simple text along with the lyrics and melody of the familiar song.   By the same author: *Tin Lizzie* (Doubleday; 1975), the life of a Model T from the time it first rolled off the assembly line in 1909 to its restoration by an antique car lover in the present day. Wonderful illustrations detail the changing countryside. Young to middle-grade readers.

A Gathering of Days: A New England Girl's Journal 1830-32   Joan Blos   (Scribner's; 1979)
    This is historical fiction describing rural life in the early 19th century, written in the form of a New Hampshire farm girl's diary. Middle-grade readers.

Guns for General Washington   Seymour Reit   (Harcourt, Brace, Jovanovich; 1990)   Young Will Knox accompanies his brother Henry, transporting the great guns from Fort Ticonderoga over the snow to Boston during the early days of the Revolutionary War. Middle-grade readers.

Hitty: Her First Hundred Years   Rachel Field   (Macmillan; 1929)   The adventures of Hitty, a little doll who was carved from a piece of ash one winter in Maine 200 years ago, and who originally belonged to Phoebe Prible, who took her everywhere. Middle-grade readers.

Indian Captive   Lois Lensky   (Harper; 1941)   A fascinating book based on the true story of Mary Jemison, captured as a child by the Seneca Indians of New York. Middle-grade readers.

Johnny Tremain   Esther Forbes   (Houghton Mifflin; 1943)   A perennial favorite for older readers, the story of the silversmith's apprentice who, after a crippling accident, becomes involved in the brewing Revolutionary War.

Jump Ship to Freedom.   James Lincoln Collier and Christopher Collier   (Delacorte; 1981)   Set in 1787, the story of young Dan Arabus, a slave boy, and his struggle to gain his freedom. Dan runs away and, after a series of heart-stopping adventures including a dramatic shipwreck, is taken into the home of a Quaker, who involves him in the Constitutional Convention and the passage of the compromise measure known as the fugitive slave law. Middle-grade to older readers. By the same authors: *War Comes to Willy Freeman*, another historically accurate story of slavery and the Revolutionary War.

Justin Morgan Had a Horse   Marguerite Henry   (Rand McNally; 1954) The story of young Joel and his colt, Little Bub, the small sturdy stallion who sired Vermont's famous Morgan horses. Middle-grade readers.

A Lion to Guard Us   Clyde Robert Bulla   (Crowell; 1981)   Amanda and her younger brother and sister travel across the ocean to find their father in the early Jamestown colony in Virginia. The trip is interrupted by disaster, when their ship is wrecked on an island in the Caribbean, but all ends happily. A short chapter book, for young to middle-grade readers.

Little House in the Big Woods   Laura Ingalls Wilder   (Harper & Row; 1973)   Based on the life of the author, this is the story of little Laura Ingalls, growing up with her Ma, Pa, sister Mary, and baby Carrie in the big woods of Wisconsin in the late 19th century. A wonderful and detailed picture of daily life long ago. Sequels include *Little House on the Prairie, On the Banks of Plum Creek, By the Shores of Silver Lake, The Long Winter, Little Town on the Prairie,* and *These Happy Golden Years.*

The Matchlock Gun   Walter D. Edmonds   (G.P. Putnam's Sons; 1969)   The book is based on the true story of young Edward Van Alstyne who, in the days of the French and Indian War, must defend his family by firing the ancient and enormous matchlock gun. Younger readers.

The One Bad Thing About Father F.N. Monjo (HarperCollins; 1970) The story of Teddy Roosevelt, as told by his youngest son, Quentin. The "one bad thing," of course, is that, as President of the United States, Quentin's father doesn't have enough time to play with his children. By the same author: *The Drinking Gourd* (see above); *King George's Head Was Made of Lead*, in which disrespectful colonists melt down the king's statue to make bullets for the Continental army; *Poor Richard in France*, the story of Ben Franklin's trip to France to ask for aid for the on-going Revolution, as told by his young grandson; *Grandpapa and Ellen Aroon*, the story of Thomas Jefferson as told by his favorite nine-year-old granddaughter; *Gettysburg: Tad Lincoln's Story* and *The Vicksburg Veteran*, tales of the Civil War; and *The Secret of the Sachem's Tree*, a story of pre-Revolutionary Connecticut. Generally appropriate for younger readers.

Ox-Cart Man Donald Hall (Viking; 1979) The 19th-century ox-cart man packs up the produce from his fields and all the goods he and his family have made during the year and travels to town to trade. Delightfully illustrated. Young readers.

Phoebe the Spy Judith Berry Griffin (Scholastic; 1989) Phoebe Fraunces, the thirteen-year-old daughter of a tavernkeeper, saves General Washington from a near-fatal plot. Young to middle-grade readers.

Pilgrim Stories Margaret Pumphrey (Rand McNally; 1961) The lightly fictionalized story of the Pilgrims, from their first flight to Holland to their first harvest in the New World. Middle-grade readers.

Rabbits and Redcoats Robert N. Peck (Walker; 1976) Young Chapter Harrow and his friend Interest Wheelock join Ethan Allen's Green Mountain Boys before the attack on Fort Ticonderoga. A good story with a happy ending. Young to middle-grade readers.

The Riddle of Pencroft Farm Dorothea Jensen (Harcourt, Brace, Jovanovich; 1989) Young Lars and his family move to an old farm near Valley Forge, Pennsylvania, where Lars meets Geordie, the ghost of an ancestor, listens to Geordie's first-hand account of the Revolutionary War, and, with Geordie's help, solves a mystery involving a missing will. Middle-grade readers.

Sam the Minuteman   Nathaniel Benchley   (HarperCollins; 1969)   The Revolutionary War begins with the Battle of Lexington, as seen through the eyes of a young boy. By the same author: *George the Drummer Boy*, a young British drummer's view of the same battle. Both have simple texts, for young readers.

Samuel's Choice   Richard Berleth   (Albert Whitman; 1990)   A young slave boy helps General Washington's army in the Battle of New York and is given his freedom as a reward. Middle-grade readers.

The Secret Soldier   Ann McGovern   (Macmillan; 1987)   The story of Deborah Sampson who, disguised as a man, fights as a soldier in the Continental Army during the Revolutionary War. Middle-grade readers.

Sing Down the Moon   Scott O'Dell   (Houghton Mifflin; 1970)   The story of Bright Morning, a fifteen-year-old Navajo girl, who is first kidnapped by Spanish slavers; then, with the rest of her people, forced by white soldiers to leave her land, on a march of 300 miles known today as the Long Walk. Bright Morning survives, and returns with her husband and baby son to live in her home canyon, hidden from the white men. Older readers.

The Slave Dancer   Paula Fox   (Bradbury; 1973)   This gripping novel tells the story of young Jesse Bollier, who was press-ganged into service on board a slave ship, bound for Africa in 1840. One of Jesse's duties is to play his flute while the imprisoned slaves exercise on shipdeck. Older readers.

Susanna of the Alamo: A True Story   John Jakes   (Harcourt, Brace, and Jovanovich; 1986)   Susanna Dickinson survived the siege of the Alamo in 1836 and then brought General Santa Anna's warning message to Sam Houston - so effectively that all Texas was roused to the cry, "Remember the Alamo!" Young to middle-grade readers.

Toliver's Secret   Esther Brady   (Crown; 1976)   During the Revolutionary War, timid ten-year-old Ellen Toliver must smuggle a secret message through the British lines when her grandfather becomes ill. Middle-grade readers.

Uncle George Washington and Harriot's Guitar   Miriam Anne Bourne   (Coward-McCann; 1983)   George Washington's orphaned niece, Harriot, longs for a guitar and writes her Uncle George asking for one. Based on a true story.

An American History Book List: True Books

Columbus Ingri D'Aulaire and Edgar Parin (Doubleday; 1955) The D'Aulaire biographies are big books, with large illustrations on every page; but there's a lot of informational text, too. Other D'Aulaire biographies include *Leif the Lucky, Pocahontas, George Washington, Benjamin Franklin,* and *Abraham Lincoln.* Appropriate for kids through the middle grades.

Commodore Perry in the Land of the Shogun Rhoda Blumberg (Lothrop, Lee & Shepard; 1985) The story of the American expedition to Japan led by Commodore Matthew in Perry in 1853, in an attempt to open a new market for Western trade. Well-written text, illustrated with period Japanese prints. Middle-grade readers.

Cornerstones of Freedom series This large collection of short books is published by the Childrens Press (Chicago): all are about 30 pages long, and each covers a specific topic in American history. Titles include: *The Story of Old Ironsides, The Story of the Liberty Bell, The Story of the Gettysburg Address, The Story of the Star-Spangled Banner, The Story of the Battle of Lexington and Concord, The Story of the Declaration of Independence,* and many, many more. The text is dry, but the facts are there. Young to middle-grade readers.

The Discovery of the Americas and *The Discovery of the Americas Activities Book* Betsy Maestro and Giulio (Lothrop, Lee, & Shepard; 1992) The book starts with the crossing of the Asia-to-America land bridge during the last Ice Age and ends with the voyage of Magellan. Text is simple and straightforward; illustrations splashy and colorful. The accompanying activity book describes over 40 "innovative" projects for the classroom. Young to middle-grade readers.

Freedom Train: The Story of Harriet Tubman Dorothy Sterling (Doubleday; 1954) A fascinating biography of Harriet Tubman, the brave and gallant woman who brought so many slaves north to freedom along the Underground Railroad.

From Path to Highway: The Story of the Boston Post Road Gail Gibbons (Thomas Y. Crowell/HarperCollins; 1988) A simple, brightly illustrated history of the famous road, from the original Indian footpath to the busy four-lane highway of today. Young readers.

If You Were There in 1492 Barbara Brenner (Bradbury Press; 1991) A new slant on the Columbus story; the theme is "What else was going on in 1492? What was life like then?" Middle-grade readers.

The Incredible Journey of Lewis & Clark   Rhoda Blumberg   (Lothrop, Lee & Shepard; 1987)   An impressively illustrated account of Lewis and Clark's landmark 19th-century journey across America. Includes many original sources: photographs of artifacts, journal quotes, and drawings. Middle-grade and older readers. By the same author: *The Remarkable Voyages of Captain Cook* and *The Great American Gold Rush*.

Indian Chiefs   Russell Freedman   (Holiday; 1987)   This is a non-fiction introduction to six great American Indian chiefs: Red Cloud, Santana, Quanah Parker, Washakie, Joseph, and Sitting Bull. The book is illustrated with impressive historical photographs. By the same author: *Lincoln: A Photobiography* and *Immigrant Kids*. The latter is a photgraphic essay on the lives of children whose families came to this country around the turn of the century. Middle-grade and older readers.

Landmark Books
    This series of history books, published by Random House in the 1950's, is targeted at kids aged 12-15. Each is about 180 pages long and deals with a specific historical topic or period. There are over 40 books in the series; sample titles include *Paul Revere and the Minute Men, The California Gold Rush, The Pony Express, The Building of the First Transcontinental Railroad, The Vikings, The Monitor and the Merrimac, The Panama Canal, Clipper Ship Days, The Barbary Pirates, The Conquest of the North and South Poles,* and *Thirty Seconds Over Tokyo*. Middle-grade to older readers.

The Landmark History of the American People   Daniel J. Boorstin   (Random House; 1970; revised 1987)   An excellent two-volume history of the United States for middle- and upper-grade kids.

The Last Known Cow on the White House Lawn and Other Little Known Facts About the Presidency   Barbara Seuling   (Doubleday; 1978)   Obscure, irresistable, and unforgettable information about the presidents. By the same author: *You Can't Eat Peanuts in Church and Other Little Known Laws*. Fun for everybody.

Many Thousand Gone: African Americans from Slavery to Freedom   Virginia Hamilton   (Knopf; 1993)   A series of short, enthralling stories and profiles that trace the history of slavery in America. Superb.   By the same author: *The People Could Fly: American Black Folktales*.

A More Perfect Union: The Story of Our Constitution   Betsey and Guilio Maestro   (Mulberry Books; 1987)   A simple history of the writing of the Constitution, with lots of large colorful illustrations. By the same authors: *The Story of the Statue of Liberty*. For young readers.

A Picture Book of George Washington   David A. Adler   (Holiday; 1989)   A very simple beginner biography for young readers. By the same author: *A Picture Book of Benjamin Franklin, A Picture Book of Abraham Lincoln, A Picture Book of Martin Luther King, Jr., A Picture Book of Christopher Columbus, A Picture Book of Eleanor Roosevelt, A Picture Book of Helen Keller, A Picture Book of John F. Kennedy*, and *A Picture Book of Thomas Jefferson*.

The President's Cabinet and How It Grew   Nancy Winslow Parker   (HarperCollins; 1991)   A cleverly illustrated explanation of the president's cabinet, including the history and function of each position. Young to middle-grade readers.

Signature Books
   This series of biographies, published by Grosset & Dunlap, each run about 180 pages long and are targeted at kids aged 9-14. Titles include *The Story of Madame Curie, The Story of Abraham Lincoln, The Story of Buffalo Bill, The Story of Stephen Decatur, The Story of Robert E. Lee, The Story of Lafayette, The Story of Florence Nightingale, The Story of Louis Pasteur*, and many more.

The Spice of America   June Swanson   (Carolrhoda; 1983)   A delightful collection of short historical stories designed to "bring out the flavor of America's past." Among others, accounts of the inventions of the doughnut, the ferris wheel, and bluejeans, of the beaver hat trade in early America, and of the writing of "Mary Had a Little Lamb." Middle-grade readers.

The Story of the White House   Katie Waters   (Scholastic; 1991)   An appealing history of the White House and the nation's capital, illustrated with photographs. Young and middle-grade readers.

And There Was America   Roger Duvoisin   (Alfred A. Knopf; 1938)   A collection of short "stories" covering the early explorers, starting with the Vikings, through the arrival of the early European settlers (Spanish, French, Dutch, and English). Lightly fictionalized, which means that there's imaginary conversation. Young to middle-grade readers.

True Stories About Abraham Lincoln   Ruth Belov Gross   (Scholastic; 1973) A collection of short one-page anecdotes about Abraham Lincoln, illustrated with attractive woodcuts. Young to middle-grade readers.

Also see individual History and Geography listings: Childhood of Famous Americans series; *The Buck Stops Here*; Foster, Genevieve; Fritz, Jean; Gonick, Larry; If You...Series; *It Happened in America*; *Kids' America*; *Kids Learn America!*; Lawson, Robert; *My Backyard History Book*; Native American Legends Series; *Paul Harvey's The Rest of the Story*; Perkins, Lucy Fitch; Quackenbush, Robert; Sloane, Eric; Time-Life; *Travelling the U.S. Through Children's Literature*; We Were There Series; *Who Put the Cannon in the Courthouse Square?*; *Yo, Millard Fillmore!*

A Book List for Geographers

All Around the World   Judy Donnelly   (Putnam; 1991)   Basic geographical concepts for early elementary-aged kids, plus an inflatable globe.

Anno's U.S.A.   Anno Mitsumasa   (Putnam; 1983)   A wordless geographical trek across America. Young readers.

As the Crow Flies: A First Book of Maps   Gail Hartman   (Bradbury; 1991)   A first look at geography as kids view the land from the points of view of a crow, an eagle, a rabbit, a horse, and a gull.

Ashanti to Zulu: African Traditions   Margaret Musgrove   (Dial; 1976)   An alphabet book with a difference, elaborately illustrating and describing many different aspects of African culture, from Ashanti, Baule, and Chaga to Xhosa, Yoruba, and Zulu. For young to middle-grade readers. Other multicultural alphabet books include *The Calypso Alphabet*   John Agard   (Holt; 1989); *A is for Aloha* Stephanie Feeney (University of Hawaii Press; 1980); *Afro-Bets: Book of Black Heroes from A to Z* Wade Judson and Valerie Wilson Wesley (Just Us Books; 1988); and *A to Zen: A Book of Japanese Culture*   Ruth Wells (Picture Book Studio; 1992).

Explorers Who Got Lost   Diane Sansevere-Dreher   (Tom Doherty;

1992) An account of explorers who didn't end up quite where they'd intended, including the stories of Bartolomeo Dias, Vasco da Gama, Christopher Columbus, John Cabot, Ferdinand Magellan, Giovanni da Verrazano, Jacques Cartier, and Henry Hudson. Includes a cartoon-illustrated fold-out map. Middle-grade readers.

Geography A-Z   Jack Knowlton   (Thomas Y. Crowell; 1988)   A "picture glossary" for beginning geographers. The text is a series of simple definitions of geographical terms, from Archipelago and Atoll to Volcano and Zone, each clearly illustrated with big, bright-colored pictures. By the same author: *Maps and Globes* (Harper & Row; 1985). The book covers ancient maps, globes, flat maps and their inaccuracies, map vocabulary terms, and different types of maps (contour, physical, political, local.) Simple no-frills text. A Reading Rainbow Selection. Young readers.

How We Learned the Earth Is Round   Patricia Lauber   (Thomas Y. Crowell; 1990)   Round earth studies from the ancient Greeks through space satellites. Simple informative text; clever and colorful illustrations. Young readers.

My World: Geography for Beginners   (Workman; 1991)   A package deal, including an inflatable globe (only the continents are labelled, in big print), a 64-page information-and-activities book, and over 100 colorful stickers, that can be pasted on the globe to show country names, the locations of rain forests, rivers, glaciers, and volcanoes, the native ranges of various animals, and the locations of famous monuments.

Paddle-to-the-Sea   Holling C. Holling   (Houghton Mifflin; 1941)   The adventurous and information-packed story of a carved Indian in a canoe, who travels across the Great Lakes and up the St. Lawrence River to the sea. Wonderful maps, diagrams, and illustrations. By the same author: *Minn of the Mississippi, Seabird,* and *The Tree in the Trail.* All are historically and geographically oriented.

Passport Sticker Books
   The Passport Sticker Books, by David Gantz, are published by Simon and Schuster: in each, a pair of traveling mice, Frannie and Joey, variously tour Japan, Britain, the (now outdated) Soviet Union, and the United States, touching on all geographical and cultural high points. There's a map on each page, marked with a red dot to show where Frannie and Joey are at any given time; and in

the back, there's a "Passport Book" for kids to assemble themselves, pasting 70 illustrated stickers in the appropriate boxes. Titles in the series include *Let's Visit Britain, Let's Visit Japan, Let's Visit the Soviet Union,* and *Let's Visit the United States.*

People   Peter Spier   (Doubleday; 1982)   A multicultural delight for younger kids, describing, through wonderfully detailed illustrations, the shapes, sizes, games, houses, costumes, foods, holidays, religions, languages, and societies of people all over the world.

Puzzle Maps   Nancy L. Clouse   (Holt; 1990)   Kids learn the names and shapes of the 50 states while solving a series of innovative puzzles, each made up of colored state-shaped pieces.

Stringbean's Trip to the Shining Sea   Vera B. Williams   (Greenwillow; 1988)   As Stringbean and his uncle travel to the West Coast, the story of the trip is told through clever illustrated postcards.

What's in a Map?   Sally Cartwright   (Putnam; 1976)   Hands-on map-making instructions for kids in grades K-3, using simple materials like sand and building blocks.

Also see individual History and Geography listings: *The Book of Where (Or How to Be Naturally Geographic); Count Your Way Books; Don't Know Much About Geography; Everything is Somewhere: The Geography Quiz Book; Geography: The United States of America; Geo-Whiz!; Kids Learn America!; Travelling the U.S. Through Children's Literature; Windows to the World.*

Chapter Five

Science

Beetles to Black Holes

Adopt a Whale

When you adopt a humpback whale through the Whale Adoption Project, you don't just adopt any nameless whale; you choose your adoptee from a list of 66 known whales, each named and studied by cetologists at the Provincetown Center for Coastal Studies. (Among the whales on the list: Patches, Churchill, Bat, Cloud, Silver, Pepper, Buckshot, and Othello.) The adoption fee is $15.00 per whale, for which adopters receive an Official Whale Adoption Certificate, a photograph of the chosen whale, a whale calendar and migration map, which enables adopters to track (approximately) their whale's movements, and a quarterly newsletter, *Whalewatch*, available in both adult and child versions. For additional information, contact the Whale Adoption Project, 70 East Falmouth Highway, East Falmouth, MA 02536; (508) 548-8328.

Adventures in Science

This is a series of individual small boxed science kits. Each includes 35 (brief) project booklets, each detailing a simple science experiment, and a smattering of hands-on supplies, to be rounded out by "readily available household items." The *Electricity* kit, for example, includes instructions for making simple electrical circuits, an electronic quiz game, and a telegraph set, and comes with a couple of small light bulbs, a bulb socket, and a roll of copper wire; the *Light* kit, which includes instructions for building a periscope, a sundial, a kaleidoscope, and a model of the human eye, comes with a prism, a mirror, and an assortment of colored plastic filters. Other kits in the series include *Magnetism* (build a compass and an electromagnet, experiment with magnetic poles), *How Things Work* (experiment with levers and pulleys, and build a balloon-powered "rocket boat"), *Sky Science* (construct a model solar system and a weather station), *Spy Science* (learn how to lift fingerprints and send messages with Morse Code), *Eco-Detective* (study acid rain and the greenhouse effect), *Backyard Science* (study insects, track the moon, experiment with solar energy), *Dinosaurs & Fossils* (make your own fossil), *Kitchen Science* (sprout seeds, make candles), and *Science Magic Tricks* (make spaghetti dance, levitate cups). Each kit costs $12.95; the series is available from several sources, including Educational Insights, 19560 S. Rancho Way, Dominguez Hills, CA 90220; (800) 933-3277 or (213) 637-2131; and Modern School Supplies, Inc. (Technology Education Catalog), P.O. Box 958, Hartford, CT 06143; (800) 243-2328 or (203) 243-9565.

Alpha Animals

In this zoological board game, players move their pieces (a small alligator, gorilla, dolphin, or elephant) around an attractive alphabet-patterned game board. The challenge is to come up with a (real) animal whose name begins with the letter the playing piece lands upon, in a category determined by a throw of the dice: mammal, reptile, bird, insect, fish, amphibian, or wildcard. For kids of all ages. *Alpha Animals* is available from game or toy stores, or from The Nature Company, P.O. Box 188, Florence, KY 41022; (800) 227-1114.

Amazing Apples, Etc.

The Amazing Apple Book (Paulette Bourgeois) is one of a series of publications by Addison-Wesley Publishing Company. All are informational activity books, targeted at kids aged 7-11. *The Amazing Apple Book*, along with much apple information, scientific, historical, literary, and superstitious, includes instructions for growing your own apple trees from seed (a very long-term project), for drying apple slices pioneer-style on strings, and for making apple prints, apple dolls, and blue candy apples. Other books in the same series include *The Amazing Egg Book* (Margaret Griffin and Deborah Seed) - in which kids dissect an egg, test the strength of eggshells, fry an egg on the sidewalk, make egg trees and egg-yolk paint, make eggnog and baked Alaska, and learn to write "egg" in Egyptian hieroglyphics; *The Amazing Dirt Book* (Paulette Bourgeois); *The Amazing Paper Book* (Paulette Bourgeois); *The Amazing Potato Book* (Paulette Bourgeois); and *The Amazing Milk Book* (Catherine Ross and Susan Wallace). Available through bookstores or from Delta Education, Inc., P.O. Box 950, Hudson, NH, 03501; (800) 442-5444.

American Nuclear Society

The American Nuclear Society publishes a free information letter for educators called *Re-actions*, issued five times yearly, plus a brochure listing an assortment of "Public Information Publications" and materials of interest to educators. Among these are a teacher curriculum guide, *Energy From the Atom* ($5.00), targeted toward grades 5 and 6, which contains student worksheets on such topics as "History of Nuclear Energy," "Radiations in Our Environment," and "Nuclear Medicine;" a board game, "Energy Chase" ($4.50), for kids aged 11 and older, in which players learn how electricity is made and win by cornering the largest energy supply; and a Personal Radiation Dose Chart ($0.15), with which students can determine their own probable annual radiation dose. Brochures are available from the American Nuclear Society, Public Communications Dept., 555 North Kensington Avenue, La Grange Park, IL 60525; (708) 579-8265. For a free subscription to the newsletter *Re-actions*, send a request to the ANS written on school letterhead stationery.

American Science and Surplus

The catalog logo is a distressed-looking airborne inventor with an array of pulleys and propellers strapped to his back - and such, one gathers, are the catalog's prime customers: basement inventors, workshop tinkerers, creative mechanics, homestyle scientists, and gimmick-lovers everywhere. The catalog consists of 60-odd closely printed pages of useful, interesting, and just plain bizarre stuff, at bargain basement prices. We, in our time, have acquired from it: a large assortment of lenses, convex and concave, for optical experiments; a set of collision balls, of the sort used in high-school physics labs to demonstrate the principle of energy transference; a popcorn rock, which, dunked in vinegar, grows puffy white crystals that look like popcorn (they're not; they're aragonite); several music box works, which our kids then encased in homemade music boxes; three pairs of red, white, and blue folding binoculars; a collection of miniature solar panels; a lot of nice cheap laboratory glassware; a stereoptical viewer (with packet of 18 stero cards, all for $6.00); and a stethoscope. For the truly self-motivated scientist. Single catalog copies cost $1.00, but once you buy some science and surplus, you'll be on their mailing list. For your copy, contact American Science and Surplus, P.O. Box 48838, Niles, IL 60714-0838; (708) 475-8440.

Ampersand Press

Ampersand Press publishes an assortment of creative science card games, among them *The Pollination Game*, *Krill*, *Good Heavens!*, *AC/DC*, and *Predator*. *The Pollination Game* consists of 72 color-illustrated cards: players use these in a game of strategy to match flowers with their proper pollinators (bees, bugs, birds). Instructions are included for several versions of the game, appropriate for kids aged 7 and up. In *Krill* ("A Whale of a Game"), players assemble Antarctic Ocean food chains using 27 illustrated cards: featured are whales, seals, squid, penguins, fish, and the shrimp-like krill, the whale's pick for dinner. *Predator* ("The Food Chain

Game") teaches players, through 40 illustrated cards, the food chain relationships in the temperate-zone forest. The simplest version of the game is a food-chain variant of "War:" each player lays down a picture card, animals take what they eat or are taken by what eats them. The owl card, for example, takes the mouse card. Predator is also available in French and Spanish. *Good Heavens!* ("Comets, Meteors, and Other Neat Sky Stuff") is an astronomy game consisting of 54 question-and-answer card (all with shiny gold backs). Answers to the questions are an education in themselves, each consisting of a paragraph or so of specific and related information. (Question: "When passing near the sun, comets are surrounded by a cloud of gas. What does this consist of?" Answer: "Hydrogen. Beyond the visible coma of a comet near the sun there is an unseen cloud of hydrogen gas. Ultraviolet light causes water to dissociate into hydrogen and hydroxyl ions, and the disc of the hydrogen cloud in 1970 is strong evidence to support the iceberg theory of the nature of the comet. The size of the cloud can be a large as a million miles in diameter.") Recommended for kids aged 10 and up; not a game for tots. *AC/DC* ("A Card Game to Electrify You") consists of 84 cards, each representing a component of an electrical circuit. Players attempt to construct workable electrical circuits without getting shocked or shorted out; these can range from the simple (power source, switch, appliance, fuse) to elaborate parallel series circuits. An informational booklet is included.

Ampersand Press also carries *The Hummingbird Game*, "a unique strategy game about the jewels of the bird world" and a wonderful resource for young ornithologists. The game consists of 60 cards, beautifully illustrated in full-color; players attempt to match hummingbirds to flowers, insects, range, and habitat. Games generally cost $8.00 to $15.00. To order, contact Ampersand Press, 8040 N.E. Day Rd West #5-A, Bainbridge Island, WA 98110; (206) 780-9015.

Anatomical Chart Company

There's an assortment of wacky stuff in here - chocolate skulls, socks patterned with foot bones, eyeball keychains - but the catalog also contains an excellent collection of resources for young scientists. There are detailed anatomical charts of all types and sizes, including a 6-foot pop-out whole-body version that turns into a 3-dimensional model in five easy steps. For the hands-on anatomist, there is a series of jigsaw puzzles based on the charts: 48 of these, including "The Skeletal System," "The Nervous System," "The Digestive System," and "The Heart." Each measures 11 x 14" and consists of 154 pieces. The catalog also carries a selection of anatomical models, including *The Kids' Bones and Skeleton Book*, which comes with a 21-piece put-together plastic skeleton and a book filled with catchy information and suggested projects and activities. Also available: anatomy flashcards and coloring books, and stethoscopes in four day-glo colors. The catalog does not restrict itself to anatomical products; there are also resources for young geologists, astronomers, physicists, and naturalists - including the "Earthlab" environmental kit, with which kids can make recycled paper, purify water, and mop up oil spills; and "Critter City," a luxury bug-box in which young entomologists can feed and observe their captured "critters." Definitely worth a look. For a free catalog, contact the Anatomical Chart Co., 8221 N. Kimball, Skokie, IL 60076; (800) 621-7500, (708) 679-4700.

Anatomy Apron

The Anatomy Apron - appropriate for kids aged 3 and up - is a vinyl apron that slips over the kid's head, patterned front and back with pre-printed outlines of internal organs. Colorful cut-out organ pieces attach to the pattern outline with velcro fasteners. On the apron front, kids can stick on lungs, heart, liver, stomach, and large and small intestines; on the back, there's an outline of the skeletal system, showing backbone, shoulder blades, ribs, and pelvic bones, with attachable kidneys. The accompanying teacher's guide lists suggestions for related learning activities. Available from the Anatomical Chart Co. (see above) or from Cuisenaire Co. of America, Inc., P.O. Box 5026, White Plains, NY 10602-5026; (800) 237-3142.

Animal Town

Despite the zoological name, Animal Town is not a scientific company; many of their excellent resources, however, are right on for the environmentally-aware young scientist. The catalog offers, for example, a series of four superbly illustrated card games: *Juniper: A Game of Trees*; *Goldenrod: A Game of Wild Flowers*; *Cinnabar: A Game of Rocks and Minerals*; and *Nautilus: A Game of Sea Shells*. All are played like rummy: players, through a process of trade, draw, and discard, assemble related four-card sets. The board games, all exquisitely designed, are even better. In *Dam Builders*, players (beavers) cooperate to build a dam and lodge and accumulate a winter food supply, while fending off wolves, forest fires, flash floods, and the depredations of The Corps, represented by a tree-chopping bulldozer; in *Nectar Collector*, players (bees) buzz through the concentric layers of a circular gameboard, storing up nectar (amber beads) in their honeycombs and racing to reach the Queen Bee; in *Save the Whales*, players cooperate to save 8 great whales from oil spills, radioactive waste, and whale catchers. An informational booklet comes with each game. All three games are appropriate for kids aged 8 and up. For a free catalog, contact Animal Town, P.O. Box 485, Healdsburg, CA 95448; (800) 445-8642.

APPMA

APPMA stands for American Pet Products Manufacturers Association, a group which is interested not only in pet foods, but in elementary education. APPMA publishes a "unique literature-based thematic unit" titled *Pets & Me*, developed in a collaboration between educators at the University of Pennsylvania Graduate School of Education and at the Purdue University School of Veterinary Medicine. *Pets & Me* is a 300-page teacher's guide, suitable for kids in grades K-5, which uses "the study of animals and pets to spark learning in language arts, oral communication, science, math, social studies, computer science, and more." The program includes a complete packet of lesson plans, plus an accompanying resource list, with annotated bibliographies and sources for hands-on materials. *Pets & Me* comes in a 3-ring vinyl looseleaf binder, and costs $15.95 plus $4.50 shipping from *Pets & Me*, APPMA, 511 Harwood Bldg., Scarsdale, NY 10583; (800) 452-1225.

Astronomy

Officially a magazine for grown-ups, but there's plenty here for younger astronomers too. The photographs are terrific; and each month a regular feature, *Sky Almanac*, provides a star map, a calendar of noteworthy astronomical events, and several pages of viewing hints. An annual subscription (12 issues) costs $17.70 from *Astronomy*, 21027 Crossroads Circle, P.O. Box 1612, Waukesha, WI 53187-1612; (800) 533-6644.

Aves Science Kit Company

Aves Science Kit Company, explains their flier, "is a science supply company specializing in homeschool laboratory science units." Their specialty is "complete self-contained laboratory units that are essentially identical to conventional laboratory exercises but are designed and packaged for the homeschooler." Each science unit comes - all equipment included, plus complete instruction sheets - in a no-nonsense little white cardboard box; the Aves people seem to be putting their money on science, not glitz. There are over 70 different kits available, covering such topics as Bacteria Staining, Blood Typing, Earthworm Study, Sheep Eye Study, Light and Seeds, Owl Pellet Study, pH Investigation, and Frog and Flower Dissections. Units can be purchased individually, for anything from about $4.00 to $7.00 apiece; or in batches, as complete laboratory programs. A Basic Laboratory Program for 12-14-year-olds, for example includes 9 science units and costs $42.75; a Natural History Program for 8-11-year-olds includes 8 units and costs $39.75. For information and a list of products and prices, contact Aves Science Kit Company, P.O. Box 220, Peru, ME 04290; (207) 562-7033.

The Backyard Scientist

Jane Hoffmann, The Backyard Scientist, is dedicated to publishing books of "exciting, challenging, and easy to understand experiments" for scientists aged 4 to 14. The experiments use supplies generally found around the average home: rubberbands, powdered Kool-Aid, flashlight batteries and tin foil, food coloring, balloons, soap, plastic bags. Experimental design is short and straightforward; each begins with a "scientific mission" or question for young investigators ("Does gravity pull all falling objects down to earth at the same rate?" "Can you change the color of ink with the electricity contained in a battery?" "Will a sugar cube dissolve faster in hot water or cold water?"), continues with step-by-step instructions, and ends with a clear scientific explanation of the experimental results. There are four books in the *Backyard Scientist* series (*The Original Backyard Scientist; Backyard Scientist, Series One; Backyard Scientist, Series Two*; and *Backyard Scientist, Series Three*); each costs $9.50 (shipping included) from The Backyard Scientist, P.O. Box 16966, Irvine, CA 92713.

Banana Slug String Band

The Banana Slug String Band - named for the bright-yellow banana slug, State Mollusk of California - sings a catchily irresistable array of nature and environmental songs for kids, all available on cassette tapes. Among them: *Songs for the Earth, Dirt Made My Lunch, Adventures on the Air Cycle*, and *Slugs At Sea*. Music here is a little bit of everything - rap, rag, reggae, and folk ballad - as are the singers, all talented songwriters, musicians, and teachers. Our kids still trail around singing, "Thanks, Earth, thanks a bunch/For my fruit, my sandwich, my milk, and my munch" or chanting, in stage whispers, "Noc-tur-nal an-i-mals: they come out at night!" Cassette and songbooks are available from the Banana Slug String Band, P.O. Box 2262, Santa Cruz, CA 95063; (408) 423-7807 or (408) 429-9806; or from Music for Little People, Box 1460, Redway, CA 95560; (800) 727-2233.

Bare Bones

Bare Bones: Everybody's Inside Out is a paper human skeleton kit designed by David Hawcock. The kit consists of a mere 20 pieces, to cut out and glue together, and the finished product is a 2/3-life-sized skeleton with articulated joints, suitable for sitting in educational positions in the family living room. The kit includes step-by-step instructions and a color-illustrated information sheet on bones. *Bare Bones* costs $15.95 and is available from the Edmund Scientific Company, 101 East Gloucester Pike, Barrington, NJ 08007-1380; (609) 547-8880.

Build Your Own Radio

With this book-and-kit set from Running Press, kids can build their own working AM radio. The included book contains step-by-step assembly instructions, along with definitions and detailed easy-to-understand explanations of the functions of all crucial parts: transistor, capacitor, speaker, potentiometer, switch, and antenna. The final product, enclosed in a fold-together turquoise cardboard case, is solid and attractive; it also works, once you provide your own 9-volt battery. Available through bookstores or directly from Running Press Book Publishers, 125 South Twenty-second St, Philadelphia, PA 19103; (215) 567-5080, (800) 345-5359.

Butterfly Garden

The Butterfly Garden is a large green cardboard box, with cellophane windows (it comes in pieces; you assemble it). It's accompanied by an instruction booklet, some butterfly feeding supplies, and a postcard for your "larval culture" - caterpillars - that must be mailed off to a supply house in California. The caterpillars, five of them, arrive promptly in a little plastic cup, food included, all set to grow. They stuff themselves for about a week, then climb up to the top of their container, hang head down, and spin chrysalises. At this point, owners transfer them gently to their cardboard Garden to wait for butterflies, which hatch out in 7-10 days. The butterflies, when they finally appear, are orange-and-black spotted Painted Ladies, very attractive: they can be kept in the Garden, fed on sugar water, or - after a few days gleeful observation - they can be released outdoors. This one is a delightful project for young scientists. The timing is just right: kids are able to participate in a long-term science experiment, but the term isn't so long that boredom sets in. It's also an active experiment: caterpillars wiggle, climb, and grow almost visibly. Growth rate, in fact, is fast enough that the caterpillars can be measured daily - ours packed on half a centimeter a day in length - and the results graphed. The Butterfly Garden costs about $20.00 and is available from a number of sources, among them The Edmund Scientific Company, 101 E. Gloucester Pike, Barrington, NJ 08007-1380; (609) 547-8880; and Insect Lore Products, P.O. Box 1535, Shafter, CA 93263; (800) LIVE BUG.

Carolina Biological Supply Company

This is a catalog and a half, over a thousand pages long with color illustrations, and a lush source of science supplies for parents and professionals. Educational biology kits of all kinds, preserved plant and animal specimens, laboratory equipment, good-quality microscopes and dissecting scopes, prepared microscope slides, charts and posters, filmstrips and videos, books, games, and puzzles, chemicals (can be sold to schools and businesses only), plus an entire section devoted specifically to "Elementary Science." A source for silkworm-growing kits, model dinosaur skeletons, human anatomy models, student dissecting kits, live chameleons and hermit crabs, and much more. The catalog itself costs $17.95, but it's worth every penny. For more information contact Carolina Biological Supply Company, 2700 York Road, Burlington, NC 27215; (800) 334-5551, or Box 187, Gladstone, OR 97027; (800) 547-1733.

Chem Matters

Chem Matters magazine is published by the American Chemical Society and is targeted at high school students - but don't write it off as a possibility for much younger chemists. It's the latest on our subscription list, and our oldest just turned eleven. *Chem Matters*, readers comment, "relates chemistry to everyday life" and "shows a side of chemistry which is fun and exciting." Topics covered in the past have included the chemical aspects of peanut brittle, charcoal briquettes, blue jean dyes, lipstick, mint, and diesel engines. Under peanut brittle, you learn that brittle, like lollipops, is chemically a *glass*, or amorphous solid. Its main ingredient - other than peanuts - is sucrose; readers learn what sucrose is and where it comes from, and discover why it turns brown when you cook it. An insert gives the chemical low-down on candy-cooking (with graph) and there's a recipe (in metric) for brittle. A supplementary Classroom Guide is available for each magazine issue, providing additional experimental suggestions, information, and references related to each article. Subscriptions to *Chem Matters* (4 issues per year) are available from the American Chemical Society, 1155 16th Street N.W., Washington D.C. 20036. A magazine subscription costs an annual $2.50; a Classroom Guide subscription, $3.00; plus $3.50 postage and handling. Single review copies can be obtained by calling (202) 872-4590.

Circulation

This board game is a journey through the human body: players move through the blood stream, collecting and delivering oxygen, and shuttling white blood cells to sites of infection. Appropriate for players aged 10 and up. *Circulation* costs $23.95 from Edmund Scientific Co., 101 East Gloucester Pike, Barrington, NJ 08007-1380; (609) 547-8880.

Cobb, Vicki

Vicki Cobb deserves special mention for better-than-the-average science books for kids - which, right there, is an understatement; these books are terrific. Her best-known books are probably *Science Experiments You Can Eat* (Harper & Row; 1972) and the sequel, *More Science Experiments You Can Eat*, both packed with science activities for the chemically curious 10-13-year-old. ("Your kitchen at home," the first book begins, "is a well-equipped laboratory.") Unlike most kids' science activity books, however, Cobb deals clearly and explicitly with the real nitty-gritty of science. Through the media of Kool-Aid, salad dressing, butter, meringue, pretzels, lemon fizz, celery, and yogurt, kids learn about solutes and solvents, colloids and emulsions, protein denaturation, fermentation, enzyme activities, and the cellular structure of plants, with detailed explanations of each.

For younger readers, Cobb has written an excellent question-and-answer series: titles include *Why Doesn't the Earth Fall Up? and other not such dumb questions about motion* (Dutton; 1988); *Why Can't You Unscramble an Egg? and other not such dumb questions about matter* (1990); and *Why Doesn't the Sun Burn Out? and other not such dumb questions about energy* (1990). Questions include "If the earth is spinning, why don't we feel it move?," "Why doesn't the moon fall to earth?," "Why does an ice cube float?," "How does wood burn?," "What does it take to move a piano?," "How does a pot holder work?," and "Why isn't the sky green or yellow? Why blue?" Anwers are short, clear, and catchy, and tie questions about familiar objects and situations to major scientific principles.

Our favorite of the Cobb books (so far), however, is *Chemically Active!* (Lippincott; 1985), one of the best books available for the young (but serious) chemist. *Chemically Active!* covers techniques of analytical chemistry (filtration, distillation, crystallization, chromatography), the mechanisms of chemical reactions, tests for specific elements, electrolytes, acids and bases, atomic structure, and the organization of the periodic table. Experiments, of which there are many - the book is chemically active in more ways than one - are challenging. Cobb-inspired kids don't simply combine vinegar and baking soda and watch it fizz; they build galvanometers, split water by electrolysis and analyze the accumulated gases, isolate carbon dioxide from soda pop, copperplate nickels. Available through bookstores.

Coloring Books

There are coloring books on the market for scientists of almost all ages. Hyperion Press (Winnipeg, Canada) publishes the Wilderness Album series, subtitled "Nature Stories for Children." There are a large number of titles in the series, among them *Birds* (I and II), *Large Mammals* (I and II), *Small Mammals, Insects, Fish, Butterflies and Moths, Wildflowers, Trees,* and *Time & Life,* which has a picture of dinosaurs on the cover. Each double-page spread includes a picture to cover, accompanied, on the facing page, with a story about the featured animal or plant, a scientific description, and directions for scientifically accurate coloring, which our children, I notice, ignored. The books cost $4.95 each, and are appropriate for 5-9-year-olds. Available through bookstores.

More detailed and better-looking is the "Start Exploring" series from Running Press: scientific titles in this series of high-quality "fact-filled coloring books" include *Oceans* (Diane M. Tyler and James C. Tyler), *Forests* (Elizabeth Corning Dudley), *Gray's Anatomy* (Freddie Stark), *Space* (Dennis Mammana), and *Insects* (George S. Glenn, Jr.). These 100+-page books include 60 illustrations to color, alternating with pages of fascinating scientific fact. In the *Insects* book, for example, coloring projects include an ancient giant dragonfly, an arthropod "family tree," a frog as seen through a many-lensed insect eye, a diagram of the parts of a grasshopper, ants approaching an ant lion's pit, a cross-section of an African termite mound, an array of butterflies, a selection of insect habitats, and an African killer bee. There are also practical hints for young insect collectors and a short bibliography. Appropriate for kids aged 7 and up. The books cost $8.95 each, and are available through bookstores or directly from Running Press Book Publishers, 125 South Twenty-second Street, Philadelphia, PA 19103; (215) 567-5080, (800) 345-5359 for orders. When ordering from Running Press, add $2.50 for postage and handling.

The Nature Press carries a complete line of Peterson Field Guide Coloring Books, based on the famous nature guides. "Once you have colored a red-eyed vireo or a yellow-blotched sawback," writes one reviewer, "you will literally never forget what it looks like." The series includes not only the *Field Guide to the Birds Coloring Book*, but equivalent coloring *Guides* to Butterflies, Dinosaurs, Fishes, Forests, Mammals, Reptiles, Seashores, Shells, and Wildflowers. Each costs $4.20 from the Nature Press, 40 West Spruce Street, Columbus, OH 43215-9300; (800) 532-6837.

For the truly advanced colorer, Coloring Concepts, Inc., produces a series of adult coloring books, among them *The Zoology Coloring Book* (L.M. Elson), *The Human Brain Coloring Book* (M.C. Diamond, A.B. Scheibel, and L.M. Elson), *The Marine Biology Coloring Book* (T.M. Niesen), *The Botany Coloring Book* (P. Young), *The Biology Coloring Book* (P. Young),*The Human Evolution Coloring Book* (Adrienne L. Zihlman), and *The Computer Concepts Coloring Book* (B.M. Glotzer). These are essentially college textbooks to color; highly detailed pictures and diagrams are keyed to a definitely adult scientific text. Our middle child, however, got *The Marine Biology Coloring Book* for his ninth birthday, adored it, and spent weeks painstakingly coloring his way coelenterates, echinoderms, crustaceans, mollusks, fish, and marine mammals. The books are published by Harper & Row (NY) and are available through bookstores. Each costs $11.95. Also available from the Anatomical Chart Co., 8221 N. Kimball, Skokie, IL 60076; (800) 621-7500.

Come With Me Science

The "Come With Me" Science Series is the brainchild of an elementary-school science teacher, who first devised these creative units for her own classroom use. The premises here are "that science is not an isolated subject and can be successfully integrated into other curriculum areas: reading, math, spelling, art, language arts, music and rhythm" and "that student involvement can be a key to learning." Music is the real key here; the series strives to teach basic life science concepts through songs.

"Come With Me" Science Units are appropriate for children in grades K-4. Each concentrates on a specific scientific topic. The current list includes "Insects," "Dinosaurs," "Sea Animals," "Birds," "Mammals of the Woods," "Reptiles/Amphibians," "Spiders and Kin," "Arctic Mammals of Alaska," "Zoo/African Mammals," "Farm Animals," "Inside of My Body," "Desert Habitat/Food Chain," and "Animals Through the Seasons." Units include a cassette tape of songs and stories, sets of small and large "teaching pictures," a match game, consisting of 20 pairs of 2-inch pictures, and a teacher's guide, with background information, song lyrics and story texts, suggestions for games and art projects, a lesson plan, and a reproducible student booklet. Complete units cost $17.00 each; individual components can be purchased separately. Additional materials are available for extra enrichment: animal stamps and puppets (including "Cell" and "Germ" puppets to accompany the "Inside of My Body" unit), books and games.

There are also literature supplements for the "Come With Me" units. A suggested companion for the "Sea Animals" unit, for example, is Eric Carle's *House for Hermit Crab*. Activities, for which the lesson plan provides detailed instructions, include making a pop-up hermit crab book, doing a hermit crab dance, making hermit crab drawings, writing a joint hermit crab poem, making a shell chart, and keeping a hermit crab "journal." Literature supplement lesson plans cost $1.50 each. For a catalog, contact Come With Me Science, Science Series Publishing Company, 3550 Durrock Road, Shingle Springs, CA 95682; (916) 677-1545.

Constellation Station

The board is a stylized map of the night sky, which, appropriately, glows in the dark. Players hop rocket-shaped pieces along the playing path learning names and locations of the constellations, plus a lot of miscellaneous star lore, while participating in "interstellar combat." Appropriate for kids aged 10 and up. The game is available from Aristoplay, P.O. Box 7529, Ann Arbor, MI 48107; (800) 634-7738.

3-2-1 Contact

3-2-1 Contact, the magazine, is a publication of the Children's Television Workshop and reflects both the content of the popular kids' science television program of the same name and that of

"Square One TV," the equally well-done children's math program. The magazine, which contains articles on science, nature, and technology, project and experiment suggestions, puzzles, games, and book and computer software reviews, is recommended for kids aged 8-14. An annual subscription costs $16.97. Order from *3-2-1 Contact*, E=MC Square, P.O. Box 51177, Boulder, CO 80321-1177; (800) 678-0613 or (303) 447-9330.

For teachers, there's an associated "Classroom Contact" program for 8-12-year-olds. The program is based on a series of 30 video-cassettes in four different scientific categories: Earth Science (examples include "Crystals: They're Habit Forming," "Fossils: Remains to be Seen," and "Volcanos: Too Hot to Handle"), Life Science (examples include "Digestion: The Inside Story" and "Flying Animals: Winging It"), Physical Science (examples include "Friction: Getting a Grip" and "Motion and Forces: Play Ball"), and Scientific Investigation (examples include "How Do You Know? Collect the Data" and "How Do You Know? Experiment!"). The accompanying Teacher's Guide includes two 40-minute lesson plans for each program, with suggested hands-on activities, cross-curriculum connections, and background information. Teacher's Guides cost $12.00; videocassettes cost $15.00 each. Order from GPN, P.O. Box 80669, Lincoln, NE 68501-0669; (800) 228-4630 or (402) 472-2007.

Cornell Laboratory of Ornithology

The Cornell Laboratory of Ornithology is "an international center for the study, appreciation, and conservation of birds." It sponsors, with the help of thousands of birdwatching volunteers, a number of nationwide bird population studies. It also, in the Lab's "Library of Natural Sounds," has amassed the world's largest collection of bird songs, over 60,000 individual recordings, representing over half of the world's bird species. Enthusiastic amateur birders can join the Cornell Laboratory of Ornithology: a $30 annual membership fee will get you a subscription to *Living Bird*, the Laboratory's quarterly magazine, and to *Birdscope*, a newsletter describing the status of current Laboratory bird research, plus discounts on bird books and supplies from the Lab's retail store and a chance to participate in Lab-sponsored birding tours.

For truly dedicated birders, the Lab offers a "Home Study Course in Bird Biology." The course, the equivalent of a college-level class in ornithology, consists of nine lessons, covering bird anatomy, behavior, development, and relationships with man.

Student progress is monitored through worksheets, which must be filled in upon completion of each lesson and sent back to the Lab for correction. The Home Study Course, which includes a one-year membership in the Lab, costs $165.00. For more information, contact the Cornell Laboratory of Ornithology, 159 Sapsucker Woods Road, Ithaca, NY 14850; (607) 254-2444.

Crayon Power

Crayon Power: The Environmental Action Journal for Concerned Kids gives kids information and news updates on environmental - notably forest - issues, plus suggestions for activities for concerned kids. Some of the recommended activities are hands-on projects: build a tree fort from recycled wood, make a mask based on the face painting patterns used by a Brazilian rainforest tribe, design an "environmental super person," start a tree-planting chain letter. Each issue also contains a number of pre-addressed "Crayon Power letters," to be colored and mailed "to tell powerful grown-ups how you feel about the way they're using the forests." Letters are variously directed to government officials, agencies, and businesses, abroad and at home.

Kids can become "Crayon Warriors" by sending a $25.00 donation to *Crayon Power*, P.O. Box 34, Jersey City, NJ 07303-0034; (201) 433-3026. In return, they receive the two annual issues of *Crayon Power* magazine and a Crayon Warrior T-shirt. Part of the donation money helps pay to print a newspaper written by kids in the rainforests of Brazil.

Creative Learning Systems

The *Transtech* catalog from Creative Learning Systems is a treasure trove of resources for young engineers. Our two youngest sons, builders from birth, are beside themselves over each new issue. "Transtech," explains the catalog publisher, stands for "transparent technology," which is what the company is aiming to create: Transtech products are intended to reveal the inner workings of things, to make "technological concepts and principles crystal-clear." Their books, accordingly, are chosen for their clarity and for the excellence of their illustrations and diagrams - Transtech is into graphics - and their hands-on materials are superb.

The catalog carries the Movit robot kits (among them a sound-sensor, a line-tracker, and a robotic arm), a complete range of Capsela kits ("see-through capsules reveal important electromechanical operations") with accompanying teachers' manuals, Meccano

Erector and Lego Technic kits, and an assortment of Fischertechnik kits, including "Computing," which which kids in grade 7 and up can build a robotic arm, a money-changing machine, a coded-card reader, a turtle, and a CD-player, all operated by (IBM) computer. For the less sophisticated, Fischertechnik offers a large number of simpler kits, such as "Cartech," which includes 230 building pieces, a motor, assorted transmission parts, and a battery holder. Transtech also carries the Ramagon Basic Builder set ("the modelling system used by NASA engineers to simulate future space stations"), and Googolplex, a 348-piece collection of architect-designed geometric shapes with which kid can create "truly spectacular structures - like rockets, space stations, racing cars, and tall futuristic robots." Books are offered on technological topics ranging from the windmill to the laser and the superconductor. For a free catalog, contact Creative Learning Systems, Inc., 16510 Via Esprillo, San Diego, CA 92127; (800) 458-2880.

Cuisenaire Company of America

Though the Cuisenaire Company is more commonly associated with math manipulatives, their catalog also carries a large array of science supplies. Categories include Measurement Materials, Teacher Resource Materials (activity and informational science books), Environmental Science, Microscopes and Magnifiers, Earth Science, Life Science, Physical Science, and Science Equipment and Supplies. The company also offers a line of pre-packaged Cuisenaire Classroom Science (CCS) kits, with enough materials for hands-on investigations by 24-30 elementary- or middle-grade-level students: these include "Balances and Equilibrium," "Water Purification," "Structures" (students build model bridges, towers, and houses), "Inks, Food Colors, and Papers," "Electricity," "Magnets and Compasses," "Liquids and Gases," and "Sound and Tone." Most components, however, are sold separately, for those educating smaller groups. An excellent source for science supplies. For a free catalog, contact Cuisenaire Co. of America, Inc., P.O. Box 5026, White Plains, NY 10602-5026; (800) 237-3142.

Delta Education

Delta Education's *Hands-On Science* catalog provides science resources "for educators who believe that children learn by doing." There's something here for young investigators in practically every scientific discipline: a "Living Wonder Habitat," with accompanying coupon for frogs, hermit crabs, goldfish, or chameleons (your pick); eight different "Anamods," three-dimensional cardboard models of various human organs; a small hand generator ("Show how mechanical energy becomes electrical energy with this amazing device"); a tornado tube kit; a model seismograph; an assortment of launchable rockets; solar system mobiles; acid rain test kits. There is also a large selection of resource books and laboratory supplies. For educators who don't have time to mix and match, Delta sells pre-assembled grade-related "Science Modules," in the fields of physical science, life science, and earth science. Each includes a detailed teacher's guide and all required activity materials, sufficient to keep a class-sized group of investigating kids busy for a month (or more).

Physical Science modules include "Properties," "Investigating Water" (for grades K-1, with included class pool), "States of Matter," "Sink or Float?," "Length and Capacity," "Electrical Circuits," "Looking at Liquids," "Powders and Crystals," "Sound," "Measuring," "Electromagnetism," "Color and Light," "Lenses and Mirrors," and "Simple Machines." This last, appropriate for kids in grades 5-6, has students building wheeled wooden cars, experimenting with pulleys, levers, and inclined planes, and learning about force, work, energy, and friction.

Life Science modules include "From Seed to Plant," "Observing an Aquarium," "Classroom Plants," "Butterflies and Moths," "Plant and Animal Populations" (kids build environments for ants, ladybugs, algae, and others), "Behavior of Mealworms," "Plant and Animal Life Cycles" (kids in grades 3-5 raise pea plants and fruitflies), "Food Chains and Webs" (kids build terraria and add organisms that variously consume, produce, and decompose), "Dinosaur Classification," "Pollution," "Fungi and Molds," "Pond Life," and "You and Your Body."

Earth Science modules include "Sunshine and Shadows," "Finding the Moon," "Soil," "Weather Watching," "Air," "Solar System," "Weather Instruments," "Earth Movements," "Water Cycle," "Rocks and Minerals," "Weather Forecasting," "Erosion," and "Solar Energy."

The modules are aimed at large groups and are, accordingly, expensive; prices range from around $100-$250 each. Teacher's manuals, which cost $9.95 apiece, are available separately. For the home-style educator, a better bet may be the "Elementary Science Kit." This includes a teacher's manual with instructions for 150 different experiments on a wide range of scientific topics: air, water,

light, sound, heat, gravity, motion, machines, magnetism, electricity, aerodynamics, earth, space, weather, plants, and food. The kit
itself, which comes packed in a red toolchest, contains an assortment of high-class scientific equipment: a prism, tuning fork, compass, spring scale, double-scale thermometer, tuning fork, Pyrex
beakers, flask, and test tubes, wooden test tube rack, doorbell and
bell wire, dry-cell battery, light bulb and holder, pulleys, magnets,
and metal ring-stand. And more. Looks to me like an education in
a box and a good buy. The entire set costs $199.95. A smaller Pri-
mary Set (100 experiments for kids in grades 1-3) is available for
$124.95. For a free catalog, contact Delta Education, Inc., P.O. Box
950, Hudson, NH 03051; (800) 442-5444.

Dinosaurs and Things
    This is a board game, playable on two levels: it can be enjoyed
both by older children and by those as young as four. Players hop
pieces along a path of colored squares (patterned with dinosaur
footprints) on the playing board; when they land on a dinosaur
picture square, they must match a cut-out replica of the pictured
animal to a picture of its skeleton. The dinosaur cut-outs are puzzle pieces, fitting into skeleton cut-outs running around the edge
of the playing board. Older kids must also answer dinosaur questions, such as "Apatosaurus used to be called by what name?" The
game costs $22.00, from Aristoplay, P.O. Box 7529, Ann Arbor, MI
48107; (800) 634-7738; or Michael Olaf's Essential Montessori, P.O.
Box 1162, Arcata, CA 95521; (707) 826-1557.

Discover
    Not a children's magazine, but an excellent resource for parents,
educators, and science-minded older kids. *Discover* readers are out
to discover the world of science; feature articles, accordingly, deal
with a wide range of scientific disciplines: physics, biology, chemistry, medicine, astronomy, anthropology, and paleontology. Each
issue includes updates on the latest in science news
("Breakthroughs") and regular columns on astronomy ("Star
Watch"), wildlife biology ("Animal Watch"), basic biology
("Biology Watch"),   medicine ("Vital Signs"), and technology
("Tech Watch.") Topics in the past have included everything from
computer viruses to the Donner Party. Well-written, entertaining,
and worthwhile. An annual subscription to *Discover* (12 issues)
costs $29.95, from *Discover*, P.O. Box 420087, Palm Coast, FL
32142-9944; (800) 829-9132.

Discovery Collections

The Discovery Collections, from Educational Insights, are advertised as "Hands-on Nature Adventures" for kids in grade 3 and up. There are four different Collections available, each containing a large and fascinating assortment of absolutely genuine samples, an identification guide, and an informational project book. "Remarkable Rocks" includes 20 different rocks and minerals, among them pumice, which floats, and is therefore a thrill for young geologists; "Super Seashells" contains 26 "authentic sea life specimens," among them a starfish, a sand dollar, some sea urchin spines, and an array of shells, both univalves and bivalves; "Colossal Fossils" contains 12 different fossil specimens, including a chunk of dinosaur bone, a trilobite, and a piece of petrified wood; and "Genuine Gems" contains 12 gemstones, including amethyst, emerald, and turquoise. The collections are enriching and absorbing tools for young investigators; there's almost endless appeal in a box full of unusual stuff. ("Look! A shark's tooth! How old is it?") Each collection costs $19.95, from Educational Insights, 19560 S. Rancho Way, Dominguez Hills, CA 90220; (800) 933-3277 or (213) 637-2131.

Earth Care Paper

Earth Care Paper offers a fundraising kit for kids who want to raise money and simultaneously encourage recyling. The project involves the sale of recycled paper products: stationery, greeting cards, and gift wrap. For full educational benefit, the company suggests that kids combine the fundraising project with a class program on recycling; there's an available Recycling Study Guide, appropriate for grades K-12 ($3.00). The Earth Care Paper products, which are truly lovely, are available through their catalog, along with a number of resources for environmentally-minded parents, teachers, and children. Among these is a Tin Can Papermaking kit, with which kids can make their own recycled paper: the kit includes screens, blotting materials, and an instruction manual; you provide the tin cans and the waste paper. Also included: an assortment of coloring and activity books based on environmental issues; and Claire Littlejohn's *The Modern Ark: The Endangered Wildlife of Our Planet*, which features, in a pocket inside the front cover, an "Earth Ark" to assemble, with 32 pairs of press-out endangered animals, all in colored cardboard. For a free catalog, contact Earth Care Paper, Inc., P.O. Box 7070, Madison, WI 53707-7070; (608) 223-4000.

Earthword

Earthword is an environmental question-and-answer game, in which players tackle 800 different questions in 16 different categories: Air, Common Sense, Dates and Data, Everyday Things, Forests and Trees, Geography, Industry, Laws and Organizations, Men and Women, Nature and Parks, Oceans and Water, Plants and Animals, Recycling, Science, Transportation, and Your Health. The game is recommended for older kids and adults, since many of the questions are quite specific. Answers, for those of you who don't remember what year the Environmental Protection Agency was formed or how many million tons of waste Americans generate annually, are found on the back of each question card. *Earthword* isn't all easy, but playing it definitely contributes to environmental education. To order, contact Earthword, Inc., 104 Church St., Keyport, NJ 07735; (908) 264-3012.

Ecol-O-Kids

The Ecol-O-Kids - the O is a blue-and-green planet earth - catalog claims to offer "the greatest selection of earth-friendly gifts, books, and educational items for kids available anywhere." They carry environmental information and activity books; environmental videos - including Dr. Seuss's *The Lorax* (a small furry creature who speaks for the trees), and *You Can't Grow Home Again*, a kid-narrated documentary on the rainforests of Costa Rica; assorted environmentally-oriented games, including *A Beautiful Place*, a board game in which players aged 4-8 cooperate to make the world a more beautiful place (by recycling, collecting litter, planting trees); a solar energy kit, with which kids can construct a solar-powered airplane, windmill, watermill, and helicopter; and an inflatable globe showing the homes of the many species of endangered wildlife. For a free catalog ("printed on recycled paper, of course"), contact Ecol-O-Kids, 3146 Shadow Lane, Topeka, KS 66604; (913) 232-4747.

Edmund Scientific Company

The Edmund Scientific Company has been selling high-quality technical equipment for over half a century now. The company is particularly noted for their optical instruments; Edmund Scientific is thus an excellent source for those in the market for good-quality student microscopes. (See Microscopes.) The catalog also offers a large and fascinating assortment of scientific kits, toys, gadgets, and books, targeted at junior scientists. Edmund Scientific sells

Sea Monkeys, Magic Rocks, gyroscopes, and optical illusion cards - and model steam engines, molecular model building kits, and, for $19.95, miniature cloud chambers. For those on a budget, Edmund Scientific carries the "Shoe Box Science" kits, covering eight different topics: Magnets, Prisms, Mirrors, Weather, Illusions, Color, Bi-Metal Discs, and Science Oddities. Each kit costs $3.99 and contains an informational background booklet, suggestions for experimental investigations, and the necessary equipment and materials. And we've all got our eyes on Edmund's "Edible Optics" kit, with which kids cast lenses out of Jello, using an assortment of petri dishes and watch glasses. Students then measure the curvature of their gelatin lenses, and determine refractive indices. For a free 100+-page catalog, contact Edmund Scientific Company, 101 East Gloucester Pike, Barrington, NJ 08007-1380; (609) 573-6260 (customer service) or (609) 547-8880 (orders).

Einstein Anderson

Einstein Anderson - his real name is Adam - is a sixth-grade science whiz, and, in this clever series of books by Seymour Simon, Einstein uses his science expertise to solve puzzles, problems, and mysteries, to trick bullies, to outsmart teenagers, and to confound parents and teachers. There are seven books in the series, all currently available in paperback (Puffin): *Einstein Anderson, Science Sleuth*; *Einstein Anderson Shocks His Friends*; *Einstein Anderson Makes Up for Lost Time*; *Einstein Anderson Tells a Comet's Tale*; *Einstein Anderson Goes to Bat*; *Einstein Anderson Lights Up the Sky*; and *Einstein Anderson Sees Through the Invisible Man*. Each book includes ten separate Einstein stories, each based on a different scientific fact or principle - with a brief pause before Einstein presents his solution to give readers a chance to solve the puzzle on their own. For those concerned about sexism in the sciences, Einstein's best friend, Margaret, has just as much scientific savvy as he does. Available through bookstores.

Environmental Organizations

Kids for a Clean Environment (Kids FACE), P.O. Box 158254, Nashville, TN 37215; Kids for Saving the Earth, P.O. Box 47247, Plymouth, MN 55447-0247, (612) 525-0002; National Audubon Society, 950 Third Ave., New York, NY 10012, (212) 832-3200; National Wildlife Federation, 1400 16th St. NW, Washington, D.C. 20036, (202) 797-6800; The Natural Resources Defense Council, 40 West 20th St., New York, NY 10011; The Nature Conservancy,

1815 N. Lynn St., Arlington, VA 22209, (703) 841-5300; World Wildlife Fund, 1250 24th St., Suite 500, Washington, D.C. 20037, (202) 293-4800.

Eureka!

Eureka! is the publications catalog from the Lawrence Hall of Science (LHS), the public science center on the campus of the University of California at Berkeley. The catalog - which carries teacher's guides, games, kits, videos, and educational software - "represents over 20 years of curriculum development." Many materials are based on exhibits that originally appeared at the Lawrence Hall of Science.

One notable LHS series is titled "Great Explorations in Math and Science" (GEMS). Most GEMS booklets cost between $5.00 and $11.00, are available for children in a range of ages, and cover a large number of scientific and mathematical topics. In *Buzzing a Hive*, for example, kids in grades K-3 study the social behavior of honeybees by making paper bees and beehives, enacting a bee play, and performing bee dances; in *Crime Lab Chemistry*, kids in grades 4-8 use paper chromatography to determine which of several pens was used to write a ransom note.

Another series - the "Outdoor Biology Instructional Strategies" (OBIS) program - is an ecosystem-based collection of science units, aimed at 10-15-year-olds and their families or teachers. OBIS modules consist of sets of related activities; each set costs $17.95. There are some 97 different activities: kids build birdfeeders and investigate bird behavior, study dragonfly perching behavior and make dragonfly decoys, hold a boat race to identify stream currents, determine food-color preferences of bluejays, make plant maps, build fly traps, weave model spider webs, and so on. For a free catalog, contact *Eureka!*, Lawrence Hall of Science, University of California, Berkeley, CA 94720; (415) 642-1016.

Explorabook

Explorabook: A Kids' Science Museum in a Book by John Cassidy and the staff of the San Francisco Exploratorium (Klutz;1991) is a book after a homeschooler's heart. "First of all," begin the introductory directions, "please do not simply read this book. If you own the *Explorabook* for more than a few hours and do not bend or smear any of its pages, nor tear open the agar packets, nor attempt to lose the attached magnet, then you are probably not using it correctly. It is a tool. Please treat it that way." The *Explorabook* is a tough, colorful, 100-page-long tool, equipped with a magnet, a Fresnel lens, a mirror, a piece of diffraction grating, a moiré spinner, a couple of packets of powdered agar for the growing of bacteria and fungi, and a lot of terrific illustrations, information, and instructions for some 50 scientific activities and experiments. With it, kids will learn the hows and whys of anti-gravity machines, rotten apples, star shapes, the Northern lights, airplane flight, and antibiotics. Our new copy is already looking damp and battered, a victim of prolonged and enthusiastic usage. It's irresistible. Available through bookstores; from the Flying Apparatus Catalogue, 2121 Staunton Ct., Palo Alto, CA 94306; (415) 424-0739; or Chinaberry Book Service, 2780 Via Orange Way, Suite B, Spring Valley, CA 91978; (800) 776-2242 (orders, cutomer service), (619) 670-5200.

Exploratorium Quarterly

The *Exploratorium Quarterly* is a publication of the San Francisco Exploratorium, the ultimate in hands-on science museums. The magazine, its staff explains, "explores the science of the everyday world - from the physics of a roller coaster ride to the biology of the dust bunny under your bed; from the mathematics of a musical scale to the structure of a suspension bridge." Each issue covers a single topic in depth, from a number of different viewpoints. Past topics have included bicycles, bridges, the eye, fire, ice, photography, electricity, food, navigation, and sports. An annual subscription (4 issues) costs $18.00; order from the Subscription Department, *Exploratorium Quarterly*, 3601 Lyon Street, San Francisco, CA 94123; (800) 359-9899.

Exploratorium Snackbook

The San Francisco Exploratorium, for those lucky enough to live within visiting range, is the end-all of hands-on science museums: let the kids loose in there long enough and they'll come out with a complete physics education. We managed two visits during our too-brief California days, and the boys were so fascinated they practically fizzed. Now that we're on the east coast, an exorbitant airplane fare away from the Exploratorium, *The Exploratorium Science Snackbook* is the next best thing to being there. The book consists of "Teacher Created Versions of Exploratorium Exhibits": 107 hands-on science projects (referred to as "snacks"), each a simple, inexpensive adaptation of an Exploratorium exhibit or demonstration. Each project is accompanied by diagrams, photographs, explanations of the scientific principle behind the project, suggestions for further activities, and sources of additional information. Sample "snacks" include building an electroscope, a fog chamber, a gas model (for which you'll need a wire-mesh screen box, a handful of pingpong balls, and a hair dryer), pan pipes, an electric motor, and a vortex tube. Recommended for students in grades K-12; users can pick and choose among science projects that range from the simple to the complex. *The Exploratorium Science Snackbook* costs $19.95 and is available from Exploratorium Publications, 3601 Lyon Blvd., San Francisco, CA 94123; (800) 359-9899.

Extremely Weird Series

This fascinating science series is written by Sarah Lovett for John Muir Publications. Each book is 48 pages long, illustrated with terrific full-page color photographs and drawings of unusual animals. The text, short and straightforward, provides both specific information about the pictured "extremely weird" subject and general information about the species as a whole. Titles in the series include *Extremely Weird Bats, Extremely Weird Birds, Extremely Weird Endangered Species, Extremely Weird Fish, Extremely Weird Frogs, Extremely Weird Primates, Extremely Weird Reptiles,* and *Extremely Weird Spiders*. Each book costs $9.95. Available through bookstores or directly from John Muir Publications, P.O. Box 613, Santa Fe, NM 87504; (800) 888-7504 or (505) 982-4078.

Eyewitness/Eyewitness Science

The Eyewitness series can best be described as picture books for big kids: these nonfiction volumes are, at heart, collections of spectacular color photographs. The result is a kid-level cross between *National Geographic* and the encyclopedia; and the effect is superb. Each Eyewitness book covers a single topic, from a variety of creative angles. Titles, of which there are many, include *Bird, Butterfly and Moth, Car, Crystal and Gem, Dinosaur, Flying Machine, Fossil, Insect, Invention, Mammal, Skeleton, Tree, Volcano,* and *Weather*. There's not much in the way of formal text; information is communicated largely through the captions of the truly terrific real-life pictures. "Like a mini-museum between the covers of a book," wrote one reviewer. An off-shoot of the original series, the Eyewitness Science books, dramatically bound in shiny silver, follows the same format: volumes include *Force and Motion, Electricity, Light, Matter, Energy, Chemistry,* and *Evolution*. Published by Alfred A. Knopf and available through bookstores.

The Flying Circus of Physics With Answers   Jearl Walker   (John Wiley & Sons; 1977)

Real-world physics problems, presented as questions, with (brief) answers in the back of the book, and a list of references for those who, crazed by curiosity, want more information. Problems deal with such physical phenomena as squealing chalk, murmuring brooks, seashell roar, superballs, Hula hoops, falling cats, boomerangs, champagne, snowballs, insects splatting on windshields, the Bay of Fundy, dust devils, rainbows, fireflies, ball lightning, water witching, and beaten egg whites. Wonderful. Available through bookstores.

Focus on Science Education

Focus on Science Education, a newsletter for teachers, is a quarterly publication of the California Academy of Sciences. Content includes short articles on current issues in science education, activity suggestions for students, and resource descriptions.   Among the resources available: "Animal Sounds," a teacher's guide and audio cassette combination in which animal sounds - made by frogs, whales, crickets, mosquitoes, songbirds, and penguins - are tied to math, science, art, and literature activities for kids in grades 2-6. An annual subscription to *Focus* costs $5.00; contact *Focus*, California Academy of Sciences, Golden Gate Park, San Francisco, CA 94118; (415) 750-7114.

For Spacious Skies

For Spacious Skies is an educational, non-profit organization aimed at promoting "an awareness of the sky." "We dwell at the bottom of the sky," begins one promotional article, "and how incredibly unaware of it we are." The For Spacious Skies program, the article continues, is intended to teach kids to see the sky as "an inspiration for learning through an interdisciplinary approach." The organization produces an activity guide for teachers and parents, plus cloud charts, in two different sizes, picturing 26 different kinds of clouds. For information, contact For Spacious Skies, P.O. Box 191, 54 Webb St., Lexington, MA 02173; (617) 862-4289.

Gonick, Larry

Larry Gonick, author of the incomparable *Cartoon History of the Universe* (see History and Geography), has not neglected the science-minded: Gonick fans now have available *The Cartoon Guide to Physics* (Larry Gonick and Art Huffman; HarperCollins; 1990), *The*

Cartoon Guide to Genetics (Larry Gonick and Mark Wheelis; Har-perCollins; 1991), and *The Cartoon Guide to the Computer* (Harper-Collins; 1983). None of these is scientifically lightweight: *Genetics*, for example, begins with a boggled shepherd figuring out the con-nection between sex and babies, and proceeds through Mendelian genetics and the DNA helix to gene cloning. *Physics* is divided into two parts: "Mechanics" and "Electricity and Magnetism." Explana-tions of the physical principles involved are delightfully clear; il-lustrations are hysterical; and it's an invaluable resource to have on hand if your kids ask awkward questions about things like su-perconductors.

Larry Gonick, according to his biographical blurb, "is the author or co-author of many books of graphic non-fiction on scientific and historical subjects. A graduate of Harvard in math, he dropped out of graduate school to pursue something really diffi-cult: rendering information in little pictures." Check out his books; you'll be tickled that he did. Available through bookstores or from A Common Reader, 141 Tompkins Ave., Pleasantville, NY 10570-3154; (800) 832-7323 or (914) 747-3388.

Heath Company
The name Heath is synonymous with "home study electronics." The company offers videos, books, computer software, and experi-mental equipment for those bent on learning electronics at home, along with an assortment of build-it-yourself electronic kits. Among these: an infrared motion sensor, an electronic dragonfly (the wings are made of piezoelectric film that changes shape when an electric current is applied), a wireless microphone, and an elec-tronic dice board. Kits come with detailed informational instruc-tions; builders learn as they assemble. For a free catalog, contact Heath Company, P.O. Box 1288, Benton Harbor, MI 49023-1288; (800) 253-0570.

The Herbarium
The Herbarium publishes a green-and-white catalog printed on recycled paper; in it, the company sells rubber stamps, environ-mental education supplies, science games and kits, and botanical supplies. The bulk of their current selection is rubber stamps: en-vironmental message stamps, teacher's stamps (with "Good Work" in three languages), a set of Rebus stamps ("great for classroom puzzles"), lots of animal stamps, and even - my favorites - an amoeba stamp and a paramecium stamp. They'll also make up

your own home-designed rubber stamp: you send in the camera-ready artwork; they turn it into a stamp. To accompany their stamps, the Herbarium sells stamping papers, glitter glue, and ink pads in every imaginable color, from scarlet and silver to smoke blue, topaz, and old rose. For a catalog: The Herbarium Rubber Stamps, P.O. Box 246836, Sacramento, CA 95825; (916) 451-9669.

How Did We Find Out About...? Series   Issac Asimov

This is a reader-friendly series of informational science books for kids in grades 5-8. Each is about 60 pages long, with black-and-white illustrations. Titles in the series include *How Did We Find Out...The Earth is Round?*, *About Electricity?*, *About Numbers?*, *About Dinosaurs?*, *About Germs?*, *About Vitamins?*, *About Comets?*, *About Energy?*, *About Atoms?*, *About Nuclear Power?*, *About Outer Space?*, *About Earthquakes?*, *About Black Holes?*, *About Our Human Roots?*, *About Antarctica?*, *About Oil?*, *About Coal?*, *About Solar Power?*, *About Volcanoes?*, *About Life in the Deep Sea?*, *About the Beginning of Life?*, *About the Universe?*, *About Genes?*, *About Computers?*, *About Robots?*, *About the Atmosphere?*, *About DNA?*, *About the Speed of Light?*, and *About Blood?* The books, published by Walker and Company, are available through libraries and bookstores. By the same author: many science titles, for readers of all ages.

Hubbard Scientific

Hubbard Scientific publishes a 40-page catalog of science education supplies - kits, models, videos, slide sets, and books - for a range of scientific disciplines: astronomy, earth science, meteorology, oceanography, environmental studies, solar energy, physical science, botany, life science, zoology, anatomy and physiology, and health science. There is a series of stereogram books for young geologists: readers wear special glasses that "provide dramatic 3-D images of special select specimens and landscape scenes." There is an assortment of games for young environmentalists: *Environmental Rummy*, the *Food Chain Game*, the *Food Webs Game*, the *Energy Management Game*, and the *Recycling Game*. There is a series of "dissectograms" for young biologists: laminated cards providing detailed step-by-step instructions for laboratory dissections of the frog, earthworm, crayfish, fetal pig, perch, grasshopper, clam, and cat. Also offered are a large number of (mostly) inexpensive kits designed for hands-on investigations in the earth and physical sciences. Included are a "Geologic History Kit," with which kids build strata with clay and recreate geologic processes; an "Evaporation Kit," which uses a single beam balance and sponge weights; an "Astrolabe Kit," and a "Molecular Size and Mass Kit." For a free catalog, contact Hubbard Scientific, Inc., P.O. Box 760, Chippewa Falls, WI 54729; (800) 323-8368.

Insect Lore Products

The Insect Lore people don't pander solely to the young ento-mologist: their black-and-white no-nonsense catalog touts the company as "The Science and Nature Specialists." Accordingly, they carry an assortment of children's science books and kits, among them a cheesemaking kit, a "Wee Sprouts" kit (kids grow five different kinds of edible sprouts), a "Fossil Factory," with which kids make reproductions of rare museum fossils, and an owl pellet kit, which contains three owl pellets; users dissect out and reassemble the skeletal remains of the owl's dinner. A good deal of the catalog is devoted to supplies for bug-lovers: there are live silkworm eggs, praying mantis eggs, and butterfly cultures, ant farms, butterfly-collecting kits, bug viewers, bug books, a build-your-own bug house kit, and a game of *Insect Lotto*, recom-mended for preschoolers through sixth-graders. For a free catalog, contact Insect Lore Products, P.O. Box 1535, Shafter, CA 93263; (800) LIVE-BUG or (805) 746-6047.

Invent America!

Invent America! is a nationwide annual contest "designed to stimulate creativity and develop problem solving skills" in which kids in grades K-8 design and build their own inventions. Inven-tions can be entered in one of several categories: there is a general grade-level category, and seven special categories, each sponsored by a major corporation, in which awards are received for "The In-vention That Best Helps the Environment," "The Most Humanitar-ian Invention," "The Invention That Best Helps People With Spe-cial Needs," "The Best Rube Goldberg Invention," "The Best Household Invention," "The Best Leisure Time Activity Inven-tion," and "The Best Safety Related Invention." Contest applicants must submit a labeled drawing and a written description of their invention, a copy of their inventor's log, detailing their research and development process, and a photograph of a model of their invention. The Invent America! starter kit includes a teacher/coordinator's handbook, which includes a series of lesson plans on development of creative thinking skills and the inventive process, student guidebooks for grades K-3 and 4-8, and a contest entry guide, with all relevant entry forms. To obtain a (free) Invent America! starter kit, send $2.95 for postage and handling to Invent America!, 1505 Powhattan, Alexandria, VA 22314.

Inventors and Scientists

These are rummy games: card decks feature, respectively, 13 famous inventors or scientists, with their portraits and brief descriptions of their accomplishments. Players, aged 7 and up, try to collect matched sets of cards. Famous inventors include Thomas Edison, Alexander Graham Bell, the Wright Brothers, and Benjamin Franklin; famous scientists include Archimedes, Louis Pasteur, and Sir Isaac Newton. Each game costs $6.00, from Aristoplay, P.O. Box 7529, Ann Arbor, MI 48107; (800) 634-7738.

Keepers of the Earth: Native American Stories and Environmental Activities for Children   Michael J. Caduto and Joseph Bruchac
(Fulcrum; 1989)

"If this book were an animal," begins the Introduction, "the stories would be its skeleton and the related activities would be the flesh and sinew on those bones." *Keepers of the Earth* pairs 24 different native American legends with detailed scientific information, discussion questions, and hands-on environmental activities. Legends and their accompanying activities are grouped into categories: "Creation," "Fire," "Earth," "Wind and Weather," "Water," "Sky," "Seasons," "Plants and Animals," "Life, Death, Spirit," and "Unity of Earth." An Inuit legend, "Sedna, the Woman Under the Sea," for example, is followed by a scientific account of the formation and composition of the ocean, a labeled diagram showing the parts of a wave, and an assortment of activity suggestions, each listing goals, procedure, necessary materials, and appropriate age range. The activities include playing "Pelagic Charades," in which players (accurately) pantomime the behaviors of specific sea animals; making a (life-sized) chart comparing ocean animal sizes; experimentally demonstrating the freezing points of fresh and salt water; making a mural of an Inuit village; and - for the very ambitious - stitching up a life-sized seal, whale, or dolphin model out of sheets stuffed with crumpled newspaper. By the same authors: *Keepers of the Animals: Native American Stories and Wildlife Activities for Children.* Available through bookstores.

Kids Discover

This magazine is described as an "easy-to-read, beautifully illustrated, educational guide to the real-life adventures of our world."

Each 20-page issue, targeted at kids aged 5-12, concentrates on a single topic in the fields of science, geography, and history. Issues to date, for example, have coveredTrees, *Bubbles, Airplanes, North and South Poles, Bridges, The Ocean,* and *Stars.* Each issue also contains puzzles, projects, and lists of suggested additional reading. The illustrations - full-color drawings, diagrams, and photographs - are terrific, and the text is both informational and catchy. An annual subscription (10 issues) costs $14.95 from *Kids Discover,* P.O. Box 54206, Boulder, CO 80321-4206; orders: (800) 284-8276.

Lab-Aids, Inc.

Lab-Aids specializes in science kits in the fields of biology and life science, chemistry, earth science, physical science, and math. Sample kits include Basic Blood Typing, Normal Mitosis, Genetic Concepts, Make-a-Gas (Oxygen, Hydrogen, or Carbon Dioxide), Basic Chromatography, Osmosis and Diffusion, Introduction to Radioactivity, Seed Structure and Enzyme Action, Identification of Chemical Reactions, Bacteria Study, Molecular Models (several kinds) and many more. As the titles imply, most are appropriate for upper-level students, in junior high or high school. Most include materials and worksheets for approximately 30 students (working in groups), plus a teacher's instruction manual. For younger kids (grades 4-8), Lab-Aids has designed the Investikits, of which their catalog so far carries four: Investigating Mirrors, Investigating Polyhedral Shapes, Investigating Human Heredity, and Investigating the Sense of Taste. Of these, the Investigating Human Heredity kit ($19.95) looks to be the most economically adaptable to small groups: using it students study selected (readily testable) human traits controlled by a single pair of genes, collecting data from family members, classmates, and friends. Using this, they learn the difference between dominant and recessive genes, phenotype (appearance) and genotype (genetic make-up), and construct a "pedigree diagram" for a single inherited trait in their own family. For a free catalog, contact Lab-Aids, Inc., 17 Colt Court, Ronkonkoma, NY 11779; (516) 737-1133.

Lakeshore Learning Materials

Lakeshore specializes in "literature-based theme packets:" familiar storybooks, plus story-related props, and teacher's activity guides for "extending the story across the curriculum." There are a number of packets with science themes, all appropriate for primary-grade children. Examples include Mary Ann Huberman's *A*

House is a House for Me, with accompanying "houses:" an egg in a nest, a plastic pond (with plastic duck), a web (with spider), a shell, and a miniature house; and Pat Hutchins' *The Wind Blew*, with accompanying pinwheel, wind sock, "balloon copter," pack of plastic "helicopter seeds," and set of small sailboats. Theme packets cost $19.95 each, from Lakeshore Learning Materials, 2695 East Dominguez St., P.O. Box 6261, Carson, CA 90749; (800) 421-5354.

Learning Alternatives

Learning Alternatives styles itself the "Hands-On Company," and the catalog - 60 packed pages of newsprint - features a large and creative range of educational math and science materials. Lots of kits, games, books, and equipment for curious kids. For a free catalog, contact Learning Alternatives, 2370 West 89A Suite 5, Sedona, AZ 86336; (800) HANDS-ON.

Learning Things, Inc.

The Learning Things, Inc., catalog concentrates on science, mathematics, and technology, carrying a large assortment of kits, games, books, and equipment for young investigators. Included are microscopes and magnifiers, dissecting tools and preserved specimens, assorted physics apparatus, chemistry labware, mathematical manipulatives, cameras and photographic supplies, construction sets, and carpentry tools for kids. There's even a "Clockworks Kit," with which kids - with help - can make a large-scale working wooden model of a pendulum clock mechanism. For a catalog send $3.00 to Learning Things, Inc., 68A Broadway, P.O. Box 436, Arlington, MA 02174; (617) 646-0093.

Let's-Read-and-Find-Out Science Series

The *Let's-Read-and-Find-Out* series was originated by Franklyn M. Branley, Astronomer Emeritus and former Chairman of the American Museum-Hayden Planetarium. There are now over 100 books in this informative and well-written series, all about 30 pages long, delightfully illustrated, and generally suitable for kids aged 5-9. Most are available in paperback. Titles in the series include: *Air is All Around You, Ant Cities, Bees and Beelines, The Beginning of the Earth, Bits and Bytes, Comets, Corn is Maize, Danger - Icebergs!, Digging Up Dinosaurs, Dinosaurs Are Different, A Drop of Blood, Ducks Don't Get Wet, Eclipse, Evolution, Fireflies in the Night, Flash, Crash, Rumble, and Roll, Fossils Tell of Long Ago, Germs Make me Sick, Get Ready for Robots!, Glaciers, Gravity is a Mystery, Hear Your Heart, How a Seed Grows, How Many Teeth?, How to Talk to Your Computer, Hurricane Watch, Is There Life in Outer Space?, Journey Into a Black Hole, Look at Your Eye, You and Your Family Tree, Meet the Computer, The Moon Seems to Change, My Five Senses, My Visit to the Dinosaurs, No Measles, No Mumps for Me, Oxygen Keeps You Alive, The Planets in Our Solar System, Rock Collecting, Rockets and Satellites, The Skeleton Inside You, The Sky is Full of Stars, Snow is Falling, Straight Hair, Curly Hair, The Sun: Our Nearest Star, Sunshine Makes the Seasons, A Tree is a Plant, Turtle Talk, Volcanoes, Water for Dinosaurs and You, What Happens to a Hamburger, What Makes Day and Night, What the Moon is Like, Wild and Woolly Mammoths,* and *Your Skin and Mine.* The series is published by Harper & Row; books are available through libraries and bookstores.

The Magic Schoolbus Series   Joanna Cole

The Magic Schoolbus is driven by Ms. Frizzle, the weirdest and most scientifically savvy teacher in school; aboard it, her classful of students, fascinated in spite of themselves, learns a great deal of extremely hands-on science. The Schoolbus shrinks the kids to the size of raindrops and takes them on a tour of the waterworks, reduces them to the size of red blood cells and sends them on a jaunt through the human body, rockets them into outer space, drills them into the center of the earth, and sinks them to the bottom of the ocean floor. Illustrations are funny and imaginative; accurate scientific information is cleverly presented in sidebars, in the form of kid-written science reports. The Magic Schoolbus books are published by Scholastic; titles to date include *The Magic Schoolbus at the Waterworks, The Magic Schoolbus Inside the Earth, The Magic Schoolbus Inside the Human Body, The Magic Schoolbus Lost in the Solar System,* and *The Magic Schoolbus On the Ocean Floor.* Available through bookstores.

Microscopes

The cruel truth about children's microscopes - the kind offered in catalogs for $30 or so - is that they are largely worthless. Parents designing a serious at-home science curriculum should plan to spend $300-$600 or more on a good-quality microscope. Optics on the cheaper models are so poor that the microscopes are of very limited usefulness, and often end up discouraging the small scientists they were meant to inspire.

Helpful hints for microscopists:

1. Don't buy plastic. Plastic cannot support the precision optics required for good microscopy. Any microscope worth its salt is made of metal. A good microscope is also heavy; lightweight models are sensitive to vibration, which makes for disrupted and unreliable viewing.

2. A binocular microscope - two eyepieces - is better than a monocular microscope. They're markedly easier to see through. Standard magnification for eyepieces is 10X (ten-fold).

3. Eyepieces set at a 45 degree angle make for much more comfortable viewing than straight-up-and-down eyepieces, and are highly recommended for those who plan to use their microscopes for any lengthy sitting. For peek-and-run types, it doesn't matter.

3. Most student microscopes have a pair of metal clips that hold the specimen slides in place on the viewing stage; to change the field of view, the slide must be moved manually. This is both awkward and imprecise; the better microscopes have mechanical stages, operated by coaxial controls: that is, pairs of knobs are turned to move the clamped slide back and forth or from side to side.

4. Total magnification of a specimen is determined by multiplying the magnification of the eyepiece (usually 10X) by that of the objective lens. Most "school-grade microscopes" have three objectives, at magnifications of 5X, 15X, and 30X. The highest magnification obtainable with such a microscope is therefore 300X (10X x 30X), which is what scientific firms mean when they advertise a "300X microscope." The more versatile microscopes have interchangeable objectives, which means that you can buy extras as experimental usage demands.

   A total magnification of 50X should give viewers a good look at pond-water microorganisms and insect parts; 150X, protozoa and tissue samples; and 300X, plant and animal cells. For views of bacteria or detailed cell studies, you'll need magnifications of 1000X or more, which requires a 100X oil-immersion objective.

5. Good-quality microscopes have both coarse and fine focusing adjustments, plus "parfocal ability," which means that there's no need to refocus when changing objectives. If you're in focus at 50X, you'll still be in focus at 150X or 300X.

6. A reflecting mirror all by itself is an inadequate light source for microscopy of any substance. Good-quality microscopes either have built-in illuminators beneath the viewing stage, or require independent illuminators, which must be purchased separately.

So where to buy a microscope? Edmund Scientific Company (101 East Gloucester Pike, Barrington, NJ 08007-1380; (609) 547-8880) carries a line of student microscopes, as does Science Kit and Boreal Laboratories (Tonawanda, NY 14150; (800) 828-7777). Science Kit and Boreal Laboratories (see National Teaching Aids, below) makes their catalog available *only* to professional teachers; if you decide to contact them, either be one or have a good story ready. A good source for *used* microscopes is a medical school; medical students are required to purchase their own good-quality microscopes and graduates are often eager to sell.

Even used, however, a good-quality microscope is just plain expensive. One possible solution to the problem is sharing: several families may all chip in to purchase a joint microscope, to be used by a pool of budding scientists. If even that is out of the question, an excellent microscope experience is provided by the Micro-Slide-Viewer (see National Teaching Aids, above), an inexpensive device with which students can view sets of photomicrographs (photographs of specimens taken through a microscope).

Books for Young Microscopists:

Close Up: Microscopic Photos of Everyday Stuff Frank B. Edwards   (Firefly Books; 1992)   A collection of 30 fascinating electron micrographs of such everyday stuff as dustballs, spiders, and breakfast cereal.

Greg's Microscope Millicent Selsam   (Harper & Row; 1963)   An "I Can Read" book about Greg's new microscope and what he does with it.

The Microscope Maxine Kumin   (HarperCollins; 1984)   The rhyming tale of Anton van Leeuwenhoek, inventor of the microscope.

Microscopes and Telescopes Fred Wilkin   (Childrens Press; 1983)
   A clear explanation of the workings of microscopes and telescopes, illustrated with big full-color photographs.

Small Worlds Close Up Lisa Grillone and Joseph Gennaro (Crown Publishers; 1978)   A collection of wonderful photomicrographs of all manner of things: salt, asbestos, a pin, the undersurface of a leaf, dandelion fluff, a fruit fly's foot, a fish scale, a bee sting, a human hair.

The Smallest Life Around Us Lucia Anderson   (Crown Publishers; 1978)   A simple account of the world of microbes, with instructions for eight experiments in which kids grow some of their own.

Mineral of the Month Club

Mineral-of-the-Month Club members receive each month a new and interesting mineral specimen, a fact sheet of information about the current specimen, and - often - suggestions for simple experiments that can be performed to demonstrate various properties of the mineral. Club Bulletins connect young geologists with like-minded penpals or with collectors eager to trade rocks, minerals, and fossils. A one-year Club membership costs $49.95; three- and six-month memberships are also available. For membership forms or additional information, send a self-addressed, stamped envelope to Mineral of the Month, Box 487, Yucaipa, CA 92399.

Modern School Supplies

Modern's "Technology Education Catalog" contains a large and highly professional assortment of supplies for young scientists and engineers. Notable among these are the Fischertechnik kits, a series of precision-engineered German-made construction kits designed to teach the principles of electricity, mechanics, and pneumatics. More advanced kits, designed to interface with a computer, introduce students to computing, sensor technology, and robotics. Also available: the Schuco Electronic Starter Lab, for introducing kids in grade 5 and up to the basics of electronics; the Schuco Physics Kits, which allow kids in grades 7 and up to perform 200 hands-on physics experiments in the fields of electricity, magnetism, electrostatics, aerodynamics, solar techology, and optics; and the Capsela Inventor Set, with which kids in grades 3-7 can build 30 different motorized models, covering the physical concepts of energy changes, electric circuits, motion energy, chain drive, gears, friction, traction, and the inclined plane. And much more. For a free catalog, contact Modern School Supplies, Inc., P.O. Box 958, Hartford, CT 06143; (800) 243-2329 or (203) 243-9565.

National Science Teachers Association

Membership in the National Science Teachers Association, should you decide to designate yourself a Science Teacher, costs

$50 a year and includes a subscription to the Association's bi-monthly newsletter, *NSTA Reports!*, "a "timely source of news on all issues of interest to science teachers of all levels," a subscription to a teaching journal of your choice, access to miscellaneous work-shops, conventions, and award programs, and a nice catalog of science publications. The Association offers four different teaching journals to card-carrying members: *Science and Children* is appro-priate for teachers of kids in grades K-8; *Science Scope* for grades 5-9; *The Science Teacher* for grades 7-12; and the *Journal of College Science Teaching* for teachers of college-level students. Each journal in-cludes ideas for classroom activities and experiments, teaching tips, current research news, and discussions of educational theo-ries and techniques relevant to science curricula.

The publications catalog - available for free, by request - con-tains a wide range of science activity books and kits. Included, for example, are all of the Smithsonian Institution's Science Activity Books: there are three of these, suitable for kids in grades K-6. Ex-periments include making home movies, ginger ale, a solar cooker capable of roasting marshmallows, and paper from grass clip-pings. There's also a long list of short books from Berkeley's Law-rence Hall of Science, ranging from *Hide a Butterfly* for pre-schoolers, in which kids make a mural of a blooming meadow, build butterfly and bird puppets, and put on a butterfly play, to *Experimenting With Model Rockets* for older kids. There's a "Fossil Activity Kit," which contains 15 different kinds of fossils, a "Stu-dent Owl Pellet Kit," (three barn owl pellets, dissecting tools, and study guide), and a "Tapes of the Night Sky" set, with which kids learn to identify constellations using star maps and audio cas-settes ("four half-hour guided tours of the heavens"). For a publi-cations catalog and membership information, contact the National Science Teachers Association, 1742 Connecticut Avenue NW, Washington, D.C. 20009-1171; (202) 328-5200.

National Teaching Aids, Inc.

National Teaching Aids offers "over 300 great low-cost teaching aids for science and health." Its prime product - and a definite sci-entific winner - is the Micro-Slide-Viewer, a nine-inch-tall, plastic, roughly microscope-shaped device, suitable for the viewing of Mi-croslides. The Micro-Slide-Viewer, however, is *not* a microscope, and the Microslides are not conventional microscope slides. Mi-croslides are strips of photomicrographs - "8 related 35 mm imag-es as photographed through a microscope." Each strip comes tucked in a protective pocket in an informational booklet, which briefly explains each photographed specimen. Well over a hundred different Microslide sets in several categories are available, appropriate for students of all ages. Categories include "Bacteria, Protozoa, and Viruses," "Plants and Fungi," "Human Biology and Health," "Reproduction, Genetics, and Heredity," and "The Biosphere." The "Introduction to the World of the Microscope" Microslide set, for example, includes photomicrographs of a printed letter "e," pollen, hydra, decay-causing bacteria, blood cells, shells of ancient animals, an earthworm cross-section, and a virus sample; the "Cells of Your Body" set includes photomicrographs of cheek cells, blood cells, lymph gland cells, bone cells, voluntary and involuntary muscle cells, nerve cells, and gland cells; the "Marine Biology" set includes photomicrographs of phytoplankton and zooplankton, sponge spicules, coral polyps, a cross-section of a jellyfish tentacle, starfish, featherworms, and shark scales. Also available: Microslide sets for Earth Science, covering such topics as "The Elements," "Minerals and Crystal Systems," and "Earth History;" and Astroslides, for young astronomers, featuring 35 mm images as photographed through a telescope or spectroscope. Photomicrographs in the Microslide sets are clear, colorful, and exquisite; and the viewing is foolproof: even the youngest scientists can get the "slides" into place and focus the Micro-Slide-Viewer. Ordinary room light is perfectly adequate for viewing; the Viewer features a white reflector that substitutes for that annoying little mirror that is supposed to provide light to inexpensive children's microscopes. This is an excellent microscope experience at a budget price: Micro-Slide-Viewers cost $7.50 each; Microslide sets, $5.00. For a free catalog, contact National Teaching Aids, Inc., 1845 Highland Ave., New Hyde Park, NY 11040; (515) 326-2555.

Nature's Blox

Parents Magazine picked this toy as "Best of the Year" in 1990. "These blocks," reads the box, "challenge the laws of nature." Nature Blox are appealingly fat rectangles, sixteen blocks to a package. The trick is that some of the blocks are internally weighted: there are four center-weighted blocks; four offset-weighted blocks, with the weight anchored solidly at one end; four sliding-weighted blocks, in which an unanchored weight shifts from one end of the block to the other when tipped; and four featherweight blocks, which contain no weights at all. The blocks can be stacked and balanced to form bizarre gravity-defying structures. A learning experience for kids aged 5 and up. Nature's Blox cost $29.95 and are available through toy stores.

The Nature Company

The Nature Company has stores nationwide, and among all the handsome gifts and supplies for nature-loving adults, the Company also carries an innovative assortment of science books, kits, and resources for kits. There are bluebird and bug houses to build; a 3-D rainforest theatre, complete with punch-out animals and three scripts; animal puzzles; kids' binoculars; and a cardboard zoetrope ("the earliest form of moving pictures"). Images are mounted inside a wheel with slits in the sides: spin the wheel, peer through the slits, and the images will appear to move. The Nature Company also sells a superb kids' video - *Aunt Merriwether's Adventures in the Backyard* - an "ant's eye-view journey through the backyard," in which kids, through ultra close-up photography, come face to face with ants, crickets, rabbits, hummingbirds, and spiders. For a catalog, contact The Nature Company, Catalog Division, P.O. Box 188, Florence, KY 41022; (800) 227-1114.

Nature Press

The Nature Press is an excellent source for field guides for both children and adults. For just-beginning naturalists, Nature Press offers the *Peterson First Guides*, to Astronomy, Birds, Mammals, Dinosaurs, and Wildflowers; these are abbreviated versions of the adult books, easy to handle, and attractively illustrated. The catalog also carries the Peterson Field Guide Coloring Books (see Coloring Books above). For a free list of publications, contact The Nature Press, 40 West Spruce St., Columbus, OH 43215-9300; (800) 532-6837.

NatureScope

The *NatureScope* activity book collection is a creative educational series published by the National Wildlife Federation. The books, 60-80 pages long, each contain a wealth of scientific information, activities variously targeted at kids in grades K-2, 3-5, and 6-8, an assortment of "Copycat" pages for student use, and a bibliography. These books are thorough. Though the (age-categorized) activities are aimed at a range of age groups, there's enough information to hold the interest of much older students. The astronomy activity book, for example, both suggests teaching little kids the names of the planets through a song, sung to the tune of "When

Johnny Comes Marching Home," and provides older kids with an explanation of the electromagnetic spectrum and the use of spectroscopy to determine the chemical composition of stars. Titles in the series include *Astronomy Adventures, Wild About Weather, Diving into Oceans, Discovering Deserts, Wading into Wetlands, Geology: The Active Earth, Endangered Species: Wild and Rare, Pollution: Problems and Solutions, Digging Into Dinosaurs, Birds, Birds, Birds, Amazing Mammals, Let's Hear it for Herps!,* and *Incredible Insects.* The books cost $7.95 apiece, from The National Wildlife Federation, 1400 16th St. NW, Washington, D.C. 20036-2266; (800) 432-6564.

The New Scientist

This is *the* best reader-friendly science journal on the market today. It's published weekly, in Great Britain, and includes short overviews of science in the news, long (and creatively illustrated) feature articles on selected science topics by experts notable for their ability to write for the general public, and science book reviews. Periodically it includes an "Inside Science" supplement, a "comprehensive and authoritative guide" to a specific subject area. These are available separately in sets, called "Fact Packs;" topics covered to date have included the Big Bang, the greenhouse effect, acid rain, gravitational theory, the nervous system, the immune system, robotics, lasers, the structure of the earth, the life of a star, and the ozone layer. A one-year subscription (51 issues) costs $140, from Quadrant Subscription Services Ltd., P.O. Box 7247-8841, Philadelphia, PA 19170-8841.

New True Books

This is an excellent series of 48-page nonfiction paperbacks, featuring a simple informational text in largish print, and lavishly illustrated with terrific full-color photographs. There are nearly 200 titles in the New True Books series, covering a wide range of fields. Titles of particular interest to young scientists include *African Animals, Airplanes, Animal Homes, Animals of Sea and Shore, The Arctic, Aquariums and Terrariums, Archaeology, Astronauts, Astronomy, Automobiles, Baby Animals, Bacteria and Viruses, Bears, Birds We Know, Birds of Prey, Bridges, Butterflies and Moths, Cats, Cells and Tissues, Comets, Meteors, and Asteroids, Computers, Dangerous Fish, Deserts, Dinosaurs, Dogs, Earthquakes, Elephants, Endangered Animals, Energy, Experiments with Electricity, Experiments with Heat, Experiments with Light, Experiments with Magnets, Fossils, Gerbil Pets and Other Small Rodents, Glaciers, Halley's Comet, Health, Helicopters,*

Horses, Insects, Jungles, Kennedy Space Center, Lasers, Machines, Marshes and Swamps, Matter, Microcomputers at Work, Microscopes and Telescopes, Monkeys and Apes, Moon Flights, Moon, Sun, and Stars, Mountains, Nutrition, Oceans, Penguins, Pets, Photography, Plant Experiments, Plants We Know, Plants without Seeds, Pond Life, Prairies and Grasslands, Predators, Reptiles, Rivers, Robots, Rocks and Minerals, Satellites, Science Experiments, Seasons, Skylab, Snakes, Solar Energy at Work, Sound Experiments, Space, Space Colonies, Space Lab, Space Shuttles, Spiders, Storms, Submarines, Television, Trains, Trees, Tropical Fish, Trucks, Underground Life, Volcanoes, Voyager Space Probes, Weather Experiments, Weeds and Wild Flowers, Whales and Other Sea Mammals, Work Animals, Your Brain and Nervous System, Your Five Senses, Your Heart and Blood, and *Your Skeleton and Skin.* The books cost $4.95 each, from Children's Press, 5440 North Cumberland Avenue, Chicago, IL 60656; (800) 621-1115 or (312) 693-0800.

Newton's Apple

This is a series of science videos based on the Emmy-winning public television program of the same name. There are six tapes in the series, each covering an interesting and unusual range of science questions. Volume 1 includes dinosaurs, bulletproof glass, sharks, and whales; Volume 2 the science of kids' everyday questions ("Why is the sky blue?" "Why do houses creak?"); Volume 3, spiders, mummies, helium, and tigers; Volume 4, cold remedies, penguins, and lie detectors; Volume 5, Einstein, cooking chemistry, bears, and muscles and bones; and Volume 6, tornadoes, plastic surgery, and high-speed bicycles. And more. Videotapes cost $19.99 from Movies Unlimited, 6736 Castor Ave, Philadelphia, PA 19149; (800) 523-0823 (orders) or (215) 722-8398 (information).

Odyssey

Odyssey, a kids' science and technology magazine, is a publication of Cobblestone Publishing, Inc. (see History and Geography for other Cobblestone magazines). Each issue focuses on a single theme, and includes related fiction and non-fiction articles, a monthly star chart and sky observation activity, books reviews, science news, and assorted puzzles and projects for young science nuts. Among the *Odyssey* themes to date: "Careers," "Famous Recent Discoveries," "Space Junk," "Robots," and "Space Colonies." A sixth-grade teacher writes: "I look for current, intelligent material to bind my curriculum to real life. *Odyssey* is ideal. It offers literature, folklore, art, pure science, and hands-on projects along the theme of earth science, drawing in my writers and artists as well as my scientists and technicians." Single copies of Odyssey cost $3.95; an annual subscription (10 issues), $19.95. To order, contact Cobblestone Publishing, Inc., 7 School Street, Peterborough, NH 03458; (800) 821-0115, fax: (603) 924-7380.

Oh! ZONE

Oh! ZONE - "A Journal By Youth of Environmental News, Art, and Opinion" - is published quarterly by a group of environmentally concerned (and active) intermediate, high school, and college students. Articles include interviews with prominent environmentalists, reports on environmental projects and progress, and pieces on such prominent environmental concerns as pollution, wilderness preservation, and endangered species of plants and animals. An annual *Oh! ZONE* membership, which includes subscriptions to the magazine and the member newsletter, plus a packet of information about environmental activism on the local level, costs $12.95, from *Oh! ZONE*, 420 E. Hewitt Ave., Marquette, MI 49855-9910.

Opportunities for Learning, Inc.

The *Discover Science!* catalog from Opportunities for Learning, Inc., contains nearly 50 pages of multimedia materials - books, workbooks, kits, models, videos, and computer software - for kids from elementary through secondary school. Included are materials for General Science, Anatomy and Physiology, Biology, Botany, Genetics, Chemistry, Physics, Earth Science, Ecology, Astronomy, and Logic and Thinking Skills. For elementary students, there's a science education in a box, the "Elementary Science Kit." This consists of an illustrated teacher's manual detailing over 150 different experiments on air, water, light, sound, heat, fire, motion, gravity, simple machines, magnetism, electricty, aerodynamics, earth, space, weather, plants, and food, and 70-plus pieces of science equipment, including a double-scale thermometer, doorbell, scale, equilateral glass prism, pulleys, light bulbs and bulb holder, tripod magnifier, beakers, flasks, test tubes and rack, and a ring stand. Total cost: $225.95. (Also see Delta Education.) The catalog also carries a series of workbooks for the "textbook-shy:" the books, organized like newsstand magazines, include articles, activities, and games; the lessons are especially designed "for teachers without a science background." There are two sets of these workbooks: *Project Earth: Science Made Practical* includes books on "The Earth," "Animals," "The Ocean," "The Weather," and "The Solar System;" *Project Explore: Science Made Practical* includes books on "The Human Body," "The Senses," "Practical Chemistry," "Energy," "Motion," and "How Things Work." Each set of six student workbooks costs $12.50; the accompanying teacher's manual, $23.50.

For older students, the majority of the materials are either on videotape or computer: there are, for example, computer programs for physics and chemistry lab simulations, a "Jr. High Life Science" series, 12 titles on 6 disks, ("Animals," "Bones, Muscle, and Skin," "Cell Theory," "Circulation and Respiration," "Control Systems," "Digestive System," "Diversity of Life," "Ecosystems," "Heredity," "Plants," "Reproduction and Growth," and "Vertebrates"), a "General Physics Series," 12 titles on 12 disks ("Vectors and Graphing," "Statics," "Motion," "Conservation Laws," "Circular Motion," "Thermodynamics," "Electricity and Magnetism," "Optics," "Atomic Physics," "Solar System," "Stellar Astronomy," and "Physics Gems"), an "Earth Science Series," 5 titles on 5 disks ("Astronomy," "Geology 1 and 2," "Meteorology," and "Oceanography"), and an "Astronomy Series," 4 titles on 4 disks ("Eclipses and Phases of the Sun and Moon," "The Solar System," "Time and Seasons," and "Telescopes"). For a free catalog, contact Opportunities for Learning, Inc., 941 Hickory Lane, P.O. Box 8103, Mansfield, OH 44901-8103; (419) 589-1700.

Orion Telescope Center
An excellent resource for the serious hands-on astronomer. While the catalog does carry a small selection of astronomy books and computer software for stargazers, Orion's prime products are telescopes and binoculars (plus accessories), of good to excellent quality, and ranging in price from the moderate to the major investment. For a free catalog, contact the Orion Telescope Center, 2450 17th Ave., P.O. Box 1158, Santa Cruz, CA 95061-1158; (800) 447-1001.

OWL and *Chickadee*
OWL, "The Discovery Magazine for Children," is targeted at children aged 8 and older; its sister magazine, *Chickadee*, is intended for younger kids, up to age 9. Both are publications of the Young Naturalist Foundation, a non-profit organization whose aim is "to interest children in their environment and the world

around them." The Foundation also produces the popular children's science-and-nature television program, OWL/TV.

OWL features interviews with naturalists and scientists, non-fiction feature articles, beautifully illustrated with color photographs, and games, jokes, puzzles, and contests for young nature-lovers. There's also a a comic-strip feature, "Mighty Mites Adventures," about a trio of kids who can shrink to any size they wish for close-up nature adventures. Subscriptions to either *OWL* or *Chickadee* cost $14.95 (10 issues) annually; to order, contact the Subscriber Service Dept. *Chickadee* and *OWL* Magazines, 255 Great Owl Ave., Buffalo, NY 14207-3082.

Poliopticon

This is an excellent optical kit for children; using it, kids can assemble a microscope, kaleidoscope, periscope, binoculars, telescope (and more) from a series of sturdy bright-yellow tubes, clamps, lenses, and eyepieces. An instruction manual, with lists of suggested activities and experiments, is included. It's attractive, educational, and irresistible; no child can fool around with this for long without acquiring a healthy knowledge of the world of optics. The complete kit costs $49.95; available from Edmund Scientific Company, 101 East Gloucester Pike, Barrington, NJ 08007-1380; (609) 547-8880.

Quantum

Quantum, "The Student Magazine of Math and Science," is a publication of the National Science Teachers Association, along with the Quantum Bureau of the Russian Academy of Sciences, the American Association of Physics Teachers, and the National Council of Teachers of Mathematics. This exalted combination turns out an excellent 80+-page magazine for high-school students, crammed with non-fiction articles detailing real-world science and math, and mathematical and scientific puzzles, problems, and contests. Topics covered in our sample copy included the mathematics of political elections, the use of physics to uncover archaeological frauds, and tactile microscopes, which "feel" with light. This is unquestionably a magazine for the upper-level kid: the math and physics articles - sprinkled with equations - are aimed at the mathematically advanced. Single issues of *Quantum* cost $5.00; a yearly subscription (6 issues), $18.00. To order, contact *Quantum*, Springer-Verlag New York, Inc., 175 Fifth Avenue, New York, NY 10010; (800) SPRINGER or (212) 460-1500.

Question and Answer Books

This series of skinny (32-page) paperbacks explains science basics to elementary-aged kids. Subjects are presented in short question-and-answer format; explanations are appealingly reader-friendly, with a scattering of related hands-on demonstrations and experiments. Titles in the series include *Air, Air, Air, All About Animal Migrations, All About Deserts, All About Islands, All About the Moon, All About Mountains and Volcanoes, All About Ponds, All About Rivers, All About Sound, All About Stars, All About Trees, Amazing Magnets, Amazing World of Animals, Amazing World of Plants, Discovering Fossils, Our Amazing Ocean, Our Amazing Sun, Our Wonderful Seasons, Our Wonderful Solar System, Rocks and Minerals, Wonders of Energy, Wonders of Water,* and *World of Weather.* Available in sets (8 books for $14.95) from Troll Learn & Play, 100 Corporate Drive, Mahwah, NJ 07430; (800) 247-6106 (orders) or (800) 942-0781 (information). Individual books are available for $2.50 apiece from Brook Farm Books, P.O. Box 246, Bridgewater, ME 04735.

Ranger Rick and *Your Big Backyard*

This pair of attractive full-color kids' nature magazines is published by the National Wildlife Federation. *Ranger Rick* is targeted at 6-12-year-olds; *Your Big Backyard* at preschoolers, aged 3-5. Both are illustrated with wonderful photographs. Text in *Your Big Backyard* is large-print and very simple, for the very small; *Ranger Rick* includes short informative articles on wildlife biology and environmental science topics, plus interviews with naturalists, catchy bits of nature trivia ("In 1937, a tornado lifted a train engine, turned it around, and set it back down on some nearby railroad tracks"), nature crafts and puzzles, and a short story (with a message) starring Ranger Rick Raccoon and his gang of woodland buddies. An annual subscription to *Ranger Rick* costs $15.00, and to *Your Big Backyard*, $12.00. Order from the National Wildlife Federation, 1400 Sixteenth St., N.W., Washington, D.C., 20078-6420; (800) 432-6564.

Rock and Gem

Ostensibly an adult magazine, but there's something here for rock hounds of all ages: nonfiction articles, color photographs, a national schedule of rock-and-mineral shows, a "Craftsman of the Month" feature, and sources for specimens, both where to dig your own and where to buy. (*Rock and Gem* readers can buy lots of inexpensive geological goodies, from Australian opals and gold nuggets to petrified wood, fossil shark teeth, and meteorites.)

This publication is aimed toward the active collector: articles in our sample issue included accounts of digging for 50-million-year-old fossil fish in Wyoming (with kids) and of unearthing geodes in California; and pieces on teaching children about minerals, hobby fossil-collecting, the minerals of Mexico and Minnesota, Arizona's Petrified Forest National Park, and mining art. An annual subscription costs $15.00 (12 issues); order from *Rock and Gem*, P.O. Box 6925, Ventura, CA 93006-9878; (805) 644-3824.

Running Press

Running Press publishes a number of terrific kits for active learners. With the *Dinosaur Hunter's Kit*, young paleontologists unearth a dinosaur fossil replica from a slab of soft clay; with the *Gem Hunter's Kit*, young geologists dig up and identify eight different gemstones; or, with the *Geode Kit*, grow their own simulated geode; and with the *Weather Tracker's Kit*, budding meteorologists assemble a snap-together plastic weather station, which includes a rain gauge, thermometer, wind-speed indicator, and wind-chill chart. There's also a cloud chart, with illustrations of 37 different cloud varieties, for skywatchers. The station is designed to be fastened to a fence post, wall, or railing; attachments (screws and a metal arm) are provided. Each kit is accompanied by an informational handbook, which provides both instructions and background information. Kits costs $14.95-$16.95, can be obtained through bookstores or ordered directly from Running Press, 125 South Twenty-second St., Philadelphia, PA 19103; (215) 567-5080, (800) 345-5359 (orders).

Save the World

"The Most Important Game You Will Ever Play," reads the cover. The playing board is a map of the world; playing pieces are stand-up cardboard photographs of endangered animals. Players move about the board answering questions on ecological issues, including endangered species, forests, water, and atmosphere. Appropriate for ages 8 and up. *Save the World* costs $24.50 from Earth Care Paper, P.O. Box 7070, Madison, WI 53707; (608) 223-4000.

Science-by-Mail

"What," asks the introductory brochure, "uses balloons, marbles, thermometers, motors, mirrors, solar cells, and ping-pong balls, includes pen pal scientists, lots of fun things to do and fits in a mailbox?" The answer is Science-by-Mail, "an international pen pal program that brings together children and scientists in science challenge problem solving." Participants receive three different science challenge packets per year (in December, February, and April), along with the name and address of a scientist penpal, to whom they send their experimental results and solutions. The packets look terrific: each concentrates on a specific scientific topic, and includes a collection of simple equipment, a 30 (or so)-page activities booklet, listing a series of related experiments, a "Big Challenge" problem, to be solved individually or cooperatively, and a suggested reading list. Our sample was titled "Evergreen Systems: A Science-by-Mail Challenge About the Environment." Listed experiments included "Plant a Tree" (seeds included), "Air Pollution Monitor" (kids make and use one), "Insulation," "Greenhouse Effect," "Lights and Energy," and "Recycle Paper." For the grand finale, in the "Big Challenge," students design an Evergreen Systems Town on the enclosed contour map, making informed decisions on construction materials, energy sources, recycling, and population distribution.

The program is intended for children in grades 4-9 (unsupervised), but younger kids should be able to manage just fine, with a spot of help here and there. There are Science-by-Mail chapters all over the country; to find the one closest to you, contact the Science-by-Mail National Office, Museum of Science, Science Park, Boston, MA 02114; (800) 729-3300 or (617) 589-0437. A family membership (limit: 4 kids) costs an annual $40.00.

Science Is...   Susan V. Bosak   (Scholastic; 1991)

The subtitle (almost) says it all: *Science Is...* is a 500+-page "source book of fascinating facts, projects and activities," targeted at kids aged 6-14. Subject areas covered include "Discovering Science," "Matter and Energy," "Humans," "The Environment," "Rocks," "Plants," "Living Creatures," "Weather," "The Heavens," and "Applying Science." Projects and activities under each subject area are further categorized as "Quickies" (next to nothing in the way of necessary materials), "Make Time" (require assorted inexpensive materials and some preparation and planning), or "One Leads to Another" (a series of challenging related activities that form an entire study unit). The book functions both as an intriguingly informational text and a how-to instruction manual, thickly spattered with diagrams, charts, clever little illustrations, stories, and truly fascinating facts: readers learn, for example, that Sir Thomas Dewar made a bubble that lasted 108 days, that the South African hercules beetle is as big as a mouse, that honeybees have taste buds on their feet, and that the largest seeds in the world come from a palm tree and are as big as beachballs. Also included: a detailed 18-page bibliography of additional resources. A real winner. Available through bookstores; from Firefly Books, 250 Sparks Avenue, Willowdale, Ontario M2H 2S4, Canada; (800) 387-5085 or (416) 499-8412; or from Scholastic, Inc., P.O. Box 7502, Jefferson City, MO 65102; (800) 325-6149.

Science Kit and Boreal Laboratories

Science Kit and Boreal Laboratories publishes a massive, full-color, 900+-page catalog for science teachers. By science teachers, they mean *teachers*; the catalog is not available to the general public. Interested home educators should keep this fine point in mind. The catalog offers a complete line of educational scientific materials: kits, laboratory apparatus and manuals, models, charts, biological specimens, geological samples, chemicals, books, and computer software. Kits are generally designed for groups of 20-30 students. To obtain a catalog, contact Science Kit and Boreal Laboratories, 777 East Park Drive, Tonawanda, NY 14150-6784; (716) 874-6020, or (800) 828-7777.

Science Through Children's Literature   Carol M. Butzow and John W. Butzow   (Teacher Ideas Press; 1989)

Science Through Children's Literature is an integrated program targeted at children in grades K-3, in which fiction books serve as "springboards to science." Over 30 well-known children's book are used for this purpose, roughly grouped into three scientific categories: Life Science, Earth and Space Science, and Physical Science. For each book is listed a selection of related science activities.

One of the fiction choices, for example, is Leo Lionni's *Swimmy*, the story of a zippy little black fish who is left alone in the sea after the rest of his school is eaten by a hungry tuna. Eventually he joins up with a school of red fish and together they come up with a clever way of protecting themselves from potential predators. Suggested associated science activities include looking at fish scales under a microscope, making a model water column showing the sea life appropriate to each depth, studying a selection of non-fish sea creatures and making a set of "Sea Creature" rummy cards, studying food chains, visiting an aquarium and a fish market, making fish prints, learning names for animal groups ("school of fish," "gaggle of geese," "pride of lions"), listening to Claude Debussy's "La Mer," and so on. Instructions are included for making a Japanese fish kite.

Activities for Alice and Martin Provensen's *The Glorious Flight*, the delightfully illustrated story of the first successful flight across the English Channel, include a demonstration of Bernoulli's Principle, building model paper airplanes and wooden gliders, making an aviation timeline, studying selected early aviators, and learning about wind currents. And much more. The book is available through bookstores; from Delta Education, Inc., P.O. Box 950, Hudson, NH 03501; (800) 442-5444; or from Teacher Ideas Press, P.O. Box 6633, Englewood, CO 80155-6633; (800) 237-6124.

Science Weekly

Science Weekly - "Put a little science in your week" - is a weekly 4-page science booklet, written at 7 different levels, for kids in kindergarten through grade 8. Each issue includes an illustrated page of information on an interesting scientific topic, followed by three pages of assorted written exercises, activities, and hands-on projects. These include a vocabulary quiz, a math problem, a writing project, a single-experiment "Weekly Lab," and a couple of science-oriented puzzles. A one-year subscription to *Science Weekly* costs $8.95; a one-semester subscription, $6.50. (If you order more than 20 subscriptions, there's a discount.) To order, contact Science Weekly Subscription Department, P.O. Box 70154-S, Washington, D.C. 20088-0154; (301) 680-8804.

Scienceland

Scienceland looks like a magazine, but its publishers describe it as a "monthly science book," recommended for children of pre-school age through third grade. Issues are designed as science picture books: each has a single theme, such as "All About Dragonflies," "All About Pinecones," "Report on Horns," or "Rabbits." Text is brief and big-print; illustrations - mostly photographs - are large, colorful, and lavish. Taken by themselves, I'd peg the *Scienceland* books as appropriate for 4-6-year-olds.

There is an option, however, for an accompanying teacher's manual, a monthly 25-page booklet, which includes a good deal of additional information about the current topic, lists of possible discussion or research questions, and suggestions for related activities or projects. This supplement can considerably extend *Science-*

land's effective age range. An annual subscription to *Scienceland* (8 issues) costs $19.95; subscriptions to the accompanying teacher's manual, $15.00. Single back issues and manuals are also available. To order: Scienceland, Inc., 501 Fifth Ave., Suite 2108, New York, NY 10017-6165; (212) 490-2180, fax: (212) 490-2187 (pause 23).

Scientific American

Scientific American, over the past years, has become increasingly inaccessible to the general public; articles are generally by professional scientists for professional scientists. It remains, however, a good source of information for advanced science students and teachers; and feature sections, "Science and the Citizen," "Science and Business," "50 and 100 Years Ago," and "The Amateur Scientist." retain their public appeal. Science-minded educators should at least keep an eye out for the December issue, which routinely includes an excellent collection of reviews of the year's new books for young scientists. Individual issues of *Scientific American* cost $3.95; an annual subscription (12 issues), $19.97. To order, contact *Scientific American*, 415 Madison Avenue, New York, NY 10017; (800) 333-1199.

Scientific Wizardry Educational Products

Scientific Wizardry has put together a lavish collection of educational books, toys, games, puzzles, and kits - and their catalog, they explain, contains only a fraction of their products; persons looking for particular items are encouraged to call and inquire. For the young scientist, Scientific Wizardry carries construction kits, entomology supplies, chemistry sets, ant farms, rock tumblers and grit, sunprint paper, crystal-growing kits, and much else. They also carry a terrific line of educational lotto and rummy games, all illustrated with beautiful full-color photographs. Animal Rummy Games, which contain 32 cards each, include *Exotic Birds, Savage Kingdom, The Vanishing Wild, Undersea World, Mysteries of the Deep, Dinosaurs, Snakes, Hidden Kingdom, North American and Arctic Wildlife, Endangered Species,* and *Animals of the Zoo*. Each costs $3.00. For a free catalog collection, contact Scientific Wizardry, 9925 Fairview Avenue, Boise, ID 83704; (208) 377-8575, fax: (208) 323-0912.

Sky and Telescope

Sky and Telescope is a magazine for the dedicated adult astronomer - articles are generally aimed at those who know their way around the business end of a telescope. It is also, however, an invaluable resource for the stargazing beginner. Each month, *Sky and Telescope* features a blow-by-blow account of the current night sky scene, complete with star maps, charts and descriptions of planetary positions, a "Moonwatcher's Corner," and descriptions of any noteworthy phenomena, such as meteor showers, planetary conjunctions, and eclipses. Single copies of *Sky and Telescope* cost $2.95; a one-year subscription (12 issues), $27.00, from *Sky and Telescope*, P.O. Box 9111, Belmont, MA 02178-9111.

SomeBody

The body in question is human: this is an anatomy game for kids aged 6-10. The puzzle-like playing boards picture a human body with superimposed outlines of the major internal organs; playing pieces are reusable colored vinyl stickers of body parts. Instructions are included for four different games, which involve teaching the names, locations, and functions of the parts of the body using the playing boards and a collection of question-and-answer cards. Sample question: "Which BODY PART has 4 chambers and carries blood through your body?" *SomeBody* costs $22.00 and is available from several sources, among them Delta Education, Inc., P.O. Box 950, Hudson, NH 03051; (800) 442-5444.

SPACE

The Game of SPACE is a question-and-answer game for 2-6 players, aged 10 and up. It consists of five packs of color-coded cards: the S cards carry questions about Stars; the P cards about the Planets; the A cards about Astronomy in general; the C cards about the Constellations; and the E cards about space Exploration. Players draw a card from one of the five packs depending on the roll of a lettered die. They earn cards by correctly answering the astronomical questions; the winner is the first person to accumulate enough cards to spell the word SPACE. The game costs $9.95 from National Science Teachers Association (NSTA) Publication Sales, 1742 Connecticut Ave., N.W., Washington, D.C. 20009-1171; (800) 722-NSTA.

Space Age Crystals

These boxed crystal-growing kits produce large lush crystal specimens, a thoroughly satisfying educational experience. Directions are simple: users simply dissolve premixed chemicals in water, add a rock (as a supporting base), and wait. Kits include an informational booklet, which includes the chemical scoop on crystals in general, plus descriptions of crystal-growing experiments conducted on board the space shuttle. Space Age Crystals are available in several varieties, including Quartz, Emerald, Citrine, and Amethyst. They are recommended for kids aged 12 or older, but younger children, with parental help, will enjoy them too. Available from the Edmund Scientific Company, 101 East Gloucester Pike, Barrington, NJ 08007-1380; (609) 547-8880.

Space Hop/Star Hop

This is a pair of astronomical board games. In *Space Hop*, player hop their playing pieces - little colored rocket ships - across the solar system, while answering questions about the sun and its planetary family. In *Star Hop*, the distances get much bigger: the board pictures the Milky Way Galaxy; and players criss-cross the known universe, answering (more difficult) questions about star types, nebulae, supernovas, black holes, and quasars. Each game costs $21.95; available from the Edmund Scientific Company, 101 East Gloucester Pike, Barrington, NJ 08007-1380; (609) 547-8880.

Spizzirri Publishing Company

The Spizzirri Publishing Company catalog (see History) carries a range of educational coloring books, with optional accompanying story cassettes, dot-to-dot books, and maze books of potential interest to young scientists. Coloring books, each 32 pages long, cost $2.25 individually, and $5.95 with accompanying cassette. They are also available in six-packs, as "Listen and Color Library" albums. The "Prehistoric Life" album, for example, includes coloring book/cassette sets titled *Dinosaurs, Prehistoric Sea Life, Prehistoric Fish, Prehistoric Birds, Prehistoric Mammals,* and *Cave Man;* the "Oceans and Seas" album includes *Atlantic Fish, Pacific Fish, Sharks, Whales, Deep-Sea Fish,* and *Dolphins;* and the "Air and Space" album, *Aircraft, Space Craft, Space Explorers, Planets, Comets,* and *Rockets.* Spizzirri also publishes the "Life Line Wall Chart," detailing 600 million years of life on earth. The chart, which unfolded stretches 70 inches long, pictures 207 different animals and plants, grouped according to proper time period. Each is identified by number, keyed to an accompanying instruction booklet. The Life Line costs $6.00 and is printed in black-and-white. The truly ambitious can color it. For a free catalog, contact Spizzirri Publishing, Inc., P.O. Box 9397, Rapid City, SD 57709; (605) 341-4451.

Star Date

Star Date is a bimonthly astronomy magazine, written for grown-ups and older students, and published by the McDonald Observatory at the University of Texas in Austin. Features, in reader-friendly fashion, cover all aspects of astronomy, from black holes to the historical use of the astrolabe. There's also a "Dear Merlin" column, which answers astronomical questions from readers, and a "Sky Calendar," with current monthly star maps and descriptions of current astronomical phenomena. The "Sky Calendar" isn't as detailed as that featured in *Sky and Telescope*, and it's a much smaller magazine - a mere 24 pages long - at least in part because it doesn't carry all those zillions of advertisements for telescopes. A one-year subscription to *Star Date* (6 issues) costs $15.00; make checks payable to the McDonald Observatory. For more information, contact *Star Date*, RLM 15.308, The University of Texas at Austin, Austin, TX 78712; (512) 471-5285.

Start to Finish Books

These 24-page science picture books are targeted at kids from preschool through grade 3. All are excellent sources for clearly answering all those "Where did it come from?"-type questions. The books are published by Carolrhoda, and written and illustrated by Ali Mitgutsch, Marlene Reidel, Annegert Fuchshuber, or Franz Hogner. Self-explanatory titles include: *From Blossom to Honey, From Blueprint to House, From Wood to Paper, From Rubber Tree to Tire, From Graphite to Pencil, From Gold to Money, From Sea to Salt, From Swamp to Coal, From Dinosaurs to Fossils, From Grain to Bread, From Egg to Bird, From Egg to Butterfly, From Sand to Glass, From Grass to Butter, From Milk to Ice Cream, From Ice to Rain, From Cotton to Pants, From Tree to Table, From Sheep to Scarf, From Seed to Pear, From Cow to Shoe, From Cement to Bridge, From Cacao Bean to Chocolate, From Beet to Sugar, From Clay to Bricks, From Oil to Gasoline, From Fruit to Jam,* and *From Ore to Spoon.* Each book costs $6.95, from bookstores or from Carolrhoda Books, Inc., 241 First Avenue North, Minneapolis, MN 55401; (800) 328-4929 or (612) 332-3344.

Stethoscopes

Every curious kid should have a chance to experiment with a stethoscope and experience the sounds of the ever-fascinating child heartbeat, adult heartbeat, pet heartbeat, and miscellaneous digestive gurgle. Luckily, stethoscopes, unlike most scientific instruments, are inexpensive. Most cost $6.00-$7.00 and are available through general scientific catalogs. The Anatomical Chart Company (see above) even carries them in assorted day-glo colors: yellow, green, orange, and hot-pink. For those who want a bit of information with their stethoscopes, Workman Publishing offers a packaged *Stethoscope Book and Kit* (Linda Allison and Tom Ferguson). The stethoscope is a relatively flimsy pop-together model, but the accompanying instruction booklet is a plus, providing over 60 suggestions for stethoscope activities. Available through bookstores or from Workman Publishing, 708 Broadway, New York, NY 10003; (212) 254-5900.

The Teachers' Laboratory, Inc.

The Teachers' Laboratory publishes a catalog of books and hands-on materials for "active learning in science and math," and an interdisciplinary teachers' newsletter, *Connect*, which contains science and technology news, suggestions for classroom science and math activities, accounts of innovative teaching techniques, and reviews of new educational resources. Among the materials offered in the catalog are the Science 5/13 Teaching Units, a series of hands-on science modules in which kids "approach the study of science through their own interests and through themes." Units are keyed to Piaget's stages of child development, which can be a bit confusing for those not up on their Piaget. Basically, "Stage 1" means little kids; "Stage 2" slightly older kids, able to handle concrete operations; and "Stage 3," kids old enough to think using abstractions. Each teaching unit includes scientific background, equipment lists, and suggestions for a wide range of creative activities, with detailed instructions. Units cost $11.50 each. Titles include "Children and Plastics," "Coloured Things," "Holes, Gaps, and Cavities," "Metals," "Minibeasts," "Ourselves," "Science, Models and Toys," "Structures and Forces," "Time," "Trees," and "Working With Wood." The catalog is free; a one-year subscription to *Connect* (8 issues) costs $24.50. Contact The Teachers' Laboratory, P.O. Box 6480, Brattleboro, VT 05302-6480; (802) 254-3457.

1001 Things You Should Know About Science   James Trefil   (Doubleday; 1992)

This book, says the author in the introduction, "is intended to be browsed. You are supposed to open it to a random page, read a bit, say 'Gee, I didn't know that' or 'How interesting,' and then put it down until next time. It's not a textbook, and you aren't supposed to read it from start to finish." It is, however, a blueprint for science education. Once you and your kids reach the point where you can flip the book open - say, to item 321, "The cell is not a blob;" or item 626, "Everything is made from quarks and leptons;" or item 886, "A neutron star is one possible outcome of a supernova" - and know in each case exactly what the author is talking about, you're definitely on your way. The book organizes its 1001 bits of scientific information into seven categories: Classical Biology, Evolution, Molecular Biology, Classical Physical Science, Modern Physical Science, Earth Science, and Astronomy. In flavor, a cross between *Trivial Pursuit* and the encyclopedia. Available through bookstores.

Tin Man Press

Tin Man specializes in creative materials to develop thinking skills. Their "Discover!" series encourages kids to do what good scientists do best: examine real-world objects from a number of different angles, make connections, and draw conclusions. There are two different "Discover!" series, each containing 12 investigative card packs. Card packs list "twenty unusual thinking challenges" concerning common everyday objects. In Series I, students discover a Pencil, a Spoon, Popcorn, Crackers, a Comb, Scissors, a Paper Clip, a Handkerchief, a Tape Dispenser, an Egg Carton, a Paper Bag, and a Table Knife; in Series II, a Button, a Shoelace, a Key, a Toothbrush, a Crayon, a Peanut, a Paper Plate, a Milk Carton, an Envelope, Notebook Paper, Aluminum Foil, and Your Hand. Sample thinking challenges: "Think of waffles and think of pancakes. Which is more like an egg carton? Why?" "Can you find the middle of a shoelace without using a ruler? Explain how you did it." "Why are most envelopes used just once?" Individual Discover! packs cost $2.25; the series is recommended for kids in grade 2 and up. For a catalog, contact Tin Man Press, P.O. Box 219, Stanwood, WA 98292; (800) 676-0459.

TOPS Learning Systems

TOPS, here, is an acronym, standing for Task Oriented Physical Science - which impressive-sounding title boils down to is a series of detailed hands-on learning units, all designed to promote active scientific research. These are some of the nicest science units around, and they're also some of the least expensive: kids use paperclips, Mason jars, aluminum foil, yardsticks, batteries, and the like in creative assemblies to investigate scientific principles. Units for kids in grades 3-10 are available as collections of student worksheets, with absolutely precise step-by-step instructions: titles, containing 20 worksheets each, include *Balancing*, *Electricity*, *Magnetism*, *Pendulums*, *Metric Measuring*, *More Metrics*, *Animal Survival*, *Green Thumbs: Radishes*, *Green Thumbs: Corn and Beans*, and *The Earth, Moon, and Sun*. The units convey the sense of real scientific laboratory investigation, rather than casual cookbook science: kids follow directions, make observations, record results in laboratory notebooks, and draw conclusions. Teacher's notes, including background information and procedural hints, are included.

For older kids in grades 7-12, accustomed to working more independently, TOPS units are presented in task card format. Each of these consists of 16 to 36 experiment cards with instructions, goals, and challenge questions for individual student use. Task card unit titles include *Pendulums*, *Measuring Length*, *Graphing*, *Balancing*, *Weighing*, *Metric Measure*, *Regularity*, *Probability*, *Floating and Sinking*, *Analysis* (introductory analytical chemistry), *Oxidation*, *Solutions*, *Cohesion/Adhesion*, *Kinetic Model*, *Heat*, *Pressure*, *Light*, *Sound*, *Electricity*, *Magnetism*, *Motion*, *Machines*, and *Rocks and Minerals*. For more information or an information-packed catalog, contact TOPS Learning Systems, 10970 S. Mulino Road, Canby, OR 97013.

Ursa Major

For avid astronomers who can't always be outdoors, Ursa Major sells Night Sky Stencils. These are truly spectacular stencils, either 8 or 12 feet in diameter, each consisting of a 400-star spread of the summer or winter sky. You stick the stencil on the ceiling, then paint in the stars using a non-toxic luminous paint (included). The paint doesn't show up in normal light; in the dark, you've got your own starry night sky. To accompany the stencils, Ursa Major also offers a 50-page booklet of night sky and science lore and a 60-minute cassette tape of night sounds - crickets, owls, and coyotes - to put indoor stargazers in the proper mood. Brochure: Ursa Major, PO Box 3368, Ashland, OR 97520; (800) 999-3433.

Van Cleave, Janice

Janice Van Cleave, professional science teacher, has published a series of quick-and-easy hands-on science books for kids aged 8-12. The books, each subtitled "101 Easy Experiments That Really Work," include *Biology for Every Kid*, *Chemistry for Every Kid*, *Earth Science for Every Kid*, *Physics for Every Kid*, and *Astronomy for Every Kid*. Format is short and sweet: each experimental description takes up two pages, and consists of a statement of purpose, an equipment list (generally simple household items), procedural instructions, a brief statement of the desired result, and a short scientific explanation. None of the experiments are especially meaty, which can be frustrating for kids who really like to tinker - "Is that *all* there is to it?" - but they do accomplish their purposes, clearly demonstrating the scientific puzzle or principle at hand. I'd put the recommended age range closer to 6-9 years. The books, published by John Wiley & Sons, are available through bookstores.

Ward's

Ward's Natural Science Establishment publishes at least two huge catalogs for educators: *Ward's Biology Catalog* and *Ward's Earth Science Catalog*. These, like the catalogs from Carolina Biological Supply and Science Kit & Boreal Laboratory, are reference works of their kind. The *Earth Sciences* catalog is close to 500 pages long; the *Biology* catalog nearly a thousand. Both carry complete lines of equipment, labware, specimens, educational kits (generally designed for groups of 25-30 students), books, charts, manuals, and computer software. Ward's does carry a smaller series of "Advanced Placement Biology Labs" in kit form, each containing enough materials for 4-6 students. Lab kits include "Osmosis/Diffusion," "Enzymatic Catalysis," "Mitosis and Meiosis," "Plant Pigments and Photosynthesis," "Cell Respiration," "Phenotype Expression and DNA Analysis," "Fruit Fly Genetics," "Population Genetics and Evolution," "Transpiration," "Physiology of the Circulatory System," "Behavior Habitat Selection," and "Dissolved O^2 and Aquatic Productivity." For some kits, additional laboratory equipment - notably a microscope and electrophoresis apparatus - is required. Kit prices range from $29 to $95. For Earth Science students, Ward's offers "Geo-logic: A Modular Teaching System for Geology," consisting of individual sets of quality geological specimens, an illustrated study guide, and sets of reproducible student worksheets. Each set contains 12 to 16 different rock and mineral specimens. Under Physical Geology, titles include "Physical Geology," "Hardness," "Cleavage, Fracture, and Parting," "Streak, Color, and Luster," "Tenacity and Special Properties," "Crystal Form," "Important Rock-Forming Minerals," "Igneous Rocks," "Sedimentary Rocks," "Metamorphic Rocks,"Energy Resources," "Metallic Mineral Resources," and "Non-Metallic Mineral Resources." Under Historical Geology, titles include "What is a Fossil?," "Types of Fossilization," "Plants and Animals of the Past," "Life of the Paleozoic Era," "Life of the Mesozoic Era," "Life of the Cenozoic Era," "Evolutionary Sequence," and "Introduction to Micropaleontology," for which last students will need a microscope. Geo-logics cost about $30 to $40 per set. Assorted collections are also available for more general studies: a "General Earth Science" collection, for example, designed for use in the Cleveland schools, contains 4 igneous rocks, 3 rock-forming minerals, 5 sedimentary rocks, 4 metamorphic rocks, and an identification key, all for $16.50. To obtain catalogs, contact Ward's Natural Science Establishment, Inc., P.O. Box 92912, Rochester, NY 14692-9012; (800) 962-2660.

The Way Things Work   David Macauley   (Houghton Mifflin; 1988)

A 384-page masterpiece which, by means of addictive and fascinating illustrations, explains the workings of machines, from the lever and the pulley to the laser, the nuclear reactor, the seismograph, the movie projector, and the electric guitar. Our kids, entranced, will pore over this one by the hour. The (absolutely clear) text explains the scientific principles behind the machinery, with the help of an endearing collection of curious wooly mammoths.

Topics covered include "The Mechanics of Movement" (the inclined plane, levers, the wheel and axle, gears and belts, cams and cranks, pulleys, screws, rotating wheels, springs, and friction), "Harnessing the Elements" (floating, flying, pressure power, exploiting heat, nuclear power), "Working With Waves" (light and images, photography, printing, sound and music, telecommunications), and "Electricity and Automation" (electricity, magnetism, sensors and detectors, computers). An essential for those whose children insist upon knowing in detail how the television, toilet, and space telescope work. Available through bookstores.

WonderScience

WonderScience, a joint publication of the American Chemical Society and the American Institute of Physics, is subtitled "Fun Physical Science Activities for Children and Adults to Do Together." This is a monthly magazine, creative, colorful, informational, and definitely curiosity-provoking, targeted at kids aged 8-12. In our sample issue, "Wonders of Water," kids learn about water cohesion through a pair of water-drop race games; make colored ice cubes and watch them melt; investigate surface tension ("How many drops of water do you think you can stack on a penny?") and capillarity; and tackle some water discussion questions: "What if water were not very cohesive? How big would puddles get?" "What if water did not dissolve things? Would ocean water be salty?" "What if water did not have surface tension? Would there be icicles?" An annual subscription to *WonderScience* (8 issues) costs $5.00, plus $2.50 postage, from the American Chemical Society, *WonderScience* Magazine, P.O. Box 57136, Washington, D.C. 20077-6702.

World of Science

There are World of Science retail stores in several states (Connecticut, Delaware, Maryland, New Jersey, New York, Ohio, Pennsylvania, Virginia, and West Virginia), and all are a thrill for the science enthusiast: science toys, books, games, kits, and equipment for the science educator and educatee. World of Science materials can also be ordered through the company catalog, 150+ black-and-white pages of science resources. Main categories include Biology, Chemistry, Earth Science, Nature, and Physical Science, with special sections on Dinosaurs, Fossils, Models, Optics, Posters, Robots, and Rockets. The company also sells microscopes and telescopes, laboratory balances, centrifuges, and glassware, chemicals ("sold to schools only"), and educational kits.

As supplements to any basic science program - "A text isn't all you need to teach science" - World of Science sells a series of boxed Science Inquiry Labs, recommended for students in grades 4-8. Lab I, "Basic Science," includes five different kits: "Plant Growth," "Air and Air Pressure," "Light," "Static Electricity," and "Sound." Each contains the materials for 12-25 different experiments, a teacher/student manual, and student worksheets (suitable for duplicating). Lab II, "Machines and Energy," also consists of five kits: "Pulleys and Inclined Planes," "Light: Reflection and Refraction," "Electricity," "Simple Machines," and "Magnetism and Electromagnetism." Lab I costs $329.95; Lab II, $469.95. Individual kits can be purchased separately. World of Science catalogs cost $2.00, from World of Science, Educational Modules, Inc., Building Four, 900 Jefferson Road, Rochester, NY 14623; (716) 475-0100.

Zoobooks

The *Zoobooks* series, published by Wildlife Education, Ltd., can be purchased either individually or by monthly subscription. These are oversized softcover booklets, 18 pages long, each featuring a different animal or group of animals. The booklets are beautifully done, heavily illustrated with spectacular photographs and drawings; and the text, though short and to-the-point, is geared toward school-aged kids, which is probably why the books are recommended for kids aged 6-10. Younger kids, however, will go for the pictures, which are worth the purchase price all by themselves. There are now over 50 different *Zoobooks* titles, among them *Alligators and Crocodiles, Animal Champions, Apes, Bears, Birds of Prey, Camels, Eagles, Elephants, Giraffes, Insects, Night Animals, Penguins, Sharks, Snakes, Spiders, Whales,* and *Wolves.* A one-year subscription (10 issues) costs $15.95 from Wildlife Education, Ltd., 3590 Kettner Blvd., San Diego, CA 92101.

Science Activity Books

Amazing Animal Senses   Ron and Atie Van der Meer   (Little, Brown; 1990) A fascinating book, crammed with diagrams, flaps, pull-tabs, and manipulatives comparing human and animal senses: vision, taste, smell, hearing, touch, navigation, reaction time. There's a pair of two-color filter glasses, and a reaction time game, with which readers can find out whether or not they're fast enough to catch a mouse. Also by the authors: *Your Amazing Senses.*

Balloon Science   Etta Kaner   (Addison-Wesley; 1989) Over fifty clever balloon experiments that demonstrate such scientific phenomena as air pressure, elasticity, static electricity, and jet propulsion. Package of balloons included. By the author: *Sound Science.*

The Big Dipper and You   E.C. Krupp   (Morrow Junior Books; 1989) An intriguing and informative account of the science and history of the Big Dipper. By the same author: *The Comet and You,* on Halley's Comet.

Bugwise: Thirty Incredible Insect Investigations and Arachnid Activities   Pamela M. Hickman   (Addison-Wesley; 1991) Lots of information and activities for young entomologists, including how to make a bug-catcher, a terrarium, an ant palace, and a "living lantern." By the same author: *Birdwise: Forty Fun Feats for Finding Out About Our Feathered Friends.*

The Curiosity Club: Kids' Nature Activity Book   Allene Roberts   (John Wiley & Sons; 1992) Information and activities on trees, green plants, soil, animals, birds, insects and spiders, and the weather; projects include making bark rubbings, growing wildflowers, identifying insects in soil samples, drawing your own (geometric) honeycomb, and making a windsock and weathervane.

Exceptional Examination of Exemplar Experiments for Exciting Teaching With Eggs   Alfred Devito   (Creative Ventures; 1982) Lots of information on the chemistry and structure of the egg. Projects include constructing a simple incubator, making an egg thermometer, and producing an eggshell-based fire extinguisher.

Flights of Imagination: An Introduction to Aerodynamics   Wayne Hoskings   (NSTA; 1990)   Eighteen projects for turning kites into science lessons.

The Fossil Factory: A Kid's Guide to Digging Up Dinosaurs, Exploring Evolution, and Finding Fossils   Niles Gregory and Douglas Eldredge   (Addison-Wesley; 1989)   Information and activities, including making a Grand Canyon in a jar and a plaster cast of your own footprint.

Gee, Wiz!: How to Mix Art and Science or The Art of Thinking Scientifically   Linda Allison and David Katz   (Little, Brown; 1983)   One of the Brown Paper School Book series. This book contains a lot of detailed scientific explanations, all supported with terrific hands-on experiments: kids investigate chromatography, soap films, capillary action, surface tension, immiscible liquids, vision, symmetry, equilibrium, and bodies in motion. Clever cartoon-like illustrations. Other science books in the series: *Only Human: Why We Are the Way We Are* (Neill Bell); *Beastly Neighbors, Or Why Earwigs make Good Mothers* (Mollie Rights); *Good for Me!: All About Food in 32 Bites* (Marilyn Burns); *The Reasons for Seasons: The Great Cosmic Megagalactic Trip Without Moving from Your Chair* (Linda Allison); *Blood and Guts: A Working Guide to Your Own Insides* (Linda Allison); *The Night Sky Book: An Everyday Guide to Every Night* (Jamie Jobb); and *The Big Beast Book: Dinosaurs and How They Got That Way* (Jerry Booth).

The House of Science   Philip R. Holzinger   (John Wiley & Sons; 1990)   Over 200 pages of projects, problems, and activities for older kids in the fields of mathematics, chemistry, physics, geology, biology, meteorology, oceanography, environmental science, geography, and astronomy.

The Kid's Nature Book: 365 Indoor/Outdoor Activities and Experiences   Susan Milord   (Williamson; 1989)   Creative nature projects for every day of the year.

Light Fantastic   Philip Watson   (Lothrop, Lee & Shepard; 1982)   This is one of the Science Club series, originally published in Great Britain. All are practical project books, beautifully illustrated in full-color. Activities include extracting chlorophyll from a green leaf, making a periscope, a color "whizzer wheel," and a color pyramid with cellophane filters, constructing a flashing badge, building a pinhole camera, and setting up your own darkroom. In the same series: *Liquid Magic, Amazing Air,* and *Super Motion.*

Look to the Night Sky: An Introduction to Sky Watching   Seymour Simon   (Puffin; 1977)   By the same author: an excellent series of short (32-page) astronomy books, each lavishly illustrated with spectacular full-color photographs. Titles include *The Sun, The Stars, Mercury, Venus, Mars, Jupiter, Saturn,* and *Uranus.*

Mr. Wizard's Supermarket Science   Don Herbert   (Random House; 1980)   Lots of fast, simple experiments with accompanying scientific explanations. Kids made gelatin gumdrops, a vinegar cannon, milk glue, aluminum-foil silver cleaner, a salad-bowl solar reflector, and a pin piano. Science, as done by Mr. Wizard, is also available on video: favorite experiments are performed in *Mr. Wizard's World: Puzzles, Problems and Imoossibilities* and *Mr. Wizard's World: Air and Water Wizardry.* Each costs $19.99, from Movies Unlimited, 6736 Castor Avenue, Philadelphia, PA 19149; (800) 523-0823 (orders) or (215) 722-8398 (information).

Mudpies to Magnets: A Preschool Science Curriculum   Elisabeth Sherwood, Bob Williams, and Bob Rockwell   (Gryphon House; 1987)   Simple hands-on activities and experiments for the very small, all more interesting and informational than most science projects for kids in this age group. Among the projects: paper chromatography, newpaper construction, an ant picnic, and dyeing flowers. By the same authors: *More Mudpies to Magnets: Science for Very Young Children.*

Naturewatch: Exploring Nature With Your Children   Adrienne Katz   (Addison-Wesley; 1986)   Nature science and craft projects. Instructions for making a potato maze, a cactus garden, a caterpillar cage, a spider web collection, and dried-seed jewelry.

The Night Sky Book   Jamie Jobb   (Little, Brown; 1977)   One of the Brown Paper School Book series. Cleverly presented astronomical information and many hands-on projects, including instructions for a tin-can planetarium, a Viking solar stone, a navigational cross-staff, an Indian medicine wheel, and a vegetable model of the solar system.

The Ocean Book: Aquarium and Seaside Activities and Ideas for All Ages   Center for Marine Conservation   (John Wiley & Sons;

1989) Puzzles, games, projects, information, and stories about all aspects of oceanography. Sample activities: kids label a map of the ocean floor, demonstrate ocean currents with colored water, make a tide mobile, make fish prints, solve a food chain crossword, make a model estuary, and clean up a sample oil spill.

Science Activity Book: 20 Exciting Activities for Parents & Kids to Do   Smithsonian Institution Family Learning Project (Galison; 1987) In the same series: *More Science Activities* and *Still More Science Activities*. Lots of interactive science activities for kids in grades K-6, among them making ginger ale, crystal gardens, marbleized paper, paper (from grass clippings), and a solar cooker capable of roasting marshmallows.

The Science Book Sara Stein (Workman; 1980) Nearly 300 pages of high-powered information and fascinating experiments for young scientists, with lots of terrific illustrations, both diagrams and photographs. By the same author: *The Body Book* and *The Evolution Book*.

Science for Kids: 39 Easy Astronomy Experiments Robert W. Wood (Tab Books; 1991) These are experiments for middle-grade kids, rather than for the very small: activities include making a spectroscope, calculating the diameters of the moon and sun, building an astrolabe and a theodolite, and making a tin-can planetarium. By the same author: *Physics for Kids: 49 Easy Experiments with Mechanics; Physics for Kids: 49 Easy Experiments with Optics; Physics for Kids: 49 Easy Experiments with Electricity and Magnetism;* and *Physics for Kids: 49 Easy Experiments with Heat*.

Science Wizardry for Kids Margaret Kenda and Phyllis S. Williams (Barron's; 1992) Over 300 pages of experiments, beautifully presented, in a fat comb-bound book that stays open on the table for easy reference. Some of the many projects include: "Create Edible Glass," "Grow a Colorful Crystal," "Create Your Own Electric Lemon," "Make Your Own Old-Fashioned Milk Paint," "Float With Ancient Greece," "Create Your Own World Clock," and "Use Plant Power to Knock Off Bottle Caps."

The Scientific Kid Mary Stetten Carson (HarperCollins; 1989) Thirty-five easy and delightful science projects and experiments for little kids, including making invisible ink and recycled paper, dipping candles, and growing sugar crystals.

Scienceworks: 65 Experiments That Introduce the Fun and Wonder of Science   Ontario Science Center   (Addison-Wesley; 1984)   Science activities, toys, and tricks, with accompanying explanations. In the same series: *Foodworks* and *Sportsworks*.

Seeing the Sky: 100 Projects, Activities & Explorations in Astronomy   Fred Schaaf   (John Wiley & Sons; 1990)   Lots of astronomical information, with accompanying activity suggestions, for middle-grade and older astronomers. Proposed activities include making a cyanometer (to measure blueness of the sky), identifying asterisms, observing variable stars, and making a moon map.

By the same author: *Seeing the Solar System: Telescopic Projects, Activities & Explorations in Astronomy* and *Seeing the Deep Sky: Telescopic Astronomy Projects Beyond the Solar System*.

Sensational Science Activities With Dr. Zed   Gordon Penrose   (Simon and Schuster; 1990)   A collection of quick and highly appealing experiments, with brief accompanying explanations. Illustrations combine photographs of experimenting kids with colorful cartoons. Activities include "Exploding Colors," "Phewy Putty," "Magic Propeller," and "Dance-Till-You-Drop Popcorn." By the same author: *Dr. Zed's Dazzling Book of Science Activities, Magic Mud and Other Great Experiments*, and *Dr. Zed's Science Surprises*.

50 Simple Things Kids Can Do to Save the Earth   The Earthworks Group   (Scholastic; 1990)   Lots of mind-sticking environmental information (the average American uses seven trees a year), along with everyday earth-protecting activities for everybody.

365 Starry Nights   Chet Raymo   (Prentice Hall; 1982)   A night-by-night account of the changing sky, plus practical instructions for stargazers, scientific information, and lore.

The Stars   H.A. Rey   (Houghton Mifflin; 1980)   A classic guide to help viewers identify the constellations, with diagrams, helpful hints, seasonal sky charts, and background information. By the same author: *Find the Constellations*, a shorter guide targeted at younger readers.

Step Into Science Series   Barbara Taylor   (Random House)   Each book lists about 25 simple experiments for young scientists, with clear instructions and big colorful illustrations. Titles in the series include *Get It in Gear: The Science of Movement, Green Thumbs Up! The Science of Growing Plants, Hear, Hear! The Science of Sound, More*

Power to You: The Science of Batteries and Magnets, Over the Rainbow: The Science of Color and Light, Seeing is Not Believing: The Science of Light and Shadow, Sink or Swim! The Science of Water, and *Up, Up, and Away: The Science of Flight.*

The Thomas Edison Book of Easy and Incredible Experiments: Activities, Projects and Science Fun for All Ages   The Thomas Alva Edison Foundation   (Thomas Alva Edison Foundation; 1988)   Over 125 pages of meaty experiments, ranging from the relatively simple to the definitely complex; instructions are included for building a portable burglar alarm, an electric motor, an electric pencil, a radio, and a cigar-box microphone.

Weatherwatch   Valerie Wyatt   (Addison-Wesley; 1990)   Lots of clever weather information, quizzes, and projects, including making a cloud in a bottle, measuring rainfall with a homemade rain gauge, making a snowflake impression, checking out the temperature on other planets in the solar system, and building a barometer.

Whales in the Classroom I: Oceanography   Larry Wade   (Singing Rock Press; 1992)   The first in a series of information-and-activity books about the ocean for kids aged 10-14. The book covers seven major oceanographic topics; background text is interspersed with maps, diagrams, charts, and murals for kids to complete themselves, interviews with famous oceanographers, problems, and puzzles.

Who Says You Can't Teach Science? Grades K-6   Alan Ticotsky   (Scott, Foresman and Company; 1985)   A large collection of short classroom-friendly experiments on air, water, dirt and rocks, the earth in space, the sun, motion, sound, light and color, simple machines, magnetism and electricity, plants, animals, and the human body.

The Whole Cosmos Catalog of Science Activities   Joe Abruscato and Jack Hassard   (Scott, Foresman and Company; 1977)   An unusual and cleverly illustrated collection of activities, experiments, information, scientific biographies, games, and puzzles. The book is divided into five parts: Life Sciences, Earth Sciences, Physical Sciences, Aerospace Sciences, and Beyond Science.

Also see individual entries under Science: *Amazing Apples, Etc.;* The Backyard Scientist; Cobb, Vicki; *Explorabook; Exploratorium Snackbook;* Microscopes: Books for Microscopists;*NatureScope; Science Is...; Science Through Children's Literature;* Van Cleave, Janice.

Chapter Six

Foreign Languages

Or Parlez-Vous Español?

Audio Forum

Audio Forum carries a large number of audio and video cassettes in different categories. Among these is an extensive and incredibly varied series of foreign language programs, described in a 36-page catalog. "Learning another language is easier than you think," states the text bolsteringly. "Use drive time or any other time when you are doing a repetitive activity - such as cooking, dog-walking, jogging - to get the practice you need to really make another language your own." Audio Forum's most prominent foreign language offering is a series of full-length introductory courses originally developed for the U.S. State Department. These consist of anything from 3 to 36 cassettes, depending on your language choice, plus a text, which includes a transcript of the spoken coversations, learning guidelines, and exercises. Emphasis here, however, is on the spoken - not written - word. Courses in 56 different languages are available, among them not only French, German, Spanish, Russian, Italian, and Japanese, but Bulgarian, Mandarin Chinese, Greek, Irish, Swahili, Tagalong, and Yoruba. For many of the languages, subsequent Intermediate and Advanced courses are available for those who complete the Introductory course.

Audio Forum also carries a number of alternative language courses, including the "No Time" (no text) series, 6- to 8-hour programs which emphasize social and business conversation; and the Phrase-a-Day program (see below) for young children. Also available: foreign language feature films on video cassette, foreign language games (French *Scrabble*, Spanish *Monopoly*), authentic ethnic music on audio cassette, and foreign vocabulary flash cards. For a foreign language catalog, contact Audio Forum, 96 Broad Street, Guilford, CT 06437-2635; (800) 243-1234 or (203) 453-9794.

Bolchazy-Carducci Publishers

The Bolchazy-Carducci people advocate the teaching of Latin. "Why offer Latin?" they write. "Students who have taken Latin tend to score higher on standardized tests than other groups of students...In the Philadelphia School District, pupils who studied Latin for 20 minutes daily at the fifth-grade level advanced one full year in standardized vocabulary tests...Latin helps one to develop good student habits and improves one's memory, factors which are vital to success in college." The Latin program they offer, Waldo Sweet's *Artes Latinae*, is ideal for independent learners: it consists primarily of a self-teaching programmed text in which material to be learned is divided into small, manageable sequential chunks, and users are continually tested to ensure mastery of the current material before being allowed to advance. Along with the programmed text, *Artes Latinae* provides a graded reader, containing poems, prose, and proverbs in Latin, a reference notebook for student use, a test booklet, a teacher's guide, and a series of text-coordinated drill cassettes, which provide students with a model for the proper pronounciation of classical Latin.

Artes Latinae Level I consists of two programmed student texts (30 teaching units) and 15 drill cassettes; Level II, two texts (24 teaching units) and 12 drill cassettes. The entire Level I program costs $260; it can also be purchased in four separate phases, which means less of an initial investment, but more in the long run. (There's a savings of $40 for purchasing the entire cassette set at once.) Also available: a Latin Pen Pal network. For information and order forms, contact Bolchazy-Carducci Publishers, 1000 Brown St., Unit 101, Wauconda, IL 60084; (708) 526-4344.

Dover Publications

Along with the *Hebrew Alphabet Coloring Book* (see Foreign Language Alphabet Books, below), Dover carries foreign language editions of Beatrix Potter's*The Tale of Peter Rabbit* (French and Spanish) and Lewis Carroll's *Alice's Adventures in Wonderland* (French, German, and Russian). Available from Dover Publications, Inc., 31 East 2nd St., Mineola, NY 11501.

Early Advantage

Early Advantage offers the Muzzy video language courses for kids aged 2-12. The programs were developed by the British Broadcasting Corporation: each consists of a six-part animated adventure, starring a fat fuzzy green creature named Muzzy and a cast of accompanying characters, including the Princess Sylvia, Bob the gardener, and the sneaky, black-caped Corvax. The program is designed to exploit each child's natural language-learning ability: kids simply listen to the programs and absorb.

Muzzy is available at two different levels, in French, Spanish, German, or Italian. Each course set contains four 45-minute videotapes (2 in the chosen foreign language, 2 in the equivalent English), 2 foreign-language audiocassettes, an illustrated foreign-language storybook with a transcript of the video program, and a clever and colorful workbook that both reinforces the vocabulary on tape and teaches additional words and phrases. The whole

Good Stuff

thing comes in a pair of sturdy plastic storage portfolios. Each course costs $155, with an option for five monthly installment payments. To order or for additional information, contact Early Advantage, 47 Richards Avenue, Norwalk, CT 06860-0220; (800) 367-4534.

First Thousand Words Series

The Usborne books, with their colorful detailed illustrations and wealth of information, are an enduring delight for educators and educatees alike. For language lovers, Usborne offers the *First Thousand Words* series, absorbing picture/word books which display, on each double-page spread, a busy familiar scene from street, home, school, city, or country. Elements from each picture (girl, boy, car, bird, house, and the like) are repeated around the page border, each labelled with its foreign-language name. Each book includes a pronounciation guide and a foreign language/English dictionary. The books are 64 crammed pages long, appropriate for readers aged 2-12. Available in the series: *The First Thousand Words in French, German, Spanish, Italian, Russian, Hebrew,* and *English.*

For those who find a thousand new vocabulary words too intimidating, there's a shorter *First Hundred Word* series for younger children, available in English, French, German, and Spanish. Also available: the *First French* and *First German* series, each of which details the adventures of the quirky Banquert family at home, at school, and on vacation, in a collection of short foreign-language storybooks. The format is simple cartoon, with dialogue in speech bubbles above the characters' heads. Usborne also publishes kids' foreign-language picture dictionaries. Available from EDC Publishing, P.O. Box 470663, Tulsa, OK 74147-0663; (800) 331-4418 or (918) 622-4522. Usborne books are also distributed by Scientific Wizardry, 9925 Fairview Ave., Boise, ID 83704; (208) 377-8575.

Foreign Language Alphabet Books

ABC: The Alef-Bet Book Florence Cassen Mayers (Abrams; 1992) A Hebrew alphabet book, illustrated with full-color photographs of art works from the Israel Museum in Jerusalem.

A to Zen: A Book of Japanese Culture Ruth Wells (Picture Books Studio; 1992) Designed to be read back to front and right to left; explains such Japanese words as *futon, origami, sushi,* and *yen.*

A Russian ABC   Florence Cassen Mayers   (Abrams; 1992)   A Cyrillic alphabet book, illustrated with full-color photographs of art works from the Hermitage Museum in Leningrad. English and Russian words included.

The Hebrew Alphabet Coloring Book by Chaya Burstein is a collection of 25 pictures to color, each featuring a letter of the Hebrew alphabet and an accompanying assortment of people/objects whose names begin with that letter. The short text teaches colorers about 250 modern Hebrew words. Available from Dover Publications, Inc., 31 East 2nd St., Mineola, NY 11501.

Jambo Means Hello: Swahili Alphabet Book   Muriel Feelings   (Dial; 1974)   An anthropological alphabet book detailing tribal life in East Africa through 26 alphabetical Swahili words.

International Linguistics Corporation

The International Linguistics Corporation produces a series of foreign language programs called "The Learnables," available in Spanish, French, German, Mandarin Chinese, Czech, Russian, and Hebrew. Programs are designed to teach language by an immersion method: the spoken language on audio cassette is keyed to a series of simple black-and-white pictures. Each lesson consists of 100 pictures, with corresponding words, phrases, or simple sentences. Kids simply looks at the pictures while listening to the cassettes. At the end of every two lessons, there's a picture discrimination test to reinforce new vocabulary.

"The Learnables" sets are available at four different levels; each consists of ten lessons, and includes a picture book and a set of 4-6 audio cassettes. For the French, Spanish, and German Learnables, a student reader/workbook, *Basic Structures*, is available to accompany Level I: it includes ten lessons with related written exercises, and 4 new audio cassettes. "The Learnables" Level I (book and five cassettes) costs $42.00. Extra picture books can be purchased separately. For a catalog, contact the International Linguistics Corporation, 3505 East Red Bridge, Kansas City, MO 64137; (800) 237-1830 or (816) 765-8855.

Learn French/German/Italian/Spanish the Fast and Fun Way

This series of books, published by Barron's Educational Series, are described as "activity kits:" each contains maps, puzzles, quizzes, a set of cut-out vocabulary flash cards, and a tear-out bilingual dictionary. The books are workbooks for independent users, designed to teach the reader the basics of the spoken and written language. Lessons conduct readers through a conversational tour of a foreign country, beginning with "Getting to Know People" and "Arrival," through "Sightseeing," "Entertainment," "Ordering Food," "At the Store," and "Essential Services." Despite this format, the books are much more than short-time survival guides for tourists: they emphasize the acquisition of a broad-based beginning vocabulary, pronounciation, conversational technique, and proper grammar. Available through bookstores.

Living Language Courses

The Living Language program encourages kids to learn a foreign language by listening to and imitating native speakers - essentially the same process by which infants and toddlers learn to speak in the first place. The Children's Living Language Courses are aimed at kids aged 5-12. Each consists of 40 lessons on 2 cassette tapes (or 4 long-playing records), a bilingual picture dictionary, and a 96-page lesson book, with text in both English and the selected foreign language. The lessons consist of short dialogues among family members and friends, plus three familiar children's stories ("The Three Bears," "The Three Little Pigs," and "Little Red Riding Hood"). The recorded conversations at first seem rapid-fire but, with repetition, comprehension sets in and young listeners sop it up. Children's Living Language Courses are available in French and Spanish. To order, contact Outlet Book Company, 40 Englehard Ave., Avenel, NJ 07001; (908) 827-2700.

Lyric Language Series

The Lyric Language series, aimed at kids aged 4-8, teaches foreign language phrases through bouncy jingles set to music, a technique also used with great success by commercial advertisers. Each set includes a 30-minute audio cassette, featuring musical phrases in both English and the selected foreign language, and a 23-page booklet of written lyrics, illustrated with the pudgy little tots from the "Family Circus" cartoon. Lyric Language audio cassette sets are available in Spanish, French, German, Italian, and Swedish. Also in the series are accompanying 35-minute live-action videos, each containing 11 simple sing-along songs. The music videos are available in Spanish, French, German, and Italian. Lyric Language audio cassette sets cost $9.98 each; music videos, $14.98. Both are available from Music for Little People, Box 1460, Redway, CA 95560; (800) 727-2233.

National Textbook Company

The National Textbook Company publishes a 175-page "Foreign Languages" catalog carrying foreign-language texts and workbooks, multicultural books (in English), foreign-language songbooks, storybooks, and graded readers, games and crossword puzzles, grammars and dictionaries, flash cards, coloring books, and audio cassette programs. Major languages covered are Spanish, French, German, Italian, Russian, and Japanese; there are also (more limited) resources available for Greek, Latin, Hebrew, Chinese, Korean, Turkish, Indonesian, Polish, Portuguese, Swedish, Scandanavian, and Hungarian.

Sample products include the *My World* coloring book series (Spanish, French, German, and Italian), designed to introduce young colorers to elementary vocabulary words; and a series of introductory activity book/audio cassette programs, variously titled *Spanish for Children*, *French for Children*, *German for Children*, *Italian for Children*, and *Japanese for Children*. The first four include two 60-minute children's audio cassettes and one teacher's audio cassette, plus an 80-page kid's story-and-activity book. Each program is divided into ten units, each dealing with a series of simple language concepts (greetings, family member names, counting, school friends, everyday objects, and so on) through conversations, songs, and stories. Stories feature the adventures of a caped hero referred to as Super Gato (Super Chat, Super Katze, Super Gatto). The Japanese format is somewhat different, including an illustrated student text, a teacher's guide, and one 17-lesson 60-minute audio cassette. Using these, kids learn some simple conversational Japanese and begin to write Japanese, using both the *hiragana* and *katakana* syllabaries. For a catalog, contact the National Textbook Company, 4255 West Touhy Ave., Lincolnwood, IL 60646-1975; (800) 323-4900 or (708) 679-5500.

Phrase-A-Day

"Phrase-a-Day French" and "Phrase-a-Day Spanish" are activity book and cassette tape sets for kids aged 5-11. The program is divided into four parts, each covering one season of the year with associated vocabulary. Kids learn by following pictures and simple text as they listen to conversation and occasional songs by native speakers. Along with assorted short sentences, users learn names of food, articles of clothing, parts of the body, names of the days and months, colors, and how to count to 100. Kids, if they can manage to operate a cassette player, can handle this one pretty much on their own. It is suggested, however, that parents/ teachers reinforce the language lessons by choosing a daily phrase from those the child has just studied and using it frequently in context throughout the day. The comb-bound activity book is about 100 pages long: pictures, captioned with the words or phrases from the tape, are in black-and-white, suitable for coloring, and there are assorted blank boxes in which kids can make their own drawings (as per the foreign language instructions). Each set (2 audio cassettes, 1 activity book) costs $19.95 from Audio Forum, 96 Broad St., Guilford, CT 06437-2635; (800) 243-1234.

Skipping Stones
   A multicultural children's magazine, almost entirely kid-written, in which foreign-language submissions appear both in the original and in English translation. See History and Geography.

Storybridges
   This is a terrific way to introduce young listeners (aged 4-8) to a foreign language. *Storybridges* sets each include 3 audio cassettes on which familiar stories are narrated in English; all the expressions and characters' conversations, however, take place in a foreign language. Kids are encouraged to participate in the story, repeating the foreign words and phrases along with the storyteller. Tape 1 includes "Goldilocks and the Three Bears" and "Little Red Riding Hood;" Tape 2, "The Turtle's Music" and "The Nightingale;" and Tape 3, "The Shoemaker and the Elves" and "Peter and the Wolf." Each *Storybridges* set costs $19.95; available in French, Spanish, and German from the Educational Record Center, Inc., 3233 Burnt Mill Drive, Suite 100, Wilmington, NC 28403-2655; (800) 438-1637, fax: (910) 343-0311.

Teach Me Tapes
   The "Teach Me" language programs are book/cassette tape sets in which a foreign language is introduced through a collection of catchy and familiar songs, interspersed with short simple conversation. Participants learn names for family members, articles of clothing, days of the week, and colors, the letters of the alphabet, and the numbers 1-10. The accompanying follow-along book is illustrated with black-and-white pictures, suitable for coloring as kids listen and sing. English translations of song and phrases are included on a separate sheet. Songs include "The More We Get Together," "Rain, Rain, Go Away," "Mary Had a Little Lamb," and "The Wheels on the Car."

"Teach Me" Tapes are available in French, Spanish, German, Japanese, Russian, and Hebrew. Additional instruction is available in the "Teach Me More" tapes. Sets cost $14.00 from Teach Me Tapes, Inc., 10500 Bren Road East, Minneapolis, MN 55343; (800) 456-4656 or (612) 933-8086.

Trivium Pursuit

Trivium Pursuit is a source for classical language materials for kids, most notably the *Greek Alphabetarion Workbook*, a 59-page black-and-white softcover that teaches beginners the shapes and sounds of the letters of the Greek alphabet, from alpha to omega, both upper- and lower-case. There's an available accompanying audio cassette to reinforce correct pronounciation.

Once kids have mastered the alphabet, they can pass on to either *Basic Greek*, a self-study workbook that introduces users to Greek vocabulary and grammar; or go whole hog with *Greek: A Programmed Primer*, a 3-volume "full course in both Classical and Biblical Greek." Generally *Basic Greek* is recommended for kids aged 10 and up; *Greek: A Programmed Primer* for junior-high or high-school students. Also available: a bibliography of classical language materials for studies of Latin, Greek, and Hebrew. For a brochure, contact Trivium Pursuit, Laurie and Harvey Bluedorn, R.R. 2, Box 169, New Boston, IL 61272; (309) 537-3641.

Chapter Seven

Arts and Crafts:

Mudpies to Mozart

Adventures in Art: Art and Craft Experiences for 7- to 14-Year-Olds Susan Milord   (Williamson; 1990)

A large collection of innovative art projects for older children, including sandcast candles, shadow puppets, paper models, topiary animals, and Japanese bound books. There's a companion volume for younger artists: Laurie Carlson's *Kids Create! Art and Craft Experiences for 3- to 9-Year-Olds*, a collection of equally attractive, but less challenging, projects, among them dinosaur sculptures, butterfly puppets, crayon cookies, snow globes, and model log cabins. Also included: eight different recipes for dough clays. Both books are available through bookstores or from Williamson Publishing, Church Hill Road, P.O. Box 185, Charlotte, VT 05445; (800) 234-8791.

Amazing Buildings   Philip Wilkinson   (Dorling Kindersley; 1993)

"See inside the great buildings of the world," reads the cover, "from castles and cathedrals to palaces and monuments." The book includes 21 large-scale illustrations of 21 famous architectural works, including the Taj Mahal, the Roman Colosseum, the Statue of Liberty, and London's House of Parliament. In each, outer walls are cut away and roofs peeled back to reveal the structure of the interior. The text describes the history of each building. A fascinating book. Available through bookstores.

Anti-Coloring Books

This series of creative coloring books was devised by artist and art teacher Susan Striker. Each contains - rather than conventional pages of pictures to color - a lavish array of creative projects for kids who like to draw. "A good solution to the problem of trying to rouse the artist in children" writes one reviewer, "without trodding on their creative impulses." There are six basic books, from *The Anti-Coloring Book* to *The Sixth Anti-Coloring Book*, in which young artists, encouraged by clever suggestions, borders, and picture starters, are encouraged to design their own playgrounds, gardens, and underwater adventures, to draw space aliens and strange new animals, to sketch their most beautiful dream or to invent a fantastic new machine. "A famous artist," reads one framed page, "needs your help. The artist started this picture but was stung on the thumb by a bee. Turn the picture any way you'd like and finish it."

There are also several specialty books: in *The Anti-Coloring Book of Exploring Space on Earth*, young architects design a future city, a snow fort, a luxury tent for very rich campers, a haunted house, an anthill, a map of an island (the kind "you'd love to be shipwrecked on"), a treehouse, an undersea community, and a houseboat (and much else); in *The Anti-Coloring Book of Red-Letter Days*, kids illustrate their New Year's Resolutions, design Valentines, invent an April Fool's joke, decorate Easter eggs and bonnets, draw their own flags, Halloween costumes, and Election Day posters, and decorate Christmas trees and holiday windows. Our favorite - and the prettiest of the series - is *The Anti-Coloring Book of Masterpieces*. Many of the art starters here are in color; and all are taken from famous paintings or sculptures, each reproduced in full (in black-and-white) in the back of the book, along with a brief biographical sketch of the artist. Kids decorate an Egyptian sarcophagus, complete a Greek vase, and decorate a medieval prayer book; they put a new face on the *Mona Lisa*, and create their own versions of paintings by Goya, Van Gogh, Manet, Degas, Mondrian, Rousseau, Cassatt, and Picasso. And more. The books, published by Holt, Rinehart, and Winston, are available through bookstores.

Archiblocks

"These correctly proportioned maple blocks," states the catalog description, "allow young builders to create classic buildings in miniature." There are several sets of Archiblocks, the least expensive of which is the catenary arch puzzle. This consists of fifteen hardwood blocks which, stacked in proper order, form a perfect and stable arch, of the sort the Romans used to build their aqueducts. Our kids have loved this one; the satisfaction of fitting in the keystone never fails. The puzzle comes with a short information sheet describing the history and physics of the arch.

More elaborate Archiblock collections come in five different sets, grouped by architectural style: these include Greek, Roman, Gothic, Santa Fe, and Post-Modern. Each set consists of 50-75 blocks, with which kids can construct stylistically correct structures, plus a teacher's guide. The catenary arch puzzle is available from Michael Olaf's Essential Montessori, P.O. Box 1162, Arcata, CA 95521; Archiblock sets from Zephyr Press, 3316 N. Chapel Ave., P.O. Box 13488, Tucson, AZ 85732-3488; (602) 322-5090.

American Art Quiz

Forty question-and-answer cards, each with a full-color reproduction of a work from the National Museum of American Art. There are eight questions on each card, designed to encourage players to study the art work at hand. Sample questions: "Is this a still life or a landscape painting?" "Name three geometric shapes in this painting. Where are these shapes repeated to create pattern?" "What colors dominate the scene?" "Is this a quiet or a noisy painting?" Since reproductions only measure about two inches square, a magnifier is included with the game, for examination of fine detail. *American Art Quiz* costs $10.95; available through book and game stores, or from RB Walter Art & Craft Materials, P.O. Box 6231, Arlington, TX 76005; (800) 447-8787.

Art for Children Series

Titles in this series of children's art books by Ernest Raboff include *Michelangelo, Pierre-Auguste Renoir, Leonardo da Vinci, Pablo Picasso, Henri Rousseau, Rembrandt, Albrecht Durer, Marc Chagall, Paul Gauguin, Frederic Remington, Van Gogh, Henri de Toulouse-Lautrec, Diego Rodriquez de Silva y Velasquez, Henri Matisse, Paul Klee,* and *Raphael.* Each volume begins with a brief biography of the artist, but the bulk of the (simple) text explains and analyzes samples of the artist's work, encouraging readers to examine and explore on their own. The books measure 8 1/2 x 11 inches and are 32 pages long; each contains numerous large full-color reproductions of the artist's works, plus many smaller black-and-white sketches. Text is attractively hand-lettered, in several colors. Available through bookstores, or from KidsArt, P.O. Box 274, Mt. Shasta, CA 96067; (916) 926-5076, (800) 959-5076; or RB Walter Art & Craft Materials, P.O. Box 6231, Arlington, TX 76005; (800) 447-8787.

Art From Many Hands   Jo Miles Schuman   (Davis; 1981)

A wonderful 250-page collection of multicultural art projects for kids in kindergarten through junior-high school. Chapters include "Arts of West Africa," "Arts of the Middle East," "European Arts," "Asian Arts, "Mexican, Central American, and South American Arts," "Arts of the Caribbean Islands," and "Arts of the United States and Canada." Following the (clear) instructions, kids can make tie-dyed dashikis, Egyptian hieroglyphic tablets, Persian miniature paintings, Swedish cookie stamps, Japanese fish prints, Indonesian shadow puppets, Cuna Indian molas, Navajo sand-paintings, and early American applehead dolls. And much more. The book is lavishly illustrated with pictures of native art work from museum collections and of student-made replicas. Available through bookstores or from KidsArt, P.O. Box 274, Mt. Shasta, CA 96067; (916) 926-5076, (800) 959-5076.

Art Rummy

There are several different sets of these attractive full-color decks of art cards, variously based on the art works in the collections of the Metropolitan Museum of Art and the National Gallery of Art. The game itself is simple: players attempt to collect sets of related cards grouped by category. Categories in the Metropolitan's *Art Rummy* game, for example, include African Art, Egyptian Art, Greek Vases, Japanese Art, Medieval Armor, Musical Instruments, Western Paintings, and Western Sculpture. More specialized card decks include *Theme Art Rummy*, in which cards are categorized by subject, such as Children in Art, Animals in Art, Sports in Art, and Dancers in Art; and *American Art Rummy*, in which categories include Portraits, Still-lifes, Folk Art, Photography, Landscapes, Miniatures, Sculptures, Abstract Works, Seascapes, and Crafts. *Art Rummy* sets are available from Michael Olaf's Essential Montessori, P.O. Box 1162, Arcata, CA 95521; (707) 826-1557; or from RB Walter Art & Craft Materials, P.O. Box 6231, Arlington, TX 76005; (800) 447-8787.

Artery

This game, for budding art critics, teaches students the language and methodology of art appreciation. The game includes 54 art reproductions, on color postcards, and a series of game cards, divided into five categories, which players use to evaluate each art image in turn. Card categories include Subject (landscape, seascape, cityscape, portrait, still-life), Sensory (line, color, shape, texture), Formal Structure (balance, unity, pattern, center of interest), Technical (artistic media: paint, pencil, print, mosaic, collage, sculpture), and Expressive (meaning, mood, theme, idea). Cards are provided for two levels of art observers (beginner and advanced); there is also an accompanying teacher's guide, with lesson plans and activity suggestions. Available in both English and Spanish from Crizmac, 3721 E. Hardy Dr., Tucson, AZ 85716; (602) 323-8555.

Art-i-Facts

Art-i-Facts, "a valuable tool for anyone who works with elementary age children," is a short monthly newsletter, supplying general information about artists and the arts, art news, and suggestions for educational art and craft activities for use at home or in school. The newsletter is 6 pages long, on heavy paper, illustrated in black-and-white. A one-year subscription (12 issues) costs $12.00 from *Art-i-Facts*, P.O. Box 67192, Topeka, KS 66667.

Arts & Activities

Arts & Activities is an art education magazine, targeted at professional art teachers, and an excellent source of background information, resource reviews, and project suggestions for all who - in one capacity or another - teach art to the young. Also included: interviews with established and young artists, a "Clip and Save" full-color art print, and a list of on-going art contests and programs for students.

A one-year subscription (10 issues) costs $20.00; order from *Arts & Activities*, 591 Camino de la Reina, Suite 200, San Diego, CA 92108; (619) 297-8032.

The Big Yellow Drawing Book   Dan O'Neill, Marian O'Neill, and Hugh D. O'Neill, Jr.

The Big Yellow Drawing Book is a workbook for young cartoonists. Using it, kids learn a long list of drawing techniques: overlapping, wraparound lines, foreshortening, perspective, shadows, the use of detail in close-up. Lots of examples and big blank spaces for kids to make drawings of their own. Available from KidsArt, P.O. Box 274, Mt. Shasta, CA 96067; (916) 926-5076, (800) 959-5076.

Blitz, Bruce

Bruce Blitz, professional cartoonist, has produced a trio of video drawing kits for young artists. Each includes a 60-minute videotape (in a bright-red or yellow box) containing step-by-step drawing instructions, a wall chart picturing selected basic lessons from the tape, and a packet of art supplies (paper, pencils, pen, pencil sharpener). The sets, which cost $19.95 each, are titled *Learn Basic Blitz Drawing, Learn to Draw Blitz Comic Strips,* and *Learn to Draw Blitz Cartoons.* Our oldest son, an avid amateur cartoonist, has been delighted with these - especially with the *Comic Strip* set, which includes a packet of professional comic strip paper, divided into blocks, with lines for dialogue. (Extra comic strip paper can be purchased separately.) Available from Blitz Art Products, Inc., P.O. Box 8022, Cherry Hill, NJ 08002.

Cherry Tree Toys

"Kits for all skill levels," advertises the catalog, which sells woodworking projects. The projects - which include banks, clocks, door harps, and whirligigs - are available as plain plans (with complete instructions, diagrams, and painting patterns), as uncut kits (all materials included; you do the woodwork and assembly), as precut kits (you sand, put together, and paint), or as assembled (but unpainted) products. Along with all this, Cherry Tree Toys sells books on woodworking projects, woodworking and painting supplies, wind-up movements for music boxes (42 different tunes), and an array of stencils. They also sell a variety of small (2 1/4 ") wooden shapes - teddy bears, apples, hearts, cows, pigs, trees, sheep, and the like - for making pins, checkers, or refrigerator magnets. A nice project for small fry. For a free catalog, contact Cherry Tree Toys, PO Box 369, Belmont, OH 43718; (800) 848-4363.

Classical Kids

These classical cassette tapes, created by Susan Hammond, are enchanting. In each, the story of a great composer is told from the point of view of a not-necessarily-enthralled child; and the narration - which is delightful - is interspersed with generous excerpts from the composer's own music. In *Beethoven Lives Upstairs*, we meet Herr Beethoven - who has four pianos and who writes in pencil on the walls - through eleven-year-old Christoph, whose mother rents Beethoven a room. The story is told through an exchange of letters between Christoph and his young uncle, a music student in Vienna; and by the end of the tape both Christoph and his listeners have come to come to love the impatient deaf composer and his music. In *Mr. Bach Comes to Call* - our favorite - Bach himself, along with an orchestra and a rambunctious boys' choir, drops in on nine-year-old Elizabeth, who hates practicing the piano. *Mozart's Magic Fantasy* is a re-creation of Mozart's opera, "The Magic Flute," with a twist - here, young Sarah, wandering backstage looking for her mother, gets caught up in the story herself and sets off for Sarastro's castle, accompanied by a dragon. *Vivaldi's Ring of Mystery* tells the story of Vivaldi and his music through young Katarina, an orphan in Venice. Cassettes run 40-50 minutes each and cost $9.95. Available from Music for Little People, Box 1460, Redway, CA 95560; (800) 727-2233; or Chinaberry Book Service, 2780 Via Orange Way, Suite B, Spring Valley, CA 91978; (619) 670-5200 or (800) 776-2242 (orders, customer service).

Clay

For kitchen-table-type potters, the cheapest way to buy clay is through a ceramics shop or pottery studio. These often sell clay in 25- or 50-pound quantities, for somewhere around 30 cents a pound. Twenty-five pounds is a lot of clay - it comes in a brick measuring about 12" x 6" x 6" - and is generally available in either

white (it looks gray) or terra-cotta (reddish-brown). The drawback
to conventional pottery clay is that objects made with it, once dry,
are very brittle - professionals refer to this as "greenware" - and
must be finished by firing in a kiln. Some professional studios will
fire homemade pottery, for a small charge per piece; others won't,
since improperly made pottery has a chance of exploding in the
kiln, thus destroying an entire batch of claywork. Hobby potters
should check with local kiln-owners; look under "Ceramics" in the
Yellow Pages of your telephone directory.

If you don't have access to a kiln, there are self-hardening clays,
which toughen up all by themselves while drying at room temperature, or clays that harden at low temperature, which can be
baked in an ordinary oven. These are generally available at art or
craft supply stores and cost around $1.50 per pound.

Our favorite along these lines is a modeling compound called
Sculpey - "Better than clay!" - which is hardened by baking in a
conventional oven at 250 F for 20 minutes. Until baking, it remains pliable. Sculpey is sold in one- or two-pound chunks, in
white - after baking it can be painted with acrylics - or in collections of smaller colored bricks. The colors are terrific - vivid and
varied. Sculpey comes in three "multipacks" containing 10 colors
each: "Colored," "Brilliant" (day-glo colors like neon-pink), and
"Metallic." Our kids use this by the hour. Each multipack (1 1/2
pounds) costs about $13.00.

A similar modeling compound called Fimo - made in Germany
- comes in an even greater array of colors; it is, however, nearly
twice as expensive as Sculpey. Sculpey and Fimo are available
from many sources, including art and craft supply stores and Flax
Art & Design, P.O. Box 7216, San Francisco, CA 94120-7216; (800)
547-7778.

Coloring Books

The "Start Exploring" series from Running Press is a collection
of "fact-filled coloring books." Among them, for young artists, are
Masterpieces (Mary Martin and Steven Zorn) and *Masterpieces of
American Art* (Alan Gartenhaus). Each contains 60 black-and-white
line drawings of famous paintings, somewhat simplified for coloring, plus - on the facing page - biographical information about the
artist and a brief discussion about the painting itself. *Masterpieces*
and *Masterpieces of American Art* each cost $8.95; the books are
available through bookstores or from Running Press, 125 South
Twenty-second St., Philadelphia, PA 19103; (215) 567-5080, (800)

345-5359 for orders. When ordering from the publisher, add $2.50 for postage and handling.

The Impressionists Coloring Book by Andy Nelson (Culpepper Press) contains 46 black-and-white line drawings of paintings by such artists as Monet, Renoir, Degas, Cassatt, Cézanne, van Gogh, Gauguin, and Toulouse-Lautrec. Opposite each picture to color is a blank framed page, on which young artists can either copy the picture or design a new version all their own. The book costs $5.95, and is available through bookstores or from Culpepper Press, 2901 Fourth St. SE, Minneapolis, MN 55414.

Dover publishes an assortment of coloring books of interest to young artists, among them the *Geometrical Design Coloring Book* (Spyros Horemis), the *Op Art Coloring Book* (Jean Archer), the *Japanese Prints Coloring Book*, the *Ancient Egyptian Design Coloring Book*, and the *Celtic Design Coloring Book* (Ed. Sibbett, Jr.). Each costs $2.95 from Dover Publications, Inc., 31 East 2nd St., Mineola, NY 11501.

Even more fine arts coloring books are available from Bellerophon Books: for musicians, Bellerophon publishes *Great Composers* (two books, "Chopin to Tchaikovsky" and "Mahler to Stravinsky"), *Early Composers, Woman Composers, Wolfgang Amadeus Mozart,* and *Ludwig van Beethoven,* plus *A Musical Alphabet,* a comprehensive A-Z book of composer portraits. For dancers, coloring books include *Great Dancers* (a history of ballet, with portraits of great dancers costumed for their most famous roles), and a trio of books on individual well-known ballets: *Sleeping Beauty, Peter and the Wolf,* and *The Nutcracker.* Available from Bellerophon Books, 30 Ancapa Street, Santa Barbara, CA 93101; (800) 253-9943.

Come Look With Me Series   Gladys S. Blizzard   (Thomasson-Grant)

This series of art books is intended to introduce young children to fine art through a series of curiosity-provoking questions about scenes in famous paintings. The books are illustrated with beautiful full-color reproductions of great works of art.

Titles in the series include *Exploring Art With Children, Exploring Landscape Art, World of Play,* and *Animals in Art.*

Available through bookstores, from the Smithsonian Institution Catalogue, Department 0006, Washington, D.C. 20073-0006; (800) 322-0344; or from the Museum of Fine Arts, Boston, P.O. Box 1044, Boston, MA 02120-0900; (800) 225-5592.

Composers Card Game

The *Composers Card Game* is a rummy-type game in which players collect sets of portrait cards, each listing one of four musical selections by a famous composer. Selections for Mozart, for example, include "Papageno the Birdcatcher's Song," "Eine Kleine Nachtmusik," "Concerto in A," and "Symphony in G Minor." The game features 13 different classical composers. The *Composers Card Game* costs $5.50, from Michael Olaf's Essential Montessori, P.O. Box 1161, Arcata, CA 95521; (707) 826-1557; or Aristoplay, Box 7529, Ann Arbor, MI 48107; (800) 634-7738 or (313) 995-4353.

Copycats and Artifacts   Marianne Ford   (David R. Godine; 1986)

The book contains 42 different creative art projects, each based on museum artifacts. For each project are included full-color photographs of the relevant museum pieces, a brief history of the art work or technique, and detailed instructions (with illustrations). Projects include marbled papers, pomander balls, a mosaic tic-tac-toe board, a shell picture frame, a bird call, a thaumatrope, and a folding ice-cream-cone fan. Available through libraries and bookstores.

Craft Catalog

The title says it all. This is a 100+-page newsprint catalog of craft - not art - supplies: stencils, paints, woodenware for decorating (including blank napkin rings, boxes, birdhouses, and some useful-looking little three-inch pawn-like people), woodburning tools, wreaths, quilting supplies, stained-glass-painting kits, and doll-making materials. For a catalog, contact Craft Catalog, 6095 McNaughten Centre, Columbus, OH 43232; (800) 777-1442.

Craft King

Craft King publishes a fat discount craft supply mail-order catalog, nearly 200 pages of materials for home craftspersons. Of particular interest to those in the market for kid projects is a supply of natural-colored, ready-to-decorate cotton "paintables:" lunch bags, tote bags, belt pouches, placemats, aprons (child and adult sizes), banners, and stuffed animals (with or without clothes). All can be decorated with fabric paints, crayons, or stencils. Also available: precut leathercraft kits, the kind you stick together with vinyl lacing; inexpensive plain T-shirts for tie-dyeing, painting, or batik; macramé supplies, beads, and tiny electronic music boxes that, when pressed, play 40+ different songs, including "Happy Birthday to You," "I've Been Working on the Railroad," and "Twinkle, Twinkle, Little Star." For a catalog, contact Craft King, P.O. Box 90637, Lakeland, FL 33804; (813) 686-9600.

Creative Learning Systems

The Creative Learning Systems catalog carries several pages'-worth of books and building kits for young architects. Among these is a classroom-sized "Bridge Model Kit," with which participating kids build various types of wooden bridges, and then test their designs in a bridge-breaking contest. The kit comes with a teacher's guide, an assortment of bridge designs and diagrams, and 360 pre-cut pieces of basswood. Presumably that's enough for 24 students, since the kit also contains 24 tubes of wood cement. There's also a "Dome Kit," suitable for kids in grade 3 and up, which produces one dome with a circumference of 39 inches. To order, contact Creative Learning Systems, Inc., 16510 Via Esprillo, San Diego, CA 92127; (800) 458-2880.

Creativity for Kids

Creativity for Kids designs wonderful activity kits for children. "We believe," states one press release, "that children learn, grow and develop in an important way from creative, imaginative experiences." The kits are beautifully boxed, and include the Sculpture Kit, with which kids can turn out three-dimensional creations made with wood, cloth, paper, soap, wire, plaster, and clay; and "The Sky's the Limit: Basic Creativity Kit," crammed with gizmos, widgets, shiny paper, feathers, cardboard tubes, glitter, and much else for sheer artistic invention. All materials are included, plus a suggestion booklet. Other kits are more directed: there's "Quilting Bee," with which kids can make eight or more patchwork projects; "The Fine and Feathery Friend Maker," with which kids can turn out a large assortment of colorful googly-eyed birds; "Jewelry Making Sampler," and "Doll Making Sampler," which includes enough equipment to make 20 or more simple dolls. A new series - the "World of Kids" kits - is multicultural, including kits for Japanese origami, native American totem poles, and Mexican piñatas. Our kids had a blast making the piñatas for Ethan's last birthday: the kit includes papier-mâché mix, balloons, paint, yards of tissue-paper fringe, collage materials, and a packet of teeny prizes.

For a current flier and purchasing information, contact Creativity for Kids, 1802 Central Avenue, Cleveland, OH 44115; (216) 589-4800.

Crizmac

Crizmac publishes a catalog of art and cultural education materials. Some of these are packaged audiovisual programs aimed at classroom use, including videotapes (or filmstrips), teacher's guides, and reproducible student activity booklets. Titles include *Haitian Visions, Gente del Sol* (the art of Mexico and Guatemala), *Tribal Design* (the art of Alaska, New Guinea, pre-Columbian Mexico, the Pacific Northwest, and Africa), and *Master Pack* (an overview of artists who have made a lasting impression on modern art: Monet, Gauguin, Kandinsky, Van Gogh, Picasso, and Chagall). The company also sells a collection of innovative art appreciation games (see *Artery* and *Token Response*, reviewed separately), full-color art posters, illustrated art history timelines, and a large number of art history resource books, many of them with multicultural themes. For a free catalog, contact Crizmac, 3721 East Hardy Dr., Tucson, AZ 85716; (602) 323-8555.

Curiosity Kits

Curiosity Kits are beyond a doubt some of the - if not *the* - best kids' craft kits on the market. For one thing, everything needed to complete the project at hand - right down to the glue and sandpaper - is included in the kit, so you never have to tear frantically through the house looking for elusive items like toothpicks or pink cellophane. If you need it, you've got it. For another, these are truly lovely crafts: the materials are high-quality, the instructions are clear, and the outcomes (trust me) are successful. There are now over 20 Curiosity Kits available.

Kits for older kids (nine and up) include a cross-stitch American sampler, a folk-art rabbit, a heart-shaped basket, shadow puppets, a weaving loom, and "Flags of the World," with which young craftspersons design and make their own heraldic banners. For younger children, there are kits for making African and American Indian masks, a bluebird house, an insect house, American Indian moccasins (fit any size foot), pottery, and rattles, and kaleidoscopes. A recent introduction is a line of craft kits for preschoolers (ages 4 and older): with these "Early Learning Adventure" kits, small people can make a skygazer's mobile, a painted police car and fire truck, to be driven on the included road map, a set of wildlife masks, or a pair of "puzzle friends."

For a free brochure and order form, write Curiosity Kits, Inc. P.O. Box 811, Cockeysville, MD 21030; (410) 584-2605.

Don't Eat the Pictures

In this delightful musical video, Big Bird and a troupe of friends from "Sesame Street" miss closing time, and spend a night accidentally locked inside the Metropolitan Museum of Art. There - in the Egyptian Gallery - they meet and help a small ghostly Egyptian prince and his (invisible) cat. The video is a great introduction to art museums and art works for kids aged 3 and up. Running time: 60 minutes.

Older kids may prefer *The Hideaways*, the movie based on E.L. Konigsberg's *From the Mixed-Up Files of Mrs. Basil E. Frankweiler*, in which two kids run away from home to live at the Metropolitan Museum of Art. The movie, made in 1973, stars Ingrid Bergman as Mrs. Basil E. Frankweiler. Running time: 105 minutes. Both movies are available from Movies Unlimited, 6736 Castor Ave., Philadelphia, PA 19149; (800) 523-0823.

Dover Publications

Dover, for paper-model architects, sells many books of cardboard cut-and-assemble buildings, among them a western frontier fort, an early American village, a selection of Victorian houses, a southern plantation, a Crusader castle, and a caveman diorama. They also carry a pair of architectural coloring books: *The American House Styles of Architecture* (A.G. Smith) and *The Victorian House Coloring Book* (Daniel Lewis and Kristin Helberg).

For young dramatists, there is a collection of cut-and-assemble toy theaters, complete with scenery, props, characters, and story synopses: these include "The Wizard of Oz Toy Theater," "The Emerald City of Oz Toy Theater," "A Peter Rabbit Toy Theater," "A Nutcracker Ballet Toy Theater," "A Peter Pan Toy Theater," and "A Fairy Tale Toy Theater," with materials for performances of "Little Red Riding Hood," "Hansel and Gretel," and "Jack and the Beanstalk."

Dover sells many do-it-yourself craft project books for kids, including a cut-and-assemble totem pole, a collection of cut-and-string antique French jumping jacks, and paper mask and puppet books. The catalog also carries assorted fine arts postcard books, with full-color reproductions of the works of famous artists. For a free catalog, contact Dover Publications, Inc., 31 East 2nd St., Mineola, NY 11501. Ask for their complete catalog first; they have dozens of free specialty title catalogs for books in the different fields of interest, including a catalog of children's books, arts and crafts titles, needlework, history, fine art, music, science, etc.

Drawing on the Right Side of the Brain   Betty Edwards   (J.P. Tarcher; 1979)

This book intends to "enhance creativity and artistic confidence," even for insecure types who think they can't so much as draw a straight line with a ruler. To do so, the author attempts to teach would-be artists to visualize objects with the right side of the brain. The right hemisphere of the brain, Edwards explains, enables artists to draw objects as they are, using spatial, relational, and comparative skills. Those of us whose horses look like crooked pigs are most likely left-brain artists, drawing symbolic pre-conceived shapes from memory. Included are numerous exercises to demonstrate and reinforce right-brain drawing techniques - notably that of "inverted drawing," which means copying an art work upside-down. (The results in our family, which includes two right-handed children and one left-handed child, were impressive.) The book also covers many technical aspects of drawing: perspective, proportion, portraits, and light and shade. Available through bookstores.

Drawing With Children   Mona Brookes   (J.P. Tarcher; 1986)

This book is subtitled "A Creative Teaching and Learning Method That Works for Adults, Too," and our family, collectively, has had a wonderful time with it. The book details a complete art curriculum, including simple starting exercises, sample lesson plans with easy-to-follow instructions, suggestions for further projects and activities, and lots of (amazing) illustrations of art work produced by kids using Brookes' techniques. By the same author: **Drawing for Older Children and Teens.** Available in bookstores.

EDC Publishing

EDC Publishing is the American source for the Usborne books (see Multipurpose Resources). Several of these detailed, colorfully illustrated, and highly informational picture books are appropriate for young artists: notably, *The Usborne Story of Painting* and *The Usborne Story of Music*, each covering these respective arts from prehistory to the present day. The effect is that of an annotated timeline, explained through the many small picture panels. Usborne also publishes a great "First Music" series, in which bright-colored blobby little cartoon characters introduce young players to the recorder, the piano, and the keyboard, while explaining the basics of musical notation. For a catalog, contact EDC Publishing, P.O. Box 470663, Tulsa, OK 74147-0663; (800) 475-4522.

Educational Record Center

This is one packed catalog, listing all categories of records, cassettes, videos, and filmstrips. There are storytapes and folksongs, patriotic songs and marches, science and math songs, sing-alongs, multicultural songs, and lullabies. For young actors (grades K-1), there's a series of musical mini-plays: each is 15-20 minutes in length and comes with a playbook and cassette tape of background music and sound effects. There are 15 titles in the series, including "The Eagle and the Turkey" (a Thanksgiving folktale), "Spider Soup" (a Halloween story), "Circus Alphabet," "Whale Watching" (an ecology tale), and "Be Kind to Each Other" (the story of Androcles and the lion). For dancers, there are multicultural folk dances, native American dances, and square dances, all with music and detailed walk-through instructions. Among the dance selections is the "Young People's Folk Dance Library," a seven-album series featuring 85 different ethnic dances from 26 countries.

There is also a large selection of classical music resources for kids, including cassettes and videotapes introducing students to the instruments of the orchestra and to the great composers and their works. Example: *Once Upon a Sound*, a 55-minute animated video which teaches kids aged 4-8 the histories, sounds, and appearances of the basic orchestral instrumental groups. Titles of individual segments include "The Horn Blower," "The Pipes of Pan," "Jubal and the Twanging String," "Bangalore and the Stump Drum," and "American Music Makers." For a free catalog, contact the Educational Record Center, Inc., 3233 Burnt Mill Dr., Suite 100, Wilmington, NC 28403-2655; (800) 438-1637, fax: (910) 343-0311.

Electronic Courseware Systems

Electronic Courseware Systems (ECS) is a music software company. Their 25-page catalog carries software appropriate for musicians of all ages, variously suitable for use with the Apple (II+, IIe, IIGS, IIc), Macintosh, Commodore-64/128, IBM (PC, XT, AT, PS/2), Atari ST, and Yamaha C-1 systems. Software programs range from simple music-reading and instrumental fingering games for beginners through composition, theory, and music appreciation exercises for older students. Something for everybody. For a catalog, contact Electronic Courseware Systems, 1210 Lancaster Drive, Champaign, IL 61821; (800) 832-4965, ext. 17 (orders) or (217) 359-7099 (information).

Emberley, Ed

Ed Emberley teaches kids to draw using a foolproof step-by-step, add-a-line technique, with which even the most artistically inhibited can soon turn out everything from penguins to pirate ships, plus a lot in between. (It's fun for the artistically uninhibited too.) Emberley end-results are clever cartoon-like little characters in all possible varieties. There are many Ed Emberley drawing books, of which the best are probably the *Big Red, Big Orange, Big Green*, and *Big Purple Drawing Books*. Each contains lots of projects: the *Big Red Drawing Book* teaches kids how to draw animals, birds, fire engines, ships, plus a large assortment of patriotic Fourth-of-July (Uncle Sam, the American eagle) and Christmas figures; the *Big Orange Drawing Book* features a large Halloween section, populated with witches, bats, owls, skeletons, and a chipper-looking devil; the *Big Green Drawing Book* includes crocodiles, snakes, dragons, monsters, and space aliens; the *Big Purple Drawing Book* includes pirates, fish, bugs, trucks, and robots. And much more. The books cost $7.95 each, and are available through bookstores or from KidsArt, P.O. Box 274, Mt. Shasta, CA 96067; (916) 926-5076, (800) 959-5076. (See *Squiggles, Dots, and Lines.*)

Eyewitness Books: Art Series

An off-shoot of the wonderful Eyewitness series (see Multipurpose Resources). The books are lavishly illustrated with full-color photographs of art works and historical artifacts; sit down on the couch with one and you'll get a homestyle trip to the art museum. Titles in the series include *Watercolor, Impressionism, Perspective, Manet, Monet, Van Gogh*, and *Gauguin*.

The original Eyewitness series includes a *Music* volume, which is a beautiful photographic introduction to musical instruments covering both types of instruments, and their structure, history, and mechanism of action. Among the illustrations, for example, are computer images of the vibration patterns of a drumhead, an ancient Egyptian harp, a dissected violin, and an Australian didgeridoo. Also of interest for artists: Eyewitness *Film* and *Costume*. Available through bookstores.

First Impressions

This is a series of biographies of famous artists, targeted at kids aged 8 and older. All are lavishly illustrated with both full-color and black-and-white reproductions of the artist's work; the text is generally catchy and appealing. The books are 92 pages in length.

Titles in the series include *Mary Cassatt* (Susan Meyer), *Leonardo da Vinci* (Richard McLanathan), *Marc Chagall* (Howard Greenfeld), *Claude Monet* (Ann Waldron), *John James Audubon* (Joseph Kastner), *Rembrandt* (Gary Schwartz), *Pablo Picasso* (John Beardsley), *Francisco Goya* (Ann Waldron), and *Andrew Wyeth* (Richard Meryman). Available through bookstores, from the Chinaberry Book Service, 2780 Via Orange Way, Suite B, Spring Valley, CA 91978; (800) 776-2242 (orders) or (619) 670-5200; or from KidsArt, P.O. Box 274, Mt. Shasta, CA 96067; (916) 926-5076, (800) 959-5076.

Fun With Architecture David Eisen (Metropolitan Museum of Art, NY)
This is a beautifully packaged rubber stamp kit. The kit includes 35 architectural stamps - walls, windows, arches, domes, roofs, and columns - plus an ink pad and an informational instruction booklet. Available through bookstores or from the Metropolitan Museum of Art, 255 Gracie Station, New York, NY 10028-9998; (800) 468-7386.

Game of Great Composers

A musical board game intended to introduce players (aged 8 and up) to "Compositional Style: Medieval to Modern." In the course of play, kids identify and locate various famous composers on the gameboard, which depicts a map of Europe. Included: 32 composer cards, each carrying a brief biographical sketch of the listed artist; 6 period cards (Medieval, Renaissance, Baroque, Classical, Romantic, and Modern); and a cassette tape of musical selections from each historical period. The game costs $30.00, and is available from Michael Olaf's Essential Montessori, P.O. Box 1162, Arcata, CA 95521; (707) 826-1557.

The General Music Store

The General Music Store's catalog is subtitled the "World's Largest Selection of Musical Instruments and Accessories." The catalog carries complete lines of recorders, percussion instruments, rhythm band sets, portable keyboards, harmonicas, student guitars, and music supplies. There are a number of musical instruments designed especially for small children: there are flutophones and tonettes, pre-school wind instruments for those with very small fingers; the Chimalong, an 8-note metallophone, played with 2 mallets, using a color-coded system of musical notes that can be read by kids of all ages; and the Music Maker, a lapharp-like stringed instrument played by plucking according to a printed "music matrix" inserted under the strings.

The Music Store also carries a series of "Musikits," musical instrument kits for children to build themselves. Finished products include a violin, viola, cello, string bass, guitar, ukelele, or banjo. "Constructing a musical instrument," explains the accompanying text, "develops and refines children's concepts of sound and how it is produced and controlled."

Also included: musical methods books, songbooks, audio cassettes, and videos for young musicians; instruction and idea books for music teachers; and an assortment of musical games. Among these last are the Galaxy board games, each of which consists of a laminated playing board, assorted playing pieces, and an instruction sheet. There are eight different Galaxy games, ranging in price from $9.50 to $13.25. Games include *Stu Stegosaurus*, in which players learn note values and musical signs while traveling through a prehistoric swamp; *Treble Trek* and *Bass Ball*, which teach, respectively, the notes of the treble and bass clefs; and *Instrument Music Match*, in which players learn to classify the instruments of the band and orchestra. For a catalog, contact The General Music Store, 19880 State Line Rd., South Bend, IN 46637; (219) 272-8266 or (800) 348-5003.

Getting to Know the World's Greatest Artists

This perfectly delightful series of biographies of famous artists, written and illustrated by Mike Venezia, is appropriate for kids aged 4-9. Each (paperback) book is 32 pages long, with a clever informative large-print text; illustrations include full-color reproductions of the artist's works plus humorous cartoon-like scenes from the artist's life. Highly recommended. Titles in the series include *Da Vinci, Rembrandt, Van Gogh, Picasso, Monet, Hopper, Cassatt, Botticelli, Goya, Michelangelo, Klee,* and *Gauguin*. The books, published by Childrens Press, are available through bookstores or from RB Walter Art & Craft Materials, P.O. Box 6231, Arlington, TX 76005; (800) 447-8787.

Gonna Sing My Head Off! American Folk Songs for Children Kathleen Krull   (Alfred A. Knopf; 1992)

A collection of 62 traditional American folk songs, including words, music (for both piano and guitar), and a paragraph of background information. Songs include "Arkansas Traveler," "Casey Jones," "The Cat Came Back," "The Erie Canal," "Go Tell It On the Mountain," "I've Been Working on the Railroad," "Old Joe Clark," "Take Me Out to the Ball Game," "We Shall Overcome," and, of course, "Yankee Doodle." Illustrated with colorful pastel drawings. Available through bookstores. Other good children's songbooks include Ruth Crawford Seeger's *American Folk Songs for Children* (Zephyr; 1970) and the Metropolitan Museum of Art's *Go In and Out the Window: An Illustrated Songbook for Children* (Holt; 1987).

Good Earth Art: Environmental Art for Kids   MaryAnn F. Kohl and Cindy Gainer   (Bright Ring; 1991)

Two hundred creative art projects for kids aged 1-10, using natural or recycled materials. Instructions are included for making natural dyes, cattail baskets, earth paints, homemade crayons, newspaper beads, and many more. Also by Kohl: *Mudworks: Creative Clay, Dough and Modeling Experiences* and *Scribble Cookies and Other Independent Creative Art Experiences for Children*.

Great Painters   Piero Ventura   (G.P. Putnam's Sons; 1984)

This is a 160-page history of art for kids, enchantingly illustrated, covering art from the days of the Roman Empire through the 20th century. Illustrations (on every page) combine Ventura's colorful, clever, and historically accurate little people with wonderful reproductions of artistic masterpieces, all drawn to scale, such that readers can readily comprehend the size of the painting relative to the size of the painter. Informative reader-friendly text. By the same author: *Great Composers,* an equivalent volume on the history of music, and *Michelangelo's World*. Available through bookstores.

Harps of Lorien

Harps of Lorien, along with exquisite harps for the adult harpist, carries an unusual and beautiful assortment of musical instruments for children. Their most popular instrument is a portable pentatonic harp, nicknamed "The Little Minstrel." This, the catalog text explains, is ideal for beginners, since all the notes of the five-tone scale harmonize with each other; thus there are *no* wrong notes. "The Little Minstrel" costs $160, and comes with a case, instruction cassette, tuning key, and stringing chart. Runner-up for most popular children's instrument is the "Kinder Lyre," a 7-string pentatonic instrument that "combines the shape of the ancient lyre with the charm and resonance of the wire-strung Celtic harp." "A wonderful first instrument," states the text, "used extensively in the Waldorf schools with the kindergarten and younger grade children." Harps of Lorien also carries a child's hammered dulcimer, child-sized bagpipes, guitars, and tambourines, Pueblo drums, harmonicas, recorders, and tin whistles, which come with instruction book and demonstration cassette. For a catalog, contact Harps of Lorien, 610 North Star Route GS, Questa, NM 87556; (505) 586-1307, fax: (505) 586-0067.

Hearthsong

A beautiful catalog for young craftspersons. Hearthsong's toys and kits are carefully chosen both for their environmental message and for their special roles in the lives of children. Products are made from all-natural materials; toys are solid and sturdy, meant to be saved and passed down from generation to generation. Hearthsong sells modelling beeswax and lap looms, silk squares in nine colors for fantasy play ("drape a house or pupper theater, make a quick cape or sash or turban, or create a lake or garden"), colored sidewalk chalk, and block crayons. There are finger-puppet kits (the puppets are made on 2 1/2" wooden bases, also sold separately) and folding puppet theatres; kits for making clay beads, pine needle baskets, beeswax candles, and sandpaintings. For small sculptors, there is a terrific Stone Sculpture Kit: it contains three quarts of "stone" mix (actually a combination of plasters and vermiculite), a pair of (blunt) carving tools, and detailed instructions. The stone mix is combined with water and poured into a mold - a one-pint cream carton works beautifully. When hard, the mix looks like concrete, but is easy to carve; our three young Michelangelos have done wonders with it. Recommended for kids aged 8 and up. For older kids, there's an option for additional advanced tools, a shaping saw and scribe, both sharp. To obtain a catalog, contact Hearthsong, P.O. Box B, Sebastopol CA 95473-0601; (800) 325-2502.

History of Art for Young People H.W. Janson and Anthony F. Janson (Abrams; 4th edition, 1992)

This is a junior version of Janson's encyclopedic classic reference work on art history, covering art from the prehistoric times to the present day. The book, 528 pages long, is richly illustrated (219 color and 300 black-and-white illustrations), impeccably researched, and includes timeline charts, equating events in art to important happenings in history, science, and literature. It's a textbook, but it's a beauty. Available through bookstores.

I Know That Building! Jane D'Alelio (Preservation Press; 1989)

Of all the architectural resources we've tracked down, this may be our favorite. The book is a beautifully-done giant paperback in full color, crammed with architectural information, games, and activities. Using it, kids can design a Victorian garden, a Morris chair, and a Frank Lloyd Wright window; make a hex sign, a gargoyle mask, and an architectural "time line;" assemble models of a skyscraper, a Queen Anne-style house, a 19th-century schoolhouse, and a covered bridge; solve a "Famous Lighthouses" puzzle; and play a card game matching famous architects with some of their best-known buildings. Available through bookstores or from Zephyr Press, 3316 N. Chapel Ave., P.O. Box 13448, Tucson, AZ 85732-3448.

I Spy: An Alphabet in Art   Lucy Micklethwait   (Greenwillow; 1991)
This unusual alphabet book contains 26 (full-color) paintings from the world's greatest museums, each containing an object to be spied out, beginning with the letters A through Z. Alphabetical object-seekers study art works by Picasso, Chagall, Rousseau, Matisse, Botticelli, Goya, Seurat, Van Eyck, Magritte, and many more. "I spy with my little eye something beginning with A," for example, faces a reproduction of Magritte's "Son of Man," the portrait of a bowler-hatted gentleman with a big green apple obscuring his face. A delight for all ages. Available through bookstores or from Chinaberry Book Service, 2780 Via Orange Way, Suite B, Spring Valley, CA 91978; (800) 776-2242 or (619) 670-5200.

Other artistic alphabets include Charles Sullivan's *Alphabet Animals* (Rizzoli; 1991), in which the letters of the alphabet are illustrated with reproductions of famous works by artists such as Marc Chagall, Andy Warhol, and Winslow Homer. Florence Cassen Mayers has written a series of museum alphabet books, all published by Abrams: these are tall skinny volumes in which each letter of the alphabet is illustrated with a big full-color photograph of a work from the collection of a famous museum. Titles in the series include *ABC: Museum of Fine Arts, Boston; ABC: Museum of Modern Art, New York; ABC: Costumes and Textiles from the Los Angeles County Museum of Art*; and *ABC: Musical Instruments from the Metropolitan Museum of Art*. In this last, alphabetical instruments begin with Accordion, Bagpipe, Clarinet, and Drum (one from Africa; one from Japan), though our kids' favorite remains the W page, Walking-Stick Instruments, which pictures an assortment of walking-sticks that variously unscrew and reassemble to produce violin bows, clarinets, and flutes. Available through bookstores.

In the Picture

This is a board game for art-lovers: players move through the galleries of the art museum, collecting clue cards each picturing a small segment of a larger painting, and answering general and specific questions about art. The winner is the first to accumulate a set of three clue cards all from the same painting, thus identifying the "missing" picture. In a variant on the original game, kids can make their own clue cards, based on the included postcard-sized reproductions of famous paintings. The game includes 12 art reproductions and 56 question-and-answer cards. *In the Picture* costs $23.95, from RB Walter Art & Craft Materials, P.O. Box 6231, Arlington, TX 76005; (800) 447-8787.

Incredible!

Targeted at young musicians, *Incredible!* is touted as "A Creative Game for Successful, Enjoyable Practicing." This game, reads the enclosed rule book, "is designed to help you learn one piece of music and to be able to play it with confidence." For long-run practice, *Incredible!* includes a "100 Days Practicing Chart" with accompanying reward stickers, and "My Incredible Repertoire Chart," with spaces for the name of each mastered piece, its composer, and the date on which it was first played correctly. For the short term, it includes tablets of black-and-white "Incredible Sections" gameboards, which the players move through during each daily practice session, marking off spaces as each section of the current lesson's musical selection is repeated. Finally, there is a colorful laminated gameboard on which each square of the playing path lists an activity to do while practicing. Players - among other activities - are told to play with their mouths open, while wiggling their toes, in the dark, or with their right hands on their heads. This, explains the rule book, helps improve the concentration. *Incredible!* costs $19.95. It is published by CPP/Belwin, Inc., 15800 N.W. 48th Ave., Miami, FL 33014; (800) 327-7643 or (305) 620-1500. CPP/Belwin ordinarily sells only to schools and businesses; call for the nearest distributor in your area. *Incredible!* is also available from Music Plus, 425 Main Street, Danbury, CT 06810; (203) 744-4344.

KidsArt

The KidsArt catalog offers art teaching books, art appreciation materials, how-to project books, art kits, art supplies, rubber stamps and inks, art history books and coloring books, and much more. A source for fine art postcard books (30 cards each; titles include *Chagall, Van Gogh, Audubon, Gauguin, Norman Rockwell, Monet, Andy Warhol, Renoir, Matisse,* and *The Impressionists*) and for the Usborne "Young Artist" series (32-page paperbacks; titles include *How to Draw Cartoons and Caricatures, How to Draw Monsters, How to Draw Spacecraft, How to Draw Animals, How to Draw Machines,* and *How to Draw Lettering*). Art supplies include powdered tempera paints in 1-pound jars, watercolors in tubes, paint without brushes for toddlers (it comes in squeeze bottles with marker tips; relatively messless for uncoordinated painters), sketch books, fingerpaint pads, bags of balsa scraps ("instant sculpture center"), and packets of plain white puzzles and bookmarks, for those who like to invent their own. KidsArt also publishes an excellent quarterly newsletter, each consisting of 16 pages of information, games, puzzles, art projects, and activities, all centered around a unifying art theme. Past issues have dealt with Folk Art, Sculpture, Wildlife Art, Ancient Greece, Outer Space, Printmaking, Leonardo da Vinci, and Traditional Arts of Africa. A one-year subscription (4 issues) costs $8.00; individual back issues are available for $2.50. For a KidsArt catalog or additional subscription information: KidsArt, Box 274, Mt. Shasta, CA 96067; (916) 926-5076, (800) 959-5076.

Kid Pix

There are many paint software programs on the market these days, all aimed at art-minded computer owners, but Kid Pix remains one of the very best: versatile, light-hearted, open-ended, and creative. Among its easy-to-use features: dozens of ready-made pictures that kids can "rubber-stamp" onto their computer-screen canvas; a talking alphabet; and an assortment of oddball tools, including "Northern Lights," "Spray Paint," "Kaleidoscope," "Trees," which generates wonderful branching fractal trees, and "Splatter," which produces a colorful Jackson Pollock effect. Users can make their own connect-the-dots pictures, paint with alphabet lines, or plaster their screen with patterned "wallpaper." Each tool comes with its own wacky sound effect: bonks, boings, beeps, and booms. Macintosh or IBM/Tandy format from Broderbund Software, Dept. 15, P.O. Box 6125, Novato, CA 94948; (800) 521-6263.

Lark in the Morning

Lark in the Morning publishes a tightly packed 70+-page catalog specializing in hard-to-find musical instruments, music, and instructional materials. ("The Lark says: 'Kill your television and play music!'") Through the catalog, interested musicians can buy African basket rattles, South American bird calls, Australian diger- idoos ("the oldest wind instrument in the world"), panpipes, pen- nywhistles, fifes, ocarinas, bagpipes, lutes, lyres, dulcimers, and harps. There is an assortment of build-your-own instruments, in- cluding dulcimer, harp, and banjo kits, and even, for the very am- bitious, harpsichord and clavichord kits.

There is also a large selection of music and instructional books, and a fascinating collection of audio cassettes and CDs. Included are recordings of Australian aboriginal music, Irish folk songs, na- tive American flute music, Russian balalaika ensembles, Scottish bagpipes, and African percussion. It's an education just to read the catalog. To obtain a copy, contact Lark in the Morning, P.O. Box 1176, Mendocino, CA 95460; (707) 964-5569.

Lives of the Musicians: Good Times, Bad Times (And What the Neighbors Thought)   Kathleen Krull (Harcourt, Brace, Jovanovich; 1993)

The fascinating (and frequently funny) biographical stories of twenty famous musicians, briefly and cleverly told. Composers covered include Antonio Vivaldi, Johann Sebastian Bach, Wolfgang Amadeus Mozart, Ludwig van Beethoven, Frederic Chopin, Giu- seppe Verdi, Clara Schumann, Stephen Foster, Johannes Brahms, Peter Ilich Tchaikovsky, William Gilbert and Arthur Sullivan, Erik Satie, Scott Joplin, Charles Ives, Igor Stravinsky, Nadia Boulanger, Sergei Prokofiev, George Gershwin, and Woody Guthrie. "Musical Notes" at the end of each chapter give more information: readers learn that Bach wrote the *Goldberg Variatiions* to relax an insomni- ac millionaire; that Igor Stravinsky once wrote a polka for fifty ele- phants wearing ballet tutus; and that Prokofiev's music was once so controversial that conductors of his symphonies received death threats. Our boys loved it. Available through bookstores.

Make Mine Music   Tom Walther   (Little, Brown; 1981)

This is one of the Brown Paper School Books series (see Multi- purpose Resources). The book, 126 pages long, is a rich source of musical information and activities, covering the science of sound, the mechanics of music, musical notation, and the history of musi- cal instruments (string, percussion, woodwind, and brass). Hands- on projects, which range from the simple to the ambitious, include making a musical bow, a lute, a spike fiddle, an Aeolian harp, a thumb piano, a bull-roarer, and a set of pan-pipes. And much more. *Make Mine Music* is available through bookstores.

Makit Products

A great series of projects for kids. The original Makit product was the "Make-a-Plate," introduced in 1976: a kid's drawing, on a plate-sized piece of paper, is sent to the Makit Products factory, where it is permanently sealed into a plastic dinner plate. Equivalent (factory-sealed) projects include Make-a-Planter, Make-a-Mug, Make-a-Pencil-Holder, Make-a-Stein, Make-a-Calendar, Make-a-Placemat, and Make-a-T-Shirt. Makit Products also offers an assortment of kits that do not require factory-processing: Christmas ornaments (trees, stars, hearts, bears, and wreaths), picture frames, pencil holders, badges, and keychains. In each case, kid's artwork is simply snapped in place, between fitted plastic pieces. Makit Products may be ordered individually, or as "Classroom Kits," which contain enough materials for 50 students. For further information, contact Makit Products, Inc., 4659 Mint Way, Dallas, TX 75236.; (214) 330-7774. Also available from KidsArt, P.O. Box 274, Mt. Shasta, CA 96067; (916) 926-5076, (800) 959-5076.

Metropolitan Museum of Art

The Metropolitan Museum of Art catalog carries an exceptional assortment of books, toys, and games for children. Notable among them is *Pablo*, a 3-dimensional modern art building kit which consists of 120 geometric cardboard building pieces in a vividly colored array of spirals, stripes, checks, and solids, plus 35 black plastic connectors. Spectacular for young artists. Also see *The Metropolitan Museum of Art Activity Book* (Osa Brown), an unusual collection of art activities based on the museum collection and illustrated with color photographs. Included are a cut-and-assemble Temple of Dendur and instructions of making a carp kite, Japanese paperdolls, a woven wall-hanging, and an imitation stained-glass window. For a catalog: Metropolitan Museum of Art, 255 Gracie Station, New York, NY 10028-9998; (800) 468-7386.

Museum of Fine Arts, Boston

A source of high-quality books, toys, and games for children, among them M.C. Escher and Joan Miró puzzle cubes (8 cubes per puzzle, each forming 6 different works of art) and optical illusion playing cards ("over 100 illusions in two decks"). For a free catalog, contact the Museum of Fine Arts, Boston, P.O. Box 1044, Boston, MA 02120-0900; (800) 225-5592.

Music for Little People

Music for Little People offers a delightful collection of audio cassettes, videotapes, and musical instruments for little people of all ages. There are lullabies and singalongs; storytapes - including Jim Hayes' "Heart Full of Turquoise," a collection of Pueblo Indian tales; folk songs; multicultural songs; environmental songs; and classical selections for kids. For hands-on musicians, Music for Little People carries folk harps, lap harps, recorders, marimbas, bodhran drums, pan pipes, thumb pianos, and small-sized guitars.

Videotapes include "I Can Dance," an introduction to ballet for kids aged 7 and up; a trio of classical ballets by professional dance companies ("The Little Humpbacked Horse," "Cinderella," and "L'Enfant et les Sortilèges"); Raffi's "Young Children's Concert;" and a large assortment of classic tales for all ages, including *The Chronicles of Narnia, The Secret Garden, Anne of Green Gables,* and *Charlotte's Web.* One of our favorite catalogs. Music for Little People, Box 1460, Redway, CA 95560; (800) 346-4445.

Music Maestro II

A board game for young musicians, subtitled "The Game of Musical Instruments, Past and Present." The playing board pictures 48 different musical instruments, from the krumhorn to the synthesizer, arranged in orchestral order; the accompanying cassette tapes introduce players to the sounds of the individual instruments, ancient and modern, and to the music of instrumental ensembles (classical, bluegrass, rock, and jazz). Instructions are included for several different levels of play, appropriate for preschoolers to adults. The game costs $25.00, and is available from Michael Olaf's Essential Montessori, P.O. Box 1162, Arcata, CA 95521; (707) 826-1557.

Music Masters

The *Music Masters* cassette tapes each contain 20 to 30 selections from the works of a great composer, interspersed with narrated information about the composer's life. Tapes are sold as sets; each set contains six cassettes covering seven different composers. Set I includes the music of Bach, Mozart, Chopin, Mendelssohn, Schubert, Schuman, and Grieg; Set II, Handel, Beethoven, Haydn, Wagner, Dvorak, Vivaldi, and Corelli; and Set III, Tchaikovsky, Brahms, Strauss, Berlioz, Verdi, Foster, and Sousa. Each set costs $25.00; all are available from Michael Olaf's Essential Montessori, P.O. Box 1162, Arcata, CA 95521; (707) 826-1557; or the Educational Record Center, Inc., 3233 Burnt Mill Dr., Suite 100, Wilmington, NC 28403-2655; (800) 438-1637.

Music Mind Games   Michiko Yurko   (CPP/Belwin; 1992)

This 430-page book contains everything you ever needed to know about teaching music to budding young musicians. The book is divided roughly into two parts: the first deals with philosophies, aims, and techniques of music teaching; the second - the real nitty-gritty - includes instructions for over 200 different creative games for teaching music theory and practice. Games are variously designed to teach the musical alphabet and intervals, the notes of the grand staff, rhythm, melodic and harmonic dictation, signs, symbols, and tempos, scales and key signatures, chords, and music-reading. The book is published by CPP/Belwin, Inc., 15800 N.W. 48th Ave., Miami, FL 33014; (800) 327-7643 or (305) 620-1500. This company ordinarily sells only to schools and businesses; contact them for the distributor closest to you. *Music Mind Games* is also available from Music Plus, 425 Main Street, Danbury, CT 06810; (203) 744-4344.

Musical Heritage Society

The Musical Heritage Society is essentially a Book-of-the-Month Club for classical music buffs: members receive copies of the Musical Heritage Review 18 times yearly, from which they select recordings on cassette, CD, or record. Selections cover every musical period - Medieval, Renaissance, Baroque, Rococo, Classical, Romantic, and Modern - and include the works of such great composers as Bach, Beethoven, Handel, Haydn, Mozart, Schubert, Telemann, and Vivaldi. For more information contact the Musical Heritage Society, 1710 Highway 35, Ocean, NJ 07712-9923.

Musopoly

It's pronounced Mu "as in music" zop' o lee and the definition, according to the box cover, is "many musicians having fun together learning to read music." This is a board game, appropriate for players over a wide range of ages, who, using it, learn the names of the notes on the grand staff and how to find them on the piano (or their own musical instrument), how to define musical symbols and identify tempos and rhythms, and how to write music dictation patterns using note symbols and the included laminated dictation slate. The brightly colored game board pathway consists of the letter names of the notes, plus assorted musical symbols; as players progress around it, they answer questions about music, thus earning "rhythm money" and (plastic) gold coins.

It's marketed as a single game, but there's a lot happening in it, on a number of different musical fronts. Along with the game-board are included blue and green grand staff note cards (bass and treble clefs), fermata cards, tempo cards, rhythm cards, and playing pieces shaped like little animals. *Musopoly* ($24.95) is published by CPP/Belwin, Inc., 15800 N.W. 48th Ave., Miami, FL 33014; (800) 327-7643 or (305) 620-1500. The company ordinarily sells only to schools and businesses; call for the distributor nearest to you. *Musopoly* is also available from Music Plus, 425 Main Street, Danbury, CT 06810; (203) 744-4344.

Once Upon the Thames

Ann Rachlin, nicknamed the "Pied Piper of London," produces narrated cassette tapes of classical music for children, delightful combinations of story, biography, and music. Tapes in the series include *Once Upon the Thames*, the life of Handel set to his music, in which listeners travel down the Thames by royal barge, and *Papa Haydn's Surprise*, the life of Haydn, from his mischievous childhood on, set to his works. The tapes are available from Michael Olaf's Essential Montessori, P.O. Box 1162, Arcata, CA 95521; (707) 826-1557; or from Music for Little People, Box 1460, Redway, CA 95560; (800) 727-2233.

The Orchestra

A terrific introduction to the orchestra for beginners and a thoroughly enjoyable musical experience for everybody. *The Orchestra*, narrated by Peter Ustinov, not only details the four instrumental families of the orchestra (strings, woodwinds, brass, and percussion), but demonstrates, in creative fashion, the breadth, depth, and sheer delight of music. Cassette tape, CD, or video: Music for Little People, Box 1460, Redway, CA 95560; (800) 727-2233.

Parent Child Press

The prime publication of the Parent Child Press is Aline Wolf's *Mommy, It's a Renoir!* This is a parent/teacher handbook for teaching art appreciation to young children, designed to be used with postcard-sized reproductions of famous paintings. Parent Child Press offers these in bound sets (you cut them out), as *Child-size Masterpieces*. To date, there are seven of these collections available, with more in preparation.

Lessons in *Mommy, It's a Renoir!* proceed sequentially, at three different levels for children of different ages. Kids first match pairs of identical paintings, then match "companion" paintings (similar, but not identical). They next sort paintings into groups of four by one artist, and then proceed to learning the names of the artists and their paintings. In the next step, they begin to learn about schools of art - Abstract, American, British, Chinese, Cubist, Dutch, French, Geometric-Abstract, Impressionist, Italian, Japanese, Post-Impressionist, Spanish, and Surrealist - and group paintings by school; and finally they construct Art Timelines, arranging postcards in chronological order on printed timelines (also available from Parent Child Press). Add an occasional trip to the art museum and you'll have it made. For more information, contact the Parent Child Press, P.O. Box 675, Hollidaysburg, PA 16648-0675; (814) 696-7512, fax: (814) 696-7510.

Philanthropist

A beautiful board game for art buffs. The game, subtitled "A Window on the World of Painting," includes a board patterned with photographs of famous international art museums, 200 full-color postcard-sized reproductions of well-known works of art from each museum's collection, playing pieces (sparkly "jewels"), and a pack of "Philanthropist Cards," each detailing an act of art philanthropy. You organize a fund for the preservation of ancient paintings, commission artists to design mosaics for parks, establish scholarship funds for art students, host guest art exhibits, and so on. The first player to perform three acts of philanthropy wins. Players collect Philanthropist Cards by answering questions about art works as they proceed around the board. As players land on museum squares, they draw an art postcard representing a work from that museum's collection, and then answer questions about it in one of six categories, to be determined by a roll of the dice: title, artist, date (within 10 years), country of artist's birth, style, and a technical or historical bonus question. (There's an option for multiple-choice answers, which helps.) The game costs about $50.00, but it's an entire art education in a box. Available through game stores or from the Metropolitan Museum of Art, 255 Gracie Station, New York, NY 10028-9998; (800) 468-7386.

Pioneer Drama Service

Ever wanted to put on a play? This (free) catalog has them all: short plays, long plays, musicals, melodramas, Christmas plays, spooky plays, simple plays, and ambitious plays. There is a series of Shakespeare adaptations for young actors (casts of 13 to 16, plus extras; performance times about one hour). There are "storyteller and participation" plays, in which members of the audience take part in the action. Examples: "Rumpelstiltskin" (cast of 5, minimal set requirements, 40 minutes long), "Snow White and the Seven Dwarves" (cast of 3, no specific set requirements, 30 minutes long), and "The Pied Piper" (cast of 6, simple area staging, 45 minutes long). For each of the many plays, there's a description of the plot, and listings of cast size, set requirements, and staging times. Single play copies run $3.00 to $4.00 apiece; and there's a royalty charge ($15 to $50) for formal performances. The company also sponsors an annual playwriting contest. For a copy of the catalog or contest guidelines, contact Pioneer Drama Service, P.O. Box 4267, Englewood, CO 80155-4267; (303) 779-4035.

Rhythm Band

Rhythm Band, Inc., sells musical instruments and teaching aids for kids. There are rhythm band instruments, sold separately or in sets, for pre-schoolers or young elementary students: rhythm sticks, jingle bells, triangles, cymbals, tambourines. There are recorders and kazoos, bellboards and harmonicas, handchimes and guitars - plus a large assortment of music books and cassettes.

Also available: a selection of musical games, including *Pulse*, a rhythm bingo game in which players aurally identify basic rhythm patterns; *Musical Magic*, a board game in which players learn the fundamentals of reading music; and *Play the Composers*, a card game designed to teach the names of famous composers and their works. To obtain a catalog, contact Rhythm Band Instruments, P.O. Box 126, Fort Worth, TX 76101-0126; (800) 424-4724.

S & S Arts and Crafts

Co-opt a few friends and this catalog is a great deal: the first section is devoted to "Group Pack Projects," craft projects sold in quantity, at substantial discounts. The selection includes Design-A-Hat, Build-A-Kite, and Make-A-Periscope kits, in sets of 12; African mask kits in sets of 15; Make-Your-Own-Yo-Yo or Pinwheel kits in sets of 24; Ojo de Dios medallions and Navajo sandpainting kits in sets of 50; and much more. Also available: beginner embroidery and latch hook kits, candlemaking and copper enameling supplies, basket-weaving and leather lace-up kits (including "budget moccasins" to assemble, in a range of sizes), ceramic tiles and mosaic projects, holiday crafts, and wood-working sets. There are six pages devoted solely to *beads* of all shapes and sizes. To obtain a catalog, contact S & S Arts and Crafts, P.O. Box 513, Dept. 2020, Colchester, CT 06415-0513; (800) 243-9232.

Squiggles, Dots, and Lines

Ed Emberley (see entry above) has made a 30-minute kids' how-to-draw video titled *Squiggles, Dots, & Lines*. In it, kids follow Emberley's instructions, using six basic shapes to assemble, step by step, increasingly complex drawings. The final products are impressive, the music is catchy, and everybody has a good time. *Squiggles, Dots, and Lines* costs $14.95 from KIDVIDZ, 618 Centre Street, Newton, MA 02158; (617) 243-7611; or Educational Record Center, Inc. 3233 Burnt Mill Dr., Suite 100, Wilmington, NC 28403-2655; (800) 438-1637.

Token Response

This is an innovative game for young art critics, designed to encourage kids of all ages to look closely at works of art, then think and talk about what they see. The game consists of an assortment of eight different colored tokens, which students select to help express their opinions about a given work of art. A light bulb, for example, means a work that is unusual or highly creative; a hand means beautifully crafted; a blue ribbon, a museum-quality masterpiece; and a clock means difficult, detailed, and time-consuming. The tokens can be used with art prints or postcards, with art books, or during museum expeditions. The game also includes a teacher's activity and discussion guide, and a set of reproducible forms, carrying all the art token symbols, which can be used for art-related activities or art journals. Available from Crizmac, 3721 East Hardy Drive, Tucson, AZ 85716; (602) 323-8555.

University Prints

University Prints supplies "scholarly and inexpensive art history visual materials." The catalog - 250 pages long, in small print - lists some 7500 different art prints, categorized by period, school, and artist. Of these, 300 are available in color, as a collection, "History of Painting in Color;" subjects range from the prehistoric to the contemporary period. The entire set, boxed, costs $45.00.

Prints may also be ordered individually, by catalog number. All measure 5 1/2 x 8" and cost 7 cents each in black-and-white, 15 cents each in color. Subjects include art history maps, architectural prints, multicultural artifacts, sculpture, and paintings of all periods. A complete catalog costs $3.00, from University Prints, 21 East Street, P.O. Box 485, Winchester, MA 01890.

RB Walter Art and Craft Materials

This catalog costs $2.00, but it's worth it: this is the Sears-

Roebuck of kids' art, 150 pages of all conceivable kinds of art and craft supplies. Included are all the standards: clay, craft sticks, collage materials, origami paper, art tissue, construction paper, markers, crayons, pastels, chalks, and paints. Other selections are more specialized: basket-weaving and candle-making supplies, metallic and glow-in-the-dark fabric paints, "multicultural" crayons and clays in (lots of) realistic skin tones, batik materials, silhouette paper, and block printing equipment. There is also a large assortment of art-related literature: art and craft activity books, instructional drawing books and videos, art history and art appreciation programs, art prints, and games. For a catalog, send $2.00 to RB Walter Art and Craft Materials, P.O. Box 6231, Arlington, TX 76005; (800) 447-8787.

Young Architects Kit

Using this packaged kit, young architects can design their own houses on paper, and then build a three-dimensional model based on their house plans, using snap-together clear acrylic pieces. Suitable for architects in grade 3 and up. The kit includes an 18 x 24" work mat, 10 sheets of drafting paper, 12 room templates, 3 furniture tracing guides, 30 clear acrylic exterior walls, 30 blue acrylic interior walls, 50 corner blocks, and assorted reusable vinyl door and window patterns. The kit costs $69.00 from Zephyr Press, 3316 N. Chapel Ave., P.O. Box 13488, Tucson, AZ 85732-3488; (602) 322-5090.

Zolo

Zolo is a wonderful resource for creative young sculptors. The set, which comes in a big wooden box with a sliding top, consists of some fifty different colorful wooden pieces: pink-and-purple spiraled balls, striped sticks, polka-dot squiggles, giant eggs, and chunky pyramids. With these, kids can assemble an almost infinite assortment of fascinating 3-D artworks. *Zolo* is expensive - the set costs about $175 - but once you've got it, it will last forever. Top quality. Available through art stores and from The Art Institute of Chicago Museum Shop, 125 Armstrong Road, Des Plaines, IL 60018; (800) 621-9337 or (708) 299-5470.

Books for All Kinds of Artists

The Art Lesson Tomie de Paola (Putnam; 1989) Tommy, who wants to be an artist when he grows up, has his first encounter with an art teacher. The experience isn't quite what he had expected.

Ballet Shoes Noel Streatfeild (Random House; 1937) The story of three young girls who are training to be professional ballerinas. This, for middle readers, is one of a series; other titles include *Dancing Shoes, Skating Shoes,* and *Theatre Shoes.*

Benjamin West and His Cat Grimalkin Marguerite Henry (Macmillan; 1947) A delightful biography of young Benjamin West, who got his start as an artist mixing his own paints from colored clay and making brushes with fur pulled from his cat Grimalkin's tail. Middle-grade readers.

Ben's Trumpet Rachel Isadora (Greenwillow; 1979) Young Ben sits on the fire escape playing his imaginary trumpet. Then one day a trumpeter from the near-by Zig Zag Jazz Club makes his musical dream real.

The Boy Who Drew Cats David Johnson (Picture Book Studio; 1991) A young Japanese artist draws wonderful magical cats who defeat the temple demon.

The Boy Who Loved Music David Lasker (Viking; 1979) Prince Esterhazy refuses to allow the court musicians to return to Vienna at the end of the summer. To solve their problem, Joseph Hayden composes his *Farewell* Symphony, in which, one by one, the musicians get up and leave the stage. Based on a true story. Young to middle-grade readers.

From Mixed-Up Files of Mrs. Basil E. Frankweiler E. L. Konigsberg (Atheneum; 1967) Claudia and Jamie run away from home and, through a variety of creative subterfuges, live at the Metropolitan Museum of Art, where they solve a mystery surrounding a statue of an angel created by (possibly) Michelangelo. Middle-grade readers.

The Girl With a Watering Can Ewa Zadrzynska (Chameleon Books; 1990) The little girl with the watering can escapes from Renoir's famous picture and takes a mischievous tour through the art museum. Young readers.

The Incredible Painting of Felix Clousseau Jon Agee (Farrar, Straus & Giroux; 1988) Felix Clousseau, a stumpy little bearded artist who wears a beret, paints incredible paintings that come alive and leave their Paris salon. Young readers.

Katie's Picture Show James Mayhew (Doubleday; 1989) On a visit to the art museum, Katie finds that she can step inside different works of art, having adventures as she goes. Young readers.

Liang and the Magic Paintbrush Demi (Henry Holt; 1980) Liang is given a magical paintbrush: whatever he paints with it comes alive. Young readers.

Linnea in Monet's Garden Christina Bjork (Farrar, Straus & Giroux; 1987) The story of a small girl who wanders through the famous impressionist's garden at Giverney. Illustrated with color drawings and black-and-white photographs of Monet and his family. Middle-grade readers.

Lion William Pène DuBois (Viking; 1956) In a white-and-silver animal factory high in the clouds, winged artists draw and paint designs for new animals. Artist Foreman (who once won a medal for inventing Worm) has a hard time with his ideas for Lion. Young and middle-grade readers.

Mouse Paint Ellen Stoll Walsh (Harcourt, Brace, Jovanovich; 1989)
   Three fat white mice fall into three primary-colored pots of paint - red, yellow, and blue - and then patter about through the puddles, mixing colors. Young readers.

The Philharmonic Gets Dressed Karla Kuskin (Harper & Row; 1982) All over the city, 105 people get (very elegantly) dressed and leave for work, finally ending up in place on stage as members of the orchestra. Young readers.

The Pottery Place Gail Gibbons (Harcourt, Brace, Jovanovich; 1987) The brightly illustrated story of a potter at work, from clay to finished product, including a short aside on the history of pottery and a nice labeled drawing showing the parts of a potter's wheel. Young readers.

Round Buildings, Square Buildings & Buildings That Wiggle Like a Fish Phillip M. Issacson (Knopf; 1988) Architecture as art and history, presented through full-color photographs of buildings from all around the world. Middle-grade and older readers.

The Second Mrs. Giaconda E.L. Konigsberg (Atheneum; 1975) The "real" story of the Mona Lisa, as told by Salai, Leonardo da Vinci's young apprentice. Illustrated with art works by da Vinci. Middle-grade and older readers.

The Story of the Nutcracker Ballet Deborah Hartzig (Knopf; 1986)   Just what the title says, for younger readers. Also see E.T.A. Hoffman's *The Nutcracker* (Crown; 1984).

Swan Lake Margot Fonteyn (Harcourt, Brace, Jovanovich; 1989) The story of the famous ballet of the same name, in which a prince falls in love with a beautiful maiden enchanted in the form of a swan. Middle-grade readers.

A Very Young Dancer Jill Krementz (Dell Yearling; 1976) A delightful photo essay about a ten-year-old girl dancing the part of Marie in the New York City ballet's production of "The Nutcracker." By the same author: *A Very Young Musician* (Simon & Schuster; 1991), a photo essay about a ten-year-old trumpet player.

A Weekend With Rembrandt Bonafoux Pascal (Rizzoli; 1991) Art history made personal. The books are written in the first-person, as though narrated by the artist, as readers spend a "weekend" learning about the painter and his works. Illustrations include wonderful full-color reproductions of famous paintings. Other books in the "Weekend With the Artist" series include *A Weekend With Degas* (Rosabianca Skira-Venturi), *A Weekend With Picasso* (Florian Rodari), *A Weekend With Renoir* (Rosabianca Skira-Venturi), *A Weekend with Leonardo da Vinci* (Rosabianca Skira-Venturi), and *A Weekend With Velazquez* (Florian Rodari). Middle-grade readers.

Visiting the Art Museum   Laurene Krasny Brown and Marc Brown (E.P. Dutton; 1986) The animated tale of one family's trip to the art museum, featuring full-color reproductions of museum works (each discussed in more detail in an appendix at the back of the book). Young readers.

When Clay Sings Byrd Baylor (Macmillan; 1972) The poetic story of ancient southwestern Indian pottery, illustrated with original designs. Young to middle-grade readers.

Wolferl: The First Six Years in the Life of Wolfgang Amadeus Mozart Lisl Weil (Holiday; 1991) Clever little line drawings illustrate this biography of the composer as a child. Appropriate for young to middle-grade readers. Also see *Letters to Horseface: Young*

Mozart's Travels in Italy by F.N. Monjo (Puffin; 1975), a collection of fictional letters written by Mozart to his sister, Nannerl, in the days when the young composer was writing his first opera; and *Mozart: Scenes from the Childhood of the Great Composer* by Catherine Brighton (Doubleday; 1990).

Chapter Eight

Creative Thinking:

Or How Is a Raven Like a Writing Desk?

Childswork/Childsplay

Childswork/Childsplay, states the catalog, is "the nation's largest distributor of psychologically oriented toys, games, and books for and about kids." The company sells materials for imaginative play: hand puppets, a folding wooden dollhouse, school and hospital playsets, complete with furniture, props, and figures, a "Family Theatre," with eight backdrops and 54 character figures, and "Kids on Stage," a simple charades game for kids aged 5-10. Games include *The Mad, Sad, Glad Game*, in which players match the appropriate feeling card (mad, sad, glad, scared) with described situations ("If someone called me stupid, I'd feel...") and *Not So Scary Things*, a colorful board game in which players aged 4-8 journey toward Mount Courage, braving thunder and lightning, monsters, the dark, spiders, bullies, and snakes along the way. There is also a wide assortment of books, targeted at specific problems such as childhood stress and deprivation, divorce, hyperactivity, illness, and sibling rivalry. For a catalog, contact Childswork/Childsplay, Center for Applied Psychology, P.O. Box 1587, King of Prussia, PA 19406; (800) 962-1141.

Creative Learning Systems

Creative Learning Systems carries a large assortment of books, activity books, and games designed to encourage creative thinking, enhance memory and concentration, and boost problem-solving abilities. Among these is a collection of books based on the "Odyssey of the Mind" competitions (featured on the PBS television series "Creativity With Bill Moyers"), which give instructions for conducting group problem-solving contests. *Art Synectics* (Nicholas Roukes) presents exercises in which kids combine imagination and analogies to transform the commonplace into the weird and wonderful: "Imagine a chair made of ping pong balls." "Creat a 3-dimensional structure based on experiments with light." "Invent symbols to replace the letters of the alphabet and use them to rewrite a well-known quotation." In *The Brain Game*, kids take a series of intelligence tests designed to demonstrate the differing abilities of the brain hemispheres. And much more.

Sample games: in *Quick Wit*, players answer questions testing logic, general knowledge, vocabulary, and problem solving abilities, and solve "visual puzzles," in which they try to identify everyday objects viewed from bizarre camera angles. *Junkyard Treasures* is a game for young inventors, inspired by the elaborate devices of Rube Goldberg: players are challenged to use invention cards, each picturing a different object, to assemble various functional contraptions. (For more on Creative Learning Systems, see Science.) For a catalog, contact Creative Learning Systems, Inc., TransTech Systems Division, 9899 Hibert St., Suite C, San Diego, CA 92131; (800) 458-2880 or (619) 566-2880.

Frames of Mind   Howard Gardner   (Basic Books; 1983)

Frames of Mind, Gardner's book on the theory of multiple intelligences, has had a lasting impact on the way many of us now view education and academic performance. The premise of the book is that there are seven basic types of intelligence, which each of us possesses or develops in greater or lesser degrees. Gardner's seven categories of intelligences are linguistic, musical, logical-mathematical, spatial, bodily-kinesthetic, and personal (both knowledge of self and knowledge of others). Each brings with it, Gardner explains, its own battery of abilities and aptitudes. The analysis of individual intelligences obviously has - or should have - a profound effect on educational techniques and approaches. Educational programs appropriate for a predominately linguistic learner, for example, will leave a bodily-kinesthetic learner out in the cold. A fascinating book for parents and educators of the multiply intelligent. Available through bookstores.

Free Spirit Publishing

Free Spirit specializes in self-help books for kids and their parents: their creative selection includes books targeted at gifted kids, learning-disabled kids, stressed-out teenagers, frustrated perfectionists, concerned social activists, and academic underachievers. Examples of Free Spirit publications: *Psychology for Kids: 40 Fun Tests That Help You Learn About Yourself* (Jonni Kincher) and *The Kid's Guide to Social Action* (Barbara A. Lewis). For a catalog ($2.00), contact Free Spirit Publishing, Inc., 400 First Avenue North, Suite 616, Minneapolis, MN 55401-1730.

The Gifted Child Today

The Gifted Child Today is a bimonthly magazine targeted at parents and teachers who deal with gifted, creative, and talented kids. Articles in each issue center around a specific topic: those covered in the past have included mentoring, accelerated learning programs, social and emotional needs of gifted children, math, science, and international programs for the gifted. Each issue also includes descriptions of enriching lesson plans and projects targeted at gifted learners, with suggestions for implementing these at home or in the classroom. A one-year subscription to *The Gifted Child Today* (6 issues) costs $30.00, from *The Gifted Child Today*, P.O. Box 8813, Waco, TX 76710-8813. Single sample issues cost $5.00.

GCT, Inc., the publishers of *The Gifted Child Today*, also produces a small catalog of activity books intended to enhance creative thinking skills and to challenge talented children. Examples include *What It Might Be Like If There Were a Tax on Intelligence...(and 1995 More Activities)*, a combination of imaginative projects and open-ended questions for kids in grades 4-9; *And There I Was...*, an activity book which encourages kids to write historical fiction; and *Design a Birdhouse for an Ostrich...(And Other Creative Activities)*, which combines clever project suggestions with fascinating facts and research challenges. Under "Curiosities," for example, kids are challenged to design a new museum dedicated to an uncommon theme. They are told that the American Museum of Natural History in New York City contains 23 acres of floor space, and are asked to find a number of equally unusual facts about museums; and are given a list of organizations to contact for museum information, among them the International Council of Museums in Paris, the Smithsonian Institution, and the Museum Programs division of the National Endowment for the Arts. They are asked to come up with a list of local resources that might be helpful in the completion of the project; and to determine what features museum of a given type should include by taking an opinion survey. To obtain a catalog, contact *The Gifted Child Today Catalog*, 314-350 Weinacker Avenue, P.O. Box 6448, Mobile, AL 36660-0448; (205) 478-4700.

Gifted Education Review

The *Gifted Education Review* is a quarterly magazine which briefly summarizes papers and articles on gifted education from recent periodical literature. There's a brief description of each magazine cited, plus subscription information: a list of chosen articles follows, with brief summaries of the content of each. Our sample issue, for example, included summaries of selections from *Agate*, the journal of the Gifted and Talented Council of the Alberta Teachers' Association, *Challenge*, a classroom activity magazine for teachers of the gifted, the *Gifted Child Quarterly*, the *Journal for the Education of the Gifted*, and *The Prufrock Journal*, an international journal for the teachers of gifted students at the secondary level.

Summarized articles range from the theoretical to the practical. When you zero in on one that looks interesting, it's up to you to track it down yourself, either from the original publisher or through a library. A one-year subscription to the *Review* (four issues) costs $30.00, from the *Gifted Education Review*, P.O. Box 2278, Evergreen, CO 80359-2278.

The Imagination Game

This is an audio cassette, featuring Charlie Brissette, Tom Armbruster, and Diane Michelle, in which music and narration combine to take kids on an imaginative journey within their minds. Young listeners imagine themselves as marionettes, snowflakes, fish, and magical traveling kites. The peaceful and relaxing tone make this an appropriate selection for bedtime. For kids aged 4 and up. *The Imagination Game* is available from the Children's Small Press Collection, 719 N. Fourth Ave., Ann Arbor, MI 48104; (800) 221-8056.

Is Your Bed Still There When You Close the Door?   Jane M. Healy   (Doubleday; 1992)

Is Your Bed Still There When You Close the Door? is subtitled "How to Have Intelligent and Creative Conversations With Your Kids." The author, Jane Healy, is a teacher and educational psychologist. The first chunk of the book is theoretical, on how children learn to think; the second practical, on how to conduct thought-provoking, mind-opening conversations with kids. The real nitty-gritty of the text is a list of mind-stretching discussion questions, with associated follow-up questions and reading lists. Questions are grouped by age level: Level One questions are appropriate for primary-aged kids through grade 3; Level Two questions for third grade through adolescence; Level Three ("Mind Bogglers") for mature middle-schoolers through adults.

A sample Level One question is "What would your life be like if you were the size of a mouse?" "By attempting to put themselves into another's point of view," writes the author, "children develop important reasoning skills." Suggestions for accompanying read-aloud books include Lynne Reid Banks' *The Indian in the Cupboard*, Mary Norton's *The Borrowers*, John Peterson's *The Littles*, and Leo Lionni's *Frederick*. Other examples: "How many things can you think of to do with a balloon?" and "What makes someone a hero or heroine?"

Level Two moves up a notch in complexity: "Imagine a world in

which everyone looked alike." "Why is it important to keep a secret?" "What if money grew on trees and people could pick as
much as they wanted?" "Do you think children should have to go
to school?" Level Three includes the classic philosophical puzzler
"Is your bed still there when you close the door?" - along with "Is
it possible to think without words?" and "Is it OK for people to
punish other people?" Our two oldest (9 and 11) seem to gravitate
toward Level Three; they spent our last trip in the car loudly discussing the mind-boggling "Do you think it is possible for something that is against the law to be morally right?" Available
through bookstores. Also see Gregory Stock's *The Kids' Book of
Questions* (Workman; 1988).

Joyful Child, Inc.

"The book that started it all" is Peggy Jenkins' *The Joyful Child: A
Sourcebook of Activities and Ideas for Releasing Children's Natural Joy.*
Joyful Child, Inc., is a non-profit organization founded to further
the principles expounded in the book. The group publishes a
small catalog of books and materials designed to promote self-
esteem, imagination, creative thinking, and natural joy; and also a
quarterly magazine, the *Joyful Child Journal*, which contains articles on parenting, reviews of educational books and materials, and
suggestions for children's activities. A one-year subscription to the
Joyful Child Journal costs $18.00 (4 issues); to order, or for further
information, contact Joyful Child, Inc., P.O. Box 5506, Scottsdale,
AZ 85261; (602) 951-4111.

Kids' Puzzle Express

The *Kids' Puzzle Express* is a bimonthly magazine for the puzzle-
minded: 30 pages of challenging puzzles, including connect-the-
dots, word scrambles and searches, crosswords, memory puzzles,
matching puzzles, mazes, rebuses, and codes. Answers are in the
back. A one-year subscription (6 issues) costs $18.00 from *Kids'
Puzzle Express*, P.O. Box 3083A, Princeton, NJ 08543-3083.

Knowledge Products

Knowledge Products is notable for its Audio Classics Series, featuring "history's greatest thinkers, ideas and events on audiocassette." Presently available series include "The Giants of Philoso-
py," a 13-part series featuring the ideas of Plato, Aristotle, St. Au-
gustine, St. Thomas Aquinas, Baruch Spinoza, David Hume, Im-
manuel   Kant,   Georg   Wilhelm   Friedrich   Hegel,   Arthur

Schopenhauer, Soren Kierkegaard, Friedrich Nietzsche, John Dewey, and Jean-Paul Sartre, "The Giants of Political Thought," featuring the works of Thomas Paine, Thomas Jefferson, Henry David Thoreau, Adam Smith, John Stuart Mill, Niccolo Machiavelli, Karl Marx, Jean Jacques Rousseau, Edmund Burke, Alexander Hamilton, James Madison, and John Jay, Thomas Hobbes, John Locke, and Alexis de Tocqueville, and "The World's Political Hot Spots," a historical, political, religious, and ideological overview of the current conflicts in the Middle East, South Africa, Central America, Germany, Ireland, Cuba, the Philippines, the (ex) Soviet Union, China, and Poland. Future series will include "Science & Discovery," a history of science from the ancient Greeks through Einstein, "The United States Constitution," from that document's creation through ratification, "The United States at War," from the American Revolution through Vietnam, and "The Great Economic Thinkers," covering economic theory from the 18th century through the present day. Each cassette runs about 90 minutes long, and all are dramatized, presenting the author's works and opinions through multiple voices (pro and con).

Audio Classics Series tapes are available by subscription: one album (two cassettes) per month for $14.95, plus shipping and handling. To order or for additional information, contact Knowledge Products, 1717 Elm Hill Pike, Suite A-4, Nashville, TN 37210; (800) 264-6441. Individual tapes in "The Giants of Philosophy" and "The Giants of Political Thought" series are available from Brook Farm Books, P.O. Box 246, Bridgewater, ME 04735.

KolbeConcepts, Inc.

KolbeConcepts sells an assortment of books and materials designed to enhance creative thinking in the fields of problem-solving, language arts, math, science, and social studies. *Ouchless Curiosity*, for example, is a small paperback filled thought-provoking "ponderables:" "If chocolate were a vegetable, would you still like it?" "Are more women than men afraid of snakes and spiders?" "Should you be paid more for doing a job because you don't enjoy it?" "Do flies do anyone any good?" Each question is accompanied by an entertaining little cartoon-like illustration. Also included: books of brainteasers and logic puzzles, literature-based activities, history and geography "quizzles," and the like. For a catalog, contact KolbeConcepts, Inc., P.O. Box 15667, Phoenix, AZ 85060; (602) 840-9770.

LifeStories/FutureStories

This pair of innovative and positively addictive games has entranced our family for weeks now. *LifeStories*, one review reads, is designed to "build bridges" between people of all ages, by encouraging the sharing of personal stories. Players progress around the game board, drawing Valuables, Memories, Etchings, and Alternatives cards, each of which elicits the telling of a story: "What was one of the first ways you earned money?" "Tell a story about a pet or an animal." "Describe a neighbor who was difficult to live with." "Describe a possession you would like to keep if all else were lost." "What is your favorite time of year? Why?" "Recall a story you heard about one of your grandmothers." "How did your parents meet?"

FutureStories is of similar format, but the stories it inspires are less personal and more imaginative. "You are a fantastic author. What will your next book be about?" "What artists of today will be remembered 100 years from now?" "What ocupation do you think will pay the highest salary in 50 years?" "How would life change if everyone saw only black and white?" "Would you like to be able to read other people's minds? How would you use that skill?" "If it were possible to have any animal now extinct as a living pet, which one would you choose and why?"

These games are a joy. Randy and I cherish Josh's reminiscences of his (no longer with us) pet hamster, Ethan's plan to power cars with the colors of the rainbow, and Caleb's desire for a pet Stegosaurus. Each game costs $29.95, plus $3.00 shipping and handling, from LifeStories, 701 Decatur Ave. North, Suite 104, Golden Valley, MN 55427; (800) 232-1873 or (612) 544-0438.

NL Associates

N L Associates styles itself "The Challenge Company;" its small catalog carries books intended to enhance creative and critical thinking. Among these are Nathan Levy's *Stories With Holes*, a collection of ten short paperbacks containing "open-ended stories for conducting inquiry training in the classroom." "Stories" are extremely short: for example, "John and Mary are on the floor. There are pieces of broken glass, and a puddle of liquid, also on the floor. Mary is dead." The correct "answer" here, printed at the bottom of the page, is that John is a cat, who has knocked over the bowl of Mary, a fish. Stories in our sample dealt largely with murder, suicide, and general disaster, which bothered our tender-hearted youngest. Also available: activity books for creative writers, guidebooks for parents and teachers of gifted children, and *Cre(Egg)tivity*, an integrated unit that teaches responsibility by having each participating child adopt and "parent" an egg. For a catalog, contact NL Associates, Inc., P.O. Box 1199, Hightstown, NJ 08520.

Philosophy for Children

Matthew Lipman's "Philosophy for Children" series has been around since 1971; and children using it, educators report, tend to be more curious, better task-oriented, and more considerate of each other, and to demonstrate improved reasoning skills. While such an evaluation seems a trifle fuzzy, the program itself does constitute a thought-provoking introduction to philosophy for kids in grades 2-12. The program consists of a soft-bound student book, 86-98 pages long, plus a teacher's instruction manual, 390-500 pages long, in a looseleaf binder. Student books include *Elfie: Getting Our Thoughts Together* (grades K-2), *Pixie: Looking for Meaning* (grades 2-4), *Kio and Gus: Wondering At the World* (grades 2-5), *Harry Stottlemeier's Discovery: Basic Reasoning Skills* (grades 4-6), *Lisa: Reasoning in Ethics* (grades 7-10), and *Mark: Reasoning in Social Studies* (grades 9-12). Student books cost $9.00; instructor's manuals, $39.95. Available through bookstores or from Zephyr Press, 3316 N. Chapel Ave., P.O. Box 13448, Tucson, AZ 85732-3448; (602) 322-5090.

Psychology for Kids Jonni Kincher (Free Spirit Publishing; 1990)

Psychology for Kids is a big purple paperback subtitled "40 Fun Tests that Help You Learn About Yourself." The tests - some admittedly of uncertain scientific reliability - really are fun; test-takers learn about body language, mood music, communication styles, ESP, photographic memory, phrenology, and handwriting analysis. Along the way, there's opportunity to pick up a lot of psychological fact and terminology: kids can determine whether they're introverted or extroverted, left-brained or right-brained, optimistic or pessimistic. They can analyze their body type (endomorphic, mesomorphic, or ectomorphic) and its (possible) relationship to personality; discover the personality traits associated with their favorite color; and interpret Rorschach blots. (Warning: listed favorite colors are red, green, orange, blue, yellow, and purple. If one of your kids picks *black*, like one of mine did, you're on your own for Test #13.) Each test section includes information about the psychological concept studied and suggestions for additional activities. Available through bookstores or from Free Spirit Publishing, 400 First Avenue North, Suite 616, Minneapolis, MN 55401; (800) 735-7323.

Six Thinking Hats

Edward de Bono's *Six Thinking Hats* (1985) describes the thinking process as a series of varied problem-solving approaches, each represented by a different colored "thinking hat." A white hat, for example, represents objective thinking; a red hat, emotional response; black, negative logical thinking; yellow, positive constructive thinking; green, creative thinking; and blue, organizational thinking. Understand, integrating, and directing these "thinking hats," de Bono argues, helps persons to become more effective thinkers.

The *Six Thinking Hats* concept has been adapted for school use by Perfection Learning; the program includes a series of problem-solving resource books with reproducible lesson sheets for kids in grades K-2, 3-5, 6-8, and 9-12. Also available: *Six Thinking Hats* student journals, in which kids are encouraged to record their daily thoughts, problems, and activities using the "hats" approach, and the *Six Thinking Hats Game*. This last is a board game: players proceed by drawing question cards and presenting their thoughts on the subject using one of the six colored hats. Sample questions: "What if people had wheels instead of feet?" "What if nothing cast a shadow?" De Bono's original book is available through bookstores, or from Zephyr Press, 3316 N. Chapel Ave., Box 13448-F, Tucson, AZ 85732-3488; *Six Thinking Hats* resource books and the *Six Thinking Hats Game* are available from Perfection Learning Corp., 1000 North Second Ave., Logan, IA 51546-1099; (800) 831-4190 or (712) 644-2831.

The Thinker's Toolbox: A Practical and Easy Approach to Creative Thinking   Pamela and David Thornberg   (Dale Seymour; 1989)

The Thinker's Toolbox introduces and explains a range of creative approaches to problem-solving: eliminate, elaborate, describe, combine, substitute, rearrange, classify, associate, exaagerate, empathize, reduce, symbolize, separate, reverse, compare, and hypothesize. For each, there is a series of intriguing examples, appropriate for thinkers over a wide range of ages. Under *eliminate*: "You are going on an airplane to spend a month at your cousin's house. You've made a list of your 12 favorite things to take along. You have room to only take four. What did you eliminate and how did you make the choices?" "The fifty states are getting too hard to handle. Eliminate 3 of them. Which did you eliminate and why?" Under *symbolize*: "As a master jeweler, you decide to create a charm bracelet that symbolizes the 21st century. Make a list of your charms, describing each one and telling what it would symbolize." The second half of the book lists a large collection of problems for thinkers to tackle with their newly-acquired problem-solving skills. Available from Activity Resources Co., Inc., P.O. Box 4875, Hayward, CA 94540; (510) 782-1300; or Bluestocking Press, PO Box 1014-GS, Placerville, CA 95667-1014; (916) 621-1122.

Ungame

The *Ungame* - "the world's favorite self-expression game" - is designed to facilitate communication and to enhance sharing and listening skills. It is available both as a full-sized board game and as a boardless pocket version. The main feature of both, however, is a pair of question card decks. Deck 1 contains generally lighthearted questions; Deck 2 deals with more serious topics. Both are aimed at encouraging talk by and among players. Example: "If you had all the power in the universe, how would you change the world?" Available from Talicor, Inc., P.O. Box 6382, Anaheim, CA 92816; (714) 255-7900; or from Childswork/Childsplay, Center for Applied Psychology, PO Box 1587, King of Prussia, PA 19406; (800) 962-1141.

Chapter Nine

Life Skills:

Learning for the Real World

Atrium Society

The Atrium Society is a nonprofit organization whose aim is to "educate the public about the fundamental causes of conflict, individually and globally," and to provide guidelines to help kids deal with conflict peacefully. Atrium's director, Terrence Webster-Doyle, has authored a number of books along these lines, grouped in the "Education for Peace" series. Notable among these is *Why is Everybody Always Picking on Me: A Guide to Handling Bullies* and *Tug of War: Peace through Understanding Conflict*. The books combine an explanatory text, filled with sample situations, with thought-provoking questions - designed to help kids analyze their own feelings and behaviors - and role-playing activities. The books can be used like workbooks; writing space is provided. For further information, contact the Atrium Society, P.O. Box 816, Middlebury, VT 05753; (802) 388-0922.

California School Fitness

California School Fitness (CSF) is a non-profit organization whose primary purpose "is to support youth fitness programming in schools." Accordingly, CSF has designed a number of kid's fitness programs, among them the "Fit-n-Caboodle" exercise workout, available on videotape. This is intended to be used in classrooms, as an adjunct to a regular physical fitness program - but is also suited to homeschools, especially those afflicted by cabin fever, rainy days, or just general antsiness. The workout, appropriate for all elementary levels, lasts 30 minutes, and involves exercises variously intended to increase cardiovascular endurance, muscle strength, and flexibility. Participating kids need just enough space to take two steps in each direction. Also available: "Take a Break," a 3-minute limbering sequence on audiocassette. "Fit-n-Caboodle" costs $29.95, plus $3.00 shipping; "Take a Break," $3.95 plus $.95 shipping. Order from California School Fitness, 6006 Wenrich Dr., San Diego, CA 92120; (619) 287-7093.

Cooking Wizardry for Kids

Cooking Wizardry for Kids by Margaret Kenda and Phyllis S. Williams is a project-packed gem: over 300 pages of clever recipes for young cooks, along with kitchen chemistry experiments and craft projects, and generous dollops of history and (non-threatening) math. There are recipes for rock candy, sourdough bread, yogurt, peanut butter, and invisible ink; there are pretzel- and butter-making projects; and, for caring pet owners, there are recipes for dog biscuits and gerbil chow. A recipe for homemade graham crackers is accompanied by the story of Sylvester Graham and his 19th-century campaign against white flour; a recipe for johnny-cake is paired with the story of Shawnee cornbread. There are also year-round holiday cooking projects, including a green milkshake recipe for St. Patrick's Day, and an Old Glory Cake, complete with stars and stripes, for the Fourth of July. There's an explanation of why onions make your eyes water, directions for growing sweet potatoes on your windowsill, and instructions for making a map of the tastebuds on your tongue. Great stuff for cooking wizards of all ages. Available through bookstores.

Cookbooks for Kids

Easy Menu Ethnic Cookbooks   (Lerner) This is a series of multicultural cookbooks for kids: each is 48 pages long, with recipes and background information, illustrated with color photographs. Titles in the series include *Cooking the Korean Way, Cooking the Japanese Way, Cooking the Indian Way, Cooking the Russian Way, Cooking the Hungarian Way, Cooking the Chinese Way, Cooking the English Way, Cooking the French Way, Cooking the Greek Way, Cooking the Italian Way, Cooking the Norwegian Way, Cooking the Polish Way,* and *Cooking the Spanish Way.*

Kids Cook! Fabulous Food for the Whole Family   Sarah Williamson and Zachary Williamson   (Williamson; 1991) Recipes for entire meals for kids to cook all by themselves.

Kids Cooking: A Very Slightly Messy Manual (Klutz Press; 1987) Lots of terrific recipes, plus a set of bright-colored plastic measuring spoons.

The Little House Cookbook Barbara Walker (HarperCollins; 1979) Over 100 authentic 19th-century recipes for foods eaten by Laura Ingalls and her family in the *Little House* series.

The Little Pigs' First Cookbook Cameron N. Watson (Little, Brown; 1987) Very simple recipes for young beginners, including dishes for breakfast, lunch, dinner, and dessert, as cooked by Charles, Bertram, and Ralph, the three little pigs.

Peter Rabbit's Cookery Book Anne Emerson (Viking Penguin; 1986) 21 recipes inspired by the Beatrix Potter books.

The Pooh Cookbook Virginia H. Ellison (E.P. Dutton; 1969) A collection of recipes linked to the Pooh books, including Cottleston Pie, Haycorn Squash, and lots of things with honey.

The Popcorn Book   Tomie DePaola   (Holiday; 1978)   Popcorn science, history, and legend, plus "Two Terrific Ways" for popping your own.

The Storybook Cookbook Carol McGregor   (Doubleday; 1967)   Recipes to accompany many children's books, among them "Heidi's Toasted Cheese Sandwiches," "Jo's New England Boiled Dinner," and "Captain Hook's Poison Cake." Book summaries and quotes included.

Childshop

Childshop sells terrific woodcraft kits for young carpenters. (We know. We've built some of them, and the boys have their eyes on more.) Childshop projects are available as several options: "Basic Plans" include building instructions and diagrams and a list of necessary tools and materials; "Discovery Plans," along with the basics, includes additional information relating to the project (how the jeep got its name, for example, on a wooden jeep) and suggestions for an activity based on the completed project; "Hardware Packages" include plans and necessary hardware (you supply the wood); and "Complete Kits" include plans, hardware, and pre-cut wood pieces, either pine or basswood. The plans are just right for kids: big print, uncluttered drawings, and crystal-clear instructions. Childshop kits include a book rack, hanging planter, wall sconce, recipe box, pet bed, clock, tool box, bird feeder, bug box, sailboat, an assortment of wooden cars, trucks, and airplanes, a doll cradle, and a step stool. And more. For a catalog, send $1.00 to Childshop, P.O. Box 597, Burton, OH 44021; (216) 834-0100.

Gardens for Kids

Our kids all started their gardening careers with a tablespoon and a packet of radish seeds, which works like a charm provided you - the sponsor - are enthusiastically willing to eat lots and lots of radishes. Radishes are perfect for beginners: they're fast and foolproof. For those who have advanced beyond the radish stage, W. Atlee Burpee offers a children's "Teepee Garden" package, which comes with six seed packets (radishes, marigolds, sunflowers, strawflowers, teeny pumpkins, and scarlet runner beans), plant labels, planting instructions, and a garden plan. The teepee - to be made out of stakes, provided by the gardener - provides support for the bean vines, which, once the beans get going, makes a leafy little playhouse. For a free catalog, contact W. Atlee Burpee & Co., Warminster, PA 18974; (800) 888-1447.

Seeds Blum of Boise, Idaho, offers a large assortment of kid-friendly "Special Garden" seed collections, including a "Child's Garden," designed to be planted compactly in a single pot; a "Show and Tell Garden," which includes broom corn, dinosaur gourds, and four-inch Jack-Be-Little pumpkins; and a "Garden Giants" collection: 14 huge seed varieties, including 13-foot-tall Bloody Butcher corn (red kernels), 4-pound Oxheart tomatoes, and monster Big Moon pumpkins. There's also a "Rainbow Garden" (weird-colored vegetables), a "Windowsill Herb Garden," a "Birdseed Garden," a "Butterfly Garden," and collections of flower and vegetable seeds suitable for windowboxes. Another surefire hit for small green thumbs: Seeds Blum sells packets of garden cress seeds for "cress writing." "Draw the letters in the soil and then sprinkle the cress seeds in the design you have 'carved.' Water and tend as usual." Catalogs cost $3.00 from Seeds Blum, Idaho City Stage, Boise, ID 83706.

Books for Young Gardeners

Eat the Fruit, Plant the Seed   Millicent E. Selsam and Jerome Wexler   (Morrow; 1980)   A how-to book for beginners, illustrated with photographs, describing six fruits whose seeds produce interesting plants.

Growing Vegetable Soup Lois Ehlert   (Harcourt, Brace, Jovanovich; 1987)   A simple book for very little kids showing where vegetables come from.

A Kid's First Book of Gardening Derek Fell   (Running Press; 1990)   The informational book comes with a 3-piece plastic greenhouse and 4 seed packets.

Kid's Gardening: A Guide to   Messing Around in the Dirt Kim G. Raferty and Kevin Raferty   (Klutz Press; 1989)   A nice bright informational book plus seed packets.

Let's Grow! Linda Tilgner   (Storey Communications; 1988)   The book is subtitled "72 Gardening Adventures With Children," and includes not only garden plans for plant-loving kids, but instructions for making an earthworm colony, growing cucumbers in bottles, making personalized pumpkins, growing catnip and making a catnip mouse for some lucky cat, and starting a beet-top/carrot-top windowsill garden.

Linnea's Windowsill Garden   Christina Bjork   (Farrar, Straus & Giroux; 1988)   Linnea, with the help of retired gardener Mr. Bloom, plants her own indoor garden. Complete directions and suggestions for windowsill gardening activities.

The Victory Garden Kids' Book: A Beginner's   Guide to Growing Vegetables, Fruits, and Flowers   Marjorie Waters   (Houghton Mifflin; 1988)   A very thorough gardening how-to book.

Games for Gardeners

In *Harvest Time*, a board game for 3-7-year-olds, players try to bring in their corn, peas, tomatoes, and carrots before the first frost. In *Back to the Farm*, players aged 8 and up attempt to establish their own organic farms. Both games are available from Animal Town, P.O. Box 485, Healdsburg, CA 95448; (800) 445-8642.

Sports Illustrated for Kids

The junior version of the adult magazine (no swimsuits). Features include informational pieces on sports and sports equipment, and interviews with athletes, both professional and amateur. For subscription information, contact *Sports Illustrated for Kids*, P.O. Box 830606, Birmingham, AL 35282-9487; (800) 992-0196.

The Teenage Entrepreneur's Guide   Sarah H. Riehm   (Surrey;1991)

The Teenage Entrepreneur's Guide is subtitled "50 Money-Making Business Ideas," all fifty of them geared toward kids who want some financial independence. Riehm knows what she's talking about; she herself was a pre-teen entrepreneur, earning $15.00 per week as an organist at the age of eight. Each business idea includes a list of necessary materials, suggestions for marketing methods, and an income estimation. Some of Riehm's possibilities for entrepreneurial kids include garage sale service, recycling, painting, latchkey service, and tutoring. And many more. A good hands-on guide for young businesspeople. The book costs $10.95 in paperback, and is available through bookstores or from Bluestocking Press, Box 1014-GS, Placerville, CA 95667; (916) 621-1123.

Toad's Tools

"*Real* tools for children who want to learn to do *real* work," write the owners, "is what we are about. And so we offer this selection of tools which won't insult your child's intelligence; tools that are made with the same care and materials as those used by 'big' people." Tools in the catalog really *are* grown-up tools: some are offered in hard-to-find small sizes; others are full-size tools appropriate for kids. These include hammer, cross-cut saw, fast-cut saw, coping saw, vise, pliers, adjustable wrench, screwdrivers, brace (with bits), and more. There's a selection of gardening tools and an assortment of carpentry and woodworking books for kids. For a catalog: Toad's Tools, P.O. Box 173, Oberlin, OH 44074.

Tooling Around

"To help small hands with big jobs," writes the proprieter, "Tooling Around carries a complete line of quality products." Many of these are the same tools used by adults, sized and weighted for kids. The company offers a complete collection of garden tools for small-sized gardeners, including rake, hoe, spade, garden fork, pruners, trowel, onion hoe, watering can, and little red wheelbarrow; there are also kids' laundry baskets and dusters, a small-sized washboard and tub, and an excellent assortment of small solid carpentry tools. Catalogs cost $2.00 from Tooling Around, 385 Delmas Avenue #A, San Jose, CA 95126-3626; (408) 286-9770.

Travel

Books on the Move: A Read- About-It, Go-There Guide to America's Best Family Destinations Susan M. Knorr and Margaret Knorr (Free Spirit; 1993) A terrific 384-page travel guide describing hundreds of destinations around the United States, with accompanying lists of related children's books to read before, during, and after, plus suggested activities to enhance the travel/book experience.

Doing Children's Museums Joanne Cleaver (Williamson; 1991) A guide to 225 hands-on discovery museums and nature centers.

Great Vacations With Your Kids Dorothy Jordan and Marjorie Cohen (Penguin; 1990)

Places to Go With Children in New England Diane Bair and Pamela Wright (Chronicle Books; 1990) A state-by-state listing of museums, historic sites, tours, activities, exhibits, parks, and restaurants, all appealing and friendly to kids. Listings include brief descriptions, hours of operation, cost, and phone numbers and mailing addresses, for those travellers who prefer to plan ahead. There are several other books in the series, for those who don't happen to live in New England: *Places to Go With Children in Southern California, Washington, D.C., Puget Sound, Miami and South Florida, Northern California, The Delaware Valley, The Southwest,* and *Orlando and Central Florida.*

Take Your Kids to Europe Cynthia Harriman (Mason-Grant; 1991) The book is subtitled "Practical, low-cost advice for families who want to go beyond superficial tourism" - which is exactly what it delivers: advice for experienced and budget-minded kid-towing travelers on everything from itinerary planning and airfares to rental houses, youth hostels, European campgrounds, and foreign grocery stores. There's also a "Totally Biased Guide" to what to see in Europe, and pages of useful resources, with telephone numbers.

Zillions

Zillions, published bimonthly by the Consumers Union, is the kid version of the adult magazine *Consumer Reports.* Like the adult magazine, *Zillions* reviews and rates various consumer products, specifically those considered to be of interest to kids. It includes, in each issue, discussions about wise money management, the value of saving, and the dangers of falling for deceptive advertising; and it clearly demonstrates the useful processes of consumer research and comparison shopping. All of this - real world economy in kid format - is appealing. On the down side, this is definitely a magazine for the mainstream consumer-minded kid. Our sample issues included articles evaluating travel games, flying disc-type toys, and marker pens, and a nice survey piece on what kids get paid for various kinds of summertime jobs - but the bulk of the consumer reporting dealt with stuff like Saturday morning TV shows, hair sprays, fast-food burgers, soda pop, and Nintendo. It's unclear whether the *Zillions* motto is "Save for a Rainy Day" or "Whoever Dies With the Most Toys Wins." A one-year subscription (6 issues) costs $16.00, from *Zillions,* P.O. Box 54861, Boulder, CO 80322-4861; (800) 234-2078.

Chapter Ten

Multipurpose Resources:

Something for Everybody

American Education Publishing

The catalog claims to carry "the newest titles of the very best in supplementary classroom materials," which basically means workbooks. Subjects include Reading, Language Arts, Math, Social Studies, and Science, and books are available at several different difficulty levels, covering grades K-12. Many of the books are cross-curricular: *Beginning Math Art*, for example, combines fundamentals of design with basic arithmetic; *Ecology Math* combines environmental information and activities with basic math for kids in fourth grade and up. A series of geography workbooks covers the United States, North America, the Continents, the Canadian Provinces, California and Washington States, South America, the Far East, and the Middle East, all recommended for kids in grade 4+; for older students (grades 7-9), there's an "American History Timelines" series (7 books, covering the pre-Revolutionary period through the 1980's); a "United States History" series (11 books); and a "History of Man" series (18 books, including *Ancient Egypt, Greece, Rome, The Medieval Period*, and *The Italian Renaissance*).

There are also assortments of books for early readers, including a "Whole Language Classroom Library," a set of 27 books for beginners in six curriculum areas (Language Arts, Social Science, Science, Math, Health and Safety, and Creative Arts). The entire collection, appropriate for kids in grades K-2, costs $363.30; individual books costs $14.95 each. For a catalog, contact American Education Publishing, 150 East Wilson Bridge Rd., Suite 145, Columbus, OH 43085; (800) 542-7833 or (614) 848-8866.

Barth, Edna

Edna Barth has authored a series of books on holiday symbols, published by Clarion Books (NY), all invaluable resources for putting an educational edge on seasonal celebrations - or for answering questions such as "Who invented jack-o-lanterns?," which so often catch parents unprepared. Books in the series include *Hearts, Cupids, and Red Roses: The Story of the Valentine Symbols, Shamrocks, Harps, and Shillelaghs: The Story of the St. Patrick's Day Symbols, Lilies, Rabbits, and Painted Eggs: The Story of the Easter Symbols, Witches, Pumpkins, and Grinning Ghosts: The Story of the Halloween Symbols, Turkeys, Pilgrims, and Indian Corn: The Story of the Thanksgiving Symbols*, and *Holly, Reindeer, and Colored Lights: The Story of the Christmas Symbols*. Each is close to 100 informational pages long, and illustrations are definitely secondary to the text; these are books for middle-graders and up. The Halloween volume, for example, covers the origin of Halloween, goblins, witches and their history, including the story of the great witch hunts of the Middle Ages, witches' familiars, cats (from ancient Egypt on), owls, bats, and toads, ghosts, skeletons (with mention of the Mexican Day of the Dead), jack-o-lanterns, fortune-telling, masquerading, and special Halloween foods.

For younger children, Carolrhoda Books (Minneapolis, MN) publishes a series of holiday history books collectively called the "On My Own Books." These are beginning readers, 40-64 pages long, but each manages to pack in plenty of fascinating facts. Titles include *Columbus Day* (Vicki Liestman), *Earth Day* (Linda Lowery), *Kwanzaa* (A.P. Porter), *Arbor Day* (Diane L. Burns), *Halloween* (Joyce K. Kessel), *Happy New Year* (Emily Kelley) (covers New Year's celebrations around the world), *Valentine's Day* (Joyce K. Kessel), *April Fools' Day* (Emily Kelley), *St. Patrick's Day* (Joyce K. Kessel), *Christmas Around the World* (Emily Kelley), *Martin Luther King Day* (Linda Lowery), *Memorial Day* (Geoffrey Scott), *Squanto and the First Thanksgiving* (Joyce K. Kessel), and *Labor Day* (Geoffrey Scott). For education year-round. Available through libraries and bookstores; the "On My Own" books can also be ordered directly from Carolrhoda Books, Inc., 241 First Avenue North, Minneapolis, MN 55401; (800) 328-4929 or (612) 332-3344.

Bits and Pieces

The Bits and Pieces catalog is subtitled "The Great International Puzzle Collection" and I nearly wrote it off when it showed up in our mailbox, since our family tends to be unfond of puzzles. Jigsaw puzzles are, of course, a predominant feature of Bits and Pieces: most are intended for serious puzzlers and consist of 1000 or more tiny little pieces. If you've got a dedicated puzzle-doer or two in your family, these are worth a look: there are, for example, a glow-in-the-dark celestial sky map puzzle, a jigsaw version of *The Last Supper*, an American history timeline puzzle, and a working jigsaw clock. And many more.

Bits and Pieces, however, contains more than standard flat-on-the-table jigsaw-type puzzles: there are also three-dimensional paper models of such international architectural landmarks as the Eiffel Tower and St. Basil's Cathedral (*not* simple); collections of mazes, ciphers, and optical illusions; *221B Baker Street, the Master Detective Game*, recommended for players aged 10 and up; a triangular Japanese mosaic puzzle that looks fiendish; and an origami collection of famous American buildings to assemble, among them the White House, the Empire State Building, and the Golden Gate Bridge. For a catalog, contact Bits and Pieces, 1 Puzzle Place, B8016, Stevens Point, WI 54481-7199; (800) JIGSAWS.

Brainboosters

These 32-page spiral-bound interactive activity books combine truly fascinating facts with clever graphics and creative puzzles: kids variously predict which animal would win the great animal race (there's a bar graph of velocities for helpful hints), match an international collection of hats to the correct foreign costume, identify artifacts unearthed from a mixed-up archaeological dig, match portraits of U.S. presidents to their campaign slogans, and match the planets in a map of the solar system to their (sometimes tricky) descriptions. Answers to each set of puzzles or questions are recorded on a plastic decoder which then "unlocks the secret answer codes," showing players where they were right or wrong.

Titles in the series include *Culture Trek, Exploring America, Prehistoric Life, Undersea Adventures, Amazing Animals, Inventions and Discoveries, Puzzles and Thinking Games, Digging Into the Past, Worldwide Wonders,* and *Outer Space Adventures.* Books cost $5.95 each; decoders - which work with all books - cost $1.50. Order from Educational Insights, 19560 S. Rancho Way, Dominguez Hills, CA 90220; (800) 933-3277 or (213) 637-2131.

Brain Quest

Want to know if your kids are keeping up with their grade-level peers? *Brain Quest* is a curriculum-based question-and-answer game, designed with the help of a large teacher advisory board. The game - subtitled "Questions and Answers to Challenge the Mind" - is basically two packs of long skinny cards, each clipped together in the lower corner by a plastic peg, which keeps them from scattering all over the place if you inadvertently drop the pack on the floor. There are ten questions per card; answer cards follow each question card, for rapid accuracy checks.

Brain Quest is available at 7 levels of difficulty, for grades 1 through 7. The Grade 1 game, appropriate for ages 6-7, consists of 750 questions, emphasizing the 3 R's, and early science and social studies; Grade 2 is heavy on spelling; Grade 3 on math; and by Grades 6 and 7, questions (1500 of them) emphasize world history and cultures, science, and technology. At each level, questions reflect the appropriate public-school curriculum content, which means that the game feels more like a test than a game. *Brain*

Quest is available through bookstores, or from Workman Publishing Company, 708 Broadway, New York, NY 10003; (212) 254-5900. Each game costs $9.95.

Brook Farm Books

Brook Farm is the bailiwick of Donn Reed and family, home-schoolers of long and talented standing. Donn is the author of *The Home School Source Book* - "the Sears catalog of home school information," says one reviewer. *The Source Book* includes a vast and varied list of educational resources in all categories, many of which can be ordered directly from Brook Farm. *The Source Book* costs $15.00, plus $1.00 postage, from Brook Farm Books, P.O. Box 246, Bridgewater, ME 04735.

Brown Paper Schoolbooks

Individual volumes of the Brown Paper School Book series (Little, Brown) are reviewed in other sections (see Arts and Crafts, History and Geography, Life Skills, Mathematics, Reading and Literature, and Science). All are creative information-and-activity books targeted at kids aged 8-12. They were written by a group of California teachers, writers, and artists, all of whom believe that "learning only happens when it is wanted, that it can happen anywhere, and that it doesn't require fancy tools." Users of their books will find such learning irresistible. Titles in the series *Beastly Neighbors, Or Why Earwigs Make Good Mothers; The Big Beast Book: Dinosaurs and How They Got That Way; Blood and Guts: A Working Guide to Your Own Insides; The Book of Think (Or How to Solve a Problem Twice Your Size); The Book of Where, Or How To Be Naturally Geographic; Everybody's A Winner! A Kid's Guide to New Sports and Fitness; Gee, Wiz! How to Mix Art and Science or The Art of Thinking Scientifically; Good For Me! All About Food in 32 Bites.; The I Hate Mathematics! Book; Make Mine Music!; Making Cents: Every Kid's Guide to Making Money; Math for Smarty Pants; My Backyard History Book.; The Night Sky Book: An Everyday Guide to Every Night; Only Human: Why We Are the Way We Are; The Reasons for Seasons: The Great Cosmic Megagalactic Trip Without Moving From Your Chair; This Book Is About Time; Word Works: Why the Alphabet Is a Kid's Best Friend.* All are available through bookstores.

Bureau of Educational Measurements

A source of standardized tests, for those whose children have to take them. Tests cannot be ordered unless the purchaser can prove him/herself to be properly qualified; orders therefore must be accompanied by a "Purchaser's Qualification Statement." The statement is a questionnaire; purchasers are required to list their purpose for using the requested test, their level of training, their relevant educational background (undergraduate or graduate courses in tests and measurements, psychological testing, educational assessment, and the like), relevant supervised training, and memberships in professional organizations. Once you have been deemed qualified, you are eligible to order any number of tests, including the California Achievement Test, the Iowa Test of Basic Skills, the Metropolitan Achievement Test, the Stanford Achievement Test, the Gates-MacGinitie Reading Test, and many others. Individual "Specimen Sets" of the tests generally run between $10.00 and $20.00. The sets include a "Norms Booklet" for self-scoring; the Bureau also provides a scoring service (you send in the completed test booklets and they do it all for you) at a cost of about $1.00 per test.

For order forms and a price list, contact the Bureau of Educational Measurements, Emporia State University, 1200 Commercial, Box 18, Emporia, KS 66801; (316) 343-1200, ext. 5298.

Calendars

Our homeschooling program is linked to celebrations: we often key our educational activities to the calendar, observing such lesser-known holidays as Edison Lamp Day, National Newspaper Week, Daniel Boone's Birthday, Galileo's Birthday, and the anniversaries of Peary's arrival at the North Pole, the opening of the Eiffel Tower, and the invention of the ice-cream cone. For other holiday-minded educators, a list of resources follows:

Day-by-Day Bonnie Bernstein, ed.   (David S. Lake, 1980)   A collection of 300 calendar-oriented projects and activities for elementary-level kids throughout the year.

Day-by-Day Trivia Almanac Gus Macleavy   (Bell; 1981)   Just as the cover claims, fascinating facts for every day of the year.

A Dictionary of Days Leslie Dunkling   (Facts on File, 1988)   Describes over 850 named days.

Every Day is Special An activity calendar for homeschooled kids, listing historical happenings, famous birthdays, and holidays for each day of the year, with suggestions for related projects. The entire calendar costs $15.00; a one-month sample is available for

$2.00. Order from Every Day is Special, 12910 Boston Ave., Chino, CA 91710; (714) 465-0090.

Timelines Paul Dickson (Addison-Wesley; 1990) A day-by-day account of historical happenings from Franklin Roosevelt's 1945 inauguration through 1989, including yearly lists of fads, trends, most famous people, and most popular bumper stickers.

Also see the listings below for: *The Kids' Diary of 365 Amazing Days* and *The New Teacher's Almanack.*

Childcraft Education Corporation

This looks like your average glitzy toy catalog, but there's more here than meets the casual eye. Some of our all-time favorites have come from Childcraft, notable among them the "Ultimate Collage Kit," which enthralled the boys for countless hours. The (conveniently boxed) kit contains a vast collection of collage materials: small and large cardboard background trays, construction paper, doilies (gold, silver, and heart-shaped), dyed macaroni, sequins, beads, glitter, feathers, colored rocks (the kind fish-owners put at the bottom of the aquarium), stickers, multicolored fabrics and yarns, and glue. There's also a "Recycled Collage Kit," which is zanier, full of plastic widgets, rubber washers, springs, spools, and fabric scraps. The "Ultimate Collage Kit" costs $19.95; the recycled version, $14.95.

Childcraft also carries the "Design-a-Dollhouse," a put-together cardboard house to be decorated, with markers, glitter, colored paper, and imagination, by the owner - plus rafts of science kits, geography games, kid-sized sports accessories, and a truly spectacular assortment of plain maple building blocks, available in sets (Beginner, Intermediate, Advanced, Deluxe, and Olympic), or individually, for block connoisseurs who like to pick and choose. For a free catalog, contact Childcraft, Inc., P.O. Box 29149, Mission, KS 66201-9149; (800) 631-5657.

Constructive Playthings

Constructive Playthings carries curriculum materials, supplies, and equipment for infants, pre-schoolers, and elementary-aged kids - and lots of each; the catalog is nearly 200 (packed) pages long. Categories include "Playground Equipment" (from the immoveably enormous to the small and portable), "Recreation," "Sand and Water Play," "Riding Toys," "Transportation," "Animals and Farm Sets," "Blocks," "School Furniture," "Housekeeping Play," "Pretend Play," "Infant Care," "Beginning Manipulatives,"

"Puzzles," "Design Perception," "Sorting and Patterning," "Shape and Size Perception," "Language Development," "Talkable Topics: The World About Us," "Readiness," "Learning About the Alphabet," "Alphabet Games," "Phonetic Reinforcement," "Number Concepts," "Math Games," "Nature Science," "Health Science," "Educational Games," "Early Childhood Resource Books," "Books for Beginners," "Social Studies," "Music," "Records and Cassettes," "Teacher Aids," "Arts and Crafts Supplies," and "Office Supplies."

This is a particularly good source for early learners: there are alphabet puzzles, magnetic and cardboard letters (upper- and lower-case), alphabet and phonics bingo games, alphabet and numbers lotto games, rhyming card games, word-and-picture flash cards, picture dominoes, and counting frames. A catalog costs $3.00, from Constructive Playthings, 1227 East 119th St., Grandview, MO 64030; (800) 832-0224 or (816) 761-5900.

Creative Home Teaching

This 48-page newsprint catalog is designed especially for the "Home School Family," and "features unique and hard to find items with a strong emphasis on creative thinking skills." All the basics are covered here: Early Learning, Math, Science, History, Geography, Language Arts, Art, and Music - plus Critical Thinking and Creative Writing. The catalog carries, for example, the complete Brown Paper School Book series (see above); *Mathematics Their Way*, a complete "activity-centered mathematical program for early childhood education," heavy on appealing manipulatives; and *I Am an Artist: Beginning to Draw Through Observation*, a collection of 22 art activities for kids in the middle grades. Also available: a pair of geography/history trivia games, *Challenge Around the World* ("Where did smorgasbord originate?" "What is the currency of China?") and *Challenge Through American History* ("Which president on Mt. Rushmore is wearing glasses?"); and *Animal Addresses*, a project unit suitable for kids in grades 3-6, which combines animal information with mapping skills ("Why don't tigers hunt zebras?"). For a free catalog, contact Creative Home Teaching, P.O. Box 152581, San Diego, CA 92195; (619) 263-8633.

Creative Teaching Associates

Creative Teaching Associates offers "quality curricular materials" for students in grades K-9, in the fields of math, language arts, and science. Their specialty is games, designed to reinforce basic academic concepts. Math resources, for example, include the "Chase Series," a set of four games that teach number place and decimals through a parcheesi-like format; fraction dominoes and tic-tac-toe; money dominoes; problem-solving bingo; *Math Around the Home*, in which arithmetical manipulations of time, temperature, money, metrics, and liquid measurement center around "problem solving challenges that occur in everyday life" (Example: "Large eggs weigh about 2 ounces. How many ounces will 1 dozen eggs weigh?"); and an assortment of consumer math board games (*Menu Math, Discount Math, Department Store Math, Bank Account Math*). Equivalent games for the language arts teach spelling, vocabulary, and the parts of speech.

Science materials include *Kitchen, Garage, and Garbage Can Science*, a book-and-videotape series for grades K-8 designed to "involve students in easy-to-do, meaningful science activities both at school and at home." Each book includes 15 reproducible student activity sheets, with accompanying teacher's pages, supplying background information and instructions. The activities involve materials commonly found in the kitchen, garage, or garbage can; topics covered include air, water, magnetism, electricity, and gravity. There are three book-and-tape sets in the series; each costs $49.95. Books are sold separately and cost $6.95 each. For a free catalog, contact Creative Teaching Associates, P.O. Box 7766, Fresno, CA 93747; (800) 767-4CTA or (209) 291-6626.

Creative Teaching Press

The Creative Teaching Press catalog offers materials for the "whole language classroom." These consist largely of literature-based activity books: there are literature-based art activities, in which well-known kid's books are correlated to hands-on art projects; literature-based cookbooks (35 recipes based on favorite books); and a series of literature-based activity books keyed to the months of the year, each containing an annotated bibliography of children's holiday books, plus an assortment of related activities involving arts, crafts, games, music, writing, drama, math, social studies, and science.

Creative Teaching Press also sells incentive charts and reward stickers, teaching calendars with assorted stickers, timelines and reference charts for intermediate science and social studies, bookmarks and bookplates, 8 1/2 x 11" world or U.S. outline maps by the pad (35 sheets for $3.50), spinners, dice, and counters for game-makers, and teacher's spiral-bound lesson plan and record books. For a free catalog, contact Creative Teaching Press, Inc., P.O. Box 6017, Cypress, CA 90630-0017; (800) 444-4CTP.

EDC Publishing

EDC Publishing is the American publisher of the Usborne books, a superb line of colorfully illustrated informational books in all fields for kids of all ages. The pictures (practically) tell it all: if you could cross the *Where's Waldo?* books with the encyclopedia, you'd get Usborne. Some examples: a series of appealing and heavily illustrated science dictionaries (*Biology*, *Chemistry*, and *Physics*), supplying all necessary basic information; the "Understanding Science" series for kids aged 11-14 (*Atoms and Molecules*, *Magnetism and Electricity*, *Machines*, *Light and Colour*, *Volcanoes and Earthquakes*, and *Seas and Oceans*); the popular "Puzzle Adventure" series, in which kids crack codes and solve puzzles while reading mystery/adventure stories (over 25 titles, including *Time Train to Ancient Rome* and *The Incredible Dinosaur Expedition*); the "Time Traveller" books, which introduce 8-11-year-olds to daily life of long ago (*Viking Raiders*, *Rome and Romans*, *Knights and Castles*, and *Pharoahs and Pyramids*); a how-to-draw series for young artists (18 different volumes); a "World Geography" series; and much more. (See entries under Arts and Crafts and Foreign Languages.) For a catalog, contact EDC Publishing, P.O. Box 470663, Tulsa, OK 74147-0663; (800) 475-4522.

Educational Insights

Educational Insights sells creative learning resources in several categories: Beginning Skills, Reading and Reading Comprehension, Critical Thinking, Mathematics, Social Studies, Science, and Electronic Teaching Aids. Resources for the very small include the *Kitty Kat* bingo games, in which the bingo cards are based on colors and shapes, numbers, the alphabet, sight words, or telling time. Counters are colored plastic kittycats. Also available: *Tub o' Letters* (upper- and lower-case) and *Tub o' Numbers*, each containing 86 plastic tiles for games and learning activities; workbook-and-cassette sets, for reinforcing alphabet and phonics skills; *Dino Checkers* ("regulation checkers with a prehistoric twist"); and *Little Riddles*, an imaginative riddle card game with four printed clues on one side and a color illustration of the answer on the other. (Example: "I have needles, but I do not sew. I am sharp on the outside and soft on the inside. Find me where it's hot and dry. I am a plant." On the reverse side, just in case you missed this one, is an illustration of a cactus.) For older kids, there are the *I.Q. Games*, quiz games on cards, packed with "hundreds of fascinating facts," in several categories, among them "Animals of the World," "Famous Places of the World," "Dinosaurs and Prehistoric Life," "U.S. Geography," "World Geography," and "U.S. History." And much more. For reviews of individual Educational Insights products, see History and Geography (Geosafari, Worldwide Penpals, Project: Earth) and Science (Adventures in Science kits, Discovery Collections). For a free catalog, contact Educational Insights, 19560 S. Rancho Way, Dominguez Hills, CA 90220; (800) 933-3277 or (213) 637-2131.

Evan-Moor

Evan-Moor sells "quality teaching materials for grades preK-6." The company also publishes a 24-page newsletter, *Helping Children Learn*. Each issue includes lesson plans for a cross-curricular theme unit, reproducible student worksheets, suggestions for hands-on math and science activities, a geography page, and ideas for literature-based projects. A one-year subscription (5 issues) costs $9.95. The 30-page catalog offers student workbooks and activity books, and teacher resource books in the categories of Math, Arts and Crafts, Early Learning, Writing, Reading, Geography, Social Studies, and Science. There is also a selection of "theme units," which include art ideas, activities designed to stimulate critical thinking, and project suggestions for math, science, and creative writing. Topics for grades 2-5 include "Who Discovered America?," "Endangered Spcies," "Sharks," and "Dragons."

Selected books include *How to Be President*, an integrated social-studies-and-language-arts unit for kids in grades 3-6; *Making Books With Beginning Writers*; *The Teacher-Friendly Computer Book*, which includes the script of a play, in which kids enact the different parts of a computer; *ABC Animal Crafts* for kids in preK-2; *Drawing Animals Around the World*, with which users draw 16 different animals, learn where they live using a world map, and read some interesting facts about each; and *The Big Book of Science Rhymes and Chants*. Some Evan-Moor books are also available in Spanish. For a free catalog, contact Evan-Moor, 18 Lower Ragsdale Drive, Monterey, CA 93940-5746; (800) 777-4362.

Eyewitness Books

The Eyewitness series, published by Alfred A. Knopf, is essentially a collection of wonderful photographic encyclopedias: each volume is dedicated to a specific topic and is heavily illustrated with spectacular full-color real-life photographs. The books are, at heart, mega-quality picture books: there is a text, but it's concentrated in the picture captions. The format works: our kids pore over these by the hour. The original (and ever-increasing) series now includes the following titles: *Amphibian, Ancient Egypt, Ancient Greece, Ancient Rome, Arms and Armor, Bible Lands, Bird, Boat, Butterfly and Moth, Car, Cat, Costume, Crystal and Gem, Dinosaur, Dog, Early Humans, Explorer, Film, Fish, Flag, Flying Machine, Fossil, Horse, Insect, Invention, Knight, Mammal, Money, Shark, Shell, Skeleton, Sports, Tree, Volcanoes and Earthquakes,* and *Weather*.

There are two off-shoots of the series: the Eyewitness Art and Eyewitness Science books (see Arts and Crafts and Science). A similar series, the Eyewitness Visual Dictionaries, is published by Dorling Kindersley: each includes hundreds of full-color (labelled) photographs illustrating the volume's subject, plus unusual enlargements, cross-sections, and cutaway views. titles include *The Visual Dictionary of Animals, Buildings, Cars, Everyday Things, Flight, the Human Body, Military Uniforms, Plants,* and *Ships and Sailing*. Available through bookstores.

Games

Great "mental caffeine," writes one educator. This bimonthly magazine contains a large collection of challenging and fascinating games and puzzles of all kinds for games fans. One example from our (already much-thumbed) sample issue was titled "Spiral Staircase" and featured a double-page spread of color photographs of *spirals*, each to be identified and matched to the proper picture caption. When I last saw it, the kids were crouched around it, eagerly identifying spirals in cinnamon bark, fiddlehead ferns, drill bits, mouse traps, and tuning keys. Also included: reviews of games and game books, and information on national gaming contests. An annual subscription (6 issues) costs $14.97 from *Games*, P.O. Box 605, Mount Morris, IL 61054-7789.

Geode

Geode Educational Options publishes a book and resource catalog of "exciting materials for teaching and parenting." It's mostly a book catalog, offering an excellent assortment of books in several categories: Thinking Skills, Change and Future Studies, Research and Reference, Interpersonal Skills, Science, Social Studies, Women's Studies, Language Arts, Mythology, Legends, and Folklore, Fine Arts, Story Books, Bibliotherapy (books that can be used to help children work through problems), and Parenting Books. There's also a large assortment of cooperative games (for little kids through adults).

The Thinking Skills section is particularly fascinating: selections include *Put Your Mother on the Ceiling*, a collection of children's imagination games by Richard de Mille; Don Rubin's *Brainstorms*, filled with "Real Puzzles for the Real Genius," one of which involves playing chess on a Mobius strip; nearly all of the wonderful Mitsumasa Anno books; *M is For Mirror*, by Duncan Birmingham, in which kids aged 4-8 solve picture puzzles by placing a mirror (included) in the right place on the page; and *Cartoons for Thinking* (Joseph P. Hester, Don R. Killian, and Doug Marlette) which, through the medium of political cartoons, inspires kids to debate contemporary ethical issues.

The catalog carries a terrific collection of science and nature books, including a large number of kids' museum activity books, crammed with appealing hands-on experiments; there's also *Tales That Aren't* (Jean Kelly), a collection of folktales with "a different attitude toward nature," in the princess refuses to marry the handsome prince if it means hurting a frog; and *Elementary, My Dear Shakespeare*, a manual for putting on Shakespearean plays with elementary-school-aged children. Catalogs cost $2.00, from Geode, PO Box 106, West Chester, PA 19381-0106.

Good Apple

Good Apple carries creative activity books for kids of all ages. Categories include Arts and Crafts, Creative Thinking, Creative Writing, Early Learning, Language Arts, Literature-Based Reading, Math, Responsibility Education, Science, and Social Studies. The company also publishes a newspaper and a trio of magazines for educators. *The Good Apple Newspaper*, appropriate for kids in grades 2-8, is published five time yearly, and includes pull-out posters, calendars, reproducible student activity pages, hands-on activities and projects in a number of fields, and suggestions for thematic teaching units. Examples from past issues include the environment, the solar system, the human body, national parks, Chanukah, and E. B. White's classic, *Charlotte's Web*. The magazines are similar in content: *Lollipops* is targeted at preschool educators; *Oasis* at teachers of children in grades 5-9; and *Challenge* at teachers and parents of gifted children, from preschool through grade 8. Single and back issues of each publication are available.

Activity books aimed at creative thinkers include *Mighty Myth*, for kids in grades 5-12, in which re-tellings of classic myths are used to spark discussions about hero worship, brain vs. brawn, peer group pressure, and other issues; *The Unconventional Inven-*

tion Book (grades 3-12), a collection of exercises for "activating student inventiveness;" and *Fact, Fantasy, and Folklore,* in which 11 classic fairytales ("Rumpelstiltskin," "Beauty and the Beast," "The Reluctant Dragon") serve as jumping-off points for debate and hands-on activities. Literature-based activity books include*Little House in the Classroom* (grades 3-5), in which the Laura Ingalls Wilder books are interfaced with other academic disciplines, through activities based on writing skills, poetry, geography, math, social studies, and art; and the "Author Connection" series, featuring projects based on the books of well-known children's writers, such as Marc Brown, Steven Kellogg, Robert McCloskey, and Ruth Heller. Social studies selections include activity books about North American Indians, famous explorers, pioneers, cultures of other countries, and ancient civilizations; there's also the "Famous Friends" series for children in grades K-4 in which, through illustrated stories, discussion questions, and follow-up activities, students learn about important American historical figures. Titles in the series include *Founders, Pathfinders, Presidential Leaders, Inventors, Legendary Heroes,* and *Outstanding Women.* For a catalog or subscription information, contact Good Apple, 1204 Buchanan St., P.O. Box 299, Carthage, IL 62321-0299; (800) 435-7234 or (217) 357-3981.

Great Kids Company

Toys, books, and games "that capture the child's interest while stimulating the imagination." The catalog carries active play equipment (tumbling mats, balance beams, and folding plastic tunnels); art supplies, including a 30 x 47" chalk mat map of the United States; building sets; sewing cards; a wooden American flag puzzle; kids' carpentry tools; and a lot of props for imaginative play: puppets, costumes, plastic food, and "Dramatic Play Hats" (policeperson, mail carrier, airline pilot, firefighter, engineer, yachter, and construction worker). They also sell some old standbys, like Lincoln logs and Tinkertoys. For a free catalog, contact the Great Kids Company, P.O. Box 609, Lewisville, NC 27023; (800) 582-1493.

Gryphon House

Gryphon House publishes early childhood teacher resources, including curriculum guides, collections of circletime activities for amusing children in groups, science, math, and arts and crafts activities books, and child development program guides. Among their selections: *Story Stretchers* and *More Story Stretchers* (Shirley C. Raines and Robert J. Canady), collections of multidisciplinary activities based on favorite children's picturebooks; and *Good Earth Art: Environmental Art for Kids* (Mary Ann Kohl and Cindy Gainer), in which kids use natural materials or common throwaways for creative art projects. Examples include "Earth Paints," "Weed Weavings," "Bark Baskets," "Car-part Wind Chime," and "Milk Carton Bird Feeder." For a catalog, contact Gryphon House, Early Childhood Books, P.O. Box 275, Mt. Rainier, MD 20712; (800) 638-0928 or (301) 779-6200.

Hirsch, E.D., Jr.

In 1987, E.D. Hirsch, Jr., hit the bestseller list with his book *Cultural Literacy: What Every American Needs to Know* (Houghton Mifflin). Hirsch defines "cultural literacy" as the body of information - fact, fable, tradition, and symbol - that educated persons share and that allows for ready communication within our national community. Acquiring cultural literacy, Hirsch states, is the key to an effective education. An appendix to the text - "The List" - lists in alphabetical order the large (and provisional) collection of concepts and terms that Hirsch and associates feel represent the core of background knowledge necessary to become culturally literate. "The List" is fun to tackle: it's 63 pages long, and runs from abbreviation, abolitionism, and abominable snowman to Zola, zoning, and Zurich. Answers, for those who fall apart midway through the list, are available in *The Dictionary of Cultural Literacy: What Every American Needs to Know* (E.D. Hirsch, Jr., Joseph F. Kett, and James Trefil); and there's also a junior version for children, *A First Dictionary of Cultural Literacy: What Our Children Need to Know*. From these have developed the "Core Knowledge Series," a grade-by-grade breakdown of the knowledge children should acquire in the first through the sixth grades. Titles include *What Your First Grader Needs to Know, What Your Second Grader Needs to Know*, and so on. Categories covered include Language Arts, Geography, World Civilization, and American Civilization, Fine Arts, Mathematics, and Natural Sciences. "Core Knowledge" volumes are not books of lists: these are collections of stories, illustrations, explanations, examples, and information - everything, in reader-friendly form, that your elementary-aged child needs to know. Available through bookstores.

Home School Supply House

The Home School Supply House sells "learning materials for all ages." The catalog carries an assortment of books on the theory and practice of homeschooling, plus close to 40 pages of carefully selected educational resources. Resources for readers range from early phonics programs and alphabet puzzles through the "Homeschool Bookshelf," a long list of literature selections, categorized by grade level (preschool through grade 12). "A variety of writing styles," states the accompanying text, "is presented through fiction, biographies, folk tales, and historical fiction - assuring your student of a sound base in literature." Selections are inexpensive and excellent; this is a good source for those in the process of building a kid-style home library. The catalog also offers books, games, and supplies for math, science, geography, history, and arts and crafts. Included are Cuisenaire rods and manuals, Miquon math materials, a selection of biographies for children, an assortment of conventional social studies textbooks, and cassette tapes of classical and contemporary music. The Home School Supply House is also a source for the "Young Discovery Library:" this series of small, colorfully illustrated books is intended for children aged 5-10. Each volume presents an overview of a specific topic; young readers can learn about everything from wool, rice, and paper to Australia, Eskimos, and ancient Rome. Each book costs $4.95. For a catalog, contact Home School Supply House, P.O. Box 7, Fountain Green, UT 84632; (800) 772-3129.

Interact

Interact's motto is "Learning Through Involvement," and their catalog, titled *Elementary Simulations*, sells a collection of learning units in which kids participate in directed group role play - which means pretending, with an educational hook. The units, or "simulations," are generally designed for large groups (10-35 students), but most look to be adaptable to - and doubtless are more enjoyable with - much smaller student numbers. Units are available for kids in grades K-9.

In one sample simulation, "Apple Valley School," participants set up a 19th-century schoolroom, receive a new Apple Valley identity (complete with name, age, family, and home, located on the included Apple Valley map), and get their education the old-fashioned way, using slates for math, holding spelling bees, playing marbles and checkers, and learning cross-stitch embroidery. Along the way, they tackle various historically-oriented "Challenge Tasks," and they polish off the simulated school year with a graduation ceremony and pioneer picnic.

In other simulations, students form a TV news team and present a broadcast, climb Mt. Olympus while studying Greek mythology, become space cadets in a future society on the brink of galactic civil war (cadet combat involves answering "Battle Questions," such as "Name the planets in order from the sun" and "On Venus, the gravitational pull is only 87% that of Earth. How much will a 200-pound earthperson weigh on Venus?"), participate in an archaeological dig in which they reconstruct an ancient civilization, travel the world to collect museum artifacts, sail to America with the Vikings, trap beaver with the mountain men, and organize a community zoo. For a free catalog, contact Interact, P.O. Box 997, Lakeside, CA 92040; (800) 359-0961 or (619) 448-1474.

The Kids' Diary of 365 Amazing Days Randy Harelson (Workman; 1979)

This over-sized paperback is the great-grandaddy of all kid's activity books; there is, as the cover advertises, "something to do every day of the year - plus lots of space to write and draw." The book can be used as a diary: there's a lined block for personal entries on each page, labeled "Dear Diary." It's also a calendar, a scrapbook, and a (delightfully illustrated) project encyclopedia. Users, during an action-packed year, will celebrate Louis Braille's birthday (by writing a coded message in Braille), George Washington Carver Day (by rooting a sweet potato), Robert Goddard's first rocket launch (by building a model rocket), Dolley Madison's birthday (by holding an egg-rolling contest), Marc Chagall's birthday (by making a "stained-glass" window), Grandma Moses's birthday (by making a family tree), Switzerland's Onion Festival (by making fried onion rings), and Walt Disney's birthday (by making a flip-book "animated cartoon"). And 357 more. Available through bookstores or from Workman Publishing, 708 Broadway, New York, NY 10003; (212) 254-5900.

Knowledge Unlimited

Knowledge Unlimited sells "materials for the discerning educator:" books, posters, videos, and filmstrips covering the fields of social studies (including "American Government and History," "American Indians," "Black Studies," "Women's Studies," "Hispanic Studies," "World Affairs and History," "Global Studies," and "Geography"), economics, science, language arts, art, and primary education.

The catalog is a real find for the educational video buff: various video series cover American history from the early colonial period through the present day; techniques used include re-enactments, still photographs, and excerpts from original newsreels or televised news programs. Viewers can hear Martin Luther King, Jr., deliver his great "I Have A Dream" speech on the steps of the Lincoln Memorial; watch Adolf Hitler's rise to power and defeat in World War II; fight the Civil War; or follow the adventures of a wagon train heading west on the Oregon Trail. For multicultural social studies programs, there are videos detailing the histories of China, Russia, the Arab nations, and Japan, plus an award-winning four-part video series on African history, geography, and culture. For map-lovers, there's a "Geography Tutor" video series: individual tapes, each accompanied by a teacher's guide, include *Map and Globe Terms*, *Types of Maps and Map Projections*, *Map Skills*, *Earth's Physical Features*, *Weather and Climate*, and *Global Problems*.

The science video selection is equally wide-ranging, and includes *Invention*, a three-part series from the Discovery Channel and the Smithsonian Institution, detailing the lives of inventors and the inventions that have shaped world history; *Our Changing World*, a five-part earth science series in which a pair of "alien scientists" introduce kids to earth's geologic, hydrologic, and atmospheric features; assorted NOVA and National Geographic videos; and episodes from Carl Sagan's PBS series, *Cosmos*.

For booklovers of all ages, there's a large collection of video versions of famous books and plays. Included are *The Diary of Anne Frank*, *The House of Dies Drear*, *Anne of Green Gables*, *Brighty of the Grand Canyon*, *The Red Badge of Courage*, and the Wonderworks production of C.S. Lewis's *The Chronicles of Narnia*.

And for younger viewers, there's an animated video series of tales from foreign lands, revealing "insights into different cultures and traditions" through stories from Europe, Asia, and Central Africa, and from the North American and Latin American Indians; and a large assortment of storybook classics, including *Aesop's Fables*, *The Velveteen Rabbit*, *Abel's Island*, *Charlotte's Web*, and *The Legend of Sleepy Hollow*.

For those who have not yet succumbed to the lure of the VCR, Knowledge Unlimited carries a range of books, creative resource guides, and activity books for educators - there is, for example, a unit on integrating art, social studies, and critical thinking through editorial cartoons - and a superb series of posters and art prints. There's a set of 10 informational posters on "Ancient Civilizations" (Sumerians, Ancient Jews, Greeks, Egyptians, Persians, Romans, Ancient India, Ancient China, Mayans, and Incas) with accompanying teacher's guide; and a series of multicultural math posters ("Math of the Navajo," "Math of Mexico," "Math of Africa," "Math of Japan"). For a free catalog, contact Knowledge Unlimited, Box 52, Madison, WI 53701-0052; (800) 356-2303.

Learning Wrap-Ups

These quickie learning manipulatives are packaged to look like firecrackers, in tubes with a "wick" sticking out the top (suitable, says the package blurb, for "explosive learning"). Each Wrap-Up set includes 10 notched problem/answer boards, plus a long heavy piece of colored string. Users wrap the string sequentially around the board, matching problem on the left to correct answer on the right. The boards are self-correcting: if answers are right, the wrapped string will match the pattern of lines on the board back. Wrap-Ups are available in a number of incarnations: Preschool/Kindergarten Wrap-Ups include Numbers, Alphabet, Phonics, and Shapes and Logic; Math Wrap-Ups include Addition, Subtraction, Multiplication, Division, and Fractions; Music Wrap-Ups, Signs and Symbols, Intervals and Chords, Rhythm and Vocabulary, and Keys and Notes. Other Wrap-Ups: Antonyms, Synonyms, Homonyms, and States and Capitals. Available from several sources including the Timberdoodle, E. 1510 Spencer Lake Road, Shelton, WA 98584; (206) 426-0672; and The Sycamore Tree, Inc., 2179 Meyer Place, Costa Mesa, CA 92627; (714) 642-6750.

Marathon

"*Marathon*," states the publisher, "was created by a father of three elementary school children who needed more attention (as every child does) from their educators (parents and teachers) to improve grades and learning abilities." Such formal goals don't communicate the sense of the game: it's appealing, competitively comfortable, informational, and - truly - fun. The game is based on 2500 question-and-answer cards on a wide range of assorted educational topics, plus 240 picture cards, featuring (cartoon-ish) portraits of famous people, maps, anatomical diagrams, animals, plants, international monuments, and geometrical shapes. Players advance along the game board by correctly answering questions. The game is appropriate for kids in grades 1-5; cards are keyed for question difficulty, with one, two, or three stars. Players (up to six at a time) do not play each other, which even among the most cooperative occasionally makes for ill feeling. Instead, each player gets two playing pieces, one representing him/herself (a smiling star) and one representing "Igg Knorantz," a caterpillar-browed character whose nose forms an upside-down question mark. The star moves ahead on the playing board for right answers, and Igg moves ahead for wrong answers, in a race for the finish line. Each player therefore challenges him/herself. Our boys, who never tire of downing Igg, love it. *Marathon* costs $29.95, plus $4.95 shipping and handling, from G. Marathon U.S.A., 12500 Network, Suite 201, San Antonio, TX 78249; (800) 992-7941 or (512) 690-9984.

Michael Olaf's Essential Montessori

This, one of our favorite resource catalogs, begins with a quote from Italian educator Maria Montessori: "Scientific observaton has established that education is not what the teacher gives; education is a natural process spontaneously carried out by the human individual, and is acquired not by listening to words but by experiences upon the environment." The catalog provides materials for furnishing this environment: musical tapes, high-quality toys and manipulatives, prints, posters, and study cards, books, cooperative games, and art supplies. The "Language" section, for example, includes a tactile alphabet book (the letters are made of red felt); a "moveable alphabet" to be ordered in a wooden box; alphabet rubber stamps; a series of "environment labels," which just-beginning readers use to label familiar objects around the house ("book," "spoon," "sink," and so on); several series of laminated picture cards ("Shells," "Composers," "Classification of Vertebrates," "Animals of Seven Continents," and more); books, from beginning readers through *Beowulf* and *The Canterbury Tales*; *Authors* card games; books of illuminated medieval letters; calligraphy kits; and dictionaries.

There is also an assortment of adult books and materials, including works on homeschooling, parenting, and the Montessori approach to education. Of particular interest to homeschoolers is a packet of "required curriculum examples." The Michael Olaf staff, the text explains, is in the process of assembling several different curricula, to give readers a broad view of what children, aged 6-12, are expected to learn in different kinds of schools. The packet of examples includes a California basic public school curriculum (translated into Montessori language) for grades K-3, a private school curriculum from a "British-influenced school in Nepal," a Waldorf-type homeschooling curriculum, and a sample of public school requirements from Japan. The packet costs $6.50. For a catalog, contact Michael Olaf's Essential Montessori, P.O. Box 1162, Arcata, CA 95521; (707) 826-1557.

Modern

"Modern," reads the catalog introduction, "is the world's largest distributor of free loan educational materials. We search for organizations willing to share curriculum relevant expertise and to sponsor video and print materials for distribution to schools. We make these videos available for group showings to students and educators requiring only a record of usage." Materials available for free loan are listed in Modern's "Free Loan Guide;" they also publish a "Special Supplement" of (purchasable) videos, software, and multimedia hardware for education.

Free loan materials must be ordered in advance (you select first and second choices for play dates); once received, you've got five days for viewing, after which you (promptly) ship it back to the company. Some materials are accompanied by free teacher's guides and student worksheets, which you keep. Some materials (VHS video cases) come with postage-paid return labels.

Free loan videos and films are available in a wide range of categories: Agriculture, Biological Sciences, Business and Economics, Education, Europe, Fine Arts, History, Home Economics, Industry and Technology, Medical and Health Sciences, Physical Education, Psychology, Religion and Philosophy, Physical Science, Social Science, and South America. Selections appropriate for elementary-aged children are marked with a little red schoolhouse; unmarked selections are generally recommended for kids in grades 7 and up. Materials for younger children include *What's Buzzin'*, a program on honeybees developed by the National Honey Board, *The Amazing Orange*, from Tropicana Products, Inc., *The Munchers: A Fable*, a claymation presentation on dental hygiene from the American Dental Association, and *Sam's Most Electrifying Account*, in which a group of puppets learn about electricity, developed by the Edison Electrical Institute. For a copy of the Free Loan Resource Guide, contact Modern, 5000 Park Street North, St. Petersburg, FL 33709; (800) 446-6337.

Play

Play, a quarterly magazine for parents, reviews "quality entertainment" for children. Our sample issue included articles on good video movies for kids (by a parent who wanted an antidote for "The Care Bears"), an article on music lessons and music-instruction programs for kids, a piece on the educational potential of CD-ROM technology, and reviews of children's books, videos, storytapes, and musical cassettes. A one-year subscription (four issues) costs $12.00; order from *Play*, 3620 N.W. 43rd St., Gainesville, FL 32606; (904) 375-3705.

Play It Smart

Play It Smart, the publisher explains, is a "non-trivial question and answer game" containing - in 3600 questions (with answers) - everything every intelligent person should know. Questions/answers are contained in a chunky 200-page book, rather than on separate cards ("great for travelling") and are divided into six categories: Business and Law, Science and Technology, History, Literature, Art/Music/Entertainment, and Various and Sundry. The game is generally (but not necessarily) aimed at a high-school-aged audience. Sample questions include: "What is a prolonged speech, commonly used in the U.S. Congress, intended to delay a vote, called?" "How many marbles are in a gross?" "How many strings do the standard forms of the following instruments have: guitar, banjo, violin?" "What is the art of carving whalebone or ivory called?" "Give the days of the week in French." The game (book, playing board, dice, and erasable pen) costs $29.95 from Play It Smart Products, 12221 Sam Furr Road, P.O. Box 2002, Huntersville, NC 28078; (800) 258-5302 or (704) 892-4263.

PlayFair Toys

PlayFair Toys publishes a catalog of nonsexist, nonviolent educational toys for all ages. The collection is wide-ranging, creative, and contains much more than toys: there are also educational games, cassette tapes, art and science kits, and books. For the very young, for example, there's *Count-A-Pig*, a count-and-match game in which players pair numbered cards to quantities of little pink plastic pigs; a clock puzzle; a squashy huggable multicolored globe; and *Go Togethers*, a game in which small players match pairs of (real) objects on laminated cards marked with object outlines: locks go with keys, babies go with bottles, cups go with saucers. For older kids: fairytales in French and Spanish; stamp-collecting kits; the "Wildflower Nature Collection," which includes a flower press, 12 pressed specimens, a wildflower identification card game, and an activity book; and a high-quality all-wood U.S. map puzzle. For a catalog, contact PlayFair Toys, P.O. Box 18210, Boulder, CO 80308; (800) 824-7255 or (303) 440-7229.

Rainbow Re-Source Center

The Rainbow Re-Source Center began as a service to home-schoolers wanting to buy and sell used educational materials, and subsequently expanded to carry new items. The Center publishes a retail catalog, in which new educational products are briefly described and reviewed, plus a fat bimonthly catalog, *The Rainbow Re-Porter*, of used educational materials, both currently available and wanted by potential purchasers. This is a Christian organization, which means that some of their science materials are questionable; many of the offered resources, however, are excellent, varied, and inexpensive. A subscription to *The Rainbow Re-Porter* costs $12.00 annually (6 issues); individual issues cost $2.50. To order or to obtain a retail catalog, contact the Rainbow Re-Source Center, P.O. Box 491, Kewanee, IL 61443.

Roots and Wings

This is primarily a book catalog, with a scattering of audiocassettes, games, kits, and truly terrific puppets, intended for use in storytelling. There's a chimpanzee puppet, for example, to accompany *Curious George*; pig, spider, and rat puppets to accompany *Charlotte's Web*; and a fuzzy green dragon to accompany *The Muffin Muncher*, Stephen Cosgrove's story of a cooperative dragon who fires up the castle ovens for muffin-baking.

There's a nice general collection of reading materials here covering arts and crafts, nature and the environment, reading and writing, and foreign languages; the catalog specialty, however, is multicultural resources. There is a particularly large assortment of native American literature, both fiction and nonfiction, plus beading loom and finger-weaving kits, a "Native Peoples of North America" map, and a teaching unit titled "American Indian Music in the Classroom," which includes 4 cassette tapes, printed song lyrics, a set of 22 photographs showing tribal dancers and singers, and a teacher's guide and bibliography. For a catalog, contact Roots & Wings Educational Catalog, P.O. Box 3348, Boulder, CO 80307; (800) 833-1787.

Shekinah Curriculum Cellar

The Shekinah Curriculum Cellar, in small print in black-and-white, publishes a 32-page catalog containing "thousands of items selected specifically for home schoolers." Categories include "Parent Helps," "Bible," "Character and Manners," "Reading," "Language Arts," "Arithmetic," "Science," "Health and Safety," "History and Geography," "Critical Thinking Skills," "Art, Drawing, and Crafts," and "Music." Materials from "Christian publishers" (many) are marked with a "c," which is helpful to educators who are biased toward such resources in one way or another. For a catalog, contact Shekinah Curriculum Cellar, 967 Junipero Drive, Box 2154, Costa Mesa, CA 92626.

Super Sleuth

Super Sleuth is a cross-curriculum research game, designed to teach kids to become good "clue detectives" through the use of reference materials, such as atlases, almanacs, dictionaries, and encyclopedias. The kit consists of a collection of 36 games, each of which takes one week to play. Games play like a bookish version of "Twenty Questions:" in each, daily clues are posted on a playing board, each giving kids another hint to help them track down the correct answer. Once a player discovers the answer, he or she writes it down on a ballot, circles the day on which the solution was reached (the earlier, the better), lists reference sources used, and drops it into a homemade classroom ballot box. Correct answers are posted on the playing board at the end of the week. The games are generally appropriate for kids in grades 4-6. Each is coded by level of difficulty: topics are given 1, 2, or 3 stars, with 1 star being the least difficult. *Super Sleuth* (36 games) costs $24.95 (shipping and handling included) from Relative Teaching Concepts, P.O. Box 8417, Richmond, VA 23226-0417; (804) 282-7842.

Sycamore Tree

The Sycamore Tree publishes a large catalog of diverse educational supplies: categories include "Bible Materials," "Reading," "Mathematics," "Penmanship," "Grammar and Composition," "Spelling," "Social Studies," "Science," "Foreign Language," "Sex Education," "Physical Education," "Arts and Crafts," "Music," "Cooking and Nutrition," "Games and Puzzles," "Felts," "References and Resources," and "Curriculum." "Christian" materials are marked with a little fish symbol, for fast identification. A useful source for many of the basics. Sycamore Tree also sells standardized tests to be administered at home: those available include the Comprehensive Test of Basic Skills (covers all academic areas) and the Gates-MacGinitie Reading Inventory (covers vocabulary development and comprehension). Completed tests must be returned to the company for scoring and evaluation. For a catalog, contact The Sycamore Tree, Inc., 2179 Meyer Place, Costa Mesa,

CA 92627; (714) 650-4466 (information) and (714) 642-6750 or (800) 779-6750 (orders and fax).

Timberdoodle
The Timberdoodle publishes a plump little newsprint catalog of resources for homeschoolers. The company covers all the basics, plus carries a nice line of supplies for budding engineers: drafting skills workbooks, Brio-Mec building kits (beechwood blocks and beams, plastic axles, wheels, and pulleys, a collection of plugs, nuts, and bolts to hold growing structures together, and an assortment of tools), Lego Technic Sets, and Fischertechnik kits ("the finest engineering lab available to the home educator," covering basic machines through pneumatics, electronics, and robotics). For a catalog, contact the Timberdoodle, E. 1510 Spencer Lake Road, Shelton, WA 98584; (206) 426-0762.

Tin Man Press
The Tin Man Press sells an assortment of inventive books and activity packs designed to encourage creative thinking. Among these is *Ideas To Go*, a collection of fifty "ready-to-use thinking challenges" for kids in grades 2-6 (in "Line Drawings," for example, kids match little squiggles to descriptive statements; in "Add Two," kids must add two lines to the drawing and two letters to the word to reach the correct answer); and *Nifty Fifty*, a creative discussion manual that gets kids to think by asking 500 mind-broadening questions about 50 everyday objects, such as sticks, stairs, roads, and socks. For a a copy of their flier, contact Tin Man Press, Box 219, Stanwood, WA 98292; (800) 676-0459. You'll like their logo.

Toys to Grow On
The Toys to Grow On catalog, in glossy full-color, sells toys, art supplies, craft kits, and let's-pretend accessories. For young entomologists, there's "The Bug Box," a company exclusive, which contains 70 plastic bugs, from giant beetles to tiny ants, plus a spectacular bright-green praying mantis; for small animal-lovers there's *Animal Match-Ups*, a gorgeous game in which 60 photo tiles - with truly stunning color animal photographs - are snapped onto a playing board. Players locate matching pairs. There's a "Bathtub Scientist" kit for water-explorers, which includes a pair of funnels connected by plastic tubing, sets of measuring cups, a hydraulic pump, a bunch of miniature boats, miscellaneous materials for in-

vestigating floating and sinking, and a collection of activity cards. Cards come with a plastic bag and clip, so that they can be safely displayed right in the midst of the action. Also available: a giant alphabet mural to color (comes in four 3-foot sections, with 20 felt-tipped markers); and *The Allowance Game* (see Mathematics) in which players hop around the board earning and spending small manageable amounts of money. The game includes realistic plastic coins and paper bills. For a catalog, contact Toys to Grow On, P.O. Box 17, Long Beach, CA 90801; (800) 874-4242.

Troll Learn and Play
The catalog carries toys, games, building sets, craft kits, and books for kids. For little kids, for example, there are magnetic picture blocks in bright primary colors, alphabet teaching toys, and Richard Scarry Press & Peel sets, with 70 reusable vinyl stickers and sturdy background playboards; for older kids, selections include a magnetic U.S. map puzzle, a coin-collecting starter set, a tabletop greenhouse (comes with 6 seed packets, 10 soil pellets, 4 pots, and a watering cup), and an assortment of inexpensive book sets. The Great Classics Library ($24.95), for example, consists of 18 paper classics for kids aged 9-14, among them *The Call of the Wild, Treasure Island, Black Beauty, The Swiss Family Robinson*, and *Around the World in Eighty Days*. There are also collections of soft-cover biographies for kids aged 7-12; each set of 10 costs $19.95. Subjects include Helen Keller, Clara Barton, John Paul Jones, Elizabeth Blackwell, Louis Pasteur, Louisa May Alcott, Babe Ruth, Sacajawea, Sequoyah, Chief Joseph, and Squanto. For a catalog, contact Troll Learn & Play, 100 Corporate Drive, Mahwah, NJ 07430; (800) 247-6106.

Video Resources

The Family Video Guide: Over 300 Movies to Share With Your Children Terry and Catherine Catchpole (Williamson Publishing; 1992) Reviews of quality classic films, both relatively new and downright old, selected with a careful eye toward films that will "enrich family time, spark lively conversations, and fascinate and stimulate (rather than baby-sit) young viewers." (You provide the popcorn.) Available through bookstores or from Williamson Publishing, Church Hill Rd., P.O. Box 185, Charlotte, VT 05445; (800) 234-8791.

Films Incorporated Video A catalog of educational quality videos for learners of all ages in the fields of Social Science, Foreign Languages, the Humanities, Language Arts for Children, Science/Mathematics, and Guidance/Health. Included: the nine-part *Story of English*, hosted by Robert MacNeil; Sir Kenneth clark's 13-part *Civilisation*; the Wonderworks Video Library; and David Attenborough's 27-part (on 14 tapes) *Life on Earth*. For a catalog, contact Films Incorporated Video, 5547 N. Ravenswood Ave., Chicago, IL 60640-1199; (800) 343-4312.

Movies Unlimited   The Movies Unlimited catalog (nearly 700 pages long, plus supplements) purports to list all videotapes currently on the market, and probably does. The catalog costs $7.95 (plus $3.00 shipping and handling), but, for movie buffs, it's worth it. Available from Movies Unlimited, 6736 Castor Ave., Philadelphia, PA 19149; (800) 523-0823 (orders) or (215) 722-8398 (customer service).

Signals   This is a catalog "for fans and friends of public television," and is thus an excellent source for better-than-average videos, among them the BBC productions of *Oliver Twist, Bleak House, Great Expectations, Jane Eyre,* and *Pride and Prejudice*. Series include *The Six Wives of Henry VIII,* Ken Burns's *The Civil War,* and *I, Claudius,* based on the novels of Robert Graves, which traces the history of the Roman Empire from 50 B.C. to 50 A.D. For a catalog, contact Signals, WGBH Educational Foundation, P.O. Box 64428, St. Paul, MN 55164-0428; (800) 669-9696.

The Video Catalog   A source for BBC and PBS videos, film classics, and performing arts videos, including selections of opera and dance.   For a catalog, contact The Video Catalog, 1000 Westgate Drive, Saint Paul, MN 55114; (800) 733-2232.

Wilcox & Follett Book Company

Wilcox & Follet publishes a sale catalog of used textbooks ("in sound, attractive condition") and new workbooks that have become available through school curriculum changes. All list at 1/3 to 1/2 of the publisher's price. The 150+-page catalog offers books from over sixty different major publishers, each listed by title only (no descriptions).   This is a good deal if you know what you're looking for. For a catalog, contact Wilcox & Follett Book Company, 5563 South Archer Avenue, Chicago, IL 60638; (800) 621-4272.

World Wide Games

A 50+-page collection of truly terrific games and puzzles. A source for Chinese checkers, parchesi, tiddlywinks, and chess, plus *Uncommon Sense*, a game "especially for word lovers," in which players tackle quips, rhymes, definitions, foreign phrases, abbreviations, spellings, and more; *Clever Endeavor*, in which players try to identify people, places, or things with the help of various clues; *Notable Quotables*, in which players try to match famous quotations with their authors; *Cathedral*, in which players use beautiful hardwood building pieces to construct a walled medieval city; and *The Sailors Game*, in which players learn about seamanship and navigation as they race their yachts around the world. For a catalog, contact World Wide Games, P.O. Box 517, Dept. 2602, Colchester, CT 06415-0517; (800) 888-0987, Dept. 2602.

Zephyr Press

The catalog describes itself, in perfect truth, as supplying "cutting-edge materials for innovative education." Categories include "Self-Directed Learning Packets" in science, social studies, and the humanities, "Mathematics," "Thinking Skills," "Whole-Brain Learning," "Science," "Arts & Humanities," "Reading & Writing," "Global Awareness," and "Self Awareness." Individual materials have been described elsewhere throughout the book (see History and Geography, Mathematics, Arts and Crafts, and Creative Thinking). This one is definitely in a class of its own. To obtain a catalog, contact Zephyr Press, 3316 N. Chapel Ave., P.O. Box 13448, Tucson, AZ 85732-3448; (602) 322-5090.

For Parents:

Book and Publications

Helpful Periodicals:

Growing Without Schooling

A bimonthly magazine for homeschoolers, founded in 1977 by educator John Holt, author of *How Children Learn* and *How Children Fail*. Includes updates on homeschooling legislation, interviews with prominent educators, and lots of informational letters from practicing homeschoolers, with comments by the editor. An annual subscription (6 issues) costs $25.00 from *Growing Without Schooling*, 2269 Massachusetts Ave., Cambridge, MA 02140; (617) 864-3100. Free books and resources catalog.

Home Education Magazine

A 68-page bimonthly magazine for homeschooling families, widely available on newstands and in bookstorres and public libraries. Includes updates on homeschooling in the news, feature articles on all aspects of homeschooling, ten regular columnists who write in every issue on topics ranging from political action to homeschooling older children, and reviews and recommendations for educational resources, children's books, computer software, and much more. An annual subscription (6 issues) costs $24.00, with special subscription prices usually available. A single current issue costs $3.00, and they offer a free informative 24-page homeschooling books and publications catalog. *Home Education Magazine*, P.O. Box 1083, Tonasket, WA 98855; (509) 486-1351

Instructor

Instructor is a magazine for elementary-level school teachers; articles include accounts of successful teaching strategies in all academic subjects, book and resource reviews, interviews with children's authors, and a pull-out monthly planner, listing events and activities for each day of the month. An annual subscription (9 issues) costs $14.95 from *Instructor*, Scholastic Inc., P.O. Box 53895, Boulder, CO 80323-3895; (800) 544-2917.

Learning

A magazine of "creative ideas and activities" for teachers, concentrating on hands-on learning units for the classroom. Also included: resource reviews, personal accounts of teachers' experiences, and a pull-out calendar of monthly events with suggested activities. An annual subscription costs $14.96 from *Learning*, P.O. Box 51593, Boulder, CO 80323-1593.

Mothering
An informative magazine carrying articles on all aspects of parenting, from pre-birth on. Reviews of resources for children and many articles on education, alternative and otherwise. An annual subscription (4 issues) costs $18.00, from *Mothering*, P.O. Box 1690, Santa Fe, NM 87504; (505) 984-8116.

Phi Delta Kappan
"The Professional Journal for Education;" articles concentrate on educational policy issues, school reform, and other controversial educational topics, of which there are many. An annual subscription (10 issues) costs $35.00, from *Kappan*, Phi Delta Kappa, P.O. Box 789, Bloomington, IN 47402-9961. Free book catalog.

Play
A glossy magazine of "quality entertainment for children." Includes reviews of books, toys, music, and videos for kids, plus articles on the educational and developmental aspects of play. An annual subscription (4 issues) costs $12.00, from *Play*, 3620 N.W. 43rd St., Gainesville, FL 32606.

Teacher
Targeted at professional teachers, *Teacher*, published by Editorial Projects in Education, is a magazine about educational trends and issues: school reform, testing, the role of parents in the public schools, multiculturalism, special needs programs. An annual subscription costs $17.94, from *Teacher Magazine*, 4301 Connecticut Avenue N.W., Suite 432, Washington, D.C. 20008; (202) 686-0800.

Recommended Books:

Arons, Stephen. **Compelling Belief: The Culture of American Schooling.** (University of Massachusetts Press; 1983.)

Colfax, David and Micki. **Homeschooling for Excellence.** (Mountain House Press; 1987.)

Cohen, Dorothy H. **The Learning Child.** (Random House; 1972.)

Gatto, John. **Dumbing Us Down: The Hidden Curriculum of**

Compulsory Schooling. (New Society; 1992.)

Guterson, David. **Family Matters: Why Homeschooling Makes Sense.** (Harcourt, Brace, Jovanovich; 1992.)

Hegener, Mark and Helen, eds. **Alternatives in Education.** (Home Education Press; 1992)

Hendrickson, Borg. **Home School: Taking the First Step.** (Mountain Meadow Press, 1989, revised edition 1994.)

Holt, John. **Teach Your Own.** (Dell; 1981.)
    Also by Holt: **Learning All the Time** (Addison-Wesley; 1989.)

Mitchell, Richard. **The Graves of Academe.** (Simon and Schuster; 1981.)

Pedersen, Anne and Peggy O'Mara, eds. **Schooling At Home: Parents, Kids, and Learning.** (John Muir Publications; 1990.)

Ravitch, Diane and Chester E. Finn, Jr. **What Do Our 17-Year-Olds Know? A Report on the First National Assessment of History and Literature.** (Harper & Row; 1987.)

Reed, Donn. **The Home School Source Book.** (Brook Farm Books; 1991.)

Smith, Frank. **Insult to Intelligence: The Bureaucratic Invasion of Our Classrooms.** (Arbor House; 1986.)

Smith, Page. **Killing the Spirit: Higher Education in America.** (Viking; 1990.)

Sowell, Thomas. **Inside American Education: The Decline, The Deception, The Dogmas.** (Free Press; 1993.)

Good Stuff

Resources Address Listing

Academy for Economic Education
125 Nationsbank Center
Richmond, VA 23277
    (804) 643-0071

Activity Resources Co, Inc.
P.O. Box 4875
Hayward, CA 94540
    (510) 782-1300

M.F. Adler Books
Box 627
Stockbridge, MA 01262
    (413) 298-3559

American Education Publishing
150 East Wilson Bridge Road
Suite 145
Columbus, OH 43085
    (800) 542-7833   (614) 848-8866

American Heritage
Book Orders
P.O. Box 10934
Des Moines, IA 50340
    (800) 876-6556

American Heritage
Subscription Department
P.O. Box 5022
Harlan, IA 51593-0522
    (800) 777-1222

American History Illustrated
P.O. Box 8200
6405 Flank Drive
Harrisburg, PA 17112
    subs: (800) 435-9610
    office: (717) 657-9955

American Nuclear Society
Public Communications Dept.
555 North Kensington Avenue
La Grange Park, IL 60525
    (708) 579-8265

American Science and Surplus
P.O. Box 48838
Niles, IL 60714-0838
    (708) 475-8440

Ampersand Press
8040 NE Day Rd West #5-A
Bainbridge Island, WA 98110
    (206) 780-9015
    fax: (206) 780-9020

Anatomical Chart Company
8221 N. Kimball
Skokie, IL 60076-2956
    (800) 621-7500
    (708) 679-4700
    fax: (708) 674-0211
    fax: (708) 679-9155

Animal Town
P.O. Box 485
Healdsburg, CA 95448
    (800) 445-8642

Aristoplay
P.O. Box 7529
Ann Arbor, MI 48107
    (800) 634-7738

Art-i-Facts
P.O. Box 67192
Topeka, KS 66667

Art Institute of Chicago
Museum Shop
125 Armstrong Road
Des Plaines, IL 60018
    (800) 621-9337   (708) 299-5470

Arts & Activities
591 Camino de la Reina
Suite 200
San Diego, CA 92108
    (619) 297-8032

Astronomy
21027 Crossroads Circle
P.O. Box 1612
Waukesha, WI 53187-1612
    (800) 533-6644

Atrium Society
P.O. Box 816
Middlebury, VT 05753
    (802) 388-0922

Audio Forum
96 Broad Street
Guilford, CT 06437-2635
    (800) 243-1234
    (203) 453-9794

Audio Memory Publishing
2060 Raymond Avenue
Signal Hill, CA 90806
    orders: (800) 365-SING
    information: (310) 494-8822

Avalon Hill Game Company
4517 Harford Road
Baltimore, MD 21214
   (410) 254-9200

Aves Science Kit Company
P.O. Box 220
Peru, ME 04290
   (207) 562-7033

Avon Books
1350 Avenue of the Americas
New York, NY 10019
   customer service: (800) 238-0658
   customer service in TN: (901) 364-5742
   orders: (800) 223-0690
   orders in TN: (901) 364-5742

Avonlea Books
Box 74, Main Station
White Plains, NY 10602
   (914) 946-5923

The Backyard Scientist
P.O. Box 16966
Irvine, CA 92713

Ball-Stick-Bird Publications, Inc.
Box 592
Stony Brook, NY 11790
   (516) 331-9164

Banana Slug String Band
P.O. Box 2262
Santa Cruz, CA 95063
   (408) 423-7807
   (408) 429-9806

Bellerophon Books
36 Ancapa Street
Santa Barbara, CA 93101
   (800) 253-9943

Betterway Books
Shoe Tree Press
1507 Dana Avenue
Cincinnati, OH 45207

Bits and Pieces
1 Puzzle Place
Stevens Point, WI 54481-7199
   (800) JIGSAWS

Blitz Art Products, Inc.
P.O. Box 8022
Cherry Hill, NJ 08002

Blue Mountain Book Peddler
15301 Grey Fox Road
Upper Marlboro, MD 20772
   (301) 627-2131

Bluestocking Press
P.O. Box 1014-Dept. GS
Placerville, CA 95667-1014
   (916) 621-1123

Bolchazy-Carducci Publishers
1000 Brown Street   Unit 101
Wauconda, IL 60084
   (708) 526-4344

Boodle
P.O. Box 1049
Portland, IN 47371

The Book Lady, Inc.
8144 Brentwood Industrial Drive
St. Louis, MO 63144
   (800) 766-READ

Book Links: Connecting Books,
Libraries, and Classrooms
American Library Association
50 East Huron Street
Chicago, IL 60611
   (800) 545-2433

Book Wise, Inc.
26 Arlington Street
Cambridge, MA 02140
   (617) 876-4014

Boomerang!
13366 Pescadero Road
La Honda, CA 94020
   (800) 333-7858

Borenson and Associates
P.O. Box 3328
Allentown, PA 18108
   (215) 820-5575

Broderbund Software
Dept. 15
P.O. Box 6125
Novato, CA 94948-6125
   (800) 521-6263

Brook Farm Books
P.O. Box 246
Bridgewater, ME 04735

Buck Hill Associates
Box 501
North Creek, NY 12853-0501

Bureau of Educational Measurements
Emporia State University
1200 Commercial   Box 18
Emporia, KS 66801
    (316) 343-1200, ext. 5298

W. Atlee Burpee & Co.
Warminster, PA 18974
    (800) 888-1447

Cahill & Company
P.O. Box 39
Federalsburg, MD 21632-0039
    (800) 462-3955

California School Fitness
6006 Wenrich Drive
San Diego, CA 92120
    (619) 287-7093

Cambridge University Press
40 West 20th Street
New York, NY 10011-4211
    (800) 872-7423

Carolina Biological Supply Company
2700 York Road
Burlington, NC 27215
    (800) 334-5551
Box 187
Gladstone, OR 97027
    (800) 547-1733

Carolrhoda Books, Inc.
Lerner Publications
241 First Avenue North
Minneapolis, MN 55401
    (800) 328-4929
    (612) 332-3344

The Center for Learning
P.O. Box 910
Villa Maria, PA 16155
    (800) 767-9090

Center for Research and Development in
Law-Related Education (CRADLE)
Wake Forest University School of Law
2714 Henning Drive
Reynolda Station
Winston-Salem, NC 27109
    (919) 721-3355
    fax: (919) 721-3353

Chatham Hill Games
Ray Toelke Associates
P.O. Box 253
Chatham, NY 12037

Chem Matters
American Chemical Society
1155 16th Street N.W.
Washington, D.C. 20036
    (202) 872-4590

Cherry Tree Toys, Inc.
P.O. Box 369
Belmont, OH 43718
    (800) 848-4363

Chickadee
255 Great Owl Avenue
Buffalo, NY 14207-3082

Childcraft Education Corporation
P.O. Box 29149
Mission, KS 66201-9149
    (800) 631-5657

Children's Book & Music Center
2500 Santa Monica Boulevard
Santa Monica, CA 90404
    (800) 443-1856
    (213) 829-0215

Children's Book-of-the-Month Club
Camp Hill, PA 17012

Children's Press
5440 North Cumberland Avenue
Chicago, IL 60656
    (800) 621-1115
(312) 693-0800

Children's Small Press Collection
719 North Fourth Avenue
Ann Arbor, MI 48104
    (313) 668-8056

Childshop
P.O. Box 597
Burton, OH 44021
    (216) 834-0100

Childswork/Childsplay
Center for Applied Psychology
P.O. Box 1587
King of Prussia, PA 19406
    (800) 962-1141

Chinaberry Book Service
2780 Via Orange Way
Suite B
Spring Valley, CA 91978
　orders, cust. service: (800) 776-2242
　all other calls: (619) 670-5200

Cobblestone Publishing, Inc.
7 School Street
Peterborough, NH 03458
　(603) 924-7209
　fax: (603) 924-7380

Come With Me Science
Science Series Publishing Company
3550 Durrock Road
Shingle Springs, CA 95682
　(916) 677-1545

Common Reader
141 Tompkins Avenue
Pleasantville, NY 10570
　(800) 832-7323

Constructive Playthings
1227 East 119th Street
Grandview, MO 64030-1117
　(800) 255-6124
　(816) 761-5900

3-2-1 Contact
E=MC Square
P.O. Box 51177
Boulder, CO 80321-1177
　(800) 678-0613
　(303) 447-9330

Cornell Laboratory of Ornithology
159 Sapsucker Woods Road
Ithaca, NY 14850
　(607) 254-2444

CPP/Belwin, Inc.
15800 N.W. 48th Avenue
Miami, FL 33014
　(800) 327-7643
　(305) 620-1500

Craft Catalog
6095 McNaughten Centre
Columbus, OH 43232
　(800) 777-1442

Craft King
P.O. Box 90637
Lakeland, FL 33804
　(813) 686-9600

Crayon Power
P.O. Box 34
Jersey City, NJ 07303-0034
　(201) 433-3026

Creative Home Teaching
P.O. Box 152581
San Diego, CA 92195
　(619) 263-8633

Creative Kids
P.O. Box 637
Holmes, PA 19043-9937

Creative Learning Systems, Inc.
16510 Via Esprillo
San Diego, CA 92127
　(800) 458-2880
　(619) 675-7700

Creative Teaching Associates
P.O. Box 7766
Fresno, CA 93747
　(800) 767-4CTA
　(209) 291-6626
　fax: (209) 291-2953

Creative Teaching Press, Inc.
P.O. Box 6017
Cypress, CA 90630-0017
　(800) 444-4CTP

Creativity for Kids
1802 Central Avenue
Cleveland, OH 44115
　(216) 589-4800

Cricket
P.O. Box 387
Mt. Morris, IL 61054
　(800) 284-7257

Crizmac
3721 East Hardy Drive
Tucson, AZ 85716
　(602) 323-8555

Cuisenaire Company of America
P.O. Box 5026
White Plains, NY 10602-5026
　(800) 237-3142

Curiosity Kits, Inc.
P.O. Box 811
Cockeysville, MD 21030
　(410) 584-2605

Delta Education, Inc.
P.O. Box 950
Hudson, NH 03051
  (800) 442-5444

T.S. Denison & Co., Inc.
9601 Newton Avenue South
Minneapolis, MN 55431
  (800) 328-3831
  (612) 888-8606

Design-A-Study
408 Victoria Avenue
Wilmington, DE 19804-2124

Discover
P.O. Box 420087
Palm Coast, FL 32142-9944
  (800) 829-9132

Dover Publications, Inc.
31 East 2nd Street
Mineola, NY 11501

Dream Tree Press
3836 Thornwood Drive
Sacramento, CA 95821
  (916) 488-4194
  orders: (800) 769-9029
  fax: (916-488-4194

Early Advantage
47 Richards Avenue
Norwalk, CT 06860-0220
  (800) 367-4534

Earth Care Paper, Inc.
P.O. Box 7070
Madison, WI 53707-7070
  (608) 223-4000

Earthword, Inc.
104 Church Street
Keyport, NJ 07735
  (908) 264-3012

Ecol-O-Kids
3146 Shadow Lane
Topeka, KS 66604
  (913) 232-4747

EDC Publishing
P.O. Box 470663
Tulsa, OK 74147-0663
  (800) 475-4522
  fax: (800) 747-4509

Edmund Scientific Company
101 East Gloucester Pike
Barrington, NJ 08007-1380
  (609) 547-8880 (orders)
  (609) 573-6260 (customer service)

Educational Insights
19560 South Rancho Way
Dominguez Hills, CA 90220
  (800) 933-3277
  (213) 637-2131

Educational Record Center, Inc.
3233 Burnt Mill Drive
Suite 100
Wilmington, NC 28403-2655
  (800) 438-1637
  fax: (910) 343-0311

Edutainment Group
1445 North Rock Road #200
Wichita, KS 67206
  (800) 752-5262
  (316) 634-0441

Electronic Courseware Systems
1210 Lancaster Drive
Champaign, IL 61821
  (800) 832-4965 ext. 17 (orders)
  (217) 359-7099 (information)

Eliza Records
1304 Rittenhouse Street N.W.
Washington, D.C. 20015

Eureka!
Lawrence Hall of Science
University of California
Berkeley, CA 94720
  (510) 642-1016

Evan-Moor
18 Lower Ragsdale Drive
Monterey, CA 93940-5746
  (800) 777-4362

Every Day is Special
12910 Boston Avenue
Chino, CA 91710
  (714) 465-0090

Exploratorium Quarterly/Exploratorium
Publications
3601 Lyon Street
San Francisco, CA 94123
  (800) 359-9899

Extra Editions
P.O. Box 38
Urbana, IL 61801-0038
  (800) 423-9872

Films Incorporated Video
5547 North Ravenswood Avenue
Chicago, IL 60640-1199
  (800) 343-4312

Firefly Books, Ltd.
250 Sparks Avenue
Willowdale, Ontario M2H 2S4
Canada
  (416) 499-8412

Fireworks Educational, Inc.
P.O. Box 2325
Joliet, IL 60434
  (815) 725-9057

Flax Art & Design
P.O. Box 7216
San Francisco, CA 94120-7216
  (800) 547-7778

Flying Apparatus Catalogue
2121 Staunton Court
Palo Alto, CA 94306
  (415) 424-0739

Focus on Science Education
California Academy of Sciences
Golden Gate Park
San Francisco, CA 94118
  (415) 750-7114

Folger Shakespeare Library
Education Programs
201 East Capitol Street, S.E.
Washington, D.C. 20003-1094
  (202) 544-7077
  (202) 675-0365

For Spacious Skies
P.O. Box 191
54 Webb Street
Lexington, MA 02173
  (617) 862-4289

Free Spirit Publishing, Inc.
400 First Avenue North
Suite 616
Minneapolis, MN 55401-1730
  (800) 735-7323
  (612) 338-2068

GPN
P.O. Box 80669
Lincoln, NE 68501
  (800) 228-4630
  (402) 472-2007

Games
P.O. Box 605
Mt. Morris, IL 61054-7789

The General Music Store
19880 State Line Road
South Bend, IN 46637
  (800) 348-5003
  (219) 272-8266

Geode Educational Options
P.O. Box 106
West Chester, PA 19381

The Gifted Child Today
P.O. Box 8813
Waco, TX 76710-8813

The Gifted Child Today Catalog
314-350 Weinacker Avenue
P.O. Box 6448
Mobile, AL 36660-0448
  (205) 478-4700

Gifted Education Review
P.O. Box 2278
Evergreen, CO 80359-2278

Globe Pequot Press
P.O. Box 833
Old Saybrook, CT 06475
  (800) 243-0495   (203) 395-0440

Good Apple
1204 Buchanan Street
P.O. Box 299
Carthage, IL 62321-0299
  (800) 435-7234   (217) 357-3981

Good Year Books
1900 East Lake Avenue
Glenview, IL 60025
  (800) 628-4480, ext. 3038

The Great Books Foundation
35 East Wacker Drive
Suite 2300
Chicago, IL 60601-2298
  (800) 222-5870
  (312) 332-5870

Great Kids Company
P.O. Box 609
Lewisville, NC 27023
    (800) 582-1493

Greathall Productions
P.O. Box 813
Benicia, CA 94510

Growing Without Schooling
Holt Associates
2269 Massachusetts Avenue
Cambridge, MA 02140
    (617) 864-3100

Gryphon House
Early Childhood Books
P.O. Box 275
Mt. Rainier, MD 20712
    (800) 638-0928
    (301) 779-6200

Guarionex Press. Ltd.
Attn: Bill Zimmerman
201 West 77th Street
New York, NY 10024
    (212) 724-5259

Hands-On History
201 Constance Drive
New Lenox, IL 60451

Harper Audio
HarperCollins Publishers
1000 Keystone Industrial Park
Scranton, PA 18512-4621
    (800) 242-7737

Harps of Lorien
610 North Star Route GS
Questa, NM 87556
    (505) 586-1307
    fax: (505) 586-0067

Hear & Learn Publications
603 S.E. Morrison Road
Vancouver, WA 98664-1545

Hearthsong
P.O. Box B
Sebastopol, CA 95473-0601

Heath Company
P.O. Box 1288
Benton Harbor, MI 49023-1288
    (800) 253-0570

The Herbarium Rubber Stamps
P.O. Box 246836
Sacramento, CA 95825
    (916) 451-9669

Historical Products
P.O. Box 403
East Longmeadow, MA 01028
    (413) 525-2250

Home Education Magazine
Home Education Press
P.O. Box 1083
Tonasket, WA 98855
    (509) 486-1351

Home School Supply House
P.O. Box 7
Fountain Green, UT 84632
    (800) 772-3129

The Horn Book, Inc.
14 Beacon Street
Boston, MA 02108-9765
    (800) 325-1170
    (617) 227-1555

Hubbard Scientific, Inc.
P.O. Box 760
Chippewa Falls, WI 54729
    (800) 323-8368

Inline Software
308 Main Street
Lakeville, CT 06039-1204
    (203) 435-4995
    (800) 453-7671

Insect Lore Products
P.O. Box 1535
Shafter, CA 93263
    (800) LIVE-BUG
    (805) 746-6047

Institute for Math Mania
P.O. Box 910
Montpelier, VT 05601
    (802) 223-5871

Instructor
Scholastic, Inc.
P.O. Box 53895
Boulder, CO 80323-3895
    (800) 544-2917

Interact
P.O. Box 997
Lakeside, CA 92040
    (800) 359-0961
    (619) 448-1474

International Learning Systems, Inc.
P.O. Box 16032
Chesapeake, VA 23328
    (800) 321-TEACH
    (804) 366-0227

International Linguistics Corporation
3505 East Red Bridge
Kansas City, MO 64137
    (800) 237-1830
    (816) 765-8855

International Reading Association
800 Barksdale Road
P.O. Box 8139
Newark, DE 19714-8139
    (302) 731-1600

Invent America!
1505 Powhattan
Alexandria, VA 22314

J C Cassettes
Box 73
Route 2
Calumet, OK 73014
    (405) 893-2239

John Holt's Book and Music Store
2269 Massachusetts Avenue
Cambridge, MA 02140
    (617) 864-3100

John Muir Publications
P.O. Box 613
Santa Fe, NM 87504
    (800) 888-7504
    (505) 982-4078

Jolie Coins
Jolie Coins Perfect Penpals
P.O. Box 68
Roslyn Heights, NY 11577-0068

Joyful Child, Inc.
P.O. Box 5506
Scottsdale, AZ 85261
    (602) 951-4111

Key Curriculum Press
P.O. Box 2304
Berkeley, CA 94702
    (800) 338-7638
    (415) 548-2304

Kids Discover
P.O. Box 54206
Boulder, CO 80321-4206
    orders: (800) 284-8276

Kids for a Clean Environment (Kids FACE)
P.O. Box 158254
Nashville, TN 37215

Kids for Saving the Earth
P.O. Box 47247
Plymouth, MN 55447-0247
    (612) 525-0002

Kids Meeting Kids
Box 8H
380 Riverside Drive
New York, NY 10025

Kids' Puzzle Express
P.O. Box 3083A
Princeton, NJ 08543-3083

KidsArt
P.O. Box 274
Mt. Shasta, CA 96067
    (916) 926-5076
    (800) 959-5076

Kidsprint Times
P.O. Box 7391
San Jose, CA 95150
    (800) 697-4537

Knowledge Products
1717 Elm Hill Pike
Suite A-4
Nashville, TN 37210
    (800) 264-6441

Knowledge Unlimited
Box 52
Madison, WI 53701-0052
    (800) 356-2303

KolbeConcepts, Inc.
P.O. Box 15667
Phoenix, AZ 85060
    (602) 840-9770

Lab-Aids, Inc.
17 Colt Court
Ronkonkoma, NY 11779
    (516) 737-1133

Ladybug
P. O. Box 592
Mt. Morris, IL 61054-0592
    (800) 827-0227

Lakeshore Learning Materials
2695 East Dominguez Street
P.O. Box 6261
Carson, CA 90749
    (800) 421-5354

Lark in the Morning
P.O. Box 1176
Mendocino, CA 95460
    (707) 964-5569

Learning
P.O. Box 54293
Boulder, CO 80322-4293

Learning Alternatives
2370 West 89A Suite 5
Sedona, AZ 86336
    (800) HANDS-ON

Learning Links, Inc.
2300 Marcus Avenue
New Hyde Park, NY 11042
    (800) 724-2616
    (516) 437-9071

Learning Things, Inc.
68A Broadway
P.O. Box 436
Arlington, MA 02174
    (617) 646-0093

LifeStories
701 Decatur Avenue North
Suite 104
Golden Valley, MN 55427
    (800) 232-1873
    (612) 544-0438

Live Home Video
15400 Sherman Way
P.O. Box 10124
Van Nuys, CA 91410
    (800) 423-7455

Long Ago & Far Away
WGBH
Print Projects
125 Western Avenue
Boston, MA 02134

Macmillan Publishing Company
Front and Brown Streets
Riverside, NJ 08075-1197
    (800) 323-9563

Makit Products, Inc.
4659 Mint Way
Dallas, TX 75236
    (214) 330-7774

Marathon U.S.A., Inc.
12500 Network
Suite 201
San Antonio, TX 78249
    (800) 992-7941
    (512) 690-9984

Math Products Plus
P.O. Box 64
San Carlos, CA 94070
    (415) 593-2839
    fax: (415) 595-0802

MECC
6160 Summit Drive North
Minneapolis, MN 55430-4003
    (800) 685-MECC, ext. 549

Merlyn's Pen
P.O. Box 1058
East Greenwich, RI 02818
    (800) 247-2027

Metropolitan Museum of Art
255 Gracie Station
New York, NY 10028-9998
    (800) 468-7386

Michael Olaf's Essential Montessori
P.O. Box 1162
Arcata, CA 95521
    (707) 826-1557

The Mind's Eye
Box 1060
Petaluma, CA 94953
    (800) 227-2020

Mineral-of-the-Month Club
Box 487
Yucaipa, CA 92399

Modern
5000 Park Street North
St. Petersburg, FL 33709
  (800) 446-6337

Modern School Supplies, Inc.
P.O. Box 958
Hartford, CT 06143
  (800) 243-2328   (203) 243-9565

Mortensen Math
Academic Excellence Institute
2450 Fort Union Blvd.
Salt Lake City, UT 84121
  (801) 944-2500

Mothering
P.O. Box 1650
Santa Fe, NM 87504
  (505) 984-8116

Mott Media
1000 East Huron Street
Milford, MI 48402
  (800) 348-6688
  (313) 685-8773

Movies Unlimited
6736 Castor Avenue
Philadelphia, PA 19149
  orders: (800) 523-0823
  customer service: (215) 722-8398

Museum of Fine Arts, Boston
P.O. Box 1044
Boston MA 02120-0900
  (800) 225-5592

Music for Little People
Box 1460
Redway, CA 95560
  (800) 346-4445

Musical Heritage Society
1710 Highway 35
Ocean, NJ 07712-9923

Music Plus
425 Main Street
Danbury, CT 06810
  (203) 744-4344

NL Associates, Inc.
P.O. Box 1199
Hightstown, NJ 08520

National Association for the Preservation
and Perpetuation of Storytelling (NAPPS)
P.O. Box 309
Jonesborough, TN 37659
  (615) 753-2171

National Audubon Society
950 Third Avenue
New York, NY 10012
  (212) 832-3200

National Council of Teachers of
Mathematics (NCTM)
1906 Association Drive
Reston, VA 22091-1593
  (703) 620-9840

National Geographic Society
Washington, D.C. 20036
  (800) 447-0647

National Science Teachers Association
(NSTA)
1742 Connecticut Avenue N.W.
Washington, D.C. 20009-1171
  (202) 328-5200

National Teaching Aids, Inc.
1845 Highland Avenue
New Hyde Park, NY 11040
  (515) 326-2555

National Textbook Company
4255 West Touhy Avenue
Lincolnwood, IL 60646-1975
  (800) 323-4900
  (708) 679-5500

National Wildlife Federation
1400 16th Street N.W.
Washington, D.C. 20036
  (800) 432-6564
  (202) 797-6800

National Women's History Project
7738 Bell Road
Windsor, CA 95492
  (707) 838-6000

National Writing Institute
7946 Wright Road
Niles, MI 49120
  (616) 684-5375

The Natural Resources Defense Council
40 West 20th Street
New York, NY 10011

The Nature Company
P.O. Box 188
Florence, KY 41022
    (800) 227-1114

The Nature Conservancy
1815 North Lynn Street
Arlington, VA 22209
    (703) 841-5300

The Nature Press
40 West Spruce Street
Columbus, OH 43215-9300
    (800) 532-6837

The New Scientist
Quadrant Subscription Services, Ltd.
P.O. Box 7247-8841
Philadelphia, PA 19170-8841

Novel Units
P.O. Box 1461
Palatine, IL 60078
    (708) 253-8200

Oh! ZONE
420 East Hewitt Avenue
Marquette, MI 49855-9910

Old News
400 Stackstown Road
Marietta, PA 17547-9300
    (717) 426-2212

Opportunities for Learning,Inc.
941 Hickory Lane
P.O. Box 8103
Mansfield, OH 44901-8103
    (419) 589-1700

Optimum Resource, Inc.
5 Hiltech Lane
Hilton Head, SC 29926
    (800) 327-1473

Orion Telescope Center
2450 17th Avenue
P.O. Box 1158
Santa Cruz, CA 95061-1158
    (800) 447-1001

Outlet Book Company
40 Englehard Avenue
Avenel, NJ 07001
    (908) 827-2700

OWL
255 Great Owl Avenue
Buffalo, NY 14207-3082

Oxford University Press
200 Madison Avenue
New York, NY 10016
    (800) 451-7566

Oxford University Press Order Department
2001 Evans Road
Cary, NC 27513
    (800) 451-7556

Parent Child Press
P.O. Box 675
Hollidaysburg, PA 16648-0675
    (814) 696-7512
    fax: (814) 696-7510

PBS Video
1320 Braddock Place
Alexandria, VA 22314-1698
    (800) 424-7963

Peninsula Booksearch
P.O. Box 1305
Burlingame, CA 94011-1305
    fax: (415) 347-0844

Perfection Learning Corporation
1000 North Second Avenue
Logan, IA 51546-1099
    (800) 831-4190
    (712) 644-2831

Pets & Me
American Pet Products Manufacturers
Association (APPMA)
511 Harwood Boulevard
Scarsdale, NY 10583
    (800) 452-1225

Phi Delta Kappan
P.O. Box 789
Bloomington, IN 47402-9961

Pioneer Drama Service, Inc.
P.O. Box 4267
Englewood, CO 80155-4267
    (303) 779-4035

Play
3620 N.W. 43rd Street
Gainesville, FL 32606
    (904) 375-3705

Play It Smart Products
12221 Sam Furr Road
P.O. Box 2002
Huntersville, NC 28078
    (800) 258-5302
    (704) 892-4263

PlayFair Toys
P.O. Box 18210
Boulder, CO 80308
    (800) 824-7255
    (303) 440-7229

Pocahontas Press
P.O. Drawer F
Blacksburg, VA 24063
    (703) 951-0467   (800) 446-0467

Poets' Audio Center
P.O. Box 50145
Washington, D.C. 20091-0145
    (202) 722-9106

Portland State University
Continuing Education Press
Contact: Tena Spears
Box 1394
Portland, OR 97207
    (800) 547-8887, ext 4891
    Oregon: (800) 452-4909, ext 4891

Puffin Books
375 Hudson Street
New York, NY 10014
    (800) 526-0275

Quantum
Springer-Verlag New York, Inc.
Journal Fulfillment Services, Inc.
175 Fifth Avenue
New York, NY 10010
    (800) SPRINGER
    (212) 460-1500

Rainbow Re-Source Center
P.O. Box 491
Kewanee, IL 61443

Rand McNally Catalog
P.O. Box 182257
Chattanooga, TN 37422-7257
    (800) 234-0679

Random House Video
400 Hahn Road
Westminster, MD 21157
    (212) 572-2683

Ranger Rick
National Wildlife Federation
1400 Sixteenth Street N.W.
Washington, D.C. 20036
    (800) 432-6564

Recorded Books, Inc.
270 Skipjack Road
Prince Frederick, MD 20678
    (800) 638-1304

Relative Teaching Concepts
P.O. Box 8417
Richmond, VA 23226-0417
    (804) 282-7842

Rhythm Band Instruments
P.O. Box 126
Fort Worth, TX 76101-0126
    (800) 424-4724

Rock and Gem
P.O. Box 6925
Ventura, CA 93006-9878
    (805) 644-3824

Roots & Wings Educational Catalog
P.O. Box 3348
Boulder, CO 80307
    (800) 833-1787

Running Press Book Publishers
125 South Twenty-second Street
Philadelphia, PA 19103
    (215) 567-5080
    orders: (800) 345-5359

S & S Arts and Crafts
P.O. Box 513, Dept. 2020
Colchester, CT 06415-0513
    (800) 243-9232, Dept. 2020

Saxon Publishers, Inc.
1320 West Lindsey Street
Norman, OK 73069
    (405) 329-7071

Scholastic, Inc.
P.O. Box 7502
Jefferson City, MO 65102
    (800) 325-6149

School Zone Publishing Company
1819 Industrial Drive
P.O. Box 777
Grand Haven, MI 49417
    (800) 253-0564

Science-by-Mail
Museum of Science
Science Park
Boston, MA 02114
    (800) 729-3300
    (617) 589-0437

Science Kit and Boreal Laboratories
777 East Park Drive
Tonawanda, NY 14150-6784
    (800) 828-7777
    (716) 874-6020

Science Weekly
Subscription Department
P.O. Box 70154-S
Washington, D.C. 20088=0154
    (301) 680-8804

Scienceland, Inc.
501 Fifth Avenue
Suite 2108
New York, NY 10017-6165
    (212) 490-2180
    fax: (212) 490-2187 (pause 23)

Scientific American
415 Madison Avenue
New York, NY 10017
    (800) 333-1199

Scientific Wizardry Educational Products
9925 Fairview Avenue
Boise, ID 83704
    (208) 377-8575
    fax: (208) 323-0912

Scott, Foresman, and Company
1900 East Lake Avenue
Glenview, IL 60025
    (312) 729-3000

Seeds Blum
Idaho City Stage
Boise, ID 83706

Shekinah Curriculum Cellar
967 Junipero Drive, Box 2154
Costa Mesa, CA 92626

Shoe String Press/
Library Professional Publications
P.O. Box 4327
925 Sherman Avenue
Hamden, CT 06514
    (203) 248-6307
    fax: (203) 230-9275

Signals
WGBH Educational Foundation
P.O. Box 64428
St. Paul, MN 55164-0428
    (800) 669-9696

Silva Orienteering Services, U.S.A.
Box 1604
Binghamton, NY 13902
    (607) 724-0411

Skipping Stones
P.O. Box 3939
Eugene, OR 97403-0939
    (503) 342-4956

Sky and Telescope
P.O. Box 9111
Belmont, MA 02178-9111

Smithsonian Institution
Department 0006
Washington, D.C. 20073-0006
    (800) 322-0344

Sourcetapes
Visual Education Corporation
14 Washington Road   Box 2321
Princeton, NJ 08543
    (609) 799-9200

Spalding Education Foundation
15410 North 67th Avenue   Suite 8
Glendale, AZ 85306
    (602) 486-5881

Spizzirri Publishing Company, Inc.
P.O. Box 9397
Rapid City, SD 57709
    (605) 341-4451

Sports Illustrated for Kids
P.O. Box 830606
Birmingham, AL 35282-9487
    (800) 992-0196

Star Date
RLM 15.308
The University of Texas at Austin
Austin, TX 78712
  (512) 471-5285

Stone Soup
Children's Art Foundation
P.O. Box 83
Santa Cruz, CA 95063-9990
  (800) 447-4569

Student Letter Exchange
630 Third Avenue
New York, NY 10017
  (212) 557-3312

Sundance
P.O. Box 1326
Littleton, MA 01460
  (800) 343-8204
  (508) 486-9201

Sycamore Tree, Inc.
2179 Meyer Place
Costa Mesa, CA 92627
  information: (714) 650-4466
  orders, fax: (714) 642-6750
  (800) 779-6750

Talicor, Inc.
P.O. Box 6382
Anaheim, CA 92816
  (714) 255-7900

Teach Me Tapes, Inc.
10500 Bren Road East
Minneapolis, MN 55343
  (800) 456-4656
  (612) 933-8086

Teacher Ideas Press
P.O. Box 6633
Englewood, CO 80155-6633
  (800) 237-6124

Teacher Magazine
4301 Connecticut Avenue N.W.
Suite 432
Washington, D.C. 20008
  (202) 686-0800

The Teachers' Laboratory
P.O. Box 6480
Brattleboro, VT 05302-6480
  (802) 254-3457

Texas Instruments
P.O. Box 53
Lubbock, TX 79408-9955
  (800) TI-CARES

Tiger Lily Books
P.O. Box 111
Piercy, CA 95587

The Timberdoodle
East 1510 Spencer Lake Road
Shelton, WA 98584
  (206) 426-0672

Time-Life
1450 East Parham Road
Richmond, VA 23280

Time-Life Video
777 Duke Street
Alexandria, VA 22314
  (800) 621-7026

Tin Man Press
P.O. Box 219
Stanwood, WA 98292
  (800) 676-0459

T'N'T
Jan Lieberman
121 Buckingham Drive #57
Santa Clara, CA 95051

Toad's Tools
P.O. Box 173
Oberlin, OH 44074

Tooling Around
385 Delmas Avenue #A
San Jose, CA 95126-3626
  (408) 286-9770

TOPS Learning Systems
10970 South Mulino Road
Canby, OR 97013

Toys to Grow On
Box 17
Long Beach, CA 90801
  (800) 542-8338
  (310) 603-8890

Traveling the U.S. Through
Children's Literature
Virginia Williams
13 Woodside Circle
Sturbridge, MA 01566

Treetop Publishing
P.O. Box 085567
Racine, WI 53408-5567
(414) 633-9228

Trivium Pursuit
Laurie and Harvey Bluedorn
R.R. 2 Box 169
New Boston, IL 61272
(309) 537-3641

Troll Learn & Play
100 Corporate Drive
Mahwah, NJ 07430
(800) 247-6106

United Art and Education Supply Co., Inc.
Box 9219
Fort Wayne, IN 46899
(800) 322-3247

U.S. Geological Survey
Earth Science Information Center
507 National Center
Reston, VA 22092

U.S. Geological Survey
Map Distribution
Federal Center Building 41
P.O. Box 25286
Denver, CO 80225

University Prints
21 East Street
P.O. Box 485
Winchester, MA 01890

Ursa Major
P.O. Box 3368
Ashland, OR 97520
(800) 999-3433

U.S. Chess Federation
186 Route 9W
New Windsor, NY 12553
(800) 388-5464

The Video Catalog
P.O. Box 64428
Saint Paul, MN 55164-0428
(800) 733-2232

R.B. Walter Art and Craft Materials
P.O. Box 6231
Arlington, TX 76005
(800) 447-8787

Ward's Natural Science Establishment, Inc.
P.O. Box 92912
Rochester, NY 14692-9012
(800) 962-2660

The WEB
Ohio State University
Room 200, Ramseyer Hall
29 West Woodruff
Columbus, OH 43210

Wff 'n Proof Learning Games
1490-JR South Boulevard
Ann Arbor, MI 48104-4699
(313) 665-2269

Whale Adoption Project
70 East Falmouth Highway
East Falmouth, MA 02536
(508) 548-8328

Wilcox & Follett Book Company
5563 South Archer Avenue
Chicago, IL 60638
(800) 621-4272

Williamson Publishing Company
Church Hill Road
P.O. Box 185
Charlotte, VT 05445
(800) 234-8791

Wonderful Ideas
P.O. Box 64691
Burlington, VT 05406
(617) 239-1496

WonderScience
American Chemical Society
P.O. Box 57136
Washington, D.C. 20077-6702

Workman Publishing
708 Broadway
New York, NY 10003
(212) 254-5900

World Almanac Education
1278 West Ninth Street
Cleveland, OH 44113-1067
(800) 321-1147

World of Science Educational Modules, Inc.
Building Four
900 Jefferson Road
Rochester, NY 14623
(716) 475-0100

World Pen Pals
1694 Como Avenue
St. Paul, MN 55108
    (612) 647-0191

World Wide Games
P.O. Box 517, Dept. 2602
Colchester, CT 06415-0517
    (800) 888-0987, Dept. 2602

World Wildlife Fund
1250 24th Street
Suite 500
Washington, D.C. 20037
    (202) 293-4800

Young Voices
P.O. Box 2321
Olympia, WA 98507
    (206) 357-4683

Your Big Backyard
National Wildlife Federation
1400 Sixteenth Street N.W.
Washington, D.C. 20078-6420
    (800) 432-6564

Zaner-Bloser
2200 West Fifth Avenue
P.O. Box 16764
Columbus, OH 43216-6764
    (800) 421-3018

Zephyr Press
3316 North Chapel Avenue
P.O. Box 13448
Tucson, AZ 85732-3448
    (602) 322-5090

Zillions
P.O. Box 54861
Boulder, CO 80322-4861
    (800) 234-2078

Zoobooks
Wildlife Education, Ltd.
3590 Kettner Boulevard
San Diego, CA 92101

Good Stuff

Indexes

Miscellaneous Index

Catalogs Index

Audio/Video Index

Books Index

Authors Index

For Additional Copies:

Good Stuff: Learning Tools for All Ages, by Rebecca
Rupp, published by Home Education Press, 1993. 392
pages, completely indexed, $14.75 plus $2.00 shipping.
Send order to Home Education Press, P.O. Box 1083,
Tonasket, WA 98855; (509) 486-1351.

A free 24 page books and publications catalog is also
available.